TERROR AND PITY

ALEKSANDR SUMAROKOV

and the Theater of Power
in Elizabethan Russia

IMPERIAL ENCOUNTERS IN RUSSIAN HISTORY

SERIES EDITOR:

Gary Marker (State University of New York, Stony Brook)

EDITORIAL BOARD:

Robert Geraci (University of Virginia, Charlottesville)
Bruce Grant (New York University, New York)
Michael Khodarkovsky (Harvard University, Cambridge, MA)
Nadieszda Kizenko (State University of New York, Albany)
Douglas Northrop (University of Michigan, Ann Arbor)
Robert Weinberg (Swarthmore College, Swarthmore, Pennsylvania)

TERROR AND PITY

ALEKSANDR SUMAROKOV
and the Theater of Power
in Elizabethan Russia

KIRILL
OSPOVAT

Boston
2016

Library of Congress Cataloging-in-Publication Data:
The bibliographic data for this title is available from the Library of Congress.

ISBN 978-1-61811-472-3 (cloth)
ISBN 978-1-61811-473-0 (electronic)

Cover design by Ivan Grave
Book design by Kryon Publishing
www.kryonpublishing.com

Published by Academic Studies Press in 2016
28 Montfern Avenue
Brighton, MA 02135, USA
press@academicstudiespress.com
www.academicstudiespress.com

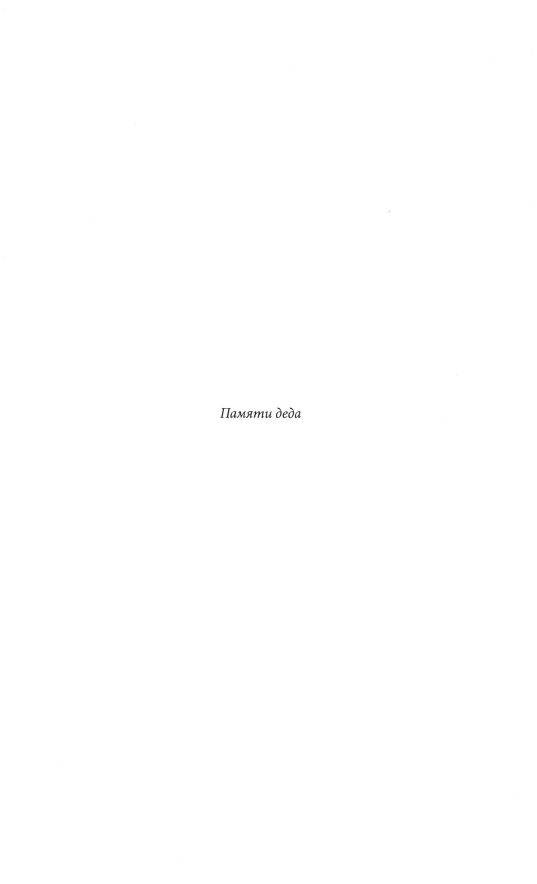

Памяти деда

CONTENTS

ACKNOWLEDGMENTS

The writing and publication of this book were made possible by the research group "DramaNet—Early Modern European Drama and the Cultural Net" at the Freie Universität Berlin, directed by Professor Joachim Küpper and funded by the European Research Council. I would like to thank Professor Küpper along with my fellow DramaNet members for the fruitful conversations, which largely shaped the outcome of my work. On its last stages, it was also facilitated by a research grant from the National Research University "Higher School of Economics" in St. Petersburg. In addition, I am grateful to Marcus Levitt for his constant support of the project from its beginnings up to the publication stage.

Parts of this work have appeared, or are expected to appear, in the volumes *EUtROPEs: The Paradox of European Empire*, edited by John W. Boyer and Berthold Molden (The University of Chicago Center in Paris, 2014); Acta Slavonica VI (Tartu: University of Tartu of Press, 2014); *Politics and Aesthetics in European Baroque Tragedy*, edited by Nigel Smith and Jan Bloemendal; and *Dramatic Experience: Poetics of Drama and Early Modern Public Sphere(s)*, edited by Tatiana Korneeva, Katja Gvozdeva, and Kirill Ospovat (both forthcoming at Brill). I am grateful to the University of Chicago, University of Tartu, and Brill Publishers for their generous permission to republish these essays in my book.

Last but not least, Alexei Evstratov has been an engaged and inspiring opponent and fellow traveler through the years. Eugenia Kapsomera Amditis has taken up the task of correcting my foreigner's English and accomplished it with grace and patience.

INTRODUCTION

Sometime around 1790, an anonymous Russian author drafted his "Commentaries" on the memoirs of Christoph Hermann von Manstein. Among other observations, the Anonym commented on the odd amusements of Empress Anna (r. 1730–1740), particularly the famous Ice Palace, where the empress's jester was locked up for a winter night together with his mock bride:

> There can be no doubt that a good government out of love for the people as well as political considerations ought to provide amusements for its subjects. Those amusements, however, should not corrupt public morals. At the time when those foolish spectacles appeared in Petersburg, the beneficent rays of education, first admitted by Peter the Great, had already begun to warm the minds of Russians. Therefore, the government could have occupied them with much more useful spectacles. It could have arranged for performances of Italian intermezzos, which were in great vogue at the time; and if the court itself would have turned to nobler diversions, maybe then already our literature could have produced dramatic works. Feofan and Kantemir would have found talents. Lomonosov and Sumarokov already lived at the time. Everywhere and at all times the court discovers, favors and fosters talents. Without royal encouragement, the finest minds and the most exquisite natural gifts will wane, perish and lapse into obscurity.[1]

---

1   "Zamechaniia na 'Zapiski o Rossii generala Manshteina,'" in *Perevoroty i voiny* (Moscow: Fond Sergeia Dubova, 1997), 444. In this study, I will include the original text for

Combining the voices of the post-Petrine generation with the attitudes and sensibilities of Catherine II's enlightened era, the Anonym apparently drew on a corpus of firsthand accounts (and, less plausibly, personal recollections) of Russian courtly politics and military events of the 1730s and 1740s. He provides an important perspective on the place that Russian literature and theater occupied in the evolving self-consciousness of the court and service nobility. While Manstein does not mention Russian literature at all, the Anonym, who also seems to be a "man of deeds" eager to demonstrate his expertise in the *arcana imperii*, the mysteries of state, chooses to include in his "Commentaries" an outline of the Russian literary canon as it emerged in the 1740s. His vision of it is shaped by two basic assumptions—the dependence of literary developments on court patronage, and the crucial political significance of public spectacles.

The emphasis on court patronage is well justified for the period in question. As Grigorii Gukovskii shows, up to the 1760s almost all literary effort was made possible by the support of the court, institutionalized in the Academy of Sciences founded in 1725 as an "auxiliary institution" to the "royal palace" and entrusted with the only secular press in the empire.[2] Moreover, as the Anonym's judgment attests, both literature and theater could be seen as necessary institutions of a well-ordered monarchy. The importance of spectacles, the main point of the Anonym's argument, was—as we shall see—widely acknowledged in early modern Europe, and largely defined the attitudes of Russian elites towards theater. In Elise Kimerling Wirtschafter's concise formulation, Peter the Great had already developed "an awareness that language could serve the cause of reform. In this context, Peter's early effort to establish permanent public theater based on a literary repertoire can be seen as a tool of social and cultural transformation. Theater not only served as the institutional locus for a new brand of public sociability, it also articulated social ideas and provided models of social behavior."[3]

Sumarokov's Russian texts and their French antecedents. With the exception of previously unpublished archival materials as well as hardly accessible or particularly important printed texts, all other textual citations will appear in English translation. In non-Russian quotations, I will preserve the spelling of the original editions, while all Russian texts will be quoted in new orthography.

2   Grigorii Gukovskii, *Ocherki po istorii russkoi literatury XVIII veka: dvorianskaia fronda v literature 1750-kh–1760-kh godov* (Moscow: Izd-vo Akademii nauk, 1936), 12–13.

3   Elise Kimerling Wirtschafter, *The Play of Ideas in Russian Enlightenment Theater* (DeKalb: Northern Illinois University Press, 2003), 4.

Interestingly, this political vision of theater defines the Anonym's picture of the emerging Russian literature in general. As its central figure, he mentions Aleksandr Sumarokov (1717–1777), a prolific poet who gained prominence as the author and stage director of the first Russian neoclassical tragedies and comedies, popular at the courts of Empresses Elizabeth (r. 1741–1761) and Catherine II (r. 1762–1796). In the view of the Anonym, other prominent Russian authors—the theologian and political and literary theorist Feofan Prokopovich (1681–1736), the poet Antiokh Kantemir (1708–1744), and the polymath and poet Mikhail Lomonosov (1711–1765)— only seem to have lived to herald the appearance of "dramatic works" in Russian or to set off Sumarokov's success. Commenting elsewhere on the founding of the Noble Cadet Corps in 1731, the Anonym specifically emphasizes that it was here that, thanks to government patronage, "Sumarokov appeared to serve Melpomene."[4] The muse Melpomene embodies tragedy, and her comic counterpart, Thalia, is not mentioned at all. In other words, after the Anonym dismisses Italian intermezzos as not sufficiently "noble," the spectacles appropriate for a dignified court and its subjects are identified with literary drama and, more precisely, tragedy.

Taking the Anonym's argument as a starting point, this study will attempt to unfold it, exploring classicist tragedy, introduced to Russia by Sumarokov (and, more specifically, his first two dramas, *Khorev* and *Gamlet*), as a literary experiment that emerged from and drew upon the political theatrics of the court, ultimately functioning as a political medium. In one of the best accounts of the political underpinnings of Russian classicist tragedy, V. N. Vsevolodskii-Gerngross draws attention to the fact that throughout the eighteenth century, tragedy was both poorly performed and poorly received outside the capitals, where it was "cultivated by the Russian aristocracy," a limited social group centered around the court and more adequately identifiable as the "court society."[5] With the tastes and interests of this group in mind, dramatic

---

4   "Zamechaniia," 447.

5   V. N. Vsevolodskii-Gerngross, *Politicheskie idei russkoi klassitsisticheskoi tragedii*, in *O teatre. Sbornik statei* (Leningrad: Iskusstvo, 1940), 107–109. A similar view of the political functions of Sumarokov's tragedy is suggested by G. A. Gukovskii in his textbook: G. A. Gukovskii, *Russkaia literatura XVIII veka* ([1939]; Moscow: Aspekt-press, 1998), 135. For a valuable discussion of the political and historical underpinnings of Sumarokov's tragedies, see E. A. Kasatkina, "Sumarokovskaia tragediia 40-kh–nachala 50-kh godov XVIII veka," in *Uchenye zapiski Tomskogo pedagogicheskogo instituta* (Tomsk: TGPI, 1955), XIII: 213–261. On the "political dialogue" between eighteenth-century Russian rulers and

writers starting with Sumarokov—and graduating for the most part from the same educational institution, the Noble Cadet Corps—developed an idiom of political allegory and allusion, which simultaneously expressed and masked the concerns of court society and the tensions permeating its social existence. Vsevolodskii-Gerngross concludes that Russian classicist tragedy was specifically tailored to negotiate "the problematic relationship between the aristocracy and the monarchy." Building on this argument, my study will explore the fundamental affinity between the poetics of classicist tragedy, both in theory and practice, and the discursive mechanics of power in autocratic Russia.

In Petersburg, as in other European capitals, theatrical performances were a central element of what Gukovskii called the "spectacle of the imperial court."[6] Richard Wortman elaborates on this concept in his work *Scenarios of Power: Myth and Ceremony in Russian Monarchy*, in which he explains:

> The sumptuous, highly ritualized presentations of Russian monarchy, produced at enormous cost of resources and time, indicate that Russian rulers and their advisers considered the symbolic sphere of ceremonies and imagery intrinsic to their exercise of power. [... T]he imperial court represented an ongoing theater of power.[7]

While theater always provided a convenient metaphor for all kinds of political representation, actual theatrical practices were commonly appropriated by early modern courts. Sumarokov's tragedies belonged to the pan-European culture of court theaters, which by the eighteenth century were firmly established as one of the crucial institutions of absolutist "culture of power" and shared a relatively uniform language of political representation, disseminated by travelling companies and individual professionals, as well as through print media.[8]

---

the elites reflected in the literary production of the time, including plays, see Cynthia H. Whittaker, *Russian Monarchy: Eighteenth-Century Rulers and Writers in Political Dialogue* (DeKalb: Northern Illinois University Press, 2003). On court society, see Norbert Elias, *The Court Society*, trans. Edmund Jephcott (New York: Pantheon Books, 1983).

6   Gukovskii, *Ocherki po istorii russkoi literatury XVIII veka*, 13.

7   Richard S. Wortman, *Scenarios of Power: Myth and Ceremony in Russian Monarchy* (Princeton, NJ: Princeton University Press, 1995), 1: 3–4.

8   Roy Strong, *Art and Power: Renaissance Festivals 1450–1650* (Woodbridge: Boydell, 1984); J. R. Mulryne, Helen Watanabe-O'Kelly, and Margaret Shewring, eds., *Europa Triumphans: Court and Civic Festivals in Early Modern Europe* (London: MHRA,

Accordingly, I consider Sumarokov's poetics from a perspective that is both historicist (or "new historicist") and comparative. On the one hand, the plays reflect cultural developments shared across early modern Europe, and on the other, they illuminate the political context of the "absolute" monarchy, its symbolic outlines, and historical practices. Stephen Orgel concludes in his pioneering account of court theatrics that "dramas at court were not entertainments in the simple and dismissive sense we usually apply to the word. They were expressions of the age's most profound assumptions about the monarchy."[9] Tragedy was particularly suited to negotiate the symbolic outlines of authority and its tensions. In his famous study, *The Origin of the German Tragic Drama*, Walter Benjamin emphasizes that for baroque tragic drama (*Trauerspiel*),

> it is … the confirmation of princely virtues, the depiction of princely vices, the insight into diplomacy and the manipulation of all the political schemes, which makes the monarch the main character in the *Trauerspiel* … The image of the setting or, more precisely, of the court, becomes the key to historical understanding. For the court is the setting *par excellence*.[10]

German baroque drama, read and performed in eighteenth-century Russia, seems to have been much more closely related to Sumarokov's plays than critics usually assume. In any case, the first Russian tragedies also dealt with historical (or mythistorical) subjects set in royal residences ("v kniazheskom dome," "v tsarskom dome") populated by "tsars, princes and magnates."[11] Far from being a mere formality, the classicist "unity of space" shaped tragedy as a political genre.

2004); Pierre Béhar and Helen Watanabe-O'Kelly, eds., *Spectaculum Europaeum: Theatre and Spectacle in Europe (1580–1750)* (Wiesbaden: Harrassowitz, 1999).

9   Stephen Orgel, *Illusion of Power* (Berkeley: University of California Press, 1975), 8.

10   Walter Benjamin, *The Origin of the German Tragic Drama*, trans. John Osborne (New York: Verso, 1985), 62, 92. Among more recent discussions of the links between early modern tragedy and the concepts of the political, see Anselm Haverkamp, *Shakespearean Genealogies of Power: A Whispering of Nothing in "Hamlet, Richard II, Julius Caesar, Macbeth, The Merchant of Venice, and The Winter's Tale"* (London: Routledge, 2011).

11   Gukovskii, *Russkaia literatura XVIII veka*, 135.

While political readings of Russian classicist tragedy are nothing new, its true relationship to autocratic politics, often obscured by tedious Soviet academic idiom, still remains largely unexplored, as even a superficial comparison with the scholarship on the Western versions of the genre affirms. Instead of accepting at face value established "progressist" narratives of Petrine Westernization or the emergence of "enlightened absolutism" as a backdrop for Sumarokov's dramatic production, this study approaches tragedy as a genre that voiced and perpetuated much more somber visions of autocracy and the traumatic collective experiences of its subjects. Operating beyond anachronistic and simplifying concepts of "propaganda" on the one hand and "oppositional criticism" on the other, I investigate the deeply ambivalent patterns of authority that relied on fear instilled by constant and often spectacular judicial terror as much as on displays of prosperity and political harmony, as outlined by Wortman.

Benjamin has linked early modern tragic drama to a vision of sovereignty as originating in extraordinary displays of power in a "state of exception" beyond any law, a vision which "positively demands the completion of the image of the sovereign, as a tyrant."[12] Elaborating on Benjamin's interpretation, Louis Marin argued that since the exceptional act of violence that lay at the foundation of royal authority, the *coup d'état*, was beyond any regulation by theoretical discourse, an absolutist "theory of politics" was in fact provided by the "practice of theater."[13] Tragedy exposed and reenacted the profoundly theatrical mechanics of autocracy, which is emphasized in more recent theoretical assessments as well. Max Weber's theory of charisma, Carl Schmitt's revival of Machiavelli and Hobbes, and Michel Foucault's discussion of public punishment all agree that authority originates in extraordinary acts of violence.[14] Specifically, the interpretation of tragedy suggested by Benjamin and Marin relies on Carl Schmitt's reading of early modern

---

12 Benjamin, *Origin of the German Tragic Drama*, 69.

13 Louis Marin, "Théâtralité et pouvoir: Magie, machination, machine: *Médée* de Corneille," in *Politiques de la représentation* (Paris: Kimé, 2005), 264–266.

14 Max Weber, *The Theory of Social and Economic Organization*, trans. A. M. Henderson and Talcott Parsons (New York: Oxford University Press, 1947); Carl Schmitt, *Political Theology: Four Chapters on the Concept of Sovereignty*, trans. George Schwab (Cambridge, MA: Harvard, 1985); Michel Foucault, *Discipline and Punish: The Birth of the Prison*, trans. Alan Sheridan (New York: Vintage Books, 1979).

political literature of "reason of state," which encouraged royal violence and was well known in eighteenth-century Russia. Just like Machiavellian political treatises, the newly imported genre of tragedy also revolved around conspiracies, death sentences, and royal pardons, unfolding the theatrical effects of sovereign acts.

Laying the ground for his analysis of Russian political symbolism, Wortman asks why Russia's rulers, "who disposed of a formidable administration and army," would require "demonstrative displays," and argues that

> such presentations, by "acting on the imagination," tied servitors to the throne as much as the prerequisites and emoluments they received from state service. To understand the persistence of absolute monarchy in Russia and the abiding loyalty of the nobility, we must examine the ways that these feelings were evoked and sustained.[15]

Poetics of theater, considered since the time of Aristotle to be a perfect medium for the manipulation of collective emotion, provided a paradigm for absolutist exercise of power, and students of European cultural history (and tragedy in particular) have amply explored this parallel.[16] Indeed, Aristotelian concepts that shaped tragedy as a genre—pity and fear, guilt, justice and punishment— were easily realigned to reflect the collective experience of an absolutist public, both in official discourse and in widely shared idioms of ego documents such as letters and memoirs. In the Anonym's account, cultural patterns of domination and submission provided the natural background for an assessment of Russian literature and theater inaugurated by Sumarokov. As my study will demonstrate, these patterns were not only the historical context for Sumarokov's tragedies but also made up the very fabric of their drama.

---

15 Wortman, *Scenarios of Power*, 1: 3–4.

16 Jean-Marie Apostolidès, *Le prince sacrifié: théâtre et politique au temps de Louis XIV* (Paris: Éd. de Minuit, 1985); Stephen Greenblatt, *Shakespearean Negotiations: The Circulation of Social Energy in Renaissance England* (Berkeley: University of California Press, 1988), 62–65; Matthew H. Wikander, *Princes to Act: Royal Audience and Royal Performance, 1578–1792* (Baltimore, MD: Johns Hopkins University Press, 1993).

❖ ❖ ❖

The book contains four lengthy parts, or chapters, which have been subdi-vided into smaller rubrics for comprehensibility's sake; however, they remain close-knit entities. The first part, "Political Theater and the Origins of Russian Tragic Drama," outlines the historical background of early Russian tragedy and its links to court theater as an institution and practice, and proceeds to discuss the fundamental symbolic structures of power and cultural patterns that informed the existence of tragedy as a genre. Its first section, "Theater at Court," inscribes the emergence of Russian dramatic theater into a broader European institutional and cultural context. The growing number of theatrical productions by foreign companies (French, German, and Italian), which made Petersburg a part of the pan-European circuit of court theaters, set the tone for the publication of Sumarokov's first tragedy in 1747 and the (re)emergence of Russian-language court theater in 1750–1756. Various dramatic genres—and tragedy above all—were inte-grated into the general mechanics of courtly ceremony and seen as a medium of political representation and signification. Contemporary dramatic theory explored the political perspective on theater and viewed neoclassical revival of drama as a political symbol, an attribute of a strong—that is to say, "abso-lutist"—monarchy. The immediate consequences of this vision for Russia are illuminated in the second section, "Sumarokov and the *réformation du théâtre*," which traces the impact of West European views of theater on Russian theatrical practice and, in particular, Sumarokov's introduction of classicist drama. Modeled on Gottsched's German reform, which aimed to revive the interest of the ruling elites for the national theater, Sumarokov's effort was driven more by the emerging culture of the court, where the arts were consciously interwoven with royal politics, than by the theoretical dogmatism traditionally ascribed to him by scholars.

The following sections, "Political Theater and the Poetics of Autocracy" and "'Scenarios of Power': The Politics of Tragic Plots," explore the deeper structures of theater—and tragedy in particular—as an institution of royal power, as outlined both in early modern criticism and contemporary schol-arship. Reflecting on commonplaces of classicist literary theory, Russian and European plays, and episodes from court history, these sections illuminate a fundamental affinity between the effects of tragedy as a spectacle and the cultural mechanics that underlay and drove royal power. Royal charisma and the public's submission to it were seen to depend on performance and representation. While this vision contradicted absolutist orthodoxy, it found its way to royal stages where the complex and ambiguous relationship between ruler and subjects could be negotiated under the guise of a fictional plot. In the last section of the first part, "Dramatic Experience: Tragedy and the Emotional Economy of the Court," I investigate the types of emotional experience that made tragic grief an intrinsic part of a ceremonial culture that we usually associate with displays of collective triumph. Tragedy was a medium for melancholy, an emotion often associated in early modern cultural theory and artistic practice with life at court, and it formed a central part of the emotional experience of Sumarokov's contemporaries. Constant fluctuations between royal favor and disgrace, triumph and despair, which were as characteristic for eighteenth-century Russia as they were for all other absolutist polities, provided an emotional matrix of terror that both empowered arbitrary royal rule and secured a cultural niche for tragedy.

Developing general points made in Part I, the two following parts offer detailed readings of Sumarokov's two first tragedies: *Khorev* (1747) and *Gamlet* (1748). Part 2, "*Khorev*, or the Tragedy of Origin," deals with Sumarokov's tragedy centered on a legendary Kievan ruler, Kii. The first section, titled "Poetry, History, Allegory," discusses the mode of representation employed in court tragedies, oscillating between poetic fiction, historical legend, and the allegories of court masques. Drawing on *Khorev*'s various contexts in Russia and Europe, the section seeks to illuminate the functions of dramatic representation that elevates singular episodes, historical or fictional, to symbolic scenarios of political order and thus asserts a central position in the monarchy's symbolic economy. The next two sections ("*Khorev* and the Scenario of Marriage" and "Pastoral Politics and Tragedy") investigate the pastoral symbolism of love and marriage, as pivotal for early modern royal myths as it was for the genre of tragedy. Defined in a politically-nuanced way, with terms such as freedom, power, and submission, love functions simultaneously as a source of dramatic interest, a metaphor of political order, and a political emotion suited to shape the monarchy's relationship to its subjects. As the final section, "The Tragedy of Suspicion," demonstrates, this pastoral utopia is threatened by royal terror, a darker facet of monarchy that is represented in *Khorev* as properly tragic. Aligning the progress of his plot with the procedure of political prosecution (and reinforcing it with allusions to actual contemporary high-profile trials), Sumarokov displays in the very first Russian literary drama the patterns of violent spectacle that tragedy as a genre shared with the practices of royal terror.

The third part, "Poetic Justice: Coup d'état, Political Theology, and the Politics of Spectacle in the Russian *Hamlet*," is concerned with *Gamlet*, Sumarokov's loose adaptation of Shakespeare's *Hamlet*. Substituting Shakespeare's final catastrophe with a happy ending (his Gamlet triumphs over Claudius and can marry Ophelia), Sumarokov turns his play into a celebration of royal triumph, an allusion to Empress Elizabeth's successful coup d'état of 1741. Although he retains some of the religious mysticism of Shakespeare's play, including the Ghost, who now appears in an off-stage dream, Sumarokov reinforces the identification of metaphysical justice with an earthly order of power established through overt violence. This is the subject of the first section, "Tragedy and Political Theology." The second, "The Drama of Coup d'état," investigates the link between tragedy and revolt, acknowledged by contemporary critics. Political theorists since Machiavelli have interpreted a spectacular and violent seizure of power as a legitimate source of authority, and tragedy was a medium suited to explore—and reenact—the dependence of political order on quasi-theatrical effects. The third section, "Anatomy of Melancholy, or Gamlet the Hero," is concerned with Sumarokov's reinterpretation of Hamlet and his famous hesitation to act: while in Shakespeare it leads away from the political, Sumarokov refashions it as a character trait appropriate for a political tactician who needs to consider his timing. Sumarokov's protagonist is thus firmly grounded in the Machiavellian "political anthropology" (Benjamin) developed in copious manuals of political conduct read and translated in eighteenth-century Russia. The fourth section, "Investigations of Malice," deals with Gamlet's adversaries, Klavdii (Claudius) and Polonii (Polonius). In depicting them as demonic "politicians" who "would circumvent God" (to quote Shakespeare), Sumarokov aligns dramatic introspection and religious interiority with the moral discipline imposed by the post-Petrine state in its claim for sacred authority. Finally, the fifth and last section, "The Catharsis of Pardon," offers a reading of the play's double ending. The triumphant Gamlet hesitantly pardons the captive Polonii, who then immediately commits suicide. Within the context of the play, Polonii's end is interpreted as an act of divine retribution. In a detailed comparison with Empress Elizabeth's judicial acts, the section explores the emotional mechanics of royal terror, adopted and perpetuated by tragedy.

The epilogue, "The Theater of War and Peace: The 'Miracle of the House of Brandenburg' and the Poetics of European Absolutism," addresses the interaction of dramatic poetics and patterns of political action from another perspective. It illuminates the cultural poetics of pan-European absolutist politics, as revealed during the Seven Years' War (1756–1763) and its outcome, known as the "miracle of the house of Brandenburg." Political self-fashioning of the war's two major actors, the Russian Emperor Peter III and Prussian King Frederick II, and their reading of events, were shaped by "scenarios of power" elaborated in tragedy and *opera seria*, the two major theatrical genres of pan-European absolutist theater specifically suited to negotiate fundamental visions of sovereignty. For Frederick, himself a man of letters and a poet, tragedy provided a paradigm of royal charisma paradoxically affirmed by the defeats threatening its very essence. In this way, theatrical interest for an unfortunate hero, the fundamental aesthetic effect of tragedy, served as a model for patriotic mobilization around the figure of the defeated rather than the triumphant king. On the other hand, the instant restitution of all conquered Prussian territory by Peter III immediately after his ascension to the throne was conceived as a spectacular gesture inaugurating a scenario of clement rule, canonized in some of the central texts of the neoclassical dramatic canon. This scenario extended to the internal policies of the new emperor, whose important measures—such as the abolishment of the terrifying secret police—relied on theatrical patterns of manipulating public emotion in favor of the "ruler-as-actor." Peter's subsequent political failure and Frederick's spectacular success stand in a complex, not to say counterintuitive, relationship to their differing yet connected "scenarios of power."

Situated on an intersection of literary criticism, political history, and cultural analysis, my study explores some of the fundamental symbolic patterns that underlay both political and literary practice in eighteenth-century Russia and early modern Europe. It draws attention to texts and events scarcely remembered outside of traditional disciplinary niches, and simultaneously aims to contribute to a broader discussion of early modern "poetics of culture" that pertains equally to literary texts and historical actions.

PART I

POLITICAL THEATER AND THE ORIGINS OF RUSSIAN TRAGIC DRAMA

THEATER AT COURT

Censuring Empress Anna's lack of cultural policy, the Anonym implicitly but clearly contrasts her reign to the much more fruitful succeeding reign of Elizabeth, which brought forth the first consistent efforts of the Russian court at literary patronage, often epitomized by the names of Lomonosov and Sumarokov.[1] Indeed, the Anonym's emphasis on court theater and public spectacle closely corresponds to the practice of Elizabeth's early years: while she originally did not show much interest in literature *per se*, and only her favorites, such as "the Russian Maecenas" Ivan Shuvalov, gradually began to encourage writers in her name, court theater experienced an immediate and powerful revival after her ascension in 1741. Expanding her predecessors' efforts, Elizabeth supported an Italian opera, hiring new singers and even her own librettist, Giuseppe Bonecchi, who received the title of an "imperial poet." A French dramatic company lead by Charles Sérigny was hired by the Russian court and arrived in Petersburg in 1743, initiating a tradition of French-language court theater that would last until the fall of the Russian empire. German companies also occasionally performed in Petersburg with royal privilege.[2]

---

1   On the patronage strategy adopted in the 1750s by Elizabeth's favorite, Ivan Shuvalov, in order to merge the competing literary efforts of the two writers into a politically informed image of Russia's benevolent monarchy, see Kirill Ospovat, "Gosudarstvennaia slovesnost': Lomonosov, Sumarokov i literaturnaia politika I. I. Shuvalova v kontse 1750-kh gg.," in *Evropa v Rossii*, ed. Pekka Pesonen, Gennadii Obatnin, and Tomi Khuttunen (Moscow: Novoe literaturnoe obozrenie, 2010).

2   On the history of court theater under Elizabeth, see Iakob Shtelin [Jacob von Stählin], *Muzyka i balet v Rossii XVIII v.* (St. Petersburg: Soiuz khudozhnikov, 2002);

From the early years of Russian court theater, Italian *opera seria* and French classicist drama, the two major genres of European court stages, became a usual part of court festivities. These festivities symbolically marked important political occasions—such as Elizabeth's coronation in 1742; the Peace of Abo, which sealed Russia's decisive victory in a short war against Sweden in 1743; and the marriage of the heir apparent Grand Duke Petr Feodorovich to Ekaterina Alekseevna, the future Catherine II, in 1745. They might also have been staged to celebrate one of the commemorative dates that dominated the yearly festive cycle: the anniversary of the empress's coronation on April 25, her name day on September 5, ascension day on November 25, and birthday on December 18. The first opera of Elizabeth's reign was Pietro Metastasio's *La Clemenza di Tito*, performed during her coronation festivities in the spring of 1742. As I will come to show, this opera, which was well suited for the occasion and was repeatedly revived over Elizabeth's reign, was meant to constitute and reenact her "scenario of power." In the next years the imperial poet Giuseppe Bonecchi composed five libretti, tailored for court festivities and extolling royal virtues in a common Metastasian allegorical idiom: *Seleuco* (Selevk, 1744), *Scipione* (Stsipion, 1745), *Mitridate* (Mitridat, 1747), *Bellerofonte* (Bellerofont, 1750), and *Eudossa incoronata* (Evdoksiia venchannaia, 1751).

Although Sérigny's productions were not limited to ceremonial occasions, they were also styled as a political medium, claiming for the Russian monarchy the theatrical symbolism associated with the glory of Versailles. The known history of Sérigny's work in Russia begins with a *divertissement* celebrating the peace with Sweden in 1744 and theatrical festivities accompanying the royal nuptials in 1745. The elaborate theatrical production

---

V. N. Vsevolodskii-Gerngross, *Teatr v Rossii pri imperatritse Elizavete Petrovne* (St. Petersburg: Giperion, 2003); Iu. A. Dmitriev, ed., *F. G. Volkov i russkii teatr ego vremeni. Sbornik dokumentov* (Moscow: Izd. Akademii Nauk, 1953); A. A. Gozenpud, *Muzykal'nyi teatr v Rossii ot istokov do Glinki: ocherk* (Leningrad: Muzgiz, 1959); L. M. Starikova, ed., *Teatral'naia zhizn' Rossii v epokhu Elizavety Petrovny. Dokumental'naia khronika*, vol. 2, bk. 1 (Moscow: Nauka, 2003), vol. 2, bk. 2 (Moscow: Nauka, 2005), vol. 3, bk. 1 (Moscow: Nauka, 2011); N. A. Ogarkova, *Tseremonii, prazdnestva, muzyka russkogo dvora, XVIII–nachalo XIX veka* (St. Petersburg: Bulanin, 2004). On the politics of eighteenth-century Russian court theater, see A. S. Korndorf, *Dvortsy Khimery. Illuzornaia arhitektura i politicheskie alluzii pridvornoi stseny* (Moscow: Progress-Traditsiia, 2011), and, in a perspective very similar to mine, Alexei Evstratov, *Le théâtre francophone à Saint-Petersbourg sous le règne de Catherine II (1762–1796): Organisation, circulation et symboliques des spectacles dramatique* (PhD diss. Paris IV, 2012).

staged by the French company on this occasion, besides a comedy ("which has recently greatly entertained the French court," as the printed description stated) and a *divertissement* written by Sérigny himself, included a play by Molière, *La Princesse d'Élide* (*The Princess of Elis*), itself composed in 1664 on the orders of Louis XIV for the arguably most famous Versailles fête, *Les Plaisirs de l'Île enchantée* (*The Pleasures of the Enchanted Island*). According to the printed account, Sérigny's luxurious performance was highly approved of by the empress and the heir apparent, and allegedly inspired the astonished foreign ambassadors to compare Petersburg to Paris.[3] The next year, in 1746, Sérigny centered his theatrical celebration of the coronation day on Voltaire's tragedy *Mérope* (1743), which was both in vogue among the European public and, as I will show in part 3, could be construed as a theatrical reenactment of Elizabeth's ascension to power in 1741. The pan-European stage idiom of ceremonial allegory shaped and informed the first perceptions of neoclassical drama, and tragedy in particular, by the Russian court society, the audience of Sérigny's productions, and the primary readership interested in West European belles lettres.

Generally, as Wortman asserts, "Literature, art, and architecture were used to express the themes of the scenario [of power] in a current cultural idiom and glorify the monarch as an esthetic and cultural ideal."[4] This political perspective on the arts fueled the practices of court patronage, and was often voiced in literary and dramatic criticism. In eighteenth-century Russia, like France under Louis XIV and other early modern monarchies during certain stages of their history, the royal court as the center of political authority claimed a dominating role in cultural production and a prerogative to establish and define the "current cultural idiom." In Nicolas Boileau's *Art poétique* (1674), the bible of European neoclassical letters translated into Russian in 1752 by Vasilii Trediakovskii, the king was entrusted with the oversight of all literary production and invested with the rights of its supreme

---

3 Vsevolodskii-Gerngross, *Teatr v Rossii pri imperatritse Elizavete Petrovne.*
4 Wortman, *Scenarios of Power*, 6–7. On the interaction between courtly politics and Russian letters in the eighteenth century, see A. L. Zorin, *Kormia dvuglavogo orla . . . : literatura i gosudarstvennaia ideologiia v Rossii v poslednei treti XVIII–pervoi treti XIX veka* (Moscow: Novoe literaturnoe obozrenie, 2001); V. Iu. Proskurina, *Mify imperii: literatura i vlast' v epochu Ekateriny II* (Moscow: Novoe literaturnoe obozrenie, 2006).

arbiter. Recently a case has been made for a specific "courtly aesthetic" engendered by the elaborate ceremonial culture of early modern monarchies.[5] Court theater would certainly be a central space of such an aesthetic, as its institutional existence was emblematic of the interpenetration of political authority and artistic refinement.

A lengthy essay on the history of the opera, published in 1738 by the highly competent Jacob von Stählin in the only Russian journal of the time, *Primechaniia na vedomosti*, contained a detailed description of fetes held at different European courts since the Renaissance and praised the "illustrious courts accustomed to magnificence, great luxury and solid view of things," among them the Russian court with its first opera productions, as primary spaces of cultural development.[6] The laudatory *Portrait naturel de l'Imperatrice de Russie glorieusement regnant* (*True portrait of the gloriously reigning Empress of Russia*), published in Hamburg by a member of the Russian court around 1746, states:

> aussi entretient elle une opera italien, des plus beaux, qui soient en Europe, et une excellente troupe de comediens françois. ... Elle a le goût exquis: ce qui paroit, non seulement dans ses ajustemens et parures, mais encore dans ses festins, et dans tous les ouvrages qu'elle ordonne; ou le bon gout et la magnificence se trouvent egalement etalés; et l'on ne voit pas en Europe une cour plus leste et plus brillante que le sienne. Elle aime les sciences et les arts; entre autres, la musique, la peinture, et les beaux tableaux, qu'elle fait recueillie de tout coté.

> She supports an Italian opera, one of the best in Europe, and an excellent troupe of French actors. ... She has an exquisite taste, which is revealed not only in her ornaments and decorations but also in her festivities and everything made on her orders where

---

5 Jörg Jochen Berns and Thomas Rahn, eds., *Zeremoniell als höfische Ästhetik im Spätmittelalter und Früher Neuzeit* (Tübingen: Niemeyer, 1995); Thomas Rahn, *Festbeschreibung. Funktion und Topik einer Textsorte am Beispiel der Beschreibung höfischer Hochzeiten (1568–1794)* (Tübingen: Niemeyer, 2006).

6 "Istoricheskoe opisanie onago teatral'nogo deistviia, kotoroe nazyvaetsia opera" [1738], in *Teatral'naia zhizn' Rossii v epokhu Anny Ioannovny*, ed. L. M. Starikova (Moscow: Nauka, 1995), 532–557, 560.

good taste and magnificence are equally on display. One does not find in Europe a court more decorous and brilliant than hers. She loves sciences and arts, among them music, painting, and beautiful images she assembles from everywhere.[7]

Similar rhetoric was adopted by Voltaire, who, seeking connections to the Russian court, eulogized Elizabeth and her father, Peter the Great, in his academic speech of 1746 and the *Anecdotes sur le czar Pierre le Grand* (*Anecdotes on Peter the Great*, 1748): "A présent on a dans Pétersbourg des comédiens français et des opéras italiens. La magnificence et le goût même ont en tout succédé à la barbarie" (There are now in Petersburg French actors and Italian operas. Magnificence and even taste have succeeded barbarism).[8]

These statements provide an important perspective on the cultural field as it emerged in Elizabethan Russia. The evolving system of courtly patronage, which subordinated theater and other forms of cultural production to the modes of cultural consumption accepted by court society and canonized under the name of "taste," at the same time recognized artistic achievement as an important source of political legitimacy and prestige.[9] In his *Temple du Goût* (*The Temple of Taste*, 1733), where a broad range of artistic production is assessed along the lines of contemporary salon tastes, Voltaire praised court architects and musicians of Louis XIV together with Colbert and his building projects, which symbolized "the glory of the nation, the prosperity of the people, the wisdom and taste of its rulers."[10] In the case of Russia, the politically informed vision of "magnificence and taste" singled out theater as the most significant cultural institution of the local court civilization. Voltaire, whose opinions were so much valued in Petersburg that in the late 1750s

---

7   *Portrait naturel de l'Imperatrice de Russie Glorieusement Régnante ...* (Hambourg: s.d.), 4–7. This text is reproduced by M. I. Sukomlinov in his annotated edition of Lomonosov's works: M. V. Lomonosov, *Sochineniia ... s ob'iasnitel'nymi primechaniiami M. I. Suchomlinova* (St. Petersburg: Imperatorskaia Akademiia Nauk, 1891), 2: 222–226, second numbering.

8   Voltaire, *The Complete Works* 46: 55.

9   On the cultural consumption of court society and the uses of "taste," see Jean Pierre Dens, *L'honnête homme et la critique du goût: Esthétique et société au 17e siècle* (Lexington: French Forum, 1981); Claude Chantalat, *A la recherche du goût classique* (Paris: Klincksieck, 1992), 29–35.

10   Voltaire, *The Complete Works*, 9: 178–179.

he was hired to write the semi-official history of Peter the Great, wrote in the dedication to his tragedy *L'orphelin de la Chine* (*The Orphan of China*, 1755):

> the Chinese, Greeks, and Romans, are the only ancient nations, who were acquainted with the true spirit of society. Nothing indeed renders men more sociable, polishes their manners, or improves their reason more than the assembling them together for the mutual enjoyment of intellectual pleasure. Scarce had Peter the Great polished Russia before theatres were established there. The more Germany improves, the more of our dramatic representations has it adopted. Those few places where they were not received in the last age are never rank'd amongst the civilized countries.[11]

In imperial Russia's constant quest for fashioning and defining itself in the idiom of the West European powers, its counterparts and rivals, theater could become a symbolic touchstone for political achievement and dignity, both for outside observers and the Russian elite itself (as the Anonym's reasoning indicates).

In his discussion of Peter the Great's civilizing accomplishments, intended to humor his daughter Elizabeth, Voltaire drew on a specific European discourse on the uses of theater, which spanned dramatic and political theory. Its foremost example was Abbé d'Aubignac's extensive treatise *La pratique du théâtre* (*The Practice of Theater*, 1657), conceived under the auspices of France's famous first minister Cardinal Richelieu, and accommodated to his vision of state-sponsored public spectacle. In his preface, d'Aubignac writes:

> All those Incomparable and Famous Genius's which, from time to time, Heaven designs for the Government of Mankind ... use to Crown all their Endeavours for the publick safety, with publick Pleasures and Entertainments, making their own glorious Labours either the means or the pretexts of all general Diversions. ...

---

11   Voltaire, *Dramatic Works*, trans. Rev. Mr. Francklin (London: J. Newbery et al., 1763), 3: 232. See also Voltaire, *The Complete Works*, 45A: 111–112.

whether to shew the greatness of a State, either in Peace or War; to inspire the People with Courage, or to instruct them in the knowledge and practice of Virtue; or, lastly, to prevent Idleness ... Princes can never do any thing more advantageous for their own Glory, nor for their Peoples Happiness, than to found, settle, and maintain at their own Charges, publick Spectacles, Games, and other Diversions, in the greatest Order, and the noblest Magnificence that their Crown will afford.[12]

The absolutist mystique of a supreme and all-embracing royal power, invested in this case in the first minister, forms the starting point for d'Aubignac's system of theatrical poetics. Literary drama, the main subject of his treatise, is discussed against the backdrop of courtly festivals and other forms of spectacle such as fireworks and ballets. At the same time, Richelieu's political authority is presented as the only force capable of implementing a neoclassical restitution of dramatic theater: "And indeed it belong'd to no body more to adorn the Kingdom with all delightful Spectacles, than to him; who every day encreas'd our Victories, and Crown'd us with new Lawrels."[13] D'Aubignac's identification of literary reform with the intrusion of political prerogative into the sphere of letters, and theater in particular, was echoed in later writings and, apparently even before Voltaire, shaped the visions of cultural developments in post-Petrine Russia.

---

12   [François-Hédelin d'Aubignac], *The Whole Art of the Stage* (London: n.p., 1684; reprint, New York: Blom, 1968), 1–2, 7. For the original, see Hélène Baby's recent critical edition: François-Hédelin d'Aubignac, *La pratique du théâtre* (Paris: Champion, 2001), 37–38, 43. For an analysis of d'Aubignac's argument, see Baby's discussion in the same volume (496–497), and, more generally, Déborah Blocker's insightful study of the political agendas behind the shaping of neoclassical theatrical practices in France under Richelieu: Déborah Blocker, *Instituer un «art». Politiques du théâtre dans la France du premier XVIIe siècle* (Paris: Champion, 2009).

13   [François-Hédelin d'Aubignac], *The Whole Art of the Stage*, 12. See also d'Aubignac, *La pratique du théâtre*, 53.

SUMAROKOV AND THE
réformation du théâtre

In 1743 Empress Elizabeth "accepted with pleasure" a dedication addressed to her by a renowned French actor and theatrical writer Louis Riccoboni and annexed to his treatise with the meaningful title *De la réformation du théâtre* (*On the Reformation of Theater*):

> I would dare to say that the establishment of a theater in Russian ... is an endeavor worthy of the glorious daughter of Peter the Great ... Thereby Russia would achieve new glory in the fine arts, and would give an example, or rather a model, to other empires who would be the more eager to follow it as they already admire the virtues of Your Imperial Majesty and would be honored to submit their prejudices to the truth proclaimed by her.[1]

While Riccoboni's project of a moralizing purgation of the dramatic canon does not seem to have had any impact on Russian practice, his conventional view of theater as a political affair and a matter of royal glory sets the conceptual framework for literary and institutional developments in Elizabethan Russia. Unlike Voltaire (who was flattered to know that Elizabeth "takes some pleasure in attending the performances

---

1   Louis Riccoboni, *De la réformation du théâtre* (Paris: n.p., 1743), vii–viii. For a Russian translation of the dedication and Elizabeth's favorable reaction to it, see Starikova, *Teatral'naia zhizn' Rossii v epokhu Elizavety Petrovny*, vol. 2, bk. 2, 149, 145.

of my plays" in the French original[2]), Riccoboni emphasized the need for dramatic performances in the national language. Only four years later, in 1747, Aleksandr Sumarokov, an officer of the guards, adjutant to the empress's favorite, Alexei Razumovskii, and the fashionable author of love songs, published his neoclassical tragedy *Khorev*, Russia's first literary drama. By 1750, Sumarokov was overseeing the performance of his plays before the empress by the distinguished youth of the Noble Cadet Corps. In 1756, "Russian theater" under his direction was officially established at court alongside French and Italian companies, a date still celebrated as the beginning of its institutional history. As D. Lang wrote in 1948,

> In establishing the St Petersburg theatre, Sumarokov and his collaborators Volkov and Dmitrievsky had to contend with a task even more formidable than that which had confronted Gottsched in Germany twenty years earlier. The only means of ensuring the continued patronage of the Empress Elisabeth, whose encourage-ment and financial support were indispensable, was to compose dramas in Russian which could compare favourably with those acted by the rival Italian and French troupes.[3]

To be sure, practices of Russian-language playwriting and performance were long in place by 1750. A tradition of court spectacle and political drama was initiated in 1672 by Elizabeth's grandfather, Tsar Aleksei, who ordered the Moscow Protestant pastor Johann Gottfried Gregorii to prepare a stage version of the Book of Esther. The ensuing play, *Artakserksovo deistvo* (*The Comedy of Artoxerxes*), a baroque tragedy centered on the figure of the *tsar*, as biblical kings were known in Russia, inaugurated a series of plays and productions that would last well into the eighteenth century, not least under the patronage of the next two generations of royal women: Aleksei's daughter and sister to Peter the Great, Natalia Alekseevna, Peter's sister-in-law Tsaritsa Praskov'ia Fedorovna, her daughter Ekaterina Ioannovna (sister to Empress Anna), and Elizabeth herself, who had apparently enjoyed performances of

---

2   Voltaire, *The Complete Works*, 93 (Correspondence, vol. 9): 273.
3   D. M. Lang, "Sumarokov's *Hamlet*: A Misjudged Russian Tragedy of the Eighteenth Century," *Modern Language Review* 43, no. 1 (1948): 69.

this sort at her own small court in the 1730s. Some of the last full-scale baroque dramas in Russian were written and staged in 1742 to commemorate Elizabeth's ascension to power.[4]

In his remarkable analysis of the first Russian plays, A. N. Robinson reveals a fundamental affinity between their theatrical poetics and the "ceremonial aesthetic" of the royal court governed by elaborate etiquette (or, in Old Russian, *chin*, "order"). According to Robinson, this affinity paralleled and anticipated the "birth of the Russian classicism," and, more precisely, Sumarokov's import of neoclassical drama together with the complex set of rules regulating it.[5] The history of Russian court theater certainly corroborates this view, and the social codes embedded in neoclassical doctrine and practice are of primary importance for a historical discussion of early Russian drama. Sumarokov's dramatic enterprise, inscribed into the courtly practices of his own age, constituted a theatrical reform, *réformation du théâtre* in d'Aubignac's if not Riccoboni's sense. As the very notion of reform suggests, his experiments in neoclassical drama both negated the older tradition and resonated with it.

Sumarokov, as Lang accurately surmises, did not act without precedent. In 1759, proclaiming his success in tragic drama and stage production, he boasted that he alone had accomplished more than the "many poets" of Germany had been able to achieve.[6] This is apparently a reference to the theatrical reform launched around 1732 by the prominent German literary theorist Johann Christoph Gottsched, a university professor at Leipzig and a leading figure in the local literary society, the *Deutsche Gesellschaft.* Until the 1750s, Gottsched's neoclassical doctrine and his criticism of baroque literary

---

4 On early Russian court theater, see P. P. Pekarskii, *Nauka i literatura v Rossii pri Petre Velikom* (St. Petersburg: Tipografiia Tovarishchestva "Obshchestvennaia pol'za," 1862), 1: 372–478; I. A. Shliapkin, *Tsarevna Natal'ia Alekseevna i teatr ee vremeni* (St. Petersburg: n.p., 1898); L. A. Itigina, "K voprosu o repertuare oppozitsionnogo teatra Elizavety Petrovny v 1730-e gody," in *XVIII vek* (Leningrad: Nauka, 1974), 9: 321–331. The volumes of the fundamental publication series *Ranniaia russkaia dramaturgiia: (XVII–pervaia polovina XVIII v.)* will be referred to below.

5 O. A. Derzhavina, A. S. Demin, and A. N. Robinson, "Poiavlenie teatra i dramaturgii v Rossii XVII v.," in O. A. Derzhavina, A. S. Demin, and A. N. Robinson, eds., *Pervye p'esy russkogo teatra* (Moscow: Nauka, 1972), 97.

6 A. P. Sumarokov, *Polnoe sobranie vsekh sochinenii* (Moscow: v Universitetskoi tipografii u N. Novikova, 1787), 6: 371–372.

practices was generally shared by the German intellectuals residing in Russia, who dominated the Academy of Sciences in Petersburg and its journals, later populated Moscow University founded in 1755, and often had personal connections to Leipzig.[7] It was through these Germans, first of all the historian and a long-time Gottsched correspondent Gerhard Friedrich Müller, that Sumarokov established his well-documented contacts with the Saxon critic. In 1753 Gottsched published in his journal a favorable review of Sumarokov's third tragedy, *Sinav i Truvor*, urging German poets to follow his example in adopting plots from national history, and in 1755 a German translation of the same tragedy was included in a collection published by the *Deutsche Gesellschaft*. In 1756 Sumarokov was elected an honorary member of this society, and on many occasions he proudly referred to his connections to Leipzig and Gottsched. Gottsched's praise for Sumarokov's playwriting openly affirmed the kinship between their projects of dramatic and theatrical revival.

Gottsched's aim was to purge the traditional repertoire of the German itinerant companies, considered low and coarse, and to replace it with neoclassical plays either translated from canonical French authors or imitating them in style and structure. To that end, Gottsched allied with the company led by Friederike Caroline Neuber (Neuberin), writing for them his first tragedy, *Der Sterbender Cato* (*The Dying Cato*, 1732), which proved a theatrical success. He encouraged his readers to write neoclassical plays, and soon there were enough of them to fill the six volumes of his *Deutsche Schaubühne* (*The German Stage*, 1741–1745). (Sumarokov must have referred to this collection when he spoke of Germany's many dramatic poets.) While Gottsched intended to supplant the older German tradition of baroque drama (the same tradition that the Moscow pastor Gregorii drew upon), his

---

7   L. V. Pumpianskii, "Lomonosov i nemetskaia shkola razuma," in *XVIII vek*, vol. 14 (Leningrad: Nauka, 1983); L. V. Pumpianskii, "Trediakovskii i nemetskaia shkola razuma," in *Zapadnyi sbornik* (Moscow: Akademii Nauk, 1937); Ulf Lehmann, *Der Gottschedkreis und Russland* (Berlin: Akademie-Verlag, 1953); Helmut Grasshoff, *Russische Literatur in Deutschland im Zeitalter der Aufklärung* (Berlin: Akademie-Verlag, 1953); G. A. Gukovskii, "Russkaia literatura v nemetskom zhurnale XVIII veka," in *XVIII vek*, vol. 3 (Moscow: Akademii Nauk, 1958), 380–415; V. P. Stepanov, "Kritika man'erizma v 'Primechaniiakh k Vedomostiam,'" *XVIII vek.*, vol. 10 (Leningrad: Nauka, 1975), 39–48.

own dramatic oeuvre has been shown to retain many of its traits.[8] His reform concept was explicitly based on d'Aubignac's *La pratique du théâtre*, translated into German in 1737, and revived its emphasis on the relevance of theater for the fashioning of polities and their ruling elites.

In a speech given in 1729, Gottsched argued for the usefulness of theatrical performances, and tragedy in particular, as a didactic medium especially fit for "monarchs, emperors, kings, princes and lords."[9] Far from being Gottsched's own invention, this line of reasoning reveals the social implications of his reform and its sources, explored in the studies of Roland Krebs and Alexander Nebrig. In fact, the French-type neoclassical tragedy, which lay at the heart of Gottschedian reformed theater, had been introduced to Germany long before Gottsched, although sporadically and with much less nationwide publicity. As Nebrig demonstrates, German verse translations of plays by Racine and other French dramatists, appearing in print and on stage since the late seventeenth century, appealed to courtly taste and patronage. In the most famous fictional account of German theatrical life in the eighteenth century, Goethe's *Wilhelm Meister*, the aspiring actor is advised that when admitted to aristocratic company he should "praise Racine, the Prince's favorite dramatist."[10] While German courts usually preferred French originals to German translations, an interest in neoclassical tragedy in the national language had developed at a very small but dynastically well connected and culturally significant ducal court of Braunschweig-Wolfenbüttel. Verse translations of several French plays made as early as the 1690s by the local court poet Christian Bressand are now considered an important point of origin for the German tradition of neoclassical tragedy. Decades later, the Braunschweig dynasty encouraged and supported Neuberin's and Gottsched's experiments in German spoken drama, and indeed the tastes of the Wolfenbüttel court formed the nucleus for Gottsched's concept of national theatrical

---

8 Peter-André Alt, *Tragödie der Aufklärung: eine Einführung* (Tübingen: Francke, 1994), 72–75.

9 Johann Christoph Gottsched, "Die Schauspiele, und besonders die Tragödien sind aus einer wohlbestellten Republik nicht zu verbannen," in Johann Christoph Gottsched, *Schriften zur Literatur* (Stuttgart: Reclam, 1972), 3–11.

10 Johann Wolfgang Goethe, *Wilhelm Meister's Apprenticeship*, ed. and trans. Eric A. Blackall (New York: Suhrkamp Publishers, 1989), 104.

reform, itself addressed to the ruling elites and court societies of the German states.[11] This development was later summarized by Herder:

> Theater came to Germany as a court festivity. The populace was allowed as rabble to learn from the magnificent cataclysms of court and state which took place behind the lamps. In some places in Germany the stage has retained this appearance and organization of a court theater, and thus remains outside of the sphere of art, as it belongs to court etiquette.[12]

The complex political and dynastic arrangement of divided Germany provided the framework for Gottsched's and Neuberin's relatively unsuccessful attempts to establish German neoclassical theater as a public medium acknowledged by the ruling groups, and at the same time procured them connections to Russia. Bressand's royal patron, Duke Anton Ulrich von Braunschweig-Wolfenbüttel, himself a prominent writer, was well acquainted with Peter the Great, whom he had introduced to Leibniz, and arranged a marriage of his granddaughter with Peter's son and heir apparent, Aleksei. The couple died before they had a chance to ascend the Russian throne, but their son shortly ruled Russia as Peter II in 1727–1730. Another ill-fated dynastic marriage, which tied Anton Ulrich's great-grandson and namesake with Peter the Great's grandniece Anna Leopoldovna in 1739, produced Russia's infant emperor Ivan VI, who inherited the throne after the death of Empress Anna in 1740. He was overthrown by Elizabeth in 1741 and, along with his parents, incarcerated for the rest of his life. In 1739, Neuberin's

---

11 Alexander Nebrig, *Rhetorizität des hohen Stils: der deutsche Racine in französischer Tradition und romantischer Modernisierung* (Göttingen: Wallstein Verlag, 2007), 30–32, 48–69, 96; see also Dirk Neufanger, *Geschichtsdrama der frühen Neuzeit, 1495–1773* (Tübingen: De Gruyter, 2005), 248–250; Roland Krebs, *L'Idée de "Théâtre National" dans l'Allemagne des Lumières* (Wiesbaden: Harrassowitz, 1985), 41, 72–73, 91–92. On the court connections of the *Deutsche Gesellschaft* in Leipzig, see Kerstin Heldt, *Der vollkommene Regent. Studien zur panagyrischen Casuallyrik am Beispiel des Dresdner Hofes Augusts des Starken (1670–1733)* (Tübingen: Niemeyer, 1997), 237–266. On the courtly views on drama in eighteenth-century Germany, see Norbert Elias, *The Civilizing Process*, trans. Edmund Jephcott (Malden, MA: Blackwell Publishing, 2003), 15–20.

12 Johann Gottfried Herder, *Briefe zur Beförderung der Humanität* (Frankfurt: Deutscher Klassiker Verlag, 1991), 311.

company was invited to play at the Russian court and was reportedly met with approval; however, after Empress Anna's death, Neuberin's stay in Russia was cut short.[13] Among the few German rulers who expressed interest in Neuberin's enterprise was Karl Friedrich von Schleswig-Holstein-Gottorf, who had been married to Peter the Great's daughter and Elizabeth's sister Anna Petrovna. Their son Karl Peter Ulrich was summoned to Russia after Elizabeth's ascension and in 1743 officially proclaimed heir apparent as Grand Duke Petr Feodorovich. He would rule Russia for six months in 1762 as Peter III before being overthrown by his wife, Catherine II, and soon afterwards killed.

In 1739, it was Duke Karl Friedrich who recommended Neuberin's company to the Russian court. Several years later, in 1744–1745, she cited the Holsteinian privilege that had been issued to her as a pretext to petition for permission to return to Russia and take part in the nuptial festivities for the Grand Duke, who after his father's death had inherited the duchy of Holstein. Elizabeth declined, but not out of aversion for the neoclassical German theater of the type that Gottsched favored: on two festive occasions in 1750—at the peak of Sumarokov's playwriting and Elizabeth's interest for Russian drama—another company produced in Petersburg Corneille's *Cinna* and Racine's *Andromaque* in German translations, preceded by allegorical prologues praising the empress. Both productions, inscribed into courtly ceremonial, were commemorated in print.[14] In 1758, Christian Gottlob

---

13 Ludmilla M. Starikova, "Die Neuberin und das 'vorliterarische' Theater in St. Petersburg," in *Vernunft und Sinnlichkeit. Beiträge zur Theaterepoche der Neuberin*, ed. Bärbel Rudin and Marion Schulz (Vogtland: Reichenbach i. V Neuberg Museum, 1999), 200–217; Berthold Litzmann, "Die Neuberin in Petersburg," *Archiv für Litteraturgeschichte* 12 (1884): 316–318.

14 On Karl Friedrich, see Krebs, *L'Idée de "Théâtre National" dans l'Allemagne des Lumières*, 80. On Neuberin's petitions, see Starikova, "Die Neuberin und das 'vorliterarische' Theater in St. Petersburg," 207–209. For the Russian translation of the prologues, see Starikova, *Teatral'naia zhizn' Rossii v epokhu Elizavety Petrovny*, vol. 2, bk. 2, 113–127, 613. The German version of *Cinna* was entitled *Die Gnade des Augustus*. On German dramatic companies in Elizabethan Russia, see, besides the works of Vsevolodskii-Gerngross and Starikova, Christiane Hartter, "Deutschsprachiges Theaterleben in Russland in der Mitte des 18. Jahrhunderts. Der Prinzipal und Geschäftsmann Johann Peter Hilferding und seine Theaterunternehmen," in *Deutsches Theater im Ausland vom 17. zum 20. Jahrhundert*, ed. Horst Fassel et al. (Berlin: International Specialized Book Service Incorporated, 2007).

Köllner, one of the German professors in Moscow, reported to Gottsched that he had been requested by Melissino, a friend of Sumarokov's and an admirer of "tragic poetry" who oversaw the German company in Moscow, to translate for its use Houdart de La Motte's tragedy *Ines de Castro*, which had pleased the empress in French.[15]

There is little wonder, then, that Sumarokov's experiments in national Russian drama were also tailored for courtly taste. The very concept of "taste," used in the mid-1740s to reenhance Elizabeth's political prestige and to fashion the image of her court and empire, made one of its earliest appearances in Russian in 1748 in Sumarokov's programmatic *Epistola o stikhotvorstve* (*Epistle on Poetry*), often described as a "manifesto of Russian classicism," combining a formal adaptation of Boileau's *Art poétique* with strong influences of Voltaire's *Temple du Goût*, as Amanda Ewington has convincingly demonstrated.[16] While a detailed analysis of the *Epistola* and its courtly contexts must be relegated to a separate study, it suffices to say here that Sumarokov encouraged his courtly readership to write poetry in Russian, providing it both with a model to imitate and an instruction to follow. Among other things, the *Epistola* contained an outline of dramatic literature centered on the neoclassical rules as illustrated by the works of a few French dramatists whose plays are summarized and commented on—Racine, Molière, Destouches, and Voltaire—while other authors are mentioned in passing (and, as P. N. Berkov has established, the comedies of Jean-François Regnard and Marc-Antoine Legrand are silently alluded to).[17] This list gains unexpected overtones if compared to Sérigny's repertoire: according to our largely incomplete data, at least four out of ten tragedies and three out of nine comedies mentioned or referred to by Sumarokov in the *Epistola* and the accompanying notes had been performed on the Russian court stage in the 1740s (and another two comedies from this list were staged in Russian translations in the 1750s). The neoclassical dramatic canon, introduced by

---

15 Gukovskii, "Russkaia literatura v nemetskom zhurnale XVIII veka," 405.

16 Amanda Ewington, *A Voltaire for Russia: A. P. Sumarokov's Journey from Poet-Critic to Russian Philosophe* (Evanston, IL: Northwestern University Press, 2010), 18–22.

17 A. P. Sumarokov, *Izbrannye proizvedeniia*, ed. P. N. Berkova (Leningrad: Sovetskii pisatel', 1957), 529.

Sumarokov to Russian literature, largely matched the practices of the French theater established several years earlier under Elizabeth's royal patronage.

This is even more conclusively affirmed by individual examples. In the text of the *Epistola* only two of Voltaire's many tragedies are mentioned, *Alzire* and *Mérope*, both staged by Sérigny in 1746. Racine's *Mithridate*, summarized in the *Epistola* even before it was performed at Peterhof in 1750, provided the basis for Bonecchi's opera produced in 1747 on the empress's coronation day. In the preface to the printed edition, Bonecchi emphasized that Racine's tragedy is "well enough known" to the local audience.[18] The affinity between the ceremonial *opera seria* and spoken tragedy (repeatedly emphasized by Stählin, in his essay on the opera as well as during the lessons he gave to Grand Duke Peter) was in fact pivotal for the reception of tragedy on Russian soil.

In an important study, Ilya Serman linked Sumarokov's early style to that of Metastasio's and Bonecchi's libretti, which were published in translations or summaries simultaneously to festive productions, becoming the first dramatic texts in Russian to be approved for print.[19] Four such editions appeared between Elizabeth's ascension in 1742 and 1747, starting with a complete translation of *Clemenza di Tito* into syllabic verse. In 1746, this series was extended to include a Russian summary of Voltaire's tragedy *Mérope*, along with a short comedy performed together with it during courtly celebrations.[20] It was against this generically heterogeneous background of court drama that the Russian public had to read Sumarokov's first tragedy, *Khorev*, separately published by the Academy in 1747 (especially since, as Trediakovskii was quick to notice, it borrowed lines from *Mérope*).

Although Sumarokov's judgments on drama are easily recognized as commonplaces of neoclassical criticism, his approach to playwriting does not seem to be of a fundamentally theoretical nature. Amanda Ewington has convincingly argued against the traditional and by now almost self-evident view of Sumarokov as a "consistent and deliberate theoretician of literature,"

---

18   Starikova, *Teatral'naia zhizn' Rossii v epokhu Elizavety Petrovny*, vol. 2, bk. 1, 124.
19   Ilya Serman, "Lomonosov i pridvornye italianskie stikhotvortsy 1740-kh godov," in *Mezhdunarodnye sviazi russkoi literatury* (Leningrad: Izd. Akademii Nauk, 1963), 112–134.
20   Kirill Ospovat, "Iz istorii russkogo pridvornogo teatra 1740-kh gg.," in *Memento vivere: sbornik pamiati L. N. Ivanovoi* (St. Petersburg: Nauka, 2009), 9–36.

since, in fact, "despite a reputation as a dogmatic classicist, Sumarokov rarely alludes to rules in his [critical] work," "does not call upon classical authority," and "does not claim strict genre boundaries, but … justifies himself on the grounds of taste and violation of nature rather than tradition or rules."[21] Unlike the university professor Gottsched, who attempted to regulate stage performance along the lines of a philosophically grounded literary doctrine, Sumarokov developed as a practitioner of the emerging court theater with its challenges and exigencies, and apparently viewed neoclassical Aristotelian theory as a guide to a specific French-type practice, in a vein suggested by the very title of d'Aubignac's *La pratique du théâtre*. In his "Opinion in a Dream about French Tragedies," written in imitation of Voltaire's *Commentaires sur Corneille* (*Commentaries on Corneille*, 1764) he expressly opposed theatrical experience to theoretical reflection: "I am listening to a tragedy and not writing a treatise."[22] Sumarokov's stance was warranted by the notion of taste and rooted in the actual tastes of the court society, not necessarily respectful of theoretical delineations.

A central issue showcasing this sometimes slight, but important difference in approach is opera. While both Boileau and Gottsched, the two highly authoritative exponents of neoclassical doctrine, dismissed opera as deficient on theoretical grounds, Sumarokov was closer in this point to court poets like Bressand who had a "simultaneous interest—as a translator, but also as a director of court festivities—for operas as well as for classicist tragedies."[23] In his version of the European literary pantheon, presented in the *Epistola* of 1748, along with playwrights as alien to neoclassical regularity as Shakespeare, Lope de Vega (criticized by Boileau), Torquato Tasso with his *Aminta*, and the seventeenth-century Dutch baroque dramatist Joost van den Vondel, he mentions Philippe Quinault, the famous court librettist under Louis XIV, praised by Voltaire and described in Sumarokov's notes as "an author of French operas, a poet of a tender lyre."[24] In 1755–1758 Sumarokov himself, following a royal order, composed the first two operas in Russian, *Tsefal i Prokris* and *Altsesta*, which were successfully performed at court. Years later, he would still cite

---

21   Ewington, *A Voltaire for Russia*, 30, 41.
22   Sumarokov, *Polnoe sobranie vsekh sochinenii*, 4: 341; Ewington, *A Voltaire for Russia*, 70.
23   Nebrig, *Rhetorizität des hohen Stils*, 96.
24   Sumarokov, *Izbrannye proizvedeniia*, 127.

Quinault as a model of dramatic style, and extol his own dramatic achievement with a claim that "among my contemporaries only Voltaire and Metastasio are worthy to be my rivals."[25] Metastasio, the most celebrated Italian librettist of the eighteenth century, ranked by Voltaire among the greatest dramatic writers of his age, served as an "imperial poet" at the court of Vienna and personified the conjunction of learned drama with the courtly fete.[26]

Most recently, Joachim Klein has emphasized that in Sumarokov's time "the staging of tragedies was an element of courtly life, a link in the endless chain of festivities and amusements," centered on the empress and her tastes.[27] Throughout his career Sumarokov affirmed time and again that it was his main function as a dramatic writer "to serve her majesty with efforts undertaken for the entertainment of the court." Moreover, Marcus Levitt has demonstrated that Sumarokov depended on court patronage for social status and advancement.[28] In 1773 he reminded Catherine that "neither the late empress [Elizabeth] nor your majesty ... have ever ordered to perform my dramas without special favor, and I have always enjoyed a distinctive treatment by your majesties which nourished my ambition."[29] Indeed, if Gottsched's most cherished albeit unfulfilled goal was a permanent "national" theater under court sponsorship, Sumarokov was certainly justified in claiming that he achieved much more success than the Germans.[30]

---

25 Sumarokov, *Polnoe sobranie vsekh sochinenii*, 10: 5; Ewington, *A Voltaire for Russia*, 21; G. P. Makogonenko, ed., *Pis'ma russkikh pisatelei XVIII veka* (Leningrad: Nauka, 1980), 108.

26 On Voltaire's praise of Metastasio and its political resonances, see part 3. On Voltaire's views of the opera as a political medium, see Denis Fletcher, "Voltaire et l'opéra," in *L'opéra au XVIIIe siècle* (Aix-en-Provence: Université de Provence, 1982), 552–553. On Metastasio and the festive culture of the Habsburg court, see Andrea Sommer-Mathis, ed., *Pietro Metastasio—uomo universale (1698–1782)* (Vienna: Verlag der Osterrichisches Akademie der Wissenschaften, 2000); Laurenz Lütteken, ed., *Metastasio im Deutschland der Aufklärung* (Tübingen: Walter de Gruyter, 2002).

27 Joachim Klein, *Puti kul'turnogo importa. Trudy po russkoi literature XVIII veka* (Moscow: Iazyki slavianskoi kul'tury, 2005), 363.

28 Makogonenko, *Pis'ma russkikh pisatelei XVIII veka*, 83; Marcus Levitt, "The Illegal Staging of Sumarokov's *Sinav i Truvor* in 1770 and the Problem of Authorial Status in Eighteenth-Century Russia," in Marcus Levitt, *Early Modern Russian Letters: Texts and Contexts* (Boston: Academic Studies Press, 2009), 190–217, 205–213.

29 Makogonenko, *Pis'ma russkikh pisatelei XVIII veka*, 162.

30 Krebs, *L'Idée de "Théâtre National" dans l'Allemagne des Lumières*, 80–81; Theodor Wilhelm Danzel, *Gottsched und seine Zeit: Auszüge aus seinem Briefwechsel* (Leipzig: Dyk'sche Buchhandlung, 1848), 135–136.

Although his short, five-year tenure as theater director (1756–1761) proved a disaster, Russian theater was now firmly established to such an extent that Elizabeth's successor, Catherine II, who witnessed Sumarokov's first productions and showed support for him after her ascension in 1762, would herself write plays for its stage. For Sumarokov, the court and the royal figure at its heart were always his primary audience. As a theater director, he had to struggle with the court chancery, which denied him subsidies, claiming his theater was licensed as a "private" (i.e., independent and commercial) enterprise rather than an institution of the court. Bitterly complaining to Shuvalov, Sumarokov wrote that if that were the case, it would be better not to perform at all. In 1768, though his standing with Catherine had by that time deteriorated, he informed her that "wishing yet to please the court and the public," he hastened to "prepare something for your coronation day on the theatrical side," namely a tragedy, two comedies, and a comic opera.[31]

In a desperate attempt to regain control over the staging of his plays, Sumarokov wrote in 1775 that his tragedies had been written "for the court" and "for my [own] glory." The unruly Moscow, the traditional seat of Russian nobility and home to Russia's emerging public, required rather "a hundred Molières,"[32] while tragedy was specifically fitted for the court (which usually resided in Petersburg) and, accordingly, came to be recognized as the principal dramatic genre. Although Sumarokov did write comedies, they were mostly *Nachkomödien*, entertainment pieces designed to accompany more earnest performances. It is not incidental that his neoclassical literary reform was inaugurated in 1747 with a tragedy. Three years later, in 1750, in a singular gesture of cultural patronage, Empress Elizabeth personally ordered each of Sumarokov's two literary rivals, Lomonosov and Trediakosvkii, to write a tragedy for court productions.[33] Their lack of success only affirmed Sumarokov's domination over the Russian tragic stage, while the royal decree itself demonstrated the symbolic significance of tragedy for the courtly "theater of power."

---

31 Makogonenko, *Pis'ma russkikh pisatelei XVIII veka*, 77, 110.
32 Ibid. 176, 122.
33 Starikova, *Teatral'naia zhizn' Rossii v epokhu Elizavety Petrovny*, vol. 2, bk. 1, 804.

POLITICAL THEATER AND
THE POETICS OF AUTOCRACY

In an important study of the French court under Louis XIV, Doris Kolesch examines the court and its spectacular entertainments as a "theater of emotions," a space where royal power was generated as an effect of elaborately orchestrated collective sensibilities of the court society, symbolically representing the whole body politic.[1] Kolesch brings attention to a notorious passage in the *Mémoires pour l'instruction du Dauphin* drafted in Louis XIV's name and under his personal supervision. The royal narrator develops d'Aubignac's lessons on the political significance of festive theater for absolutist monarchy, and coins his own term for the appropriate kind of emotional community, "society of pleasures":

> A prince or a king of France may find something more in the public entertainments which are devised less for us than for our court and all our people. There are nations where the majesty of kings derives for the most part from their refusal to reveal themselves, and that can be reasonable among minds accustomed to slavery who can only be governed by fear and terror, but that's not the spirit of our Frenchmen ... it was necessary to conserve and cultivate with care

---

1 Doris Kolesch, *Theater der Emotionen: Ästhetik und Politik zur Zeit Ludwigs XIV* (Frankfurt and New York: Campus Verlag, 2006). See also Kathryn A. Hoffman, *Society of Pleasures: Interdisciplinary Readings in Pleasure and Power during the Reign of Louis XIV* (New York: St. Martin's Press, 1997).

all that which, without diminishing my authority and the respect which is due to me, linked my people, and especially the people of quality to me ... This society of pleasures, which gives the courtiers an honest familiarity with us, touches and charms them more than one could say. The people, on the other hand, enjoy spectacles, at which we, in any event, endeavor always to please, and all our subjects in general are delighted to see that we like what they like or that at which they succeed the best. By this we hold their minds and their hearts, sometimes more strongly than we do by rewards and kindnesses. And, for foreigners, in a State that they see flourishing and well regulated, what we spend on those things that might seem to be superfluous creates for them a very advantageous expression of magnificence, of power, of richness and grandeur.[2]

Following a logic that foreshadows Wortman's analysis of court theatrics, the king's ghost writer describes courtly festivities and the "society of pleasures" they shaped as a practically effective remedy against dissent and mutiny among the "people" and the "persons of quality," as well as a symbolic embodiment of the monarchy's benevolent relationship to its subjects, its primary guarantee for perpetual stability. The same issues framed the genre-specific discussion of tragedy that famously had been integrated into court celebrations under Louis XIV. Racine's classic, *Iphigénie*, was first performed in Versailles in the course of summer festivities of 1674, and more than a century later Goethe's Wilhelm Meister would emphasize that on reading Racine he "can always picture a poet residing at a brilliant court, with a great king before his eyes."[3] D'Aubignac insisted in his treatise that the success of a play depended on its conformity to the collective sensibilities of the public, which, in turn, had to be shaped by theatrical productions following d'Aubignac's own precepts. This circular argument was powered by a vision of an audience of subjects representative of the political nation

---

2   *Mémoires de Louis XIV pour l'instruction du Dauphin*, ed. Charles Dreyss (Paris: Didier, 1860), 2: 567–568. English translation partially quoted from Hoffman, *Society of Pleasures*, 173–174.

3   Goethe, *Wilhelm Meister's Apprenticeship*, 104.

and reinforced by their theatrical experience in an emotionally charged loyalty to the crown:

> Thus the Athenians delighted to see upon their Theatre the Cruelties of Kings, and the Misfortunes befalling them, the Calamities of Illustrious and Noble Families, and the Rebellion of the whole Nation for an ill Action of the Prince, because the State in which they liv'd being Popular, they lov'd to be perswaded that Monarchy was always Tyrannical, hoping thereby to discourage the Noble Men of their own Commonwealth from the attempt of seizing the Soveraignty, out of fear of being expos'd to the fury of a Commonalty, who would think it just to murther them. Whereas quite contrary among us, the respect and love which we have for our Princes, cannot endure that we should entertain the Publick with such Spectacles of horror; we are not willing to believe that Kings are wicked, nor that their Subjects, though with same appearance of ill usage, ought to Rebel against their Power: or touch their Persons, no not in Effigie; and I do not believe that upon our Stage a Poet could cause a Tyrant to be murder'd with any applause, except he had very cautiously laid the thing: As for Example, that the Tyrant were and Usurper, and the right Heir should appear, and be own'd by the People, who should take that occasion to revenge the injuries that had suffered from a Tyrant.[4]

Despite his absolutist stance and the apparently non-political focus of his work, d'Aubignac does not shy away from addressing the most prominent threats to the monarchical order, embedded in its own structure: tyranny and revolt. Expressing faith in the stability of the French monarchy, he nevertheless does not resort to the usual overconfident and loud-mouthed propagandistic idiom but instead links the "respect and love" inspired by sovereigns to a precarious dynamic of illusion: modern subjects are expected to willingly ignore the flaws of kings and the evidence of their abusive power, while the tempting notions of popular prerogative, disputed but backed by the influential example of ancient republicanism, still loom in accepted

---

4   [François-Hédelin d'Aubignac], *The Whole Art of the Stage*, 70; see also d'Aubignac, *La pratique du théâtre*, 119–120.

discourse. Riccoboni brings up similar issues in his *Dissertation sur la Tragédie Moderne* (*A Dissertation on Modern Tragedy*, 1730):

> Among the Greeks, the People having a great Share in the Government, nothing interested them so much as the Revolutions of Kingdoms: They were pleased to see the Passions drawn in such a manner as to occasion them, and to hear the Theatre adopt political Maxims. ... The French, contented with their happy Government, through a long Succession of Years under the wise Direction of their Princes, are less touched with Pictures resembling the Intrigues of Ambition: They with Joy behold Love and Jealousy keep Possession of their Stage ... Why may they not make their Princes represent Dramatic Heroes, as the English have done?[5]

If the predilection of French audiences for amorous themes was a reliable sign of the voluntary withdrawal of the people from the political sphere and their concession of power to the monarchy, then absolutist order had to be fragile: the public interest in the ruin of the powerful and "intrigues of ambition" might have been weakened but certainly was not extinguished, as canonical seventeenth-century plays such as Corneille's *Nicomède* (ca. 1650) and Racine's *Britannicus* (1669), among others, attest. Riccoboni's own sympathy for English-type political drama emphasizes the relevance of tragedy as a medium where royal power is (re)negotiated, and the community of subjects, consigned to passivity by absolutist political theory, reclaim their indubitable and threatening power over their rulers. Hélène Merlin-Kajman draws attention to an episode in *Nicomède*, where a popular revolt against an unworthy king is triggered by a perceived threat to Nicomède, the esteemed and valorous heir apparent. The rebels kill two henchmen involved in an intrigue against the prince, and continue to rage (5.4):

> Le peuple par leur mort pourrait s'être adouci;
> Mais un dessein formé ne tombe pas ainsi:

---

5 Louis Riccoboni, *An Historical and Critical Account of the Theatres in Europe, together with ... A Comparison of the Ancient and Modern Drama* (London: T. Waller, 1741), 329–330; see also Louis Riccoboni, *Histoire du théâtre italien ... et une dissertation sur la tragedie moderne* (Paris: André Cailleau, 1730), 1: 314–315.

Il suit toujours son but jusqu'à ce qu'il l'emporte;
Le premier sang versé rend sa fureur plus forte;
Il l'amorce, il l'acharne, il en éteint l'horreur,
Et ne lui laisse plus ni pitié ni terreur.

The peoples rage no further might pretend
But form'd designs have seldom such an end,
They press as what they have contriv'd before
The first bloodshed opens the way to more.
Fleshes, and hardens, does all horror chace
And unto fear or pitty leaves no place.

Nicomède's appearance appeases the mutinous subjects, and he restores their obedience to the lawful king, his father (5.9):

Tout est calme, seigneur: un moment de ma vue
A soudain apaisé la populace émue.

All's quiet sir, my sight did soon asswage
The peoples fury and has balmed their rage.[6]

As Merlin-Kajman notes, during the revolt the populace is freed from the constraints of pity and fear, the two emotions that according to Aristotle had to be inspired and manipulated by a tragedy in order to achieve catharsis, a "purgation," or "purification of passions."[7] In the seventeenth and eighteenth century, Aristotle's enigmatic doctrine and its diverging interpretations famously provided the groundwork for dramatic theory, including Corneille's own *Trois Discours sur la poésie dramatique* (*Three Discourses on Dramatic*

---

6   [Pierre] Corneille, *Oeuvres completes* (Paris: Éditions du Seuil, 1963), 538–540; Pierre Corneille, *Nicomede: a tragi-comedy*, trans. John Dancer (London: Francis Kirkman, 1671), 48, 54.

7   Hélène Merlin-Kajman, *L'absolutisme dans les lettres et la théorie des deux corps. Passions et politique* (Paris: Champion, 2000), 66–67. See also Alexander Pleschka's very recent study developing Merlin-Kajman's argument on the complex relationship between theatrical audiences and the politically empowered public in the absolutist era: Alexander Pleschka, *Theatralität und Öffentlichkeit: Schillers Spätdramatik und die Tragödie der französischen Klassik* (Berlin: De Gruyter, 2013).

Poetry, 1660). In *Nicomède*, the emotional mechanics of tragedy summarized in the notion of *catharsis* are identified with the workings of royal authority, which brings about the restitution of the disciplining effects of pity and fear among rebellious subjects, and is itself construed as a fundamentally theatrical phenomenon. At the same time the theatrical paradigm secured a privileged role for the political nation, the audience of the spectacle of monarchy and the ultimate judge of its success, on and off stage.

The discourse on theater developed on the crossroads of Aristotelian theory and theatrical practice by d'Aubignac, Corneille, Riccoboni, and the like saw the collective attitudes of the public as the most important measure of dramatic writing. At the same time, it suggested that monarchy depended on a voluntary concession of power by the subjects in and through a semi-aesthetic illusion, "suspension of disbelief." In his *Art poétique*, Boileau would later recommend that Racine model his tragic heroes on the king, thus identifying royal charisma with theatrical engagement. In *Nicomède* the rebellious "people" are indeed invested with the power to judge the prince's performance, while their uprising cannot be dismissed as illegitimate, as it is aroused by real crimes and fueled by loyalty to a future king; in fact, the rebels save the day and secure the tragedy's happy ending. Their instantaneous submission to Nicomède, a reinstatement of monarchical order, is driven by *admiration*—an emotion introduced by Corneille as a core element of his poetics in the *Examen de Nicomède*, and calculated to unite the theatrical audience of the play with the politically self-conscious subjects on stage. Tragedy could function as a ritualized reenactment of the original compact between monarchy and its subjects, and it is this role that it came to play in eighteenth-century Russia. Indeed, this is how the goal of tragedy is defined in what is possibly the earliest existing account of the genre in Russian, included in the 1728 manuscript translation of Trajano Boccalini's famous seventeenth-century serialized pamphlet, *Ragguagli di Parnasso* (in Russian, *Vedomosti parnasskiia*). Dedicating a separate issue to an imaginary performance of a political tragedy, Boccalini asserted that its goal was to teach fear to rulers, and loyalty to subjects.[8]

---

8   *Vedomosti parnaskiia gospodina Traiana Bokkalini rimlianina . . . Siia kniga . . . na rossiiskii perevedena Andreem Vasil'evym v Sanktpiterburge 1728 godu.*—OR RGB, fond 310, number 885, ll. 32ob.-34, 46ob-48. On this and other Russian translations of Boccalini,

Conventional concepts of neoclassical literary theory, more closely associated with political idiom than usually assumed by students of eighteenth-century Russian literature, allowed for reflection on tragedy's political functions. While no systematic treatises on drama were translated or composed in Russia during the period in question, an interesting case of an explicitly political reading of literary and dramatic poetics is found in John Barclay's famous neo-Latin novel *Argenis*, published in 1751 on Elizabeth's orders in Trediakovskii's Russian translation as *Argenida*. At one point the author explains through his alter ego, the courtly writer Nicopompus, the idea of his novel, conceived as a royalist remedy against the disasters of political chaos. A crisis of monarchy, with "the people disobedient to the prince, to both their ruins" (Barclay was referring to the last tumultuous years of the Valois rule in France), can be resolved with the help of fictional representation and its manipulative effects. To this end, Nicopompus designs "a stately fable, in manner of a history," which will attract the curiosity of the politically active public who will be led to acknowledge their errors at the same time as they "love my book above any stage-play or spectacle on the theatre."

While Barclay seems to dismiss theater as a diversion lacking the political gravity appropriate for his novel, it in fact serves as a model for his vision of political didactics that heavily relies on classical discussions of theatrical poetics. It was drama that Horace referred to in his famous precept that Barclay elaborates upon: "He has won every vote who has blended profit and pleasure, at once delighting and instructing the reader."[9] (Trediakovskii quoted those verses in the preface to his translation.) He further bases his techniques of enticement on a reading of Aristotle's *Poetics* emphasizing the link between tragic emotions and poetic justice: "I will stir up pity, fear, and horror ... I will figure vices and virtues, and each of them shall have his reward." Finally, Barclay resorts to a theatrical simile in order to express his idea of an edifying effect:

> ... they shall meet with themselves and find in the glass held before
> them, the show and merit of their own fame. It will perchance

---

see M. A. Iusim, *Makiavelli v Rossii: moral' i politika na protiazhenii piati stoletii* (Moscow: Institut vseobshchei Istorii RAN, 1998), 93–97.

9   Horace, *Satires, Epistles and Ars poetica*, trans. H. Ruston Fairclough (London: Heinemann, 1961), 478–479.

make them ashamed longer to play those parts upon the stage of this life, for which they must confess themselves justly taxed in a fable.

The very conventional concept of "the stage of this life," which makes drama the perfect mirror of political existence, serves in Barclay's rendering to align its chaotic developments with a certain vision of state order. Identifying "rebellion" with "irreligion," he overtly links divine justice—both in fiction and outside it—to the royalist cause, doomed to triumph over aristocratic faction. Consequently, the didactic encouragement of "virtues" aims for the reinstatement of the "traditional" hierarchy of unconditional rule and obedience, undermined by the "vices" of political actors:

> How much better had it been (I speak the plainlier amongst my friends) for the King to look back upon his Ancestors, and to prevent mischiefes by the example either of their wiser resolutions, or their errors, then after the wound received, to stand in need of physique? But these Traitors now up against him, what title, what colour will they find for their Rebellion, which hath not been long before infamous by the like troubles? ... I will discover, how the King hath done amiss: and what anchor the history of former times doth yet offer him in his now near ship-wrack. Then will I take off the mask from the factious subjects, that the people may know them: what they are like to hope, what to fear: by what means they may be reclaimed to virtue, and by what means continuing obstinate, they may be cut off.[10]

While individual rulers and their actions are not exempt from criticism, the moralizing effects of fiction help to revive and to renegotiate the absolutist compact between monarchy and its subjects, devoid of any constitutional

---

10 John Barclay, *Argenis*, ed. and trans. Mark Riley and Dorothy Pritchard Huber (Assen: Royal van Gorcum, 2004), 1: 333, 337; see also John Barclay, *Argenida: Povest' geroicheskaia ... perevedennaia ... ot Vasil'ia Trediakovskago* (St. Petersburg: Pri Imp. Akademii nauk, 1751), 1: 416–417.

limitations on royal power. In Lev Pumpianskii's terms, *Argenis* contained "a complete code of absolutist morals."[11] Literary reminders of "wiser resolutions" of historical kings as well as their "errors" are seen as crucial for the healthy functioning of monarchy as an institution and its dignity in the eyes of its subjects. Revealing the dramatic overtones of Barclay's poetics of political fiction, Aleksandr Karin in his 1760 epistle used a similar argument to describe the genre of tragedy, locating it in the spaces of royal power:

Трагедия пример Влыдыкам и Князьям,
Как должно сыскивать им путь в безсмертной храм.
В ином там славится щедрота иль геройство,
В другом, в владении восставил что спокойство.
В ином правдивой суд или великой дух:
Описан всякаго по мере вид заслуг:
Иного бедствия представлены злощастны,
Или в желаниях успехи как нещастны. . . .

Tragedy gives an example to sovereigns and princes how they should find their way into the temple of immortality. One is famed for his liberality or valor, another for having restored peace in his realm, yet another for his justice or magnanimity. The merits of each are dutifully listed, as well as the misfortunes of others or their misguided wishes. . . .[12]

Denying subjects any direct political rights, Barclay quite importantly recognizes their role as the audience of the "public spectacles" of political action, fictional or not. "The people" (and he certainly means the political class), in its double role as a nation of subjects and the readership of the novel, are the ultimate judges of emotional techniques employed in order to persuade them to identify virtue with obedience and accept the sweeping denunciation of political resistance. Since the

---

11 Pumpianskii, "Lomonosov i nemetskaia shkola razuma," 6.
12 A. Karin, "Pis'mo," *Poleznoe uveselenie* 12 (1761): 11.

novel's readers are themselves guilty of "credulity" towards the rebels and have assumed shameful roles on "the stage of this life," it is only through the effects of fictional representation that they can be refashioned as worthy subjects and reminded of their duty. Indeed, this was the expressly recognized goal of drama. Following Horace, who in his *Ars poetica* (twice translated into Russian in 1752–1755) stated that dramatic art had to rely on the knowledge of "what is imposed on senator and judge, what is the function of a general sent to war," Riccoboni wrote in his dedication of the *De la réformation du théâtre* to Elizabeth that through theater she "will teach the youth a sensible morality, suited to fashion wise politicians, courageous soldiers, good citizens, magistrates upright and zealous in state service."[13]

Apart from Wortman, emotional patterns of power and submission have attracted little attention from the students of eighteenth-century Russian letters. Among notable exceptions are Jelena Pogosjan's thesis on the political ode of the 1730s–1760s, which introduces the notion of "political emotion" as a crucial element of the literary poetics of the period, and Andrei Zorin's analysis of Catherine II's comic operas and their court performances as a paradigm for the emotional bond between the nation of subjects and royal authority.[14] Most recently, this perspective has been developed in Alexei Evstratov's two theses, and corroborated by Andrei Kostin's archival find of a detailed description of the street masquerade "Minerva Triumphant," which inaugurated Catherine's reign in 1763.[15] It was prepared and staged by a team

---

13 Horace, *Satires, Epistles, and Ars poetica*, 476–477; Riccoboni, *De la réformation du théâtre*, viii. On the political didacticism of Russian tragedy, see Cynthia H. Whittaker, *Russian Monarchy: Eighteenth-Century Rulers and Writers in Political Dialogue* (DeKalb: Northern Illinois University, 2003), 144. On tragedy as medium of absolutist social discipline, see Ruedi Graf, *Das Theater im Literaturstaat: literarisches Theater auf dem Weg zur Bildungsmacht* (Tübingen: Walter de Gruyter, 1992).

14 Jelena Pogosjan, *Vostorg russkoi ody i reshenie temy poeta v russkom panegirike 1730–1762 gg.* (Tartu: Tartu Ulikooli Kirjastus, 1997); Andrei Zorin, "Catherine II versus Beaumarchais: The Scandal at the St. Petersburg Court at Time of the French Revolution," in *Russia and The West. Missed Opportunities. Unfulfilled Dialogues* (Brussels: Konninklijke Vlaamse Akademie van Belgie, 2006).

15 A. G. Evstratov, "Ekaterina II i russkaia pridvornaia dramaturgiia v 1760-kh–nachale 1770-kh godov," (PhD diss. Russian State University for the Humanities, 2009); Evstratov, *Le théâtre francophone à Saint-Petersbourg sous le règne de Catherine II*

of actors and writers, many of whom over two previous decades had made crucial contributions to the emergence of Russian court theater, including Sumarokov himself. The preface to the description once again draws on d'Aubignac's argument and elaborates on the political benefits of spectacles for absolutist power, emphasizing the new empress's involvement in the entertainments shared with her subjects. Luxurious feasts and dramatic plays staged for the noble public and duly rewarded with "respect and love" for the monarch are deemed no more important than performances intended for the "great number of the poor," the serfs, who admittedly constitute "all the might of this flourishing state." To reward them who are (or are expected to be) "proud to live as her slaves" since "her yoke is for them light, agreeable and preferable to liberty, which will never diminish the beloved power," Catherine feels a need to ensure that they "share the common amusement" during the masquerade.[16]

Among the plays staged during the festivities of 1763 was Sumarokov's tragedy *Semira* (1751), written for Elizabeth's court about a decade earlier. As Alexei Evstratov has convincingly demonstrated, the play proved a convenient scenario for a performance that reenacted the newly negotiated compact between the new empress, whose legitimacy could be seen as doubtful, and her court.[17] Indeed, *Semira* showcases the mechanics of a revolt simultaneously subdued by force and appeased by the clemency of Russia's ancient ruler, Oleg. Apparently, the threat of revolt was a central issue for the genre of tragedy as it was perceived and practiced in Russia. As early as 1716, the Hannoverian diplomat Friedrich Christian Weber describes in his famous account of Petrine Russia, *Das veränderte Russland* (*Russia Transformed*), a performance of a tragedy personally written and staged for Peter the Great by his sister, Princess Natalia. Its "subject related to one of the late Rebellions in Russia, represented under disguised Names," and the tragedy concluded "with a Moral, reflecting on the Horrors of Rebellion, and the unhappy Events it

(*1762–1796*); Andrei Kostin, "Moskovskii maskarad 'Torzhestvuiushchaia Minerva' (1763) glazami inostrantsa," *Russkaia literatura* 2 (2013): 80–112.

16   Kostin, "Moskovskii maskarad 'Torzhestvuiushchaia Minerva,'" 95–98.
17   Evstratov, *Ekaterina II i russkaia pridvornaia dramaturgiia*, 25–79.

commonly issues in." In the next lines, Weber links the performative practices newly imported to Russia to "a blind Obedience among these People towards their superiors."[18] The same themes were reiterated in Sumarokov's neoclassical dramas: all of his tragedies, written between the 1740s and the 1770s, dealt with conspiracies and revolts—successful, abortive, or only fearfully anticipated—and interrogated the outlines and inner workings of the monarchy's political order.

---

18 Friedrich Christian Weber, *The Present State of Russia* (London: W. Taylor, 1722), 1: 189–190.

"SCENARIOS OF POWER": THE POLITICS OF TRAGIC PLOTS

The affinity between operative political scenarios and dramatic plots was neither superficial nor incidental. Specific political allusions, which we might or might not discern in individual dramatic texts, were only symptomatic of more fundamental structures of political thinking that were both revealed and shaped by the imported genre of tragedy. As Walter Benjamin demonstrates in *The Origin of the German Tragic Drama*, for baroque tragedy (*Trauerspiel*) "historical life, as it was conceived at the time, is its content, its true object." Its vision of history is centered on the figure of the sovereign, its "principal exponent" and "representative," and thus "the main character of the *Trauerspiel*."[1] Aristotle—to quote an early English translation—required that tragedy should represent the actions of

---

1   Walter Benjamin, *The Origin of the German Tragic Drama*, trans. John Osborne (London: Verso, 1985), 62–63. For recent reassessments of Benjamin's argument, see Romain Jobez, *Le théâtre baroque allemand et français. Le droit dans la littérature* (Paris: Classiques Garnier, 2010); Bettine Menke, *Das Trauerspiel-Buch: der Souverän—das Trauerspiel— Konstellationen—Ruinen* (Bielefeld: transcript, 2010). Stage versions of German baroque dramas discussed by Benjamin were performed and even translated in early eighteenth-century Russia. N. S. Tikhonravov, ed., *Russkie dramaticheskie proizvedeniia 1672–1725 godov* (St. Petersburg: n.p., 1874), has published a surviving Russian version of Daniel Casper von Lohenstein's *Sophonisbe* (1665), and Andreas Gryphius's *Großmütiger Rechtsgelehrter, oder Sterbender Aemilius Paulus Papinianus* (*The Magnanamious Jurist, or the Dying Aemilius Paulus Papinianus*, 1659) is also known to have been produced in Russia in Petrine times. It was also performed in Riga by Hilferding's company in the 1750s, with a short description of the performance (now in BAN) supposedly printed in Petersburg. See *Svodnyi katalog knig na inostrannykh iazykakh, izdannykh v Rossii v XVIII veke* (Leningrad: Nauka, 1985), 2, no. 1332.

those "who are of Eminent Quality, and of Great Reputation."[2] D'Aubignac reiterated his precept:

> Tragedy represented the Life of Princes and great People full of disquiets, suspicions, troubles, rebellions, wars, murders, and all sorts of violent passions, and mighty adventures ... that word, in its true signification, meaning nothing else but a Magnificent, serious, grave poem, conformable to the Agitations and sudden turns of fortune of great people.[3]

As an image of monarchy in crisis, tragedy, or *Trauerspiel*, was in place in eighteenth-century Russia, with its constant rebellions and palace revolutions. The early years of Peter the Great's reign were marked by two uprisings of the *streltsy* regiments stationed in Moscow in 1692 and 1698. Between Peter's death, in 1725, and 1801, supreme power was usurped four times with the help of the guards regiments, including Elizabeth's coup in late 1741 and Catherine's in the summer of 1762. This pattern, which involved the violent deaths of three emperors—Peter III, in 1762; Ivan VI, in 1764; and Peter III's son Paul I, in 1801—was summarized as early as 1764 by Eléazar de Mauvillon: "everyone knows that Russia has always been a stage for tragic scenes, revolutions, conspiracies, and interior tumults."[4] It might have been Mauvillon's book that inspired an obscure German cleric to make the secret history of the Russian palace revolutions of 1740–1741, amalgamated with Mirovich's failed revolt of 1764, into a French tragedy, *L'Innocence opprimée, ou La mort d'Iwan Empereur de Russie* (*The Oppressed Innocence, or the Death of Ivan, Emperor of Russia*) published in 1765.[5]

---

2 *Aristotle's Art of Poetry: Translated from the Original Greek ... Together with Mr. D'Acier's notes from the French* (London: D. Browne and W. Turner, 1705), 186–187; see also *La Poétique d'Aristote traduite en françois avec des remarques critiques ... par André Dacier* (Paris: Claude Barbin, 1692; reprinted Hildesheim: Olms, 1976), 182.

3 [François-Hédelin d'Aubignac], *The Whole Art of the Stage*, 140; see also d'Aubignac, *La pratique du théâtre*, 210–211.

4 Eléazar de Mauvillon, *Histoire de la vie, du règne et du détrônement d'Iwan III, empereur de Russie, assassiné à Schlüsselbourg dans la nuit du 15 au 16 juillet (NS.) 1764* (London: n.p., 1766), xi. On palace revolutions in eighteenth-century Russia, see the recent comprehensive study by I. V. Kurukin, *Epokha "dvorskikh bur'": Ocherki politicheskoi istorii poslepetrovskoi Rossii, 1725–1762 gg.* (Riazan': NRIID, 2003).

5 Léopold-Frédéric Fallot, *L'Innocence opprimée, ou La mort d'Iwan Empereur de Russie: Tragédie ...* (n.p., 1765). On Fallot and his play, see Charles Duvernoy, *Ephémérides du comté de Montbéliard ...* (Besançon: Imprimerie de Charles Deis, 1832), 403–404.

Palace revolutions exemplified the state of exception that is considered the basis of sovereignty in Carl Schmitt's legal theory and has been viewed as central for the representations of power in early modern drama, first by Benjamin and later by Marin. This was most certainly true for eighteenth-century Russia, where palace revolutions were not only easily accomplished but afterwards for decades revived in collective memory by the yearly celebrations of the royal "ascension day." In fact, revolts were the focal issue of what Stephen Greenblatt calls in a similar context "paradoxes, ambiguities, and tensions of authority."[6] Together with the conspiracies they arose from, the coups inevitably had a dual status in contemporary discourse, official and semi-private. On the one hand, successful coups were repeatedly praised during the ensuing reigns as salutary and divinely sanctioned acts of popular will, whose legitimacy was proven by their very success. Speaking in Wortman's terms, they called forth "scenarios of rejoicing" inaugurated and perpetuated in ceremonial festivities. On the other hand, any kind of political dissent was simultaneously recognized as a heinous crime and an imminent danger to the state. This opposition to the regime had to be constantly contained with biblical precepts of unconditional obedience, and at the first suspicion persecuted with all the excessive and unchecked might of Russia's repressive machinery, operated by the Secret Chancery and other similar agencies responsible for political crimes. In 1764, two years after Catherine's triumphant ascension to the throne and two decades after Elizabeth's de facto ban on capital punishment, the officer Vasilii Mirovich was executed in Petersburg after a failed attempt to free and enthrone the long deposed ex-emperor Ivan VI, who was also killed in the process. The tension between opposing and mutually exclusive views of what had become an established succession procedure, which threatened to undermine the moral foundations of the current order, could not be resolved in the official normative discourses, which mostly avoided critical scrutiny of the status quo. Instead, it was drama with its polyphonic techniques of performance and representation where this tension could be constantly negotiated, and the revolting subjects could be silently but clearly shown and acknowledged as the mute

---

6   Stephen Greenblatt, *Shakespearean Negotiations: The Circulation of Social Energy in Renaissance England* (Berkeley: University of California Press, 1988), 65.

yet powerful force commanding the monarchy's fate, beyond forensic taxonomies and verdicts of the established idioms of containment.[7]

As we have seen, the temptations of republicanism associated with the very genre of tragedy were perpetuated in the dramatic idiom of the *tragédie classique* at least since Corneille, who linked them to the feudal and aristocratic dissent of the Fronde, and through this aesthetic representation established an actual presence in Russia, where they were otherwise consistently suppressed. Manstein describes the fall of the "counsellor of state, De Fick, whom Peter I had, in 1716, sent to Sweden," where he "contracted a taste for republican government; and when, after the death of Peter II the council of state entered on the plan of limiting the royal authority, he tried to get himself listened to." Not surprisingly, "when the Empress Anne declared herself absolute sovereign … he was arrested, and, without being examined on any one article, was sent off to Siberia."[8] While Russia's own "Fronde of the nobility" may not have existed as a consolidated political force after 1730, as Gukovskii would have it, the phantom of aristocratic revolt—with good reasons—continued to haunt the imaginations of the Russian court. Voltaire's tragedy *Brutus*, dramatizing the heroic beginnings of the Roman republic and the abolishment of monarchy, is known to have been performed in the late 1750s, and the manuscript rendering of his *Mort de César* (*The Death of Caesar*, 1736) might have been among the earliest dramatic translations into Russian.[9] Reviewing *Brutus* in his "Opinion in a Dream about French Tragedies," Sumarokov revived d'Aubignac's assumption that the reaction of theatrical audiences to a play depended on the specific political and religious consensus they represented,

---

7   On the importance of revolt for Sumarokov's tragedies, see Gukovskii, *Russkaia literatura XVIII veka*, 137–138; Kasatkina, "Sumarokovskaia tragediia 40-kh–nachala 50-kh godov XVIII veka," 223. On similar trends in early modern German drama, see Arnd Beise, *Geschichte, Politik und das Volk im Drama des 16. bis 18. Jahrhunderts* (Berlin: Walter de Gruyter, 2010). On the ambiguous status of the Russian palace revolutions, which fitted the legal definition of high treason, see E. V. Anisimov, *Dyba i knut. Politicheskii sysk i russkoe obshchestvo v XVIII veke* (Moscow: Novoe literaturnoe obozrenie, 1999), 42; and Kurukin, *Epokha dvorskikh bur'*, 345, specifically linking this issue to Sumarokov's dramatic practice.

8   Cristoph Hermann Manstein, *Contemporary Memoirs of Russia* (London: Longman, Brown, Green, and Longmans, 1856), 52–53.

9   Voltaire, *Smert' Cezarja. Eine anonyme frühe russische Übersetzung von Voltaires Tragödie* (Munich: Fink, 1967).

and he remarked prophetically that Voltaire's Roman tragedy "might become more fashionable in Paris sometime in the future, for monarchies can turn into republics."[10]

In 1790, when in the wake of the French Revolution Catherine II came to view literary writing as a potential source of revolutionary threat, she persecuted the successful dramatist Iakov Kniazhnin for the tragedy *Vadim Novgorodskii*, which depicted a legendary republican revolt against ducal rule in mediaeval Russia, although she herself had written and staged a play on the same subject several years earlier. Princess Dashkova, Catherine's one-time friend and Knyazhnin's patron, attempted to protect him by pointing out that *Vadim* "was less dangerous to sovereigns than many a French tragedy acted at the Hermitage," the empress's own small and exclusive palace theater, separated by then from the more public stages.[11] William Edgerton has argued that the long-standing debate on whether Catherine misunderstood Kniazhnin's intentions or if he did indeed express republican sentiment is misguided since the play is consistently ambiguous in its treatment of political principle, autocratic or republican. Commenting on this argument, Marcus Levitt notes that "such ambiguity—the clash of irreconcilable truths—is on some level inherent in the zero-sum confrontations that make up the substance of [Russian] classicist tragedy."[12]

The ambivalence of the Russian tragedy and its representation of authority and dissent emerged early in its history. In Sumarokov's *Artistona* (1750), a family of grandees, compelled to rebel against the despotism of King Darius, are defeated but pardoned by the king after persuasively asserting their right to revolt:

Я скипетр дал тебе, а ты за ту услугу
Отъемлешь без стыда Оркантову супругу. ...
Я вижу, что тебе мучительство природно,

---

10 Sumarokov, *Polnoe sobranie vsekh sochinenii*, 4: 350–353.

11 Quoted in Marcus Levitt, *The Visual Dominant in Eighteenth-Century Russia* (DeKalb: Northern Illinois University Press, 2011), 121.

12 William Edgerton, "Ambivalence as the Key to Kniazhnin's Tragedy 'Vadim Novgorodskii,'" in *Russia and the World of the Eighteenth Century*, ed. Roger Bartlett, Anthony G. Cross, and Karen Rasmussen (Columbus, OH: Slavica, 1988), 306–315; Levitt, *Visual Dominant in Eighteenth-Century Russia*, 122.

И умереть готов, когда тебе угодно.
Вели различное мученье вымышлять,
Рви тело, но души не мни поколебать:
Отан не знает свойств малейшия боязни.
Дай смерть разбойничью: мне место злыя казни
Не может мнимого бесчестия принесть;
Бездельство, а не казнь отъемлет нашу честь.[13]

I have given you the scepter, and you return the favor by shame-lessly taking Orkant's spouse. ... I see that tyranny is natural to you, and I am prepared to die at your pleasure. You can have different kinds of torture devised for me, tear my body apart, but do not hope to shake my soul: Otan does not know even the smallest symptoms of fear. Punish me with a thug's death: a place of brutal execution cannot be dishonorable for me; evil deeds rather than punishment take away our honor.

Elizabeth's palace revolution of 1741 (successfully imitated by Catherine in 1762) itself followed a profoundly theatrical logic and was in many ways inscribed into the actual theatrical and ceremonial culture of the court, as Jelena Pogosjan has demonstrated in an insightful study.[14] On the night of the coup, November 25, Elizabeth, accompanied by a small group of followers and wearing a cuirass over her usual dress along with a mask, walked into the barracks of the Preobrazhenskii guards regiment (established by her father, Peter the Great): "As soon as she arrived there—reads a reliable official account—she appeared before the soldiers, a sword in her hand, and told them in a few words that they saw in her a legitimate empress and those who loved her had to follow her immediately." Elizabeth's explanations referred both to the mask that hid her face and to her alleged status as a rightful but disowned heir to her father's throne. In fact, given that Peter's

---

13 A. P. Sumarokov, *Dramaticheskie sochineniia*, ed. Iu. V. Stennik (Leningrad: Iskusstvo, 1990), 181.

14 Jelena Pogosjan, "Masks and Masquerade at the Court of Elizabeth Petrovna (1741–1742)," in *Russian and Soviet History: From the Time of Troubles to the Collapse of the Soviet Union*, ed. Steven Usitalo and W. B. Whisenhunt (Lanham, MD: Rowman and Littlefield, 2008).

law of succession gave each ruler the right to choose their successor and thus abolished all dynastic rights, Elizabeth's claim to power had no legal ground but mainly depended on her performance of the role assumed that night. First of all, she had to act the part for the benefit of the guards in the barracks, who did quickly recognize her as their empress and followed her to arrest the infant Ivan VI and his parents. Over the following night and the next days, she rehearsed her new role for the Petersburg public that came to the palace to greet and assess the new empress, Russia's third monarch in a year. Her performance was a success. The French ambassador, the Marquis de la Chétardie, who enjoyed Elizabeth's favor and had firsthand knowledge of the events at court, reported that Elizabeth's conduct toward her visitors "succeeded in winning her everyone's hearts."[15]

Apparently, Elizabeth relied on the same patterns of theatricality of royal charisma that was explored and exposed in Corneille's *Nicomède*. Appearing in person before armed guards, who had already proved themselves dangerous to their rulers during the overthrow of the regent Johann Ernst Biron several months earlier, Elizabeth claimed the same immediately theatrical power over her future subjects that befitted a true heiress and secured her charismatic authority over the head of the lawful but unworthy ruler. In 1760, the anniversary of Elizabeth's ascension was celebrated with a performance of Metastasio's opera *Siroe, Re di Persia* (1725), which adapted Corneille's portrayal of the imperious heir apparent in the face of popular revolt that simultaneously shakes political order and establishes his personal power. If Corneille's prince magnanimously cedes this power to his weak-spirited father, in *Siroe* he is called upon to accept the crown, and is honored with an apotheosis projected in the Russian performance onto the coup of 1741. Not surprisingly, a similar pattern of events reappeared in Sumarokov's tragedies. In the last one, *Mstislav* (1774), the populace revolts after the grand duke decides to execute his rebellious but valorous brother and vassal. The uprising is suppressed by force, but the younger prince receives pardon and is reinstated in his rights. More importantly, in Sumarokov's second tragedy, *Gamlet* (1748), a remake of Shakespeare's play provided with a happy ending and

---

transformed into a veiled celebration of Elizabeth's coup, the Danish prince leads a successful revolt against Klavdii (Claudius): "All of the citizens did rally to support me ... all expressed the wish to crown me king of Denmark" (5.5).[16] In part 3, I will offer a detailed reading of the tragedy, exploring (among other issues) the affinity of Sumarokov's dramatic poetics to the mechanics of charismatic authority as outlined by Max Weber.

Reenacting the production of royal charisma through the collective feelings of the audience of subjects for a political actor—empathy that could be understood in Aristotelian terms as pity for the protagonist (an oppressed heiress, for example) and fear for her fate, or identified with other emotional components of the *tragédie classique* such as admiration or love—Russian court drama was crucial for negotiating the relationship between the ruler and her immediate social milieu, including the military, responsible for the palace revolutions. Interestingly enough, in the early years of her court theater Elizabeth had to impose it on the public: the orders she issued to the courtiers and their wives to be present at theatrical performances sometimes had to be enforced by the Petersburg police.[17] These performances were arranged as ceremonial occasions calculated to steer and shape the mutual gaze of the ruler and the political nation, on and off stage, and the plays were intrinsic to this process.

Even before the emergence of neoclassical tragedy in the 1740s, the political significance of the medium of theater was displayed on stage. In *Stefanotokos* (*The Crown-bearer*), a dramatic allegory of Elizabeth's ascension performed in her presence at the Novgorod seminary in December 1742, the allegorical figure of Loyalty, sunk in despair, is comforted by Hope, who stages a play within a play on the subject of the biblical book of Esther, immediately followed by Stefanotokos's triumph. We do not know whether Elizabeth or her followers did indeed seek assurance in a performance of this kind before the coup, but either way, this episode is meaningful. In the eyes of the early Russian court society the book of Esther seemed to provide an archetypical plot for a political drama. Besides the fragment in *Stefanotokos*, three different pre-classicist dramatic treatments of the subject are extant,

---

16   A. P. Sumarokov, *Selected Tragedies*, trans. Richard and Raymond Fortune (Evanston, IL: Northwestern University Press, 1970), 132.

17   *Istoricheskii vestnik* 21, no. 8 (1885): 416.

including the first Russian play of 1672 and an allegorized composition presumably linked to the rise to power of Elizabeth's mother, the future Catherine I, culminating in her coronation as empress in 1724.[18]

The story of Esther, king Artaxerxes's wife of a relatively humble descent (as Romanov royal brides tended to be until the mid-eighteenth century), who was able to outwit and overthrow her husband's omnipotent favorite, Haman, and substitute him with her guardian, Mordecai, summarized the temptations and dangers of life at court and allowed for an imposing display of absolute autocratic authority possessing and exercising total control over the fates of all protagonists. In one of the two early eighteenth-century plays, Artaxerxes's power is shown to depend on the circular dynamics of vision, performance, and impression connecting the king to his subjects. Having come to see the king without his request, in a direct violation of the law, Esther professes to be terrified by a possible death sentence. After he reassures her of his favor, agrees to her wishes, and she finally leaves, the king proudly speaks to the "senators" around him of the fear that he is able to inspire: "She was seized by fear when she came to me, but her beauty pleased me. You see the frightful fame I have amongst you. If my wife would not be encouraged by my words, she would hardly be alive; but my hand is in fact beneficent to all," and the senators respond with praise for his might and protestations of loyalty.[19]

Not only does this scene contain in a nutshell the whole Esther plot—she is admitted to the king and achieves her ambitious aims through a display of humility—but it also reveals the fundamentally theatrical vision of royal power, generally manifested in early drama. The brute fear expressed by Esther, the model subject, is certainly authentic but simultaneously conforms to the established protocols of "political emotion" and, in the dramatic reenactment of a biblical exemplum, is inscribed into the ceremonial idiom of obedience. Instead of eliminating this fear, Artaxerxes rewards it with signs of benevolence in what he himself explains to be an instructive performative act engaging the spectator-subjects by manipulating emotional tensions. Clemency and benevolence are only worthy of an autocrat if they

---

18   O. A. Derzhavina, A. S. Demin, and A. N. Robinson, eds., *P'esy stolichnykh i provintsi-al'nykh teatrov* (Moscow: Nauka, 1975), 641–648.

19   Ibid., 280–281.

do not appear self-evident but rather are seen to blaze in spectacular and arbitrary gestures that reaffirm by contrast general fear as the basic principle of monarchic order and showcase the unpredictable omnipotence of royal authority.

This pattern of power was itself perpetuated as a ritualized economy of exchange between ruler and subjects, as the story of Esther shows. Aside from dramas, where the monarchy's dangerously eruptive powers were both displayed and reduced to conventional theatrics, this dynamic of fear and encouragement appeared in the more immediately ceremonial performances. In a panegyric declamation recited before Elizabeth (elsewhere praised as the "New Esther") by the students of the Trinity seminary in the fall of 1743, the two speakers are first shown to be seized by "fear and terror" at the need to express their ardent feelings for the empress in her presence. In the course of the declamation, this fear is heightened by the exposition of Elizabeth's might, but then the speakers are relieved to be reminded of her clemency, and the piece finishes with exclamations of love for Elizabeth.[20]

Sovereignty, as it functions in early Russian theater, fulfills itself in the gaze of the royal spectator, itself staged as a public spectacle of power. As Artaxerxes explains to the senators, he was kind to Esther because he was "glad to see the beauty of his queen" (this is especially telling since, as the dramatic versions of the biblical story do not fail to reiterate, Artaxerxes's first wife fell out of favor after she refused to show herself to the king and his guests). During the performances of the 1672 *Comedy of Artaxerxes*, which inaugurated Russian court theater as an institution, Tsar Aleksei was the only sitting spectator, though many courtiers were standing in the audience and on stage as a part of his retinue, and the royal women were allowed to watch from a secluded space. In the final scenes of *La forza dell'amore e dell'odio* (*The Power of Love and Hatred*), the first opera staged in Russia at the court of Empress Anna in 1736, the king Sofit is seen sitting on a throne facing an amphitheater filled with the inhabitants of a rebellious and reconquered city, solemnly announcing pardon to all except the instigator of the revolt. This scene of mutual observation of the ruler and his people, informed on both sides by intense political anxiety, which ends one of the first dramatic texts

---

20   Ibid., 502–506; on the "New Esther," see ibid., 512.

ever published in Russian, can be seen as a starting point for Russian tragedy as a literary genre and theatrical form where, in Marcus Levitt's words, "the ruler's sight is often crucial to a tragedy's outcome," while at the same time the "limits of this vision are interrogated."[21] The power of royal gaze was staged and reaffirmed in theatrical spaces where the hierarchical distinction between the sovereign and subjects was both reproduced—as it was usual for court theaters across Europe, Elizabeth and the royal family occupied privileged sitting positions—and suspended.

---

21 Levitt, *Visual Dominant in Eighteenth-Century Russia*, 99.

DRAMATIC EXPERIENCE: TRAGEDY AND THE EMOTIONAL ECONOMY OF THE COURT

Louis Marin elucidates the fundamental paradox behind absolutist political theater: the ostentatious ceremonial display on stage and during state rituals functions as a representation of power emanating from the closed space of the royal palace inaccessible to most of the subjects.[1] Tragedy—German baroque drama as well as the French *tragédie classique*—gives its audiences insight into *arcana imperii*, the inner workings of power. In the words of Wilhelm Meister,

> Corneille, if I may put it thus, portrays great people, but Racine portrays persons of quality. … Whenever I study his Britannicus or his Bérénice, I have the sense of being at court myself, of being privy to things great or small in these dwellings of the gods of this earth, and through the eyes of a sensitive Frenchman I perceive kings adored by all nations, courtiers envied by multitudes, all in their natural shape with all their defects and sorrows.[2]

---

1   Louis Marin, "Théâtralité et pouvoir: Magie, machination, machine: *Médée* de Corneille," in Louis Marin, *Politiques de la représentation* (Paris: Kimé, 2005), 266–267.

2   Goethe, *Wilhelm Meister's Apprenticeship*, 104. See also Volker Schröder, *La tragédie du sang d'Auguste: politique et intertextualité dans Britannicus*, 53–60. On the "idealization of courtly world" in French classical drama, see Volker Kapp, "Die Idealisierung der höfischen Welt im klassischen Drama," in *Französische Literatur in Einzeldarstellungen*,

As the students of early Russian drama have amply demonstrated, the notion of theater as a metaphor for political and historical achievement belonged to the political idiom imported into Russia through Petrine translations of works such as Wilhelm Stratemann's *Theatrum historicum* (*Featron, ili Pozor istoricheskii …*, 1724), and its use was linked to the gradually consolidating absolutist poetics of representation.[3] Conversely, the theatrical interest of tragedy was produced on the threshold of the enclosed and secretive sphere of court politics, appealing both to those who were excluded from it—such as the Petersburg "populace" (*narod*), which was in 1757 allowed to attend a performance of Sumarokov's tragedy along with the empress—and those who inhabited it.[4] D'Aubignac claims that

> in the French Court, Tragedies take a great deal better than Comedies … for in this Kingdom the persons of good Quality, and Education, have generous thoughts and designs, to which they are carried either by the Motives of Vertue or Ambition, so that their life has a great Conformity with the Characters of Tragedy. …[5]

The prevalence of tragedy over comedy on court stage—more symbolical than practical, but still asserted in one of the first essays on drama, published in Russian in 1733—derived from its resonance with the collective modes of emotionality adopted by the court society to deal with the anxieties of its day-to-day political experience; the audiences of court theaters often "found themselves confronting riddling treatments of the pitfalls and dangers of courtly life."[6] Norbert Elias, in his classic *The Court Society*, linked

---

ed. Peter Brockmeier and Hermann H. Wetzel (Stuttgart: Metzler, 1981), 1: 115–176. A direct link between the fortunes of neoclassical tragedy and the public fascination for "the royal role" has been suggested by Matthew H. Wikander, *Princes to Act: Royal Audience and Royal Performance, 1578–1792* (Baltimore, MD: Johns Hopkins University Press, 1993), 12.

3   O. A. Derzhavina, A. S. Demin, and A. N. Robinson, "Rukopisnaia dramaturgiia I teatral'naia zhizn' pervoi poloviny XVIII v.," in *P'esy liubitelskikh teatrov* (Moscow: Nauka, 1976), 48–50.

4   Starikova, *Teatral'naia zhizn' Rossii v epokhu Elizavety Petrovny*, vol. 3, bk 1, 162.

5   [François-Hédelin d'Aubignac], *The Whole Art of the Stage*, 72; see also d'Aubignac, *La pratique du théâtre*, 122.

6   Wikander, *Princes to Act*, 7.

the courtly taste for tragedy with a specific emotional economy of the absolutist elites, shaped by the constant competition for power and favor.[7] Both
A. N. Robinson in his analysis of Petrine drama and Iurii Lotman in his
more broadly conceived studies on the poetics of eighteenth- and early
nineteenth-century Russian culture, have shown that in the wake of Petrine
reforms, theater came to function in Russia as a fundamental paradigm of
social and political existence at court and in state service.[8]

According to Aristotle, in order for tragedy to achieve its emotional
effects, spectators have to identify with characters on stage, who have to
be "like ourselves."[9] In neoclassical theory—Corneille's *Discours de la
tragédie*, Dacier's commentary to his translation of Aristotle, and
Gottsched's speech on the uses of tragedy that largely followed Corneille—
two different interpretations of this precept were debated. On the one
hand, similarity could be seen as an issue of social rank; all three authors
cite the opinion of an earlier commentator who "applies it only to kings
and princes, maybe because tragedy can only make us fear misfortunes
which have happened to someone like us, and if they occur only to kings
and princes, this fear will only effect those of a similar standing." In all
three cases, this reading of Aristotle's is disputed: a prince on stage is in
fact an "ordinary man," and, consequently, his fate can be instructive to
anyone, or, more specifically, to "persons of middling state," according to
Gottsched.[10] While the two opposing interpretations might seem mutually exclusive, they amount together to a vision of tragic poetics that
simultaneously reaches across social boundaries and hierarchies and reaffirms them, arranging the emotional reactions of the audience according
to status and inscribing them into the overall mechanics of absolutist
polity. Another influential neoclassical literary theorist, René Rapin, in

---

7 Norbert Elias, *The Court Society*, trans. Edmund Jephcott (New York: Pantheon Books,
   1983), 111–113.
8 Derzhavina, Demin, and Robinson, "Rukopisnaia dramaturgiia i teatral'naia zhizn' pervoi
   poloviny XVIII v.," 25–52 (section by A. N. Robinson); Iurii Lotman, "Poetika bytovogo
   povedeniia v russkoi kul'ture XVIII veka" and "Teatr i teatral'nost' v stroe kul'tury nachala
   XIX veka," in Iurii Lotman, *Izbrannye stat'i*, vol. 1 (Tallinn: Aleksandra, 1992).
9 *Aristotle's Art of Poetry*, 186; see also *La Poétique d'Aristote*, 181.
10 Corneille, *Oeuvres completes*, 830–831; *Aristotle's Art of Poetry*, 209–210; *La Poétique d'
   Aristote*, 188–189; Gottsched, "Die Schauspiele," 7–8.

his Aristotelian *Réflexions sur la poétique de ce temps* (*Reflections on the Poetics of Our Times*, 1674–1675), well known in Russia (they were quoted by Grigorii Teplov in his 1755 "An Essay on the Qualities of a Poet"), wrote on the subject and the aims of tragedy:

> For it makes Man modest, by representing the great Masters of the Earth humbled; and it makes him tender and merciful, by shewing him on the Theatre the strange Accidents of Life, and the unforeseen Disgraces to which the most important Persons are subject. But because Man is naturally timorous and compassionate, he may fall into another Extreme, to be either too fearful, or too full of Pity; the too much Fear may shake the Constancy of Mind, and the too great Compassion may enfeeble the Equity. 'Tis the Business of Tragedy to regulate these two Weaknesses; it prepares and arms him against Disgraces, by shewing them so frequent in the most considerable Persons; and he shall cease to fear ordinary Accidents, when he sees such extraordinary happen to the highest Part of Mankind. But as the End of Tragedy is to teach Men not to fear too weakly the common Misfortunes, and manage their Fear; it makes account also to teach them to spare their Compassion, for Objects that deserve it not. For there is Injustice in being mov'd at the Afflictions of those who deserve to be miserable.[11]

Rapin's vision of tragedy emphasizes its mastery of what Greenblatt calls "techniques of arousing and manipulating anxiety," "a dread bound up with the fate of particular situated individuals." As Greenblatt argues, the employment of those techniques in drama was related to the fact that early modern ruling elites, both clerical and secular, "believed that a measure of insecurity and fear was a necessary, healthy element in the shaping of proper loyalties," and this view pervaded "public maiming and executions," as well as the royal pardons that they paved the way for: "Salutary

---

11   René Rapin, "Reflections upon Poetry," in *The Whole Critical Works*, trans. Basil Kennet (London: J. Walthoe et al., 1731), 2: 204–205; see also René Rapin, *Les réflexions sur la poétique de ce temps, et sur les ouvrages des poètes anciens et modernes* (Geneva: Droz, 1970), 97–98.

anxiety, then, blocks the anger and resentment that would well up against what must, if contemplated in a secure state, seem an unjust order."[12]

The terrifyingly sudden overthrow and public prosecution of the great and powerful, a forceful reminder of the risks and dangers of life at court, was a constant feature of Russian politics during the first decades of the eighteenth century, even after the death of Peter the Great, who set the highest and hardly attainable mark in the formal prosecution of his only son and heir to the empire, Tsarevich Alexei, which involved torture and resulted in the tsarevich's death (supposedly under Peter's own hands) in 1718. The fall of Peter's omnipotent favorite, Aleksandr Menshikov, stripped of all his posts and exiled to Siberia by Alexei's son Peter II in 1727, was followed under Empress Anna by the ruin and execution of Menshikov's sworn enemies, the powerful noble clan of the Princes Dolgorukii, in 1730. It made such an impression that the Spanish ambassador, the Duke of Liria, considered their fate "tragic," and his good friend, the wife of the British resident, Jane Rondeau, agreed that it would "make a pretty story for a tragedy."[13]

The ruin of the Dolgorukiis was followed by the fall of the Princes Golitsyn in 1736 and the brutal execution of Anna's cabinet minister Artemii Volynskii and several members of his circle in 1740 (Volynskii's tongue and hand were cut off on the scaffold before he could be beheaded). Political trials continued after Elizabeth's ascension to power in 1742. One of her first measures was to prosecute the ministers of the previous reigns allegedly responsible for the suppression of her succession rights, including Russia's most experienced diplomat, Count Andrei (Heinrich Johann Friedrich) Ostermann, and her most famous general, the charismatic and popular Field Marshal Count Burchard Christoph von Münnich. They were sentenced to death and led to the scaffold, where they were given royal pardon, substituting permanent Siberian exile for capital punishment.

---

12   Greenblatt, *Shakespearean Negotiations*, 133, 138.

13   *Zapiski diuka Liriiskago i Bervikskago vo vremia prebyvaniia ego pri imperatorskom rossijskom dvore* ... (St. Petersburg: n.p., 1845), 103; Jane Vigor, *Letters from a lady, who resided some years in Russia, to her friend in England* (London: J. Dodsley, 1777), 64. On her friendship with Liria, see Jane Vigor, *Eleven additional letters from Russia, in the reign of Peter II* (London: J. Dodsley, ca. 1785), 51–52, 65.

Writing a generation later, Manstein's anonymous commentator outlined the effects that judicial terror had on Russian society:

> Considering the chronicles of Russian history in the eighteenth century, we notice with astonishment the striking turns of fate. The ascension of every new sovereign overthrows those who had risen by the predecessor's power, and with a mighty hand attempts to elevate the confidants of the new ruler. Observing the atrocious examples of the favorites of fortune and other men of deed and counsel each in their own turn either perish or fall into oblivion, all minds were naturally seized by involuntary fear, all talent and noble ambition had to vanish in obscurity.[14]

The fall of the great (central for Rapin's understanding of tragedy) is seen by the Anonym as a central theme in the "chronicles of Russian history"—the semi-historical works such as the memoirs by Manstein that he was commenting upon and the ones by Ernst von Münnich, the field marshal's son, that he heavily used, as well as the field marshal's own *Ebauche du gouvernement de l'Empire de Russie* (*An Outline of the Government of the Russian Empire*, 1762–1764). Both father and son mentioned "many death sentences for glorious and illustrious persons" as important traits of Anna's reign.[15] Public interest in these episodes of court history was also reflected in publications commemorating Münnich's own "grievous fall" along with that of Ostermann.[16]

Rapin's analysis of tragic effects had to be digested in Russia—as elsewhere in the absolutist era—by a public accustomed to constant fear as a regular element of political existence. As Evgenii Anisimov shows in his study of Russia's secret police in the eighteenth-century, any oral comment on Russia's rulers, past or present, state policies, or episodes of political

---

14 "Zamechaniia na 'Zapiski o Rossii generala Manshteina,'" in *Perevoroty i voiny* (Moscow: Fond Sergeia Dubova, 1997), 475.

15 Minikh [Münnich], "Zapiski," 388.

16 *Leben, Thaten, und Betrübter Fall des Weltberufenen Russischen Grafen Burchards Christophs von Münnich* (Bremen: Nathaniel Saurmann, 1742); *Merckwürdiges Leben und trauriger Fall des russischen Staats-Ministers Andreae Grafen v. Ostermann* (Bremen: Nathaniel Saurmann, 1742).

history could be prosecuted as a state crime, especially (but not exclusively) if it came from someone of low rank.[17] Indeed, *fear*—primarily as the "fear of God," *strakh bozhii*, associated with the Last Judgment, in Russian called the "Terrible Judgment" (*Strashnyi sud*)—was commonly recognized in various official discourses (state-sponsored political treatises, sermons, and royal decrees) as an important source of social order. "Fear of God" was the subject of the first chapter of Peter I's *Artikul voinskii* (1716), a code of military law that for decades dominated the procedures of criminal prosecution in Russia.[18] At the same time, quite understandably, *fear* occupied a significant place in informal reflections on the current order. Before his fall, Volynskii, then a high-standing and powerful official, contrasted the position of Russian dignitaries to the freedoms of Polish senators who did not have to fear even their king, while "here we have to fear everything."[19]

Since the pastor Gregorii, the shaky position of the most powerful was a central issue for Russian political drama and its depictions of courtly life. The fall of Haman, time and again reiterated in the Esther dramas, offered a universal pattern of a career at court. Trials over those in power were staged in other early dramas as well. In the *Act of the Glorious Queen of Palestine Lands,* the king, acting on a not altogether groundless suspicion of marital unfaithfulness, tries, convicts, and exiles his spouse together with their children. This play, linked by L. A. Itigina to Elizabeth's court theater of the 1730s, might as well be related to earlier episodes from the reign of Peter the Great, who divorced his first wife, banishing her into a convent, and presided over a trial and execution of his second wife's lover. Another play, also possibly linked to Elizabeth's private

---

17   E. V. Anisimov, *Dyba i knut. Politicheskii sysk i russkoe obshchestvo v XVIII veke* (Moscow: Novoe literaturnoe obozrenie, 1999), 54.

18   *Polnoe sobranie zakonov Rossiiskoi imperii s 1649 g.* The complete laws of the Russian empire, [Sobranie I] ([St. Petersburg]: 1830), vol. 5 (1713–1719): 320–321, no. 3006. The code was republished in 1748.

19   D. A. Korsakov, *Iz zhizni russkih deiatelei XVIII veka* (Kazan': Tipografiia Imperatorskogo Universiteta, 1891), 309. According to the Anonym, the Field Marshal Prince Dolgorukii, who at times occupied the highest military posts, was twice exiled and imprisoned only on the grounds of his inappropriate oral remarks ("Zamechaniia," 442). Even when inaccurate, reports of this kind testify to the atmosphere of arbitrary terror that the Russian subjects and courtiers endured.

theater, the *Comedy of the Count Farson* (which, curiously enough, seems to draw on the Earl of Essex plot) narrates the rise and fall of a royal favorite, finally condemned in a formal trial by the senators envious of his power. The opera *Clemenza di Tito*, a centerpiece of the festive celebrations of Elizabeth's coronation in 1742, staged the trial of a courtier accused of conspiring against his emperor.

In the following parts, I will illuminate the proximity between dramatic poetics and the procedures of political persecution that was central for classicist Russian tragedy inaugurated by Sumarokov in 1747 and that loomed large in the consciousness of the courtly public. In 1765, the tutor to Grand Duke Paul Semen Poroshin recorded a remark by Grigorii Teplov, a reader of Rapin and a well-educated statesman who contributed to Catherine II's first manifestos. Teplov noted that the fate of Tsarevich Alexei would be an appropriate subject for a tragedy; indeed, all French tragedies of that period that dealt with Peter the Great concentrated on his relationship with his unfortunate son.[20] Poroshin also records the traumatic memories that the courtiers still had of the Volynskii trial two decades after the event. This episode was so important for the political experience of the Russian elite that Catherine II (who had not even come to Russia by 1740) took pride in the fact that no trials of this kind were possible under her reign. Even later, in the first decade of the nineteenth century, Vladislav Ozerov, the last Russian dramatist to achieve significant success with classicist tragedies, conceived a play representing Volynskii's fall. Admitting to his patron, Aleksei Olenin, that the tragedy could never be performed on public stages, he still asked him for access to the trial records, and went on to elaborate on his plan to treat "the justice of the Russian boyar, the duties of a magnate and senator" whose ruin symbolized the "unfortunate state of the people under a weak and suspicious government."[21] Both Ozerov and the Anonym disapproved of the harsh autocratic practices of Anna's reign, which were discarded, as the Anonym

---

20 S. A. Poroshin, "Zapiski, sluzhashchie k istorii velikogo kniazia Pavla Petrovicha," in *Russkii Gamlet* (Moscow: Fond Sergeia Dubova, 2004), 348; Kirill Ospovat, "Petr i Aleksei: k literaturnoi semantike istoriograficheskogo siuzheta," in *Sobranie sochinenii. K 60-letiiu L. I. Soboleva* (Moscow: Vremia novostei, 2006), 442–455.

21 *Russkii arkhiv* 1869, 143.

insists, in the enlightened era of Catherine the Great; quite importantly, though, Ozerov's never-accomplished plan and the Anonym's biased but competent narration outline a dynamic of terrifying spectacle and public fear that was common to political trials and theatrical productions in the first half of the eighteenth century.

Evidently, there were the immediately theatrical effects of public executions, conceptualized by Michel Foucault as crucial rituals of sovereignty, and considered in early modern discussions of drama up to Edmund Burke and Friedrich Schiller as an archetype for the engagement of public emotion.[22] According to the Anonym, Volynskii was beheaded "among the multitude attracted by curiosity and trembling in horror." The Saxon diplomat Petzold, who witnessed the pardon of Osterman and Münnich, wrote that after "this spectacle" (*dieses Schauspiel*) "among Russian nobles there were few who left the square indifferent or without compassion."[23]

The anatomy of this emotion is revealed in the memoirs of Prince Iakov Shakhovskoi, who had earlier served under Münnich and was ordered in 1742 to arrange for his voyage into exile. Seized by awe and compassion ("в удивительных и сожалительных сих восторгах находясь"), he contemplated the contrast between Münnich's previously successful career and his current misery: "Alas! This spectacle is a persuasive proof for me that one can never fully rely on one's reason and fortune in one's deliberations and enterprises."[24] The occasion that Shakhovskoi is commenting on was not in itself spectacular (he had to enter the barracks where Münnich was kept), but he still views it as a "spectacle" (*zrelishche*) that through emotional impact conveys to him as a spectator a lesson of self-discipline and common wisdom immediately related to his own position as a courtier and servitor. While Shakhovskoi's reaction does not necessarily have to be considered "theatrical," it certainly exemplifies the emotional mechanics that were exploited and appropriated by tragedy,

---

22 Carsten Zelle, "Strafen und Schrecken. Einführende Bemerkungen zur Parallele zwischen dem Schauspiel der Tragödie und der Tragödie der Hinrichtung," in *Jahrbuch der deutschen Schillergesellschaft* 28 (1984): 76–103.

23 Ernst Herrmann, *Geschichte des russischen Staates* (Hamburg: Friedrich Perthes, 1853), 5: 5.

24 Ia. P. Shakhovskoi, "Vospominaniia," in *Imperiia posle Petra* (Moscow: Fond Sergeia Dubova, 1998), 49.

focused—according to neo-Aristotelian dramatic theories—on the fall of the great and its disciplining effects on the audience.

The first Russian-language essay on drama, published in 1733 in the *Primechaniia na vedomosti,* stated that in the fifth act of a tragedy "the whole plot takes a very sad and pitiful end, which consists for the most part in the executions and murders of the most illustrious persons of the tragedy."[25] As Benjamin notes, in baroque versions of Aristotle's theory, fear and pity are identified with the "participation in the fate of the most outstanding characters. Fear is aroused by the death of the villain, pity—by the death of the pious hero."[26] Hans-Jürgen Schings demonstrates in his detailed survey of those various and often conflicting readings that the Aristotelian notion of a *catharsis* of passions was conventionally understood to signify a technique of emotional discipline, useful for the polity insofar as it teaches the public to cope with the anxieties of political existence symbolized by the fall of the prince.[27] Schings summarizes his conclusions with a phrase from the *Meditations* of Marcus Aurelius, translated into Russian as early as 1740:

> Tragedies were first introduced, to put Men in mind, of the Accidents which happen in their Live; to Inform them that they must necessarily Come, and teach them, that those things which they see with so much Delight on the Stage, should not appear insupportable in the Grand Theatre of the World ...[28]

---

25 "O pozorishchnykh igrakh, ili komediiakh i tragediiakh," in *Teatral'naia zhizn' Rossii v epokhu Anny Ioannovny,* ed. L. M. Starikova, 524.

26 Benjamin, *Origin of the German Tragic Drama,* 61.

27 Hans-Jürgen Schings, "Consolatio Tragoediae. Zur Theorie des barocken Trauerspiels," in *Deutsche Dramentheorien. Beiträge zu einer historischen Poetik des Dramas in Deutschland,* ed. Reinhold Grimm (Frankfurt am Main: Atheneum, 1971). A more recent study argues that the interpretation of *Poetics* centered on the notion of catharsis, universally accepted by the European scholarly tradition almost to this day, was actually elaborated in Medici Florence in concert with the doctrines of social and political discipline sponsored by the emerging principate: Déborah Blocker, "Dire l'«art» à Florence sous Cosme I de Médicis: une *Poétique* d'Aristote au service du Prince," *AISTHE* 2 (2008).

28 Quoted in Dacier's commentary on Aristotle, and its English translation: *Aristotle's Art of Poetry,* 78. For the Russian version of Marcus Aurelius, see *Zhitie i dela Marka Avreliia Antonina tsesaria rimskago: A pri tom sobstvennyia, i premudryia evo razsuzhdenii o sebe*

To quote Greenblatt once again, "precisely because this anxiety was pervasive and unavoidable, those in power wanted to incorporate it ideologically and manage it. Managed insecurity may have been reassuring both to the managers themselves and to those towards whom the techniques were addressed."[29]

In his turn, Norbert Elias linked the poetics of neoclassical tragedy to the strategies of emotional self-regulation and self-control, imposed by the specific rationality of the court society.[30] "An integral part of social life at court," classicist drama existed in the tension between the clear-sighted common wisdom of everyday political existence and the highly artificial allegorical poetics of courtly fetes. The "connection between spectacle proper and allegory," reflected in the "allegorical character of the figures," "in courtly respect ... precisely defined," as revealed by Benjamin, was certainly in place in eighteenth-century Russia.[31] In 1761, Chancellor Mikhail Vorontsov sent to his young daughter in Vienna a translation of Metastasio's latest libretto, *Alcide al bivio (Alcides at a Crossroads)*, in order to prepare her to attend its performances, but more importantly to ensure that she receives "a moral lesson for a young person's behavior, good notions of virtue." To that end, the loving father substituted the protagonists' "invented names," some of them overtly allegorical, with "direct words"—a "young man" for Alcide, "reason" for Fronimo, "virtue" for Aretea.[32]

Besides celebrating a certain ruler or dynasty, court festivities were designed to engage its public in an all-embracing emotional economy, which intertwined political conformity with moral self-discipline in the name of "virtue." Tragedy was directly linked to the theatrical aesthetic of this kind. The 1733 essay, published both in Russian and German, insisted that tragedy's only goal was to teach virtue, for the first time introducing Russian

---

samom, S nemetskago na rossiiskoi iazyk perevel ... Sergei Volchkov (St. Petersburg: Pri Imperatorskoi Akademii nauk, 1740).

29 Greenblatt, *Shakespearean Negotiations*, 137–138.

30 Elias, *Court Society*, 112.

31 Benjamin, *Origin of the German Tragic Drama*, 191. Benjamin's idea of a profoundly allegorical poetics of early modern drama has been recently developed in Jane K. Brown's valuable book-length study, *The Persistence of Allegory: Drama and Neoclassicism from Shakespeare to Wagner* (Philadelphia: University of Pennsylvania Press, 2007). For a discussion specifically on allegory in Metastasio and *opera seria* and its relationship to contemporary tragedy, see her chapter 6. On the allegorical foundations of representation in classical French theater, see also Blocker, *Instituer un «art»*, 194–202.

32 P. I. Bartenev, ed., *Arkhiv kniazia Vorontsova* (Moscow: Tip. A. I. Mamontova, 1872), 4: 165.

readers to neoclassicist commonplaces propagated among others by Gottsched.[33] Paraphrasing Aristotle and Rapin, Gottsched suggested that tragedies had to offer allegorical illustrations of a moral precept:

> The Poet wishes to teach truth through fables, and prepare the spectators for their misfortunes by displaying the grievous fall of the powerful. ... The Poet chooses a moral maxim, which he wishes to inculcate in his spectators. He then designs a generalized fable which illustrates the truth of this maxim. He then searches the history for such famous men who have experienced something similar: and he adopts their names for the actors of his fable in order to invest them with esteem.[34]

Control over anxieties produced by common political experience had to be established through dramatic techniques in order to assure the audience's acceptance of the "justice" of current order. The importance of this emotional mechanic for the poetics of tragedy is revealed in a scene from Shakespeare's *Hamlet*, a play in many ways paradigmatic for early modern tragic drama and explicitly concerned with the functioning of theater at court. *Hamlet* was very much relevant in mid-eighteenth century Russia: a French translation published in the second volume of Pierre Antoine de La Place's *Le Théâtre Anglois* (1746) was well known to the Russian public and inspired Sumarokov to produce his own reworking of the play in 1748 (see part 3). Sumarokov is also known to have worked with the English original in the 1685 edition, and later engaged in a debate with Trediakovskii on the differences and similarities between his play and Shakespeare's. During a ceremonial speech in the first scenes of *Hamlet*, Claudius announces his marriage to Gertrude and encourages the young prince to temper his grief (1.2):

> Though yet of Hamlet our dear brother's death
> The memory be green, and that it us befitted

---

33 "O pozorishchnykh igrakh, ili komediiakh i tragediiakh," 520.
34 Gottsched, *Versuch einer Critischen Dichtkunst*, in Gottsched, *Schriften zur Literatur*, 161.

To bear our hearts in grief and our whole kingdom
To be contracted in one brow of woe,
Yet so far hath discretion fought with nature
That we with wisest sorrow think on him,
Together with remembrance of ourselves.
Therefore our sometime sister, now our queen,
The imperial jointress to this warlike state,
Have we, as 'twere with a defeated joy,
With an auspicious and a dropping eye,
With mirth in funeral and with dirge in marriage,
In equal scale weighing delight and dole,
Taken to wife . . .

'Tis sweet and commendable in your nature, Hamlet,
To give these mourning duties to your father;
But, you must know, your father lost a father;
That father lost, lost his; and the survivor bound
In filial obligation for some term
To do obsequious sorrow. But to persever
In obstinate condolement is a course
Of impious stubbornness; 'tis unmanly grief . . .
'tis a fault to heaven,
A fault against the dead, a fault to nature,
To reason most absurd, whose common theme
Is death of fathers, and who still hath cried,
From the first corpse till he that died to-day,
"This must be so."[35]

Benjamin suggested in his gnomic manner that "for the *Trauerspiel* Hamlet alone is a spectator by the grace of God."[36] Indeed, we see him as a responsive, if confused, spectator to a profoundly theatrical narration of his father's death delivered by an "apparition," which "assume[s] my noble father's

---

35   William Shakespeare, *Hamlet*, ed. G. R. Hibbard (Oxford: Oxford University Press, 1987), 154–155, 160.

36   Benjamin, *Origin of the German Tragic Drama*, 158.

person" and simultaneously arouses and moderates Hamlet's pity (*"Hamlet.* Alas, poor ghost!—*Ghost.* Pity me not") and fear ("I could a tale unfold whose lightest word, / Would harrow up thy soul, freeze thy young blood … / But this eternal blazon must not be / To ears of flesh and blood"), manipulating them in order to incite him to political action (1.5).[37] The theatrical ("tragic") pattern behind this "apparition" is revealed by Hamlet himself, as he arranges for the Ghost's story to be reenacted on the court stage as *The Murder of Gonzago*, relying on the emotional force of theatrical reactions.

Conversely, Claudius in the monologue quoted above, which precedes the Ghost's entry in a weak anticipation of its solemnity, attempts to contain Hamlet's "unprevailing woe"—and, possibly, that of all other subjects, the "Lords and Attendants" who are present during his speech in "a room of state" and might also harbor dissent—along the lines of the ceremonial logic of succession. Illuminating the fundamental kinship between "funeral pageantry" and tragedy, Michael Neill remarks that "[f]or Claudius … Hamlet's willful ostentation of these 'trappings' of grief is … an implicit denial of the due succession meant to be affirmed in the pageantry of funeral custom," a threat to political order that has to be pacified and brought to conformity: "This must be so."[38] Grief can only be "commendable" in the form of "mourning duties," which have to be succeeded by the celebration of the new ruler, merging "delight and dole" in a ceremonial cyclic scenario of eternal renovation of the monarchy's cosmos, here symbolized by the ritual of royal wedding. Whatever his personal flaws, Claudius certainly relied on a valid symbolical pattern, which helps explain the functioning of tragedy at absolutist courts and its paradoxical integration into the ceremonial idiom of rejoicing. In Roland Barthes's Nietzschean formulation, "out of *spectacle* of failure [tragedy] believes it can create a transcendence of failure, and out of the passion of the immediate, a mediation. When all things are destroyed, tragedy remains a *spectacle*, that is, a reconciliation with the world."[39]

---

37 Shakespeare, *Hamlet*, 185–186.

38 Michael Neill, *Issues of Death: Mortality and Identity in English Renaissance Tragedy* (Oxford: Clarendon Press, 1997), 300. I owe this reference to Susanne Wofford. See, even more generally, Naomi Conn Liebler, *Shakespeare's Festive Tragedy: The Ritual Foundations of Genre* (London: Routledge, 1995).

39 Roland Barthes, *On Racine*, trans. Richard Howard (Berkeley: University of California Press, 1992), 60.

Tragedy and the closely related *opera seria* were intrinsic to a ceremonial aesthetic that made constant oscillation between joy and grief ("With mirth in funeral and with dirge in marriage, / In equal scale weighing delight and dole") one of the principal sources of pleasure. The 1733 essay on drama specifically addressed the paradox of the theatrical success of tragedies, "which rather induce the spectators to grief than to joy," and illuminated it through an analogy (also reminiscent of Nietzsche) with the European-type music recently imported to Russia and closely associated with court entertainments. Tragedy is similar to musical dissonance, which, though itself unpleasant to the ear, in skillful combination with the pleasant consonances provides for more "delight and admiration" than the consonances alone.[40]

Apparently, tragedy integrated the inevitable experience of anxiety (grief, pity, fear) into festive scenarios of triumph and domesticated it in accordance with the emotional pattern outlined by Shakespeare's Claudius. In Sumarokov's 1748 version of *Hamlet*, Ofeliia's confidante, Flemina, consoling her, elaborates on the benefits of misfortune:

Приятней солнца свет, когда пройдет ненастье,
И слаще сладка жизнь, когда пройдет несчастье.
Кто знает для чего случаи таковы …(4.1)

More brightly shines the sun after foul weather passes,
And life seems sweeter in the wake of our misfortune.
Who knows the purposes of happenings like this.[41]

If this is so, the spectacle of grief sets off and reenhances the ostensible harmony of political cosmos, as confirmed by the happy endings of most of Sumarokov's tragedies, including *Gamlet*: the prince of Denmark punishes the regicides, reconquers his throne and, apparently, expects to be united with Ofeliia after she performs her "mourning duties" to her criminal father ("pays the last debt to nature," as Sumarokov puts it). Fashioning political calamities, *happenings like this*, as Aristotelian peripeteia ("Peripetie is a

---

40   "O pozorishchnykh igrakh, ili komediiakh i tragediiakh," 518.
41   Sumarokov, *Polnoe sobranie vsekh sochinenii*, 3: 98; Sumarokov, *Selected Tragedies*, 118.

change of one fortune into another"[42]), tragedy offered the spectators an emotional framework for their very real political experience, inscribing it into the ceremonially affirmed dynamic of grief and joy. In fact, the patterns of emotional oscillation, elaborated and canonized in drama, could frame the public perceptions of crucial political events and scenarios of imperial power. Days after Elizabeth's death in December 1761, Lomonosov praised her successor, Peter III, in verses reminiscent both of Shakespeare's Claudius and Sumarokov's Flemina:

> Сияй, о новый год, прекрасно
> Сквозь густоту печальных туч.
> Прошло затмение ужасно;
> Умножь, умножь отрады луч.
> Уже плачевная утрата,
> Дражайшая сокровищ злата,
> Сугубо нам возвращена.
> Благополучны мы стократно:
> Петра Великого обратно
> Встречает Росская страна.[43]

> Shine, o new year, beautifully through the thickness of mournful clouds. The terrible eclipse is over: oh strengthen the ray of joy. The sorrowful loss, more valuable than the gold of treasures, has been restored double to us. Our prosperity is hundredfold, the Russian land welcomes back Peter the Great.

Several weeks earlier, he used a similar rhetoric to recall Elizabeth's coup d'état of 1741 in a celebration of its twentieth anniversary:

> Красуйся в сей блаженный час,
> Как вдруг триумфы воссияли;
> Тем вяще озарили нас,
> Чем были мрачнее печали.

---

42 *Aristotle's Art of Poetry*, 162.
43 M. V. Lomonosov, *Izbrannye proizvedeniia* (Leningrad: Sovetskii pisatel', 1986), 162–163.

О радость, дай воспомянуть!
О радость, дай на них взглянуть!
Мы больше чувствуем отрады,
Как скорби видим за тобой:
Злочастья ненавистны взгляды
Любезный красят образ твой.[44]

O shine at this blessed hour, when the triumphs have blazed and have illumined us the stronger, as the woes were dark. O joy, let me remember! O joy, let me look at them! We feel more delight when we see sorrows behind us. Misfortune's heinous gazes only adorn your image.

Behind the two ascensions, foundational for the political order (and, as was the case with the 1741 coup, often reenacted in operas and tragedies, including Sumarokov's *Gamlet*), Lomonosov's panegyric rhetoric—in line with the generic poetics of the solemn ode, as described by Pogosjan—revealed the fundamental patterns of absolutist "political emotionality" and aligned them with ceremonial logic. In accordance with the tragic aesthetic outlined above, the ubiquitous "scenario of rejoicing," which, as Wortman has amply demonstrated, informed most public celebrations of Russian monarchy, was in fact inseparable from "woes" and "sorrows," experienced by individual and collective political actors and revived in the ceremonial idiom as a necessary source of triumph. While in his many descriptions of Elizabeth's coup Lomonosov (along with other panegyric writers) relegated the "woes" and "terrors" to the previous reign, a coexistence of emotional extremes was in fact at any time intrinsic to the subjects' relationship to autocracy. For example, after the 1741 coup, public joy was not in fact so universal, as, according to Manstein, "upon every face might be seen consternation depicted; everyone was in fear either for himself or some member of his family, and complete confidence was not restored till some days afterwards." Describing Empress Anna, he wrote that she "was naturally gentle and compassionate, never liking to use severity," and it was her favorite, Biron, who was to blame for "a great number of bloody executions, without

---

44 Lomonosov, *Izbrannye proizvedeniia*, 157.

reckoning an infinity of persons—and some of them of the highest distinction—who were sent to Siberia without her knowing anything of it."[45]

While this distinction between the empress and her minister can seem naïve, it clearly conveys a deeply ambiguous vision of autocracy shared by the Russian political class and fundamental for political drama, since, as Benjamin has established, "the theory of sovereignty which takes as its example the special cases in which dictatorial powers are unfolded, positively demands the completion of the image of the sovereign, as tyrant."[46] In Russia, this inherent ambiguity of tragic treatments of monarchy was played out in a well-known historical episode. When in 1785 the Moscow Governor General Iakov Bruce suggested to Catherine to suppress Nikolev's tragedy *Sorena i Zamir*, which he considered subversive because of its repeated attacks against tyranny, Catherine replied: "It surprises me ... that you have halted the representations of tragedy evidently met with general approval by the public. The sense of the verses that you have noticed does not relate to your sovereign. The author opposes the despotism of tyrants, while you call Catherine your mother."[47] On the one hand, a double reference to the public approval of the play and the empress ("you call Catherine your mother") suggests—in a logic reminiscent of d'Aubignac—a relationship of mutual reinforcement between monarchy and drama that both make use of theatrical mechanics of collective engagement to fashion images of rule. On the other hand, only the absolute royal will (endowed with but not limited to sovereignty over textual interpretation) can draw and uphold the distinction between tyranny and benevolent monarchy, apparently blurred even for zealous servitors like Bruce. In Greenblatt's words, "the enhancement of royal power is not only a matter of the deferral of doubt: the very doubts that [a tragedy] raises serve not to rob the king of his charisma but to heighten it, precisely as they heighten the theatrical interest of the play."[48]

Consequently, in early Russian plays royal clemency was time and again balanced with terrifyingly unexpected outbursts of excessive violence. While on other occasions the kings consult their councilors and weigh their

---

45 Manstein, *Contemporary Memoirs of Russia*, 323, 272.

46 Benjamin, *Origin of the German Tragic Drama*, 69.

47 *Russkii vestnik* 4 (1810): 119.

48 Greenblatt, *Shakespearean Negotiations*, 63.

decisions, in some of the central episodes they are seen to undergo a sudden change of heart that leads them to brutal persecution of those closest to them—the favorite Haman in the Esther plays, or the queen in the *Act of the Glorious Queen of the Palestine Lands*. The same proximity of opposites is characteristic of Sumarokov's stage rulers: in both *Khorev* (analyzed in part 2) and *Sinav i Truvor*, an admittedly benevolent monarch ends up bringing about the ruin of his valorous brother and heir, and in *Artistona* the tyrant Darius in one of the final scenes instantly renounces his intention to marry the heroine against her will and execute her rebellious lover. As A. N. Robinson has shown, the dynamic of emotional oscillation between joy and grief, associated with the dangerous unpredictability of royal will, was central to Russian political drama since its beginnings.[49] The prologue to the *Act of the Glorious Queen* explains that everyone, whatever their social status, has to suffer misfortunes:

> we will see it, to tell the truth, in the persons of highest dignity, like princes and magnates are not exempt from grief, which is also used to living in royal residences ... But the Lord is merciful, he shows his goodness to man after his woes and brings him to joy. And we, benevolent spectators, have decided to present this wonder to your eyes on our half-witted theater ...

In the last scenes of the play, the experience of political persecution is overtly interwoven into the theatrics of royal triumph. In its final scenes, the king returns his queen from exile and celebrates their reconciliation with a feast, calling on musicians to "play for our joy and delight, / In order not to think of the sorrow that was before." His senators, however, insist that it is "impossible not to remind truthfully of the sorrow" experienced by those who witnessed the fall of their queen. The king urges the queen to narrate her misfortunes, "fear and terror," but then all of them conclude that "it is today only appropriate to amuse the queen for her delight so that she could forget all her sorrow." The recollection of the queen's "extreme woe" serves in the ritualized logic of the feast to set off and emphasize the ceremonial public

---

49   Derzhavina, Demin, and Robinson, "Rukopisnaia dramaturgiia," 95.

"joy," and thus fulfills a function similar to the role of the drama itself in the festive culture of the court.[50]

Walter Benjamin has explored the notion of grief, or mourning (*Trauer*), as crucial for the cultural poetics of baroque drama, *Trauerspiel*. This German term—which, in Benjamin's view, stands for a dramatic form distinctively different from ancient *tragedy*—was current in the eighteenth century and applied to neoclassical dramas, whether Racine's, Gottsched's, or Sumarokov's. In the 1733 essay it was literally translated into Russian as "mournful play," *pechal'naia igra*.[51] The paradox behind the combination of the two concepts was not incidental to German terminology, and was recognized by dramatic theory elsewhere. In his famous *Préface* to *Bérénice*, Racine stated that his goal was to produce "cette tristesse majestueuse qui fait tout le plaisir de la tragédie" ("that majestic grief which forms all the pleasure of tragedy"). *Bérénice*, Racine's most harmless tragedy, could boast "[le] bonheur ... de ne pas déplaire à Sa Majesté" ("the good fortune ... to have pleased his majesty") and was a clear case of courtly aesthetic. Written in the language of gallantry and alluding to an amorous episode from Louis XIV's youth, it staged the monarch's power over his own feelings, intertwining the ensuing "tristesse majestueuse" with an exaltation of royal omnipotence.[52]

Benjamin emphasized "the relationship between mourning and ostentation," inherited from Italian theater that itself "emerged from pure ostentation, from the *trionfi*, the processions with explanatory recitation which flourished in Florence under Lorenzo de Medici," and inherent in the dramatic genre whose "very name ... already indicates that its content awakens mourning in the spectator," "[f]or these are not so much plays which cause mourning, as plays through which mournfulness finds satisfaction: plays for the mournful." The first spectator in this theater is the prince, in Benjamin's words "the paradigm of the melancholy man." This point is illustrated with a passage from Pascal's *Pensées*, suggesting that a king, if left alone, would find himself "a man full of miseries, and one that feels them as well as any other common person," and in order to avoid that "there never fails to have near the persons

---

50 Derzhavina, Demin, and Robinson eds., *P'esy liubitelskikh teatrov*, 406, 435.

51 "O pozorishchnykh igrakh, ili komediiakh i tragediiakh," 518.

52 [Jean] Racine, *Théâtre complet*, ed. Jean-Pierre Collinet (Paris: Gallimard, 1983), 1: 374.

of kings, a great many that continually watch to make divertissements succeed after business ... to supply them with pleasures and pastimes."[53]

Indeed, the interest in tragedy, whether read or performed, highlighted the constant presence of *grief* in the symbolic idiom of royal display: in Sumarokov's dramas, themselves aligned with courtly festivities, tragic action, sometimes leading to the death of the protagonists, often plays against a ceremonial backdrop of a planned royal wedding. As a courtly genre, tragedy must have appealed to an established sensibility of grief, apparently accepted in Russia—as elsewhere—as an important "political emotion" associated with court existence. In a letter to Empress Anna that brought about his fall, Volynskii drew a sinister picture of courtly mores and requested a grant of money, complaining that he was "brought to such an extreme condition of my mind that at times nothing in the world pleases me, even my very life, and judging with my weak mind, it seems sometimes that it would be better to die than to lead this restless and harmful life in such sorrow."[54] Anna's all-powerful favorite, Ernst Johann von Biron, considering Volynskii's letter as a direct threat to his power, demanded a criminal inquiry in a formal petition to the empress that did not neglect to mention that for him, too, his high rank "is not very pleasant, especially given the flux of fortunate and unfortunate events which accompanies human fate."[55] Over a decade later, Empress Elizabeth's favorite, Ivan Shuvalov, a powerful patron of the arts and artists including Sumarokov, admitted to a hypochondriac state of mind amidst the pleasures and dangers of the court.[56] Russian rulers of the era were also prone to melancholy. The short-lived emperor Peter II, mostly remembered by historians as a dissolute youth whose love of entertainments directed him away from education and state business, during his coronation had, according to the future Jane Rondeau, "a very grave look; if I were not speaking of a monarch, I should say, a surly one; so much so that even the bloom of youth loses its pleasingness by it."[57]

---

53 Benjamin, *Origin of the German Tragic Drama*, 118–119, 140, 142–144.
54 RGADA, fond 6, op. 1, ed. khr. 195, ll. 6ob-7.
55 RGADA, fond 6, op. 1, ed. khr. 196, l. 1ob.
56 Bartenev, *Arkhiv kniazia Vorontsova*, 6: 287.
57 Jane Vigor, *Eleven additional letters*, 72.

Both Ernst von Münnich and the Anonym mention the peculiar literary predilections of Anna Leopoldovna, the mother of the infant emperor Ivan, who ruled Russia as a regent in 1740–1741 before she was overthrown by Elizabeth, and could have enjoyed Neuberin's performances. In the Anonym's words,

> Reading, especially of dramatic works, was her most pleasant occupation; once during such pastime she said that her attention was mostly attracted to those writings where an unfortunate princess was shown to suffer her miseries and chains with a noble pride and magnanimity. That would give one grounds to think that she had a presentiment of the ill fate that awaited her, but it would be more reasonable to conclude that those words sprang from a mind given to mournful contemplation.

In the very act of reading plays, the regent fashions her own political identity in the terms of tragic drama outlined by Benjamin. A ruler over one of the world's largest empires, she displays melancholy ("mournful contemplation"), attributed in plays and treatises to monarchs and princes like Hamlet, and associated with a distrust of courtly ways. According to the Anonym, on one occasion she was charmed by an account of the private life led in Hamburg by those who had withdrawn from society, and exclaimed: "Oh my god! Why could not I live in Hamburg, far from the vanity of pompous palaces and grandeur of all kind!"[58] The history of her own fall—during the coup of 1741 she was captured and subsequently kept in prison until her death five years later—seamlessly fitted into the pattern of a genre that customarily dealt with situations "where heroic greatness meets its downfall, and the court is reduced to a scaffold."[59] More specifically, the misfortunes of princesses were a topic often explored by early modern playwrights.[60] Anna, who reportedly had good knowledge of French and perfect German, could

---

58 "Zamechaniia," 474, 403.
59 Benjamin, *Origin of the German Tragic Drama*, 93.
60 Peter-André Alt, *Der Tod der Königin: Frauenopfer und politische Souveränität im Trauerspiel des 17. Jahrhunderts* (Berlin: Walter de Gruyter, 2004).

have had in mind German plays like Andreas Gryphius's *Catharina von Georgien* (1657), where Russian politics plays a prominent role, or French works such as Voltaire's 1724 *Hérode et Mariamne*, listed by Sumarokov among his masterpieces in 1748. Fallot's 1765 play, which dramatized current (and largely accurate) accounts of Anna's own fall, returned both her fate and her sensibility—expressly described as "Melancolie"—to the realm of tragic drama:

> *La Duchesse [Anna].*
> … Car souvent la fortune aux grandeurs nous éléve,
> Et bientot inconstante elle nous les enléve.

> *The Duchess [Anna].*
> For fortune often raises us to greatness
> And soon takes it away to us with its usual inconstancy.[61]

The "melancholic" vision of life at court and its dangers, associated with tragedies, was not peculiar to Anna Leopoldovna but rather constituted a usual feature of the courtly "theater of power." Anna's dramatic tastes were apparently shared by the nine-year-older Elizabeth; the two princesses were exposed to a very similar political and cultural experience, growing up at the often menacing Russian court and gradually working their way to the throne. No wonder, then, that the plays about "unfortunate princesses" were as much appreciated by the triumphant empress as they were by her ill-fated predecessor. Even if the *Act of the Glorious Queen of Palestine Lands* cannot be reliably linked to Elizabeth's private theater, as Itigina would have it, we can refer to a similar German play, performed and published in Moscow by Johann Christoph Siegmund, the head of a German dramatic company who could boast a lifelong acquaintance with the new empress, on the occasion of Elizabeth's ascension day in 1744. The play, *Die unterdrückte aber durch die siegende Weißheit wieder erhobene Gerechtigkeit (Justice Oppressed and Restored by Triumphant Wisdom)*, was conceived as a fictionalized but recognizable reenactment of the hardships that Elizabeth (Ermilda) had to endure under

---

61   Fallot, *L'Innocence opprimée*, xxxiii.

Empress Anna and Anna Leopoldovna (Olmirena) on her way to the ancestral throne.[62]

The play's last scene stages Elizabeth's triumph and the downfall of Anna Leopoldovna. While Anna's son, the legitimate emperor Ivan, was sealed off from the world in a distant prison and all references to his name were forbidden, all documents containing his name confiscated and destroyed, Elizabeth's compassion for his mother was made a matter of public display. Besides Siegmund's play, which emphasized the new empress's clemency towards Anna, this became evident after her death in 1746 when Anna's body was brought to Petersburg for public mourning, shared and encouraged by the empress, while the semi-official *Portrait naturel de l'Imperatrice de Russie* publicized this episode:

> Avec quelle grandeur d'ame, relevée par des marques d'humanité et de compassion, en reflechissant sur l'inconstance des choses de ce monde, ne l'avons-nous veue assister, et verser des pleurs, aux funerailles, qu'elle fit a la princesse Anne, ci-devant regente, au couvent de St. Alexandre Nevski—suivant l'exemple d'Alexandre le Grand, qui pleura amerement la mort de Darius, son plus grand ennemi.

> What a greatness of spirit, exalted by the signs of humanity and compassion at the thought of the inconstancy of worldly things did she show when she wept at the funeral of princess Anne, the former regent, at the St. Alexander Nevski Monastery, following the example of Alexander the Great who bitterly bemoaned the death of Darius, his greatest enemy.[63]

Mournful contemplation of the "inconstancy of worldly things" is integrated into Elizabeth's "scenario of power," the ceremonial demonstration of triumph over her rival, and the role of the first spectator at the grave of the fallen princess is added to her royal roles. This role was important enough to Elizabeth that she became the first Russian monarch to make theatrical production of tragedies a regular element of courtly life. Theatrical

---

62 See the Russian translation in Starikova, *Teatral'naia zhizn' Rossii v epokhu Elizavety Petrovny,* vol. 2, bk. 2, 29–72.

63 *Portrait naturel,* 6.

perceptions of tragedy—as well as *opera seria* already introduced under Empress Anna—were clearly linked to a demonstrative sensibility of grief, complicating our view of the courtly amusements famously favored by Elizabeth. Sumarokov had the courtly taste in mind when he composed tragedies where "virtue in distress is embodied by an innocent heroine, often imprisoned [or] facing a forced marriage to an evil tyrant."[64] Assessing the dramatist's achievement on the verge of the nineteenth century, Nikolai Karamzin wrote that his mournful scenes were designed to "draw tears from the eyes of the sensible Elizabeth."[65] Royal tears, shown to the audience of subjects, themselves constituted a spectacle of "humanity and compassion" that was meant to reenhance the emotional bond between the empress and her subjects. This pattern of political emotionality had been already employed by Empress Anna, as Jane Rondeau reported in 1734 from her court:

> I have often seen her melt into tears at a melancholy story, and she shews such unaffected horror at any mark of cruelty, that her mind to me seems to be composed of the most amiable qualities that I have ever observed in any one person; which seems a particular mark of the goodness of Providence, as she is possessed of such power.[66]

When Christian Wilhelm von Münnich, steward of the court under Elizabeth and possibly the author of the *Portrait naturel*, noticed the tears shed by the empress at another 1746 funeral, he remarked: "I admit that I always see it with pleasure and am always assured that I am very fortunate to serve a sovereign who has a tender and a sensible heart."[67] It was this political spectacle of royal sensibility that court theater with its various spaces and genres, along with other ceremonial forms, was fashioned to manage and perpetuate.

---

64 Ewington, *A Voltaire for Russia*, 136.

65 N. M. Karamzin, *Sochineniia* (Leningrad: Khudozhestvennaia literatura, 1984), 2: 112.

66 Jane Vigor, *Letters from a lady*, 90.

67 K. A. Pisarenko, ed., "Pis'ma ober-gofmeistera Kh. V. Minikha Ioganne-Elizavete printsesse Angal't-Tserbstskoi, 1745–1746 gg.," in *Rossiiskii Arkhiv: Istoriia Otechestva v svidetel'stvakh i dokumentakh XVIII–XX vv.* [Vol. XVIII] (Moscow: Studiia Trite, 2009), 78.

PART II

KHOREV, OR THE TRAGEDY OF ORIGIN

POETRY, HISTORY, ALLEGORY

Sumarokov's *Khorev*, Russia's first classicist drama, builds upon a legend. According to ancient Russian chronicles, Kiev, "the mother of Russian towns," was founded by Kii, who ruled there as the oldest of three brothers, the other two being Khorev (chosen by Sumarokov as his protagonist) and Shchek (the play mentions him in passing as deceased). Except for the foundation of Kiev and a military raid on Byzantium (characteristic for the first generations of historical Russian rulers), no details of the brothers' actions are reported. Using this scarce data as his starting point, Sumarokov devised a complex dramatic plot. In his version, Kii had conquered Kiev from its previous ruler, Zavlokh, whose infant daughter, Osnelda, was captured and grew up in Kiev as a prisoner of war. At the start of the play, it is announced that Zavlokh is back at Kiev's walls demanding nothing but the release of his daughter, while Osnelda, by now nubile, is passionately loved by Khorev, Kii's heir, and reciprocates his feelings. The lovers forge a plan to marry, thereby ending all hostilities and reuniting the Kievan nation, up to then split into Kii's victorious people and their prisoners, Zavlokh's former subjects. Before they reveal their plan to Kii, a generally benevolent ruler expected to approve of it, Osnelda, faithful to her filial obligations, sends a secret messenger to Zavlokh requesting his permission to marry. Meanwhile, Kii's counselor Stalverkh, having heard of the young couple's secret accord but unaware of its exact purpose, relates to Kii his suspicion of a conspiracy possibly planned by the popular Khorev to overthrow the elderly ruler with the help of Zavlokh and his troops. Kii hesitates to doubt the loyalty of his faithful subjects and his valorous brother, but, enraged with

Stalverkh's report of his secret dealings, refuses a peaceful settlement of the matter, sending Khorev into battle with Zavlokh to restore his hitherto unblemished "glory." Meanwhile, Zavlokh's letter forbidding the marriage arrives, and Osnelda burns it on the spot in desperation. Having learned of the secret correspondence, Kii summons Osnelda and confronts her with the accusation of political conspiracy; she lacks the evidence to prove her innocence, and Kii sentences her to death by poison. Kii fears that Khorev will turn his troops against him, but instead Khorev returns triumphant, bringing Zavlokh as his prisoner. Finally convinced of his innocence, Kii tries to repeal Osnelda's death sentence, but it is too late. Stalverkh off stage and Khorev on stage commit suicide, while Kii and Zavlokh regret their cruelty towards the young lovers.[1]

It might seem to be a paradox that for the first time introducing to Russia a markedly "foreign" literary form—a French-type five-act neoclassical tragedy, strictly observing the notorious unities—Sumarokov chose national history for his subject, in an apparent contradiction to the authoritative French usage. In a comparison of ancient Greek and contemporary French tragedy, attached to his widely read *Théâtre des Grecs* (1730), a collection of classical dramatic texts in French translation, Pierre Brumoy complained that, while both the Greeks and the French took dramatic subjects from history or "popular traditions, which are living annals," the French tragedy

> borrows its materials from abroad; and very seldom takes them from the history of our own country. ... As to the antiquity of our monarchy, the grandeur of our most remarkable events, and the exploits of our heroes, they are subjects that give us pleasure in history: they are naturally interesting to us from the love we bear to our native country: but whether it is that our vanity startles at seeing

---

1   Scholarship on *Khorev* refers without exception to the abridged and revised version of the play published by Sumarokov in 1768 and reproduced by Novikov in the posthumous *Polnoe sobranie vsekh sochinenii* and in all subsequent printings. This is also the text translated by Richard and Raymond Fortune in Sumarokov's *Selected Tragedies* (Evanston, IL: Northwestern University Press, 1970). I will refer to the original 1747 version: Aleksandr Sumarokov, *Khorev. Tragediia* (St. Petersburg: Pri Imperatorskoi Akademii nauk, 1747), citing the page number in parenthesis. When possible I will use the Fortunes' English text with necessary emendations, also citing the page numbers.

truths in pure theatrical pieces, assume the appearances of fables …
we are not easily reconciled to domestic themes upon our theatre.

The Greeks, on the contrary, drew upon "history or the fables of their own
country," which "were to them inexhaustible, nay, their only funds," so that
"there is not a city, a festival, nor a monument among the Grecians, which
was not celebrated by one or more theatrical entertainments."[2]

Brumoy's influential remarks provide an important background for some
of the subsequent attempts to adapt episodes from national history for the uses
of tragedy. As if to make up for the deficiencies he described, the original patriotic functions of the genre could be revived and adopted to the monarchical
sentiment of modern polities. An important case in point is the German
dramatist Johann Elias Schlegel (1719–1749), a one-time disciple of Gottsched,
who published in the 1740s two "national" tragedies: *Hermann* (1743), the
only German tragedy ever mentioned by Sumarokov,[3] and *Canut* (1746).
Canut, which only preceded Sumarokov's dramatic debut by a year, provides a
striking parallel to his experiments in tragedy. It was written in Denmark in a
conscious effort to inaugurate a local "national" theater under court patronage,
encouraged by a group of educated courtiers that included the Russian envoy
Johann Albert von Korff, and was quickly followed by a treatise making a
theoretical case for the choice of national subjects for dramatic works.[4] *Canut*
focuses on the eponymous medieval king whose considerable military and
political achievements made him a ready national paragon for successful royal
rule. A quasi-dynastic parallel between Canute the Great and the ruling Danish
king Frederick V, whose ascension made possible the reestablishment of theater
in Copenhagen, was affirmed in Schlegel's dedicatory poem, styled as Canute's
own speech to Frederick from beyond the grave.[5]

---

2 Pierre Brumoy, *The Greek Theatre* (London: Mess. Millar, 1759), 1: ciii–civ; see also Pierre
Brumoy, *Théâtre des Grecs* (Paris: Lottin, 1785), 1: 183–185.

3 Sumarokov, *Polnoe sobranie vsekh sochinenii*, 10: 97.

4 On court patronage behind Schlegel's experiments in Danish theater, see Johann Elias
Schlegel, *Aesthetische und dramaturgische Schriften*, ed. J. von Antoniewicz (Heilbronn:
Gebr. Henninger, 1887), clxii–clxiii; on Schlegel's relationship to Korff, see Eugen Wolff,
Johann Elias Schlegel (Kiel & Leipzig: Lipsius & Tischer, 1892), 107.

5 Johann Elias Schlegel, "Anrede Canut des Großen an Se. Majest. Friedrich den Fünften,
König in Dänemark, Norwegen etc.," in *Werke*, vol. 1 (Kopenhagen and Leipzig: Christian
Gottlob Prost, 1761), 219.

Besides theoretical considerations, Schlegel's use of tragedy for the representation of royal history could draw on recent developments in another genre of court performance, the festive *opera seria*. Christian Seebald's book-length study traces the emergence of the "medieval" dynastic opera as an important subgenre on German stages since the late seventeenth century. It was inaugurated in 1689 with Agostino Steffani and Ortensio Bartolomeo Mauro's *Henrico Leone,* produced on the orders of the Welf Duke of Hannover (who employed Leibniz as his court historiographer) and tailored to display his dynasty's political ambitions through the figure of its potent twelfth-century ancestor. From there, dynastic opera spread to other Welf courts at Wolfenbüttel and London, as well as Dresden, where the nuptial festivities of the royal heir in 1719 included the performance of Stefano Pallavicino and Antonio Lotti's *Teofane*, an opera celebrating the tenth-century Saxon emperor Otto II and the claims of the contemporary Saxon electors to imperial succession.[6]

Sumarokov's dramatizations of early Russian history certainly fall within this pattern, outlined for the Russian public in Jacob von Stählin's 1738 essay on the history of court opera (which becomes even more relevant in Russia given its dynastic ties to Wolfenbüttel and a long-standing political alliance with Saxony).[7] Bringing to the stage a legendary forefather and giving him the anachronistic title of "the prince of Russia" ("kniaz' Rossiskii," 4), Sumarokov—as if following the path suggested by Brumoy—constructs his drama as a medium for the commemoration of a national past identified with royal history, "the antiquity of our monarchy." Similar to the Greeks who composed their tragedies in celebration of national events and sites, Sumarokov chooses as his setting the ancient capital associated with the beginnings of a unified Russian monarchy and its adoption of Christianity. The festive resonance of this choice must have been evident in 1747. Three years earlier, in 1744, a year and a half after her ascent to the throne, Empress Elizabeth, accompanied by her recently proclaimed heir apparent, Grand Duke Petr Feodorovich, and his future spouse, undertook a trip to Kiev, obviously laden with political symbolism, as

---

6   Christian Seebald, *Libretti vom "Mittelalter": Entdeckungen von Historie in der (nord) deutschen und europäischen Oper um 1700* (Tübingen: Walter de Gruyter, 2009).

7   "Istoricheskoe opisanie onago teatral'nogo deistviia, kotoroe nazyvaetsia opera" [1738], in *Teatral'naia zhizn' Rossii v epokhu Anny Ioannovny*, ed. L. M. Starikova (Moscow: Nauka, 1995), 546.

the ensuing ceremonial events and official publications duly revealed. One of the principal sites visited by the empress was the Kievan Academy, a church-run institution of classical learning whose cultural importance far outgrew the confines of what was by then a depopulated provincial town. Sermons delivered by the academy's teachers (and later published in Petersburg, the actual imperial center) outlined the continuous tradition of royal power that linked Elizabeth to the medieval rulers of Kiev, and pageantry was employed to convey a similar message. As one source reports,

> От Киевской Академии помощию выписанных машин и своего изобретения деланы Государыне разныя удивительныя явления к ея удовольствию; между прочим выезжал за город важный старик самаго древняго виду, великолепно прибранный и украшенный короною и жезлом, но сделанный с молодаго студента. Колесница у него была божеский фаетон, а в него впряжены два пиитические крылатые кони, называемые пегасы, прибранные из крепких студентов. Старик сей значил древняго основателя и Князя Киевскаго, Кия. Он встретил Государыню на берегу Днепра, у конца мосту, приветствовал ее важною речью и, называя ее своею наследницею, просил в город, яко в свое достояние, и поручал его и весь народ Руский в милостивое ея покровительство. В продолжение приемов Государыни от чинов и народа Малоросийскаго, с живейшими чувствованиами непритворнаго их усердия и полной радости, примолвила однажды Государыня, окруженная безчисленным народом: "Возлюби мя, Боже, так в царствии небесном, как я люблю сей благонравный и незлобивый народ!"

The Kievan academy with the help of imported and locally designed machinery presented the Empress with various curious shows for her pleasure; among other things, out of the city came a grave old man of the most ancient age, magnificently decorated and invested with a crown and staff, represented by a young student. His chariot was a divine phaeton driven by a pair of poetic winged steeds named Pegasus, chosen from robust students. The old man signified the ancient founder and prince of Kiev, Kii. He met the Empress on the bank of Dnepr, at the end of the bridge, welcomed her with a solemn speech and, calling her his heiress, invited into the city as his dominion, and surrendered it and the whole Russian people to her gracious protection. During the banquets prepared for the Empress by the estates and the people of Little Russia with the most vivid sentiments of genuine zeal and boundless joy, the Empress said once amidst innumerable people: "I wish, oh Lord, you would love me as much in the heavenly kingdom as I love this well-minded and gentle people!"[8]

Kievan students staged a royalist version of national memory, using theatrics to revive the vital link between the current political order and its original point of constitution. Sumarokov's *Khorev*, conceived both as a work of literature worthy to be printed and to enter into the national canon and as a script for court productions, did not only adopt the central figure of Kii, but also developed and explored the symbolic and poetic effects aimed for by the ceremonial performance. While I will later discuss at length the political implications of Sumarokov's historicism, for now I would like to illuminate its repercussions for dramatic poetics.

The figure of Kii, however naïvely schematic it might appear both in the masque and in the tragedy, points towards a set of issues fundamental for early modern dramatic treatments of history. Aristotelian doctrine—readily available to Sumarokov in André Dacier's annotated translation of the *Poetics* into French, and to the Kievan scholars in the influential Latin textbook *De arte poetica* (*On Poetic Art*, ca. 1705), composed for use at the academy by Feofan Prokopovich during his tenure there—framed the discussion of dramatic plot by a seemingly clear-cut but in fact complex distinction between "poetry," and "history" as fiction and non-fiction: "an Historian Writes what did happen, and a Poet what might, or ought to have come to pass … Poetry … treats of general, and History relates only particular things."[9] This distinction is immediately complicated in

---

8   "Istoriia Russov," *Chteniia v Obshchestve istorii i drevnostei rossiiskikh,* no. 4, otd. 2 (1846): 244. Volumes of this series will be further referred to by the abbreviation COIDR.

9   *Aristotle's Art of Poetry*, 137–138.

Aristotle's argument by an ambiguous notion of the "received legends" (or "known Fables," in eighteenth-century English), which serve as possible sources for tragic plots and, more importantly, provide a paradigm of oscillation between truth and fiction. The classical scholar Brumoy draws on Aristotelian language when he refuses to distinguish between the two in his definition of the national memory of the Greeks as "history or the fables of their own country."

The bulk of actual historical lore available to a dramatist, whether ancient or modern, is not confined by the strict Aristotelian definition of "history" but equally pertains to "poetry." This was acknowledged in the emerging Russian historiography (a discourse quite relevant for Sumarokov, as his own undated attempts at a history of Moscow and the mutinies of the Petrine reign confirm). Vasilii Tatishchev, who was circulating the first manuscript copies of his *History of Russia*, a monumental compilation of Russian medieval chronicles, around the same time as Sumarokov was writing his first historical dramas, faithfully reproduced medieval origin legends but flouted the evident falsehoods propagated by the annalistic tradition, sarcastically comparing early chroniclers to classical epic authors, standard examples of poetic fiction. One of the evident cases in point was the story of Kii, reported by Tatishchev and immediately denounced in a separate note as fictitious.[10] The producers of the Kievan masque, professionally versed in classical idiom, conveyed a similar message by entrusting Kii's chariot to "a pair of poetic winged steeds named Pegasus."

If history is itself "poetry," then tragedy as defined by Aristotle provides a paradigm for its proper reading. According to *Poetics*, tragedy combines the opposing principles of "history" and "poetry," for when the dramatist "also exposes true Incidents on the Stage, he no less deserves the Name of a Poet, since nothing hinders, but that the Incidents which did really happen, may have all the verisimilitude, and all possibility which Art requires." A generalizing, "philosophical" perspective is put in place that is all but indifferent to the truth of fact and thus assures the value of *mythos*, a concept that simultaneously refers to "received legends" and dramatic plots. It is this perspective that makes Kii, clearly a figment of false etymology, an acceptable and even appropriate protagonist for political drama. Sumarokov adopts a technique recommended by Aristotle, who expressly allows for tragedies where "one or two Names ... are known, and all the other invented." The discourse of

---

10   Vasilii Tatishchev, "Istoriia rossiiskaia," in *Sobranie sochinenii*, vol. 2 (Moscow: Ladomir, 1995), 30; vol. 4 (Moscow: Ladomir, 1994), 44, 110, 391.

"history" may be subdued, and yet not necessarily dissolved, by the more complex logic of "poetry," "a general thing, is that, which every Man, of such or such a Character, necessarily or probably ought to say, or do, which is the aim of Poesy, even when it imposes names on the Persons."[11]

Feofan Prokopovich elaborates this point in a typically baroque fashion: establishing a direct link between Aristotle's poetic doctrine and political philosophy, "judge and ruler over all arts and sciences," and drawing a parallel between the poet and the political philosopher, who both teach their readers lessons of political duty, he identifies the "law of probability or necessity" that must dominate a tragic plot with a theory of political action:

> wise rule over a state, prescription of laws, judicial action, verdicts and the distribution of rewards—those are the actions of a sovereign, and it is they that make it possible to recognize him as such … The actions of the last kind I consider "general," for they befit any sovereign since he is one.[12]

In Dacier's terms, Aristotle suggests a poetics of tragedy that is "neither Historical nor Particular, but General and Allegorical," and indeed his interpretation of Aristotle clearly resonates with Benjamin's important conclusion that in early modern drama "a series of types such as is formed by king, courtier, and fool, has an allegorical significance."[13] In the *Dictionnaire de l'Académie française* (1694) the meaning of "allegorie" was explained as follows: "It is also said of paintings and bas-reliefs which represent moral objects in the human or animal figures."[14] This is the function that Kii, in fact nothing more than a name, could easily assume both in the masque and the tragedy. Without disturbing the logic

---

11 *Aristotle's Art of Poetry,* 138–139.
12 Feofan Prokopovich, "De arte poetica," in *Sochineniia* (Moscow and Leningrad: Izd. AN SSSR, 1961), 233, 406.
13 *Aristotle's Art of Poetry,* 146–147; *La Poétique d'Aristote,* 141; Benjamin, *Origin of German Tragic Drama,* 191. Dacier's authoritative interpretation of Aristotelian dramatic poetics as allegorical seems to complicate the clear-cut distinction, accepted by Jane Brown, between the "mimetic" notion of representation heralded by neo-Aristotelianism, and the allegorical poetics associated with its opposite: Neoplatonism. On a more general level, though, it confirms her principal conception of the constant interplay of the two in the early modern period, while Brown herself acknowledges that "heavily Platonist discourse was readily intertwined with Aristotle's critical language" (Jane Brown, *The Persistence of Allegory,* 52–60).
14 *Dictionnaire de L'Académie française* (Paris: Coignard, 1694), 28.

of festive representation with historical particulars, he served as an allegory of royal power and monarchical political order. It was the allegorical generalization behind the name that resonated with Elizabeth's enthusiastic protestations of mutual love between her and her subjects during the Kievan festivities, and, later, with the voice of Sumarokov's Kii: "Vladychestvo moe liubov'iu utverzhdeno" (2.1.18; "My sov'reignty in love stands steadfast without challenge," 54).

The emerging Russian tragedy drew upon a poetics of political allegory, a specific mode of representation and reading that was taking root in Russia along with court culture itself. It embraced genres as distant as narrative historiography, translated political novels, and court pageantry, and was outlined in Trediakovskii's lengthy preface to his 1751 court-sponsored translation of the *Argenis*. Elaborating on Barclay's own ideas of instruction through parable (quoted in part 1), Trediakovskii juxtaposed an elucidation of the novel's direct allusions to the French Wars of Religion with a generalizing interpretation suggesting that Barclay's characters were fictional creations, so that "in the person of Meleander the author represents a clement king rather than Henri III, and Cleobolus refers to a skillful politician rather than Villeroy." Trediakovskii recommends this second reading for its "utility for the Russian people," since, taken in this perspective, Barclay's "tale would be common to all centuries, and all nations; and, consequently, it would by equal right be ours." At the same time, he expressly refuses to see the two readings as contradictory, thus blurring the distinction between history, fiction (Aristotelian "poetry"), and allegory.[15]

Sumarokov's dramatic poetics was permeated by a similar mixture of topical allusion (sometimes mistakenly identified in the relevant scholarship with allegory as such), political generalization, pure fiction, and allegorical conceit. Adopting a common technique of baroque drama, outlined by Benjamin and meticulously explored by Albrecht Schöne,[16] in *Khorev* Sumarokov employs the language of the emblem—an allegorical mode generally popular in early modern Europe, and favored in Russia since Peter the Great—to frame his discussion of royal power:

> Те люди что закон давать произведенны,
> Закону своему и сами покоренны.

---

15   Barclay, *Argenida*, 1: xxxxvii–xxxxviii. On Barclay's poetics of historical allegory, see John Barclay, *Argenis*, 1: 22–26.

16   Albrecht Schöne, *Emblematik und Drama im Zeitalter des Barock* (Munich: Beck, 1993).

И есть ли согрешат, малейший оных грех,
Винняе их творит подверженных им всех.
Великих камни гор, что волны отрывают,
Высоки древеса что ветры низвергают,
Шумняй других вещей малейших им падут,
Толь большую хулу пороки нам влекут.
Хула то малая что многим неизвестна,
А наша и хула как похвала всеместна. (3.3.41)

The princes who hold power by which laws are created are subject, even they, to their commandments. And if they sin, their slightest error makes them more guilty than all of their subjects. Stones torn by waves from mountains, great trees uprooted by winds fall more loudly that smaller things; similarly vices attract more blame to us. Blame which is ignored by many is not great, but our blame, like praise, is known everywhere. (66)

Through the image of the falling stone as an emblem for royal glory, Khorev evokes a centuries-old topos of monarchs as open to all eyes, while the emblematic identification of royal glory with physical sound reappears in Kii's praise of Khorev:

Строптивые соседы
По северу гласят до волн его победы.
Сармация дрожит руки его меча,
Орда как ветра прах бежит его плеча.
Недавно от него безстрашные народы
Текли через леса, чрез горы и чрез воды.
Казалось им, что он всю землю мог потрясть,
И всю вселенную России дать под власть. (2.1.19)

Our stubborn hostile neighbors, voice all his victories up to the northern waters. Sarmatia trembles at the swinging of his sword. The Tartars flee from him, even as dust from wind. It was not long ago when from him the fearless nations, in terror fled through woods, through mountains and through rivers. It seemed they felt his

mighty grip shaking the earth entire, placing the universe beneath
our Russian rule. (54)

The many anachronisms contained in these lines highlight their allusive
significance, emphasized by the chronological indication "not long ago." In
fact, we are confronted with praise for Russia's (this term is itself anachronistic here) military successes in the 1730s and 1740s. Sarmatia has been
already recognized to be a reference to Poland, while the Horde—properly
the common name of the Tatar nomadic states that dominated Russian lands
in the medieval period—apparently stands for the Ottoman empire, politically associated in Sumarokov's time with Russia's other traditional enemy,
the Tatar khanate in Crimea. The well-known *Sinopsis,* a seventeenth-century
history of Russia, identified the Tatars with the Turks, and Sumarokov
himself in one of his historical essays, losing sight of actual chronology,
described the medieval Tatar rulers of Russia as subjects to the Ottoman
empire.[17] Indeed, in the 1730s Russian troops led a series of successful military
campaigns first in Poland, where they secured the throne for the Petersburg-
backed candidate, and then against the Turks and Tatars in Crimea, achieving
much-celebrated victories under the command of Field Marshal Münnich.
Russian victories in those two theaters were recognized as symbolic of the
empire's new dominating position in the north of Europe. A 1738
German-language pro-Russian pamphlet, sponsored by the Russian envoy in
Paris, Antiokh Kantemir, read:

> From now on the states of the north have begun to view the Russian
> empire with different eyes than before, and other European powers felt
> strong respect for the Russian monarchy and the Russian nation. What
> a great importance did the gloriously reigning empress ascribe to the
> affairs of the north and how magnificently did she accomplish the
> military operations in Poland, before the eyes of the world! She has
> successfully re-conquered Azov which, as the Muslims thought, would
> forever remain in their possession. She has shown the significance of

---

17 A. P. Sumarokov, *Dramaticheskie sochineniia,* ed. Iu. V. Stennik (Leningrad: Iskusstvo,
1990), 457; *Sinopsis* (Kiev: n.p., 1681; Köln and Wien: Böhlau, 1983), 154; Sumarokov,
Polnoe sobranie vsekh sochinenii, 10: 116.

the Russian empire to the Turks, as well as the Tatars of Crimea, Noga, Kuban' and other regions …[18]

Apparently, the "Scythian war," where Khorev had recently earned his "laurels" (2.2.21; 56), also alludes to the Crimean campaign, whose veterans constituted an important segment of Sumarokov's original readership. Khorev's victories reach not only to the southwest but also "up to the northern waters." Besides a general reference to the "north" as a theater of Russian domination, this seems to be a specific allusion to the short Russian-Swedish war (1741–1743), triumphantly won by the Russian troops and concluded by the Peace of Abo. This peace, Russia's first international success under Empress Elizabeth, was lavishly celebrated and assumed an important part in Elizabeth's "scenario of power," as it was staged in the early 1740s.

Besides the coup d'état of November 1741, the third important event constitutive of this scenario, and accordingly celebrated with allegorical performances, was the wedding of Elizabeth's heir apparent, Petr Fedorovich, to the future Catherine II in 1745. The peace and the wedding were accompanied by a series of intertwined festivities that included Italian operas (*Il Seleuco* in 1744 and *Scipione* in 1745) and French *divertissements* written and staged especially for each occasion that conformed in their main political message: the praise of the new empress. Individual political events that we consider as hard facts, which can be represented or distorted by court pageantry, were themselves refashioned in their ceremonial reenactments into allegorical signs of a common symbolic truth, a virtual "scenario of power" that fused and recast the very notions of war and peace or love and marriage, thereby overshadowing and complicating their immediate referentiality. Characteristic for the court semantics is a letter sent in 1746 by Christian Wilhelm von Münnich, Empress Elizabeth's steward of the court, to Johanna Elisabeth of Anhalt-Zerbst, the mother of Grand Duchess Catherine, in Berlin:

Since Your Highness has informed me of your wish to go to Berlin to enjoy somewhat the carnival which takes place there, I suppose this

---

18 [A. D. Kantemir and Ch. F. Gross], "Tak nazyvaemye 'Moskovitskie pis'ma,'" *Rossiia i Zapad: gorizonty vzaimopoznaniia. Literaturnye istochniki XVIII v. (1726–1762)* (Moscow: Nasledie, 2003), 243.

letter will find you amidst amusements and entertainments. There is a good reason to indulge in them at such a court where the king has concluded a hard and bloody war with a peace as unexpected as it was longed for and with equal advantage and glory. Her Imperial Majesty, my august sovereign, has set an example to the king of Prussia since the very beginning of her most fortunate reign. Peace enjoyed by this vast empire since that time and the successfully concluded marriage which most clearly represents a more constant stability of the throne than any battles and victories, has provided no lesser occasion for festivities, and the inauguration of a masquerade in this city, which I mentioned in my previous letter, allows for a diversity of amusements, which would be lacking if they only took place at court.[19]

Professionally responsible for the functioning of the court, Münnich uses courtly festivities in Berlin and Petersburg as a symbolic framework for the discussion of the political achievement of the two rising powers. Their different situations are conflated in a single scenario of political stability, "a hard and bloody war" necessarily succeeded by the "longed-for peace." However, peace—not only a matter of foreign relations but an all-embracing foundational principle of political order—is engendered less through the actual cessation of hostilities, "battles and victories," than through court-sponsored rituals of public joy. Specifically, Münnich names the royal nuptials: they bring a promise of dynastic continuity and, more importantly, as a festive action constitute an allegory in their own right, a representation and a performative reenactment of the "constant stability of the throne" that they are expected to provide for.

From this ceremonial poetics, with its constant tension between the literal and the virtual, action and meaning, politics and performance, the court tragedy emerged. While the plays did not necessarily depend on specific ceremonial occasions, they perpetuated the overall semantics of courtly spectacle, exploring and interrogating the central notions of royal representation in their fictional plots. In particular, the Elizabethan "scenario of power" provided a point of origin for *Khorev*, where a monarchy's fate is also decided between a successful war and the promises of a royal wedding.

---

19   Pisarenko, "Pis'ma ober-gofmeistera Kh. V. Minikha," 64.

KHOREV AND THE SCENARIO
OF MARRIAGE

Sumarokov first came into vogue in the 1740s as an author of love songs fashionable among Petersburg society, and his debut as writer of tragedies certainly built upon his success as a poet of love. For the rest of his life Sumarokov would first enjoy, and later furiously contest, the reputation of a "tender" poet. According to Klein, "during the reign of Elizabeth the life of the Russian court abounds in gallant amusements. Following Racine's example and exploring the subgenre of love tragedy, Sumarokov thus pursues the most natural road to success."[1] This development was not incidental to Russia; by the time Sumarokov started out as a playwright, it had become a commonplace that, in Louis Riccoboni's words, the great French dramatists of the seventeenth century "thought proper to soften the Severity of Tragedy, in order to recommend it to the Liking of their young King and Court; and for this Purpose they made Love the Master and Controuler of their Stage."[2]

Evidently, the allegorical idiom of the "gallant amusements," exported from France to other European courts by way of fashion, played an important role in the discourses of absolutist domination. A sober-minded French representative in Russia indicated as much when he chose to inform his

---

1   Joachim Klein, *Puti kul'turnogo importa*, 363.
2   Louis Riccoboni, *An Historical and Critical Account of the Theatres in Europe, together with ... A Comparison of the Ancient and Modern Drama* (London: T. Waller, 1741), 294–295. See also Riccoboni, *Histoire du théâtre italien*, 1: 268.

court that Empress Elizabeth "loves everything which has the air of gallantry."[3] The political idiom of *galanterie* relied on what Melissa E. Sanchez calls "the commonplace early modern equation of political and erotic unions—the claim that sovereign and subject, like husband and wife, are bound as much by reciprocal love as by law or necessity."[4] This claim, as scholarship has amply demonstrated over the last decades, was crucial for conceptions of marriage and power as well as for their treatments in pageantry and drama across early modern Europe, and certainly occupied a central position in Sumarokov's dramatic poetics.

As what John D. Lyons terms a "tragedy of origins," *Khorev* intertwined love and politics in a historically unsubstantiated but conceptually charged representation of the beginnings of the Russian state, as symbolized by Kii and Kiev.[5] Sumarokov operated in the same mode of historical allegory that allowed Tatishchev—also in a commonplace way—to refashion a theoretical model of the origin of society adapted from current political philosophies as a narrative segment within his chronicle-based history of Russia in the chapter "On ancient Russian government and other governments in comparison." In Sumarokov's play Kii is credited with building walls around Kiev, thus transforming a settlement into a polity. His relationship to the younger Khorev, whom he had instructed "in the art of war" and who eventually replaced him at the head of troops (21–22), corresponds to Tatishchev's argument that one of the primeval forms of political power was a compact between older men "with sufficient property and wisdom" but lacking physical strength or progeny for their protection, and "others, young, healthy and physically capable of labor" who lacked experience and required instruction. Another, and yet earlier, model and paradigm of social order is, for Tatishchev, marriage, described as a compact that not only refers to "sincere love" but by force of tradition implies relations of domination, since "no community, small or large, can exist without supervision and power," assigned in this case to the husband as "the head and the lord" of his wife. This double

---

3   *SIRIO* 105 (Iur'ev, 1899): 474.

4   Melissa E. Sanchez, *Erotic Subjects: The Sexuality of Politics in Early Modern English Literature* (Oxford: Oxford University Press, 2011), 3. On love and politics as the two primary topics of Sumarokov's tragedies, see Klein, *Puti kul'turnogo importa*, 361–376.

5   John D. Lyons, *The Tragedy of Origins: Pierre Corneille and Historical Perspective* (Stanford: Stanford University Press, 1996).

signification of love, simultaneously construed as tangible reality, a thing in itself, and as a sign, an allegory of power, was crucial for the genre of tragedy as it was practiced by Sumarokov.[6]

In his essay "On Racine," Roland Barthes argues that "in Racine, sex itself is subject to the fundamental situation of the tragic figures among themselves, which is a relation of force … The essential relation is one of authority, love serves only to *reveal* it."[7] Barthes's reading of Racine—both reinforced by more recent insights into early modern literary discourse and divested of its once scandalous anti-historicism—seems to be valid for the *tragédie galante* and its allegorical language in general, and relevant for Suma-rokov's dramatic treatments of love in particular. Reviewing *Khorev* in his lengthy critique of Sumarokov's oeuvre in 1750, the competent and attentive Trediakovskii noted that the main dramatic interest of the play was focused on the female protagonist Osnelda and the mutual passion that bound her to Khorev: "Khorev had only loved her, and could not bear parting with her: that's why he exhausted all ways to keep her in Kiev. But when he learned that she was dead, he killed himself in greatest sorrow."[8] Indeed, the issue of Osnelda's sojournment in Kiev and her possible departure is discussed in the very first lines of the tragedy by Osnelda and her confidant Astrada:

Астрада
Княжна! сей день тебе свободу обещает,
Отец твой воинством весь город окружает
И хощет иль тебя из плену свободить,
Иль всех своих людей под градом положить.

Оснельда
… Астрада! Мне уже свободы не видать,

---

6   Vasilii Tatishchev, "Istoriia rossiiskaia" (Moscow: Ladomir, 1994), 1: 359–360; E. A. Kasatkina, "Sumarokovskaia tragediia 40-kh–nachala 50-kh godov XVIII veka," 225–228.

7   Roland Barthes, *On Racine*, trans. Richard Howard (Berkeley: California University Press, 1992), 13, 24.

8   V. K. Trediakovskii, "Pis'mo, v kotorom soderzhitsia rassuzhdenie o stikhotvorenii, ponyne na svet izdannom … pisannoe ot priiatelia k priiateliu," *in Kritika XVIII veka*, ed. A. M. Ranchin and V. L. Korovin (Moscow: Olimp, 2002), 92.

Я здесь осуждена под стражею страдать,
Хотя я некую часть вольности имею,
И от привычки злой претерпевать умею. (1.5)

Astrada
Princess! this day promises you freedom. Your father has surrounded the city with his troops, willing either to free you from captivity or to lose all his men under the walls.

Osnelda … Astrada! I will never see freedom, I am doomed to suffer here under guard, although I have partial freedom and am accustomed to endurance from vicious habit.

Astrada's promise of freedom, at first apparently welcome to Osnelda and the play's audience, is immediately overturned by the heroine's premonition, later justified by the course of events. The very possibility of freedom is dismissed, while its opposite, captivity, moves to occupy a central place in the play's development. In Barthes's words, "[t]he division of the Racinian world into strong and weak, into tyrants and captives, covers in a sense the division of the sexes: it is their situation in the relation of force that orchestrates some characters as virile and others as feminine."[9] Accordingly, Osnelda's captivity shapes her identity as a tragic heroine and provides a potent metaphor for her amorous relationship to Khorev: bringing the two notions together, she confesses to having first "experienced love in captivity" ("liubov' v plenenii poznala," 33) and describes it as "toils with no escape" ("neiskhodimy seti," 8). Of course, Osnelda speaks the conventional language of gallantry, employed among others by Sumarokov in his love songs:

Прешли те дни, как я был волен;
Но их я не могу жалеть.
Неволей я своей доволен,
И серцу не пречу гореть.

Over are the days of my freedom, but I cannot regret them. I am satisfied with my bondage, and do not prevent my heart's ardor.

---

9   Barthes, *On Racine*, 13.

Ты довольно силы в плен взять приложила

Я своей неволи сам ищу …

Я тебе подвластен быть хочу …

You were powerful enough to capture me, I desire my own captivity
… I wish to be your subject. [10]

The metaphorical parallel between amorous devotion and political submission, realized in the dramatic plot, develops in tragedy into a double paradigm of public and private emotion, as Osnelda's role showcases. (To Sumarokov's first audiences the amorous princess living at a court once ruled by her father but deprived of her ancestral throne could have resembled Elizabeth before her coup; although one of her lovers was persecuted by Empress Anna, Elizabeth was proud to recall, by way of a lesson of obedience for the young Peter, that "in the time of the Empress Anne, she had never failed in giving her the respect due to a crowned head, anointed of the Lord."[11]) Voluntary renunciation of freedom, and enthusiastic acceptance of "captivity" and submission formed the core of what Ziad Elmarsafy in his study of seventeenth-century French treatments of the topic calls "the erotic contract" between monarchy and its subjects: "If desire makes absolute monarchy possible, nay palatable, it also attenuates the relationship between subjugation and slavery … Love for the master effaces the servile implications of being a subject."[12] Love for her master is exactly the passion that consumes Osnelda. Calling Kiev her "cherished dungeon" ("liubeznaia temnitsa," 9), she employs a gallant paradox appropriate for her amorous feelings, and simultaneously voices a formula of royal domination. Around the same time *Khorev* was written, Sumarokov's rival Lomonosov in a similar fashion addressed Empress Elizabeth:

Пусть мнимая других свобода угнетает,

Нас рабство под твоей державой возвышает.

---

10   Sumarokov, *Polnoe sobranie vsekh sochinenii,* 8: 208, 238.

11   [Catherine, Empress of Russia], *Memoirs of the Empress Catherine II* (London: Trübner, 1859), 55.

12   Ziad Elmarsafy, *Freedom, Slavery, and Absolutism: Corneille, Pascal, Racine* (Bucknell, PA: Bucknell University Press, 2003), 31.

Let pretended freedom oppress others,
We are honored by enslavement under your dominion.[13]

Speaking to Kii later in the play, Osnelda identifies her feelings for Khorev with the collective loyalty of the whole populace to the heir apparent:

Одналь ево чту я? Он мил всему народу,
А мне содержанной в плену, давал свободу. (4.7.58)

Do I alone respect the prince? To all the nation
He has endeared himself; to me in that he freed me. (75)

In a meaningful transposition Osnelda personally admits to a politically appropriate "esteem" for Khorev, while the erotically charged "endearment" for him is relegated to the community of subjects: the two affects are in fact identical. She then refers again to the paradox of "freedom in captivity," which permeates her accounts of her relationship to Khorev, and—as Elmarsafy's study demonstrates at length—is crucial for the visions of power, both political and erotic, in the absolutist age.

Indeed, the commonplaces explored in French plays resonated in Russia with authoritative local discourses of domination and love. Surveying various marital customs in a separate chapter of his *History of Russia*, Tatishchev maintained that the Russian word for marriage, "brak," "properly means an act of choice," which may only be performed "with the common consent of both parties," and referred to Petrine legislation that specifically forbade forced marriages and guaranteed "freedom in this respect" ("v tom byt' svobode").[14] Marriage was thus officially proclaimed a rare sphere where subjects of the Russian empire, who customarily had to identify themselves as "slaves" in their dealings with the state regardless of their actual social position, possessed "freedom" to decide for themselves. However, as the very idea of marriage implies, this freedom, amalgamated with love, could only fulfill

---

13 M. V. Lomonosov, *Izbrannye proizvedeniia* (Leningrad: Sovetskii pisatel', 1986), 209.

14 Tatishchev, "Istoriia rossiiskaia," 1: 387, 389; *Polnoe sobranie zakonov Rossiiskoi imperii s 1649 g.*, [Sobranie I] (St. Petersburg, 1830), vol. 4 (laws from 1700–1712), 191–192, no. 1907.

itself in the self-negating act of voluntary subjugation, a reconstitution of the established order of power.

This politically charged vision of love and marriage informed the French gallant aesthetic and its adoption at the Russian court beginning in the 1730s. One of the immediate models for *Khorev* was Voltaire's immensely popular tragedy *Zaire*, which was performed at the Russian court by the same cadet company that would soon thereafter inaugurate the tradition of Russian-language neoclassical theater with Sumarokov's first tragedy. Sumarokov translated the first scene of the play into Russian, and later praised it for its "gallant taste" ("vkusa schegolskogo"), echoing Lessing's contemporaneous judgment in the *Hamburgische Dramaturgie*: "Love itself has dictated Zaire to Voltaire, says a critic civil enough. He should have rather said: gallantry."[15] In this scene the beautiful Zaire, held captive at the court of the sultan Orosman, is encouraged by her confidant to hope for freedom but instead admits that she is in love with the sultan, who has promised to marry her:

> garde-toi de penser
> Qu'à briguer ses soupirs je puisse m'abaisser,
> Que d'un maître absolu la superbe tendresse
> M'offre l'honneur honteux du rang de sa maîtresse,
> Et que j'essuie enfin l'outrage et le danger
> Du malheureux éclat d'un amour passager...
> son superbe courage
> A mes faibles appas présente un pur hommage;
> Parmi tous ces objets à lui plaire empressés,
> J'ai fixé ses regards, à moi seule adressés;
> Et l'hymen, confondant leurs intrigues fatales,
> Me soumettra bientôt son cœur et mes rivales.

> Think not I mean to stain my spotless honor,
> Or stoop to be the mistress of a tyrant;

---

15 Gotthold Ephraim Lessing, *Hamburgische Dramaturgie* (Stuttgart: Reclam, 1981), 82. My understanding of *shchegolskoi* as an equivalent of the French *galant* rests on the usage of Trediakovskii's 1730 translation of Paul Tallemant's *Le voyage de l'isle d'Amour*, where *galanterie* is rendered as *shchegolstvo*.

That I will ever hazard the quick change
Of transitory passion; no, my friend …
I have subdued his haughty soul to love
Most pure, and most refined: amidst the crowd
Of rival beauties that contend for Osman,
I, I alone have fixed his wand'ring heart,
And Hymen soon, in spite of all their deep
And dark intrigues, shall make the Sultan mine.[16]

In Voltaire's work, the traditional Oriental forms of amorous captivity, imposed on powerless concubines by the coercive violence of the master's desire, are supplanted by love and marriage. However, Zaire's prospective marriage does not restore her freedom to leave the palace but only refashions Orosman's sway over her, reenhancing his ever-present authority as monarch and captor with emotional obligation.

Both in *Khorev* and in the Russian court performances of the 1740s this rhetoric of marriage was reinvested with political signification.[17] For the royal nuptials of 1745, Sérigny's French company prepared an allegorical *divertissement* titled *Soedinenie liubvi i braka* (*The Alliance of Love and Marriage*) that staged a solemn reconciliation of Amour and Hymen at Peter's and Catherine's conjugal altar and exalted the empress:

Любовь

Поистине я тебе обещаюсь,

Что никогда не оставлю сих высоких Супругов:

Я клянусь окончить для них войну,

Которая от давних времен разлучала меня с тобою:

Потщимся совокупно о спокойствии всея Земли,

Сопрягая толь слаткий союз.

---

16   Voltaire, *The Complete Works*, 8: 433–434; Voltaire, *The Dramatic Works*, trans. Rev. Mr. Francklin (London: J. Newberry et al., 1762), 5: 6–7. For Sumarokov's assessment of the scene, see *Polnoe sobranie vsekh sochinenii*, 4: 352; for its translation, 1: 296–299.

17   On the affinities between *Khorev* and *Zaire*, see Eveline Vetter, *Studien zu Sumarokov* (PhD diss. Freie Universität Berlin, 1961), 68; Iu. V. Stennik, *Zhanr tragedii v russkoi literature. Epokha klassitsizma* (Leningrad: Nauka, 1981), 42.

Брак

Позабудем нашу ссору, будем неразлучны,

Двух любящихся супругов утвердим благополучие …

Представим нашу ревность пред очи Государыне,

Которая державствует в сих странах;

Чтоб каждой старался ей угодить …

Благополучной народ! …

Пой, прославляй Империю

Августейшаго Ея Величества:

Под ее законами ничто не может быть докучно,

Живи в тишине

Слатко быть управляемым

От разума и милости.[18]

Love

I promise you truly that I will never leave this exalted couple. I swear to end for their sake the war waged since ancient times between you and me. Let us together strive for the tranquility of the world, while we conclude such a delightful union.

Marriage

Let us forget our strife and never part again. Let us secure the fortune of the two loving spouses … Let us represent our zeal before the eyes of the Empress who rules in these lands, so that everyone wishes to please her … O most fortunate people! … Sing, exalt the dominion of her august majesty: under her laws nothing is burdensome. Live in peace, it is delightful to be ruled by reason and clemency.

As was customary for early modern Europe, the rhetoric of the celebrations was tailored to represent the "domestic bliss of the royal marriage" as an image of "the relation of sovereign and subject as one of love and affection rather than coercion."[19] Proposing to Osnelda in similar language, Khorev

---

18 L. M. Starikova, ed., *Teatral'naia zhizn' Rossii v epokhu Elizavety Petrovny. Dokumental'naia khronika. 1741–1750,* vol. 2, bk. 1 (Moscow: Nauka, 2003), 101.

19 Victoria Kahn, "The Passions and the Interests in Early Modern Europe: The Case of Guarini's *Il Pastor fido,*" in *Reading the Early Modern Passions: Essays in the Cultural History*

suggests that submission to duty can and should be reinforced, rather than subverted, by love:

Оснельда, есть ли брак любви не разрушает
И должность пламени в крови не угашает,
Почто нам приключать друг другу вечный стон
И что препятствует взойтить тебе на трон,
Который ждет меня? (1.3.14)

Osnelda, if marriage is not opposed to love, and duty does not suppress the flame of passion, why should we inflict eternal pain on each other, and what is it that hinders you from ascending the throne that awaits me?

Khorev's intended marriage to Osnelda—singled out by Trediakovskii as the play's most important plotline—mirrors the symbolic scenario of the 1745 nuptials and puts on display the political implications of the gallant idiom of love. Elizabethan court theater commonly employed love as an allegory of political triumph; already the peace with Sweden in 1743 was styled in a serenade as "un Lien que l'Amour et la Fidélité rendront indissoluble" ("a bond which love and faithfulness will make indissoluble")—an apt allegory, given that Elizabeth's nephew and heir apparent, Grand Duke Peter, was born into a dynastic marriage between the ruling families of Sweden and Russia.[20] In the opera *Il Seleuco*, written and staged by Giuseppe Bonecchi for the same occasion, the final reunion of heroic lovers under the protection of the mighty and victorious ruler presented a transparent allegory of the peace itself. Not surprisingly, then, similar allegorical themes were employed by Bonecchi for the actual wedding of Grand Duke Peter. In the finale of his 1745 opera *Scipione*, the imperious Roman hero "in order to augment popular rejoicing orders a public celebration of the marriage of Sifaks and Nirena." In fact, Sifaks (Siface), the model young hero and the scenic alter ego of the Grand Duke, shows

---

of Emotion, ed. Gail Kern Paster, Katherine Rowe, and Mary Floyd-Wilson (Philadelphia: University of Pennsylvania Press, 2004), 234.

20   V. N. Vsevolodskii-Gerngross, *Teatr v Rossii pri imperatritse Elizavete Petrovne* (St. Petersburg: Giperion, 2003), 34.

significant similarities to Khorev in that he also combines tender love with military valor and "gloriously reaffirms his dominion and his ancestral throne" with military feats.[21] In Khorev's Kiev, his possible marriage to Osnelda would also stand for public peace, as Khorev himself makes clear:

> наш союз народ от пагубы избавит,
> Которою остр меч с обеих стран грозит ...
> пленники своих покинут тягость уз,
> Когда нас сопряжет желанный сей союз. (1.3.16–17)

> our union will save the people from the woe which a mutually waged war would bring ... the captives will leave their heavy chains when we are united by the longed-for marital bonds.

While referring to specific political circumstances—Zavlokh's siege of Kiev and the imprisonment of his former subjects—Khorev employs allegorically charged terms, once again linking marriage to the notions of "freedom in captivity" and political reconciliation of the ruling family with its subjects. The 1745 nuptials were celebrated in largely similar language; Lomonosov appealed to the royal couple in his ode: "Ot vas Rossiia ozhidaet / Schast-livykh i spokoinykh let" ("Russia awaits from you / Years of peace and prosperity").[22] In the revised later version of the play, Khorev thus concludes his vision of the future peace: "I bran' okonchitsia liubov'iu, ne mechem" ("The battle shall be won by love, not by sword," 53).[23] Similarly, a *divertissement* staged in 1744 on the occasion of the Peace of Abo read:

> Пришли часы оставить брань
> И гнев смягчить в кипящей крови,
> Покорствуйте теперь любови
> И естеству несите дань.[24]

---

21 Starikova, *Teatral'naia zhizn' Rossii v epokhu Elizavety Petrovny*, vol. 2, bk. 1, 92.

22 Lomonosov, *Izbrannye proizvedeniia*, 103.

23 Sumarokov, *Dramaticheskie sochineniia*, 44.

24 *Uveselenie, sochinennoe i predstavlennoe ot ... frantsusskikh komediantov po vsenarodnom torzhestvovanii ... vechnago mira* (Moscow: Tipografiia Imperatorskoi Akademii nauk, 1744), 3.

The time has come to abandon warfare and temper the wrath raging in the veins. From now on subdue to love and pay tribute to nature.

The antithesis of "love" and "war" ("bran'"), elaborated in the political allegories of the 1740s, came to occupy a central position in the verbal texture of Sumarokov's drama and the construction of its plot. Decades later, arguing against the common view that his poetic scope was limited to "tender" themes, Sumarokov exclaimed: "can a Hercules represented in drama resemble the tender Sylvia or Amarillis sighing in Tasso or Guarini!"[25] Distancing himself from the tradition of the dramatic pastoral exemplified by its two most famous specimens, Torquato Tasso's *Aminta* (1573) and Battista Guarini's *Il pastor fido* (1585), he asserted that a stage hero endowed with masculine valor ("Hercules") should not display feminine "tenderness." Curiously enough, his early dramas seem to be strongly indebted to the pastoral pattern denounced here. Among the model French tragedies summarized in his 1748 *Epistle on Poetry*, Sumarokov listed Racine's *Phédre*, singling out as its central episode Hippolyte's declaration of love to Aricie. This monologue, along with the entire role of Aricie, was famously added to the ancient plot by Racine, transforming Euripides's impregnably chaste character into a gallant lover.

Besides translating Hippolyte's lines into Russian, Sumarokov closely imitated them in Khorev's amorous speech to Osnelda:

> Я мнил, что я рожден к единой только брани,
> Противников карать, и налагати дани;
> Но бог любви тобой ту ярость умягчил,
> Твой взор меня вздыхать и в славе научил …
> Против тебя, против себя вооружался …
> Я тщился много раз, чтоб мне тебя забыть,
> И мнился иногда уже свободен быть.
> Но вспомнив о тебе, я чувствовал что страстен.
> Сей гордый дух тебе стал вечно быть подвластен. (1.3.11)

---

25 Sumarokov, *Polnoe sobranie vsekh sochinenii,* 9: 219.

I thought I was destined to wage war, to subdue the enemy and impose contribution; but the god of love has appeased this fury and taught me to sigh despite my glory. . . . I have sought weapons against you and myself . . . Often I have attempted to forget you, and sometimes thought myself to be free. But then I would remember you and feel my passion again. This proud spirit is forever your subject.

Substituting war for Hippolyte's hunt, Sumarokov molds the motifs of court performances into the verbal core of his principal character. Khorev's emotional self emerges from a complex interplay between the allegorically charged notions of war, love, freedom, and subjection. A vision of political power as a constant thrust for military violence ("fury") and conquest is reinforced by Khorev's metaphorical recourse to emotional "weapons against you and myself." The literal (political) and allegorical (erotic) planes of this metaphor—so important for Sumarokov that he inserted it in his translation of Hippolyte's harangue—are reconciled when Osnelda comments on Khorev's possible military action against her father: "Oruzh'e ia sama protiv sebia dala" ("I have myself given you a weapon against me," 15). Elaborating on this conceit, in her speech that inverts his account of the victory of love over fury, Osnelda paints Khorev as the exact opposite of the loving self he professes to be, as someone like Sumarokov's hard-hearted Hercules. She then offers herself as a flesh-and-blood victim for his actual, if quite phallic, weapon:

И есть ли славно быть таким тебе Героем,
Чтоб ты не умягчен любезной током слез
Оружие свое на кровь ея вознес;
Насыть свой алчный меч, напейся кровью жадно,
И ежели еще оружье будет гладно,
Вот грудь моя, вонзи свой меч ты и в нее … (2.6.30)

And if it brings glory to be such a hero who, unappeased by the tears of his beloved, draws a weapon against her kin, then satisfy your bloodthirsty sword, drink as much blood as you wish, and if your weapon is not satisfied, here is my breast, pierce it with your sword.

This tense image of the horrors of war in fact builds upon a common-place gallant metaphor of love as a wound, more specifically a wound to the heart or "breast." One of Sumarokov's own love songs reads:

Цели мою рану, что ты мне дала,
Или не льзя,
Мне грудь пронзя,
Стесненному духу отрады подать? [26]

Heal the wound that you have inflicted on me, or it is impossible, having pierced my breast, to give relief to the suffering spirit?

The development of this metaphor will take a tragic turn in the play's finale, with Khorev stabbing himself with his victorious sword out of love for the deceased Osnelda; as Benjamin puts it, "the dagger becomes identical with the passions that guide it."[27]

In the first scenes, however, we are confronted with a rhetoric—familiar to us from Münnich's letter—that aims to contain the anxiety of armed violence through the idiom of love and marriage. Khorev's battle with Zavlokh, presaged by erotic metaphors in the lovers' speech, does end in triumph and civic reconciliation, if at an extreme personal price. In Khorev's original declaration of love, the "fury" associated with primeval "pride" and "freedom" is replaced by submission (he "at times thought myself to be free" but in fact "this proud spirit fell a slave to you forever," 11; 50), mirroring Osnelda's emotional language and identified with a promise of civic peace. Elsewhere, Khorev produces a related formula of their political marriage while refusing to release Osnelda from Kiev in defiance of Kii's orders:

Я сим величество твое изображу,
А после сам тебя на трон твой посажу.
Потомки возгласят что я владел страною,
Но царствуя страной, я царствовал собою,
И быв сугубый царь тебе подвержен был. (3.3.42)

---

26 Sumarokov, *Polnoe sobranie vsekh sochinenii*, 8: 236.
27 Benjamin, *Origin of German Tragic Drama*, 133.

I will thus pay tribute to your majesty, and later myself lead you to your throne. Posterity will say that I have ruled the country and simultaneously myself and that doubly a czar, I was your subject.

What at first seems to be little more than a reference to the play's fictional circumstances can be construed as a discussion of the central issues of power due to the allegorical signification of the terms employed. Once again, Sumarokov develops a series of more or less overt tropes to explore royal marriage as a paradigm of political order. As is the case in *Zaire*, the future marriage reconciles Osnelda's prolonged *captivity* with her royal *majesty*, and the two combine in a paradoxical definition of royal power. Accordingly, Khorev diminishes the absolute power provided to him by armed force through voluntary submission to duty and "laws": "The princes who hold pow'r by which laws are created / Are subject, even they, unto their own commandment" (3.3.41). This vision of power, which makes the sovereign both ruler and subject ("I have ruled the country and simultaneously myself") translates into Khorev's emotional bond with Osnelda, itself fashioned as the ultimate gallant paradox of domination and submission: "doubly a czar, I was your subject."[28] Khorev's decision to keep Osnelda in Kiev reduces both of them to a common *captivity*, in what is simultaneously a virtual "pre-enactment" of their longed-for marital vows and an ideal scenario of royal rule.

---

28 Commenting on Sumarokov's later use of a similar paradox, I. Z. Serman recognized its importance for the seemingly transparent, yet in fact intricate, verbal texture of his tragedies. See I. Z. Serman, *Russkii klassitsizm. Poeziia. Drama. Satira* (Leningrad: Nauka, 1972), 143. The frequency of this motif in French drama as well as its political implications are discussed by Elmarsafy, *Freedom, Slavery, and Absolutism*, 23.

PASTORAL POLITICS AND TRAGEDY

Much more than an incidental encomiastic conceit, representations of marriage as a foundational act of a monarchical political order were the focus of a long-standing tradition of the dramatic pastoral, inaugurated by Tasso's *Aminta* and Guarini's *Il pastor fido*. Indeed, both popular Renaissance plays were intrinsically related to the poetics of courtly fetes and hugely influenced their development, intertwining the language of love and politics in ways that would remain relevant for eighteenth-century *galanterie*. Guarini's Arcadia is freed from a divine curse by a happy marriage, fulfilling an ancient oracle: "Your woe shall end when two of Race Divine / Love shall combine."[1] The seventeenth-century English translator of the play, the royalist Sir Richard Fanshawe, who worked on his adaptation during the Civil War and dedicated it to the future king Charles II, recalled the occasion for the original production of Guarini's play and the political scenario behind its fictional plot. The occasion was a wedding "of two of Divine (that is Royall) extraction . . . from which fortunate Conjunction hee [Guarini] prophesies a final period to the trouble that had formerly distracted the State." Fanshawe then suggests that this could be a symbolic model for the restoration of the English monarchy, "thereby uniting a miserably divided people in a publick joy."[2]

While this dedication was certainly not known to Sumarokov and his audience, it reveals a deep undercurrent of political symbolism that largely

---

1 Giovanni Battista Guarini, *A Critical Edition of Sir Richard Fanshawe's 1647 Translation of Giovanni Battista Guarini's "Il pastor fido,"* ed. Walter F. Staton and William E. Simeone (Oxford: Clarendon Press, 1964), 24.

2 Ibid., 4–5; Kahn, "The Passions and the Interests in Early Modern Europe," 235–237.

shaped pastoral drama as a genre. Its tradition had certainly established a presence in mid-eighteenth century Russia. Stählin's 1738 essay praised Guarini's *Il pastor fido* alongside *Ercole amante*, an opera staged for the young Louis XIV and an apparent source for Sumarokov's later reference to an amorous Hercules as an emblem of poetic "tenderness."[3] In 1756 Voltaire professed to know "that almost everyone in Stockholm and Petersburgh, know whole scenes of the *Pastor Fido* by heart."[4] The pastoral strain was evident both in Bonecchi's Italian libretti, a genre directly descendant from Guarini's drama, and in French spoken plays such as Molière's "comédie galante" *La Princesse d'Élide* staged by Sérigny for the wedding celebrations of 1745.

Originally produced during a Versailles fête, Molière's play was designed as an allegorical celebration of Louis XIV's political and amorous successes. Its plot, according to the summary included in the official printed account of the Petersburg festivities, focuses on a princess who "remains constant in her wish not to love anything but hunt," but then "the virtue of the prince of Ithaca acquires so much power over the heart of the princess that she cannot defend herself anymore."[5] Her male counterpart undergoes a similar evolution and describes his newly found allegiance to love in politicized terms anticipating both Racine's Hippolyte and Sumarokov's Khorev:

Si de l'amour un temps j'ai bravé la puissance,
Hélas ! . . . il en prend bien vengeance . . .

If for a while I defy'd the Power of Love, alas . . . it takes full Vengeance for it now . . . [6]

Of course, the marriage of the prince and the princess gives occasion for an "allégresse publique" ("public joy") blurring the boundary between the fictional space of the play and the festivities outside it. The Petersburg production was preceded by a ballet where "Joys and laughs come together

---

3   "Istoricheskoe opisanie onago teatral'nogo deistviia," in Starikova, *Teatral'naia zhizn' Rossii v epokhu Anny Ioannovny*, 538, 551.

4   Voltaire, *The Works*, vol. 30 (London: J. Newbery et al., 1763), 20; Voltaire, *The Complete Works*, 25: 294.

5   Starikova, *Teatral'naia zhizn' Rossii v epokhu Elizavety Petrovny*, vol. 2, bk. 1, 106–107.

6   Molière, *Œuvres*, vol. 4 (Paris: Hachette, 1878), 145; Molière, *The Works* (London: John Watts, 1748), 10: 69.

to the tune of Marriage, and lead all the peoples of kingdoms and provinces which are fortunate enough to be ruled by Her Imperial Majesty."[7] Evidently, the pastoral idiom of love provided a paradigm for the "aesthetic ideology" developed, according to Terry Eagleton, by eighteenth-century absolutism:

> If absolutism does not wish to trigger rebellion, it must make generous accommodation for sensual inclination. ... What is at stake here is nothing less than the production of an entirely new kind of human subject—one which, like the work of art itself, discovers the law in the depths of its own free identity, rather than in some oppressive external power. The liberated subject is the one who has appropriated the law as the very principle of its own autonomy, broken the forbidding tablets of stone on which that law was originally inscribed in order to rewrite it on the heart of flesh.[8]

Drawing upon the notion of "aesthetic ideology," Victoria Kahn concludes in her insightful analysis of Guarini's pastoral and its resonances that "*Il Pastor fido* is political both because it places the *satisfaction* of the passions (both the characters' and the reader's) at the center of a newly aestheticized social order and because it makes the aesthetic ideology itself an object of rhetorical analysis and thus, potentially, of political interest."[9]

Similarly, in eighteenth-century Russia the recently imported literary idiom of love, pastoral or "gallant," certainly functioned as an "aesthetic ideology" that helped refashion and renegotiate the current order both in the erotic and the political realms. The idiom of romance was first introduced in 1730 into printed Russian letters, controlled by the state and the Academy of Sciences, by Trediakovskii, who, relying on the patronage of the influential diplomat Prince Aleksandr Kurakin, published his translation of Paul

---

7   Starikova, *Teatral'naia zhizn' Rossii v epokhu Elizavety Petrovny,* vol. 2, bk. 1, 103. On *La Princesse d'Élide,* its festive contexts and significations, see Kristiaan Aercke, *Gods of Play: Baroque Festive Performances as Rhetorical Discourse* (Albany: SUNY Press, 1994), 188–198; Alain Viala, *La France galante. Essai historique sur une catégorie culturelle, des ses origines jusqu'à la Révolution* (Paris: Presses Universitaires de France, 2008), 84–111; J. Morel, "Sur *La Princesse d'Élide,*" in *Agréables mensonges. Essais sur le théâtre français du XVIIe siècle* (Paris: Klincksieck, 1991).

8   Terry Eagleton, *The Ideology of the Aesthetic* (Oxford: Oxford University Press, 1990), 19.

9   Kahn, "The Passions and the Interests in Early Modern Europe," 230.

Tallemant's French erotic prose allegory *Le voyage de l'isle d'Amour*, along with a selection of his own poems. J. Pogosjan has revealed the political overtones of this edition, which, along with love lyrics, included poetic encomia to Russia, Peter the Great, and the reigning Empress Anna, and more generally resonated with the language of sensibility adopted by then at the Russian court.[10] One of Trediakovskii's poems, characteristically entitled *Stikhi o sile liubvi* (*Verses upon the Power of Love*), clearly identified erotic and political domination:

> … та царит царями,
>
> Старых чинит та ж молодцами,
>
> Любовь правит всеми гражданы,
>
> Ту чтят везде и поселяны,
>
> Та всчинает брани,
>
> Налагает дани.
>
> Не без любви мир, договоры;
>
> А прекращал кто б иной ссоры?[11]

[Love] rules over kings, makes old men young, rules the cities, is venerated by peasants, starts wars and imposes contributions. Without love there are no peace treaties, who else would stop hostilities?

Trediakovskii's gallant idiom closely echoed the politicized visions of love perpetuated by the pastoral tradition since Guarini, who described it as "a Powerfull Law" armed with an "amiable violence."[12] Not surprisingly, this conceit reappears with an immediately political function in Trediakovskii's panegyric song set to music and sung before Empress Anna:

> Любовь все удостоят,
>
> Сердца к оной пристроят;
>
> Жить имеет в нас тая,

---

10 J. Pogosjan, *Vostorg russkoi ody i reshenie temy poeta v russkom panegirike 1730–1762 gg* (Tartu: Tartu Ülikooli kirjastus, 1997), 34ff.

11 V. K. Trediakovskii, *Izbrannye proizvedeniia*, ed. L. I. Timofeev (Moscow and Leningrad: Sovetskii pisatel', 1963), 82–83.

12 *Giovanni Battista Guarini's "Il pastor fido,"* 37.

Умрет ненависть злая,—
Счастием богом данны
Самодержицы Анны.

К правде склонен всяк будет,
Лжи и след весь забудет;
Трона зрим одесную
Уж мы правду святую:
На троне богом данна
Самодержица Анна.

Трусил Марс и с войною
Пред нашей тишиною;
А российскую силу
Превознесет бог милу,—
Счастием богом данны
Самодержицы Анны …

И министры советны
Поживут безнаветны,
Зло усмотрят проклято,
Научат всех жить свято,—
Счастием богом данны
Самодержицы Анны.[13]

Everyone will honor love in their hearts. She will live in us, and vicious hatred will be extinct thanks to the fortune of the god-given autocrat Anna. Everyone will be inclined to truth and forget the traces of deception. Near the throne we see already the sacred truth, and on the throne the god-given autocrat Anna. Mars with his wars was subdued by our peace, and the Lord will extol the Russian amiable might, thanks to the fortune of the god-given autocrat Anna. … Councilors and ministers will live without ruses, will

---

13 Trediakovskii, *Izbrannye proizvedeniia*, 413–414.

spot evil and teach everyone to live in virtue, thanks to the fortune of the god-given autocrat Anna.

Foreshadowing the symbolism of Sumarokov's tragedies, "love" is assigned a central place in the vision of political justice and peace. Erotic overtones of royal charisma were reinvigorated at the ascension of the younger and personally captivating Elizabeth. In an ode written soon after the coup d'état of 1741 Trediakovskii was quick to explore the pastoral dynamic of love and submission:

Коль светло сидит на престоле!
Величество в императрице,
Красоту же мы зря в девице,
С почтением падаем доле.

Но, о сердец наших всех пламень!
О Элисавета Петровна!
Почто сердце ти было камень,
Зря росса толь к тебе любовна?
Почто не скоряй воцарилась? …

Сим дух твой непоколебимый
Хотя и не мог не терзаться,
Но так изволил обращаться,
Будто б народ не был любимый.[14]

What a bright majesty has mounted the throne in our empress! We see in her feminine beauty and we fall before her with even more veneration. But oh the flame of our hearts! Oh Elizabeth! Why was your heart indifferent like a stone when it saw the Russian so enamored by you? Why did you not ascend to the throne earlier? … Your immutable spirit could not but torment itself, but you feigned that you did not love your people.

---

14 Trediakovskii, *Izbrannye proizvedeniia*, 137–138.

Lomonosov, the best poet of his generation, followed the lead in 1746, once again giving a poetic account of the coup:

Не всяк ли скажет быть чудесно,
Увидев мужество совмесно
С толикой купно красотой?
Велико дело есть и знатно
Сердца народов привлещи,
И странно всем и непонятно
Пол света взять в одной нощи!
Но кое сердце толь жестоко,
Которо б Сей Богини око
Не сильно было умягчить?
И кая может власть земная,
На Дщерь и дух Петров взирая,
Себя противу ополчить?[15]

Will not anyone say it is a wonder, seeing such virility combined with such beauty? It is a great feat to attract the hearts of the peoples, and it is astonishing that half the world can be conquered in one night! *Where is a heart so savage which would not be softened by the looks of this goddess?* And which worldly power could arm itself against Peter's daughter and his spirit?

In both cases, the success of Elizabeth's coup is grounded in the relation of mutual reinforcement between her political power and erotic charm that assures her the "hearts" of her subjects, just as the Princess of Elis, Aricie, and Osnelda took sway over the hearts of Euryale, Hippolite, and Khorev. Sumarokov himself referred to this motif in a later ode, praising the divine beauty of the empress's body and assuring her that Russia "melts in love" for her.[16] Indeed, the gallant idiom of love was so important for Elizabethan language of power that it was employed directly after the coup by the French envoy

---

15   Lomonosov, *Izbrannye proizvedeniia*, 109.
16   A. Sumarokov, *Ody torzhestvennyia. Elegii lubovnyia. Reprintnoe vosproizvedenie sbornikov 1774 goda* (Moscow: OGI, 2009), 34, second numbering.

Chétardie, who stood very close to the new empress, to describe her success in an official dispatch to his court: "une princesse aimable, héritière légitime de la couronne, et qui par les agréments de sa personne, autant que par les qualités de son âme, captivait l'amour de tout l'empire" ("an amiable princess, legitimate heiress to the throne who has captivated the hearts of the whole empire by her charms as much as by the qualities of her spirit").[17] Once again, these uses of political eroticism are firmly grounded in the pastoral visions of power. Guarini praises love in the following terms:

> With Reason therefore man (that gallant creature,
> That lords it over all the works of Nature)
> To thee as Lady Paramount payes Duty,
> Acknowledging in thine, thy Maker's beauty.
> And if thee Triumphs gain, and Thrones inherit,
> It is not because thou hast lesse of merit;
> But for thy glory: since a greater thing
> It is to conquer, than to be a King.[18]

This almost enigmatic sequence provides a rhetorical framework for the relations of power. The very act of succession or conquest is seen as driven by love, construed elsewhere in *Il pastor fido* as "an Act / mixt of Conquest and Compact."[19] Guarini simultaneously contests the traditional moral philosophy that censures love, degrading it beyond and below political action, and extols the act of conquest rather than stability of order: a coup d'état. Furthermore, it is love that secures the subjection of men who "pay duty" to "Lady Paramount," Love herself or Empress Elizabeth as her incarnation.

As Victoria Kahn has demonstrated, the uneasy mix of court aesthetics and moral heterodoxy in *Il pastor fido* was acknowledged in Traiano Boccalini's account of Guarini's play in his *Ragguagli di Parnasso*, rendered into Russian in 1728 as *Vedomosti parnasskiia*. *Il pastor fido* is represented there as a "Pastoral tart" offered by a shepherd to Apollo, the ruler of Parnassus; when someone remarks the tart is "disgustingly sweet" he is severely rebutted on the grounds that "in

---

17 *SIRIO 96* (St. Petersburg, 1896): 662.
18 *Giovanni Battista Guarini's "Il pastor fido,"* 96
19 Ibid., 161.

time of *Carneval*, it was lawfull to commit exorbitances." According to Kahn, Boccalini implies that "aesthetic sweetness—the aesthetic pleasure of reading—can itself persuade to unlawful behavior," but at the same time "seems to view this potential for unlawful exorbitance at court in positive terms."[20]

If the pastoral "aesthetic ideology" aimed to reconcile the principles of pleasure and passion with the moral order, its very relevance attested to the fundamental tension between the two. Cardinal Bellarmine is reported to have complained that "the *Pastor Fido* was responsible for the depravity of countless women,"[21] and centuries later the pastoral rhetoric of sovereignty employed in Elizabethan Russia could be still seen as profoundly problematic. Elizabeth's rival on the European theater of power, Frederick II of Prussia, left the following account of her ascent to the throne in his private *Histoire de mon temps*:

> The regent [Anna Leopoldovna] had rendered herself odious, by the weaknesses she had indulged in favour of a foreigner, the handsome count Lynar, envoy from Saxony. Yet her predecessor, the empress Anne, had more openly distinguished Biron, a native of Courland and a foreigner likewise. So true it is that the same things cease to be the same, when they happen in other times, or to other persons. If love was the downfall of the regent, a more general love, which the princess Elizabeth taught the Preobraszenskoi guards, raised the latter to the throne. These princesses each had the same inclination for voluptuousness. The former concealed it under the veil of prudery; her heart only betrayed her: but it was carried by Elizabeth even to the excess of debauchery. . . . She preferred liberty to the ties of marriage, which she held to be too tyrannical. The better to confirm her government, she appointed her nephew, the young duke of Holstein, to the succession . . .[22]

This version of events—certainly biased yet far from groundless, since Frederick relied on the intelligence supplied by his astute and

---

20 Kahn, "The Passions and the Interests in Early Modern Europe," 231–232. For the Russian translation of this episode, see OR RGB, fond 310, no. 885, l. 67.

21 Quoted in Nicolas J. Perella, *The Critical Fortune of Battista Guarini's "Il pastor fido"* (Florence: Olschki, 1973), 28–29.

22 [Frederick II], "History of my Own Times," in *Posthumous Works of Frederic II King of Prussia*, trans. Thomas Holcroft (London: Robinson, 1789), 1: 170–172.

well-informed envoy in Russia, Axel von Mardefeld—reads as a malicious parody of the pastoral scenario of Elizabeth's ascension. From this perspective, the mutual love between the empress and her people is reinterpreted as base depravity but is still identified as the main reason for her success. According to Frederick's account, the 1741 coup marked a shift not only in court politics but also in public morals, the spirit of the "times." In fact, Elizabeth's notorious sexual licentiousness was seen by many as a touchstone for the central issues of public morality during her reign. In 1742 an officer of the royal guards, who might well have known what he was talking about, complained about the dissolute love life of recent Russian rulers, including Elizabeth, and concluded: "look what monarchs do, how can the common folks avoid it?"[23]

The successful adoption of the Western "gallant" language of love in Russia, first by Trediakovskii in his translation of Tallemant and its accompanying poems and then by Sumarokov in his tragedies, songs, and elegies, was both made possible by and strongly contributed to a developing current of public sensibility that favored a certain freedom of amorous choice and extramarital relationships. Tracing this trend in his famous "secret history" of the Russian court, the essay *O povrezhdenii nravov v Rossii* (*On the Corruption of Morals in Russia*, 1787), Mikhail Shcherbatov later remarked that it was under Elizabeth that "women began to desert their husbands." Anna Buturlina, for example, "after leaving her husband, married her lover. After publicly contracting this adulterous and unlawful marriage, they lived together openly." Another case highlighting the role of the Western-type theater as a space particularly encouraging of the equality of sexes involved Countess Anna Apraksina, who was allowed to divorce her husband after he was arrested "for an alleged attempt to do her some insult in a German play." As Shcherbatov emphasizes, "this divorce was decided by a civil, not an ecclesiastical authority" and was allowed "for no other reason than that her father … enjoyed a certain favor at Court."[24] The half hidden but acutely felt conflict between the amorous behavior accepted, or at least tolerated, by the officially pious Russian court (similar in this respect to other European courts) and the norms of traditional morality is illustrated by yet another case in point, that

---

23 Quoted in Kurukin, *Epokha dvorskikh bur'*, 351.

24 M. M. Scherbatov, *On the Corruption of Morals in Russia*, trans. and ed. Antony Lentin (Cambridge: Cambridge University Press, 1969), 227.

of Natalia Lopukhina, famed as one of the most beautiful women at the Russian court, who conducted a longtime affair with Count Löwenwolde. When Jane Rondeau congratulated Lopukhina's husband in 1738 on the birth of a child, he referred her to Löwenwolde, and frankly explained that "all the world knows it is true, nor does it disturb me ... I can neither love nor hate her, but continue in a state of indifference; so why should I be disturbed at her making herself easy with a man she likes, since, to do her justice, she behaves with as much decency as the affair will admit of." Further complicating the original "confusion" she experienced after Lopukhin's confession, Rondeau admits to her correspondent: "I hate myself for the ill nature I am guilty of," and thus vividly reveals the strong tension between the accepted decorum and the amorous ethic gradually emerging as a new norm.[25]

This conflict, which informs both Frederick's and Shcherbatov's perspective on Elizabeth and her reign, was one of the major topics of dramatic pastorals and was constantly negotiated in *Il pastor fido* and in various offsprings of the pastoral tradition, including Molière's *La Princesse d'Élide*, Racine's *Phèdre*, and Sumarokov's *Khorev*. Benjamin's intuition that dramatic pastoral and early modern tragedy "have a latent impulse to combine," while the "antithesis between the two is only a superficial one," has been confirmed by later scholarship. For example, Karl Maurer's study traces the history of a heterogeneous genre from Guarini, who amalgamated courtly aesthetic with authoritative Aristotelian doctrine and references to ancient models, to seventeenth-century France where the influence of Guarini's example work "was able to catalyze the emergence of an independent court tragedy."[26] In *Il pastor fido*, a mutual passion of two young lovers is considered illicit and condemned by theocratic authority as a crime against public welfare until a recognition scene reveals that their marriage is in fact divinely sanctioned: "Pleasure, that is, is reconciled to virtue and passion is aligned with public interest."[27]

---

25 Jane Vigor, *Letters from a lady, who resided some years in Russia, to her friend in England* (London: J. Dodsley, 1777), 177–179.

26 Benjamin, *Origin of German Tragic Drama*, 94; Karl Maurer, "Die verkannte Tragödie. Die Wiedergeburt der Tragödie aus dem Geist der Pastorale," in *Goethe und die romanische Welt* (Padeborn: Schöningh, 1997), 222. On the pastoral overtones of Racinian tragedy, see also Perella, *The Critical Fortune of Battista Guarini's "Il pastor fido,"* 53–55; Morel, "Pastorale et tragédie," in *Agréables mensonges*.

27 Kahn, "The Passions and the Interests in Early Modern Europe," 226.

Until this last moment, however, the characters—and the readers—of the play are left to grieve for the happy primeval times when love was seen as a "lawfull flame," while "Husband and Lover signifi'd one thing," and to resent the fatal enmity between passion and established law.[28] Their collision is the focus of one of the central scenes of *Khorev*, where Osnelda's guardian servant Astrada eloquently asserts the rights of love:

> Тебе ль последовать безумным предрассудкам? …
> Чтоб наше естество суровствуя страдало,
> Обыкновение то в людях основало.
> Обычай, ты всему устав во свете сем,
> Предрассуждение правительствует в нем,
> Безумье правилы житья установляет,
> А легкомыслие те правы утверждает …
> Любовь без следствиев худых незапрещенна,
> Сей слабостию вся исполненна вселенна.
> Не свету, одному покорствуй божеству …
> Девица, разве жить между зверей в пустыне,
> Подверженна всегда во младости своей
> Всеобщей слабости, что царствует над ней. (3.2.35–36)

> Is it for you to obey insane prejudice? … Custom is the reason for severe suffering inflicted on our nature, custom is the law of this world, where prejudice rules, insanity establishes rules of life, and folly confirms them. … Love without bad consequences is not illicit, the universe is full of this weakness … Do not obey the world, but only the deity … A girl who does not live in the wilderness among animals is always in her youth subject to the common weakness which rules over her.

Astrada's monologue—an outright apology of adultery—clearly follows a pastoral pattern. The *Princesse d'Élide* opens with a chorus specifically urging young girls to fall in love ("Quand l'amour à vos yeux offre un choix agréable, /

---

28 *Giovanni Battista Guarini's "Il pastor fido,"* 126.

Jeunes beautés, laissez-vous enflammer"). Euyriale's tutor, Arbate, upon hearing his amorous confessions does not condemn his pupil but praises his affection as a worthy principle of political action ("C'est une qualité que j'aime en un monarque"), discarding the strictures of traditional morality ("chagrin des vieux jours").[29] Similarly, in *Phédre* Hippolyte's tutor, Théramène, encourages his love for Aricie:

> D'un chaste amour pourquoi vous effrayer?
> S'il a quelque douceur, n'osez-vous l'essayer?
> En croirez-vous toujours un farouche scrupule?

> And, after all, why should a guiltless passion
> Alarm you? Dare you not essay its sweetness,
> But follow rather a fastidious scruple?[30]

However, Astrada offers a much more consistent and elaborate critique of the current moral order, because she fundamentally questions the legitimacy of established moral law and the power of popular beliefs that maintain constraints on love over the socially and intellectually superior inhabitants of the "prince's palace." This argument is echoed elsewhere by Khorev:

> К чему природа нас безвредно понуждает,
> Те страсти в нас одно злодейство охуждает (3.3.42).

> Harmless passions inspired in us by nature are only condemned by villainy.

Sumarokov seems to draw on the famous lines from *Il pastor fido*:

> Whom Love hath joyn'd, why dost thou separate,
> Malicious Fate! And two divorc'd by Fate,
> Why joyn'st thou perverse Love! How blest are you
> Wild beasts, that are in loving ty'd unto

---

29 Molière, *Œuvres*, 4: 131–132, 143–144.

30 [Jean] Racine, *Théâtre complet*, 2: 285; Jean Racine, *The Dramatic Works … A Metrical English Version by Robert Bruce Boswell* (London: G. Bell and Sons, 1897), 2: 211.

No lawes but those of Love! whilst humane lawes,
Inhumanely condemn us for that cause …
Nature too frail, that do'st with Law contend!
Law too severe, that Nature do'st offend![31]

Guarini's verses aroused a debate that extended far beyond matters of literary style. Censured by many conservative critics as outright impious, they reappeared in Pierre Bayle's *Dictionnaire historique et critique*, in the article "Guarini," where he maintained that in these lines the poet "touches upon one of the most incomprehensible mysteries of nature": "How is it possible that under such a Being [a single God] men should be drawn to evil by a bait that is almost unsurmountable, I mean, by the sense of pleasure, and are deterred from it by the fear of remorse, infamy, or several other punishments."[32] Astrada attempts to resolve this mystery by dismissing the restrictions on erotic freedom as meaningless prejudice, false opinions of the "world" opposed in fact to the true divine will which favors love. Apparently, this line of reasoning did not appear either neutral or harmless. In exposing Astrada as an unworthy "philosopher," the erudite Trediakovskii—echoing the tone of criticisms leveled against Guarini himself—in an irate critique condemned her speech as "false," "impious," and "harmful to good morals." Furthermore, he identified her arguments with the blameworthy "atheistic" doctrines of Spinoza and Hobbes, and contravened them with a series of philosophical arguments in support of an orthodox vision of an innate moral discipline common to all, compelling enough for Sumarokov (who had no training in philosophy) to strike Astrada's speech altogether from a later version of the play.[33]

As Trediakovskii's wording suggests, what was at stake was much more than an academic issue. Expressly defending commonplace morality questioned by Sumarokov as the ultimate foundation of social order, Trediakovskii did in fact come close to "charging him with subversion."[34] Indeed, the

---

31 *Giovanni Battista Guarini's "Il pastor fido,"* 78.

32 Pierre Bayle, *The Dictionary Historical and Critical* (London: J. J. and P. Knapton et al., 1736), 3: 261. On the heated critical debate around the moral implications of *Il pastor fido*, and specifically the verses just quoted, see Perella, *The Critical Fortune of Battista Guarini's "Il pastor fido,"* 28–32, 57–62.

33 Trediakovskii, "Pis'mo," 95–98.

34 Marcus Levitt, "Slander, Polemic, Criticism: Trediakovskii's 'Letter … from a Friend to a Friend' of 1750 and the Problem of Creating Russian Literary Criticism," in *Early Modern*

renegotiation of divine and human law proposed by Sumarokov's Astrada and her predecessors was pivotal for the pastoral tradition, making it attractive, deeply problematic, and immediately relevant for the conflicted sensibilities of post-Petrine Russian elites. In Racinian tragedy, much like Guarini's pastoral, "the Past is a right," and the central figures "are defined by the refusal to inherit" (for example, the hereditary feud, as in *Khorev*): "Their effort of disengagement is opposed by the inexhaustible force of the Past; this force is a veritable Erinys that prevents the institution of the new Law, in which everything would at last be possible."[35]

Pastoral plots, laden with allegory, offered a pattern for the resolution of this conflict: while passionate lovers—construed as models of subjectivity, both erotic and political—assert their freedom of choice, the figures of authority accommodate this new freedom to the notions of duty and obedience in acts of reconciliation, thereby subduing its potential for subversion and containing it within the bounds of the existing order of power. This was the scenario chosen by Elizabeth for the marriage of her heir apparent, both on and off stage. In 1746 Sérigny produced Philippe Poisson's one-act comedy *L'Impromptu de campagne* (*A Country Impromptu*), which recycled pastoral commonplaces. The play staged a story of a young couple who fell in love seemingly against the wishes of their parents, only to discover that they were intended for each other in the first place, but not before the reasonable Isabelle could give a lesson of restraint:

> Aux volontés d'un père il faut bien se résoudre.
> Puis-je faire autrement? ...
> Il faut bien sur soi faire un effort.

> One has to comply with a father's will.
> Could I have acted differently? ...
> One has to constrain oneself.

Finding Catherine in tears soon after the wedding, Elizabeth, in Catherine's own account, claimed that she had been assured that "I had no repugnance

---

Russian Letters: Texts and Contexts, 69.

35 Barthes, *On Racine*, 47–48.

to marrying the Grand Duke; that, besides, she had not forced me; that, as I was married, I must not cry any more." Catherine herself referred to similar notions of marital duty when she commented on her miserable marriage to Peter: "Had he wished to be loved, I should have found no difficulty in loving him. I was naturally well disposed, and accustomed to fulfill my duties."[36]

This vision of marital harmony based on the identification of love and duty, that Elizabeth wished to stage in the Grand Duke's private chambers, as attested both by the rhetoric of the festivities and by the secret instructions received by the courtiers assigned to Peter and Catherine, resonated not only with pastoral fictions but also with the official discourse on marriage. A decree issued by Peter I on January 5, 1724, expressly forbade parents and serf owners to force their children and serfs to marry "without their heartfelt wish," and obliged them to take an oath during the marriage ceremony confirming that their dependent "wishes with my permission to lawfully wed on his own accord, true and unconstrained."[37] Pretending to abolish the barbaric customs of forced marriage, denounced later by Tatishchev and Sumarokov's Astrada, this decree sought to refashion paternalistic authority, symbolically harmonizing it with the subjects' "own accord" without in fact diminishing its legal powers of control, the right to give or withdraw "permission."

This political symbolism informed the themes of Elizabethan court theater, which time and again extolled benevolent rulers who approve and sponsor the marriage of heroic lovers, sometimes at the cost of personal sacrifice. This motif dominates the finale of the festive operas beginning with *La Clemenza di Tito* staged in 1742 and imitated by Bonecchi in *Il Seleuco* and *Scipione*. Similarly, in the *Princesse d'Élide* the royal father assures his daughter:

> je me plains de toi, qui peux mettre dans ta pensée que je sois assez mauvais père pour vouloir faire violence à tes sentiments, et me servir tyranniquement de la puissance que le ciel me donne sur toi.

---

36 Philippe Poisson, *L'Impromptu de campagne,* in *Répertoire du Théâtre François . . .* (Paris: P. Didot l'aîné, 1804), 20: 484; [Catherine, Empress of Russia], *Memoirs of the Empress Catherine II*, 59. On this dramatic motif and its political symbolism, see Déborah Blocker, *Instituer un «art». Politiques du théâtre dans la France du premier XVIIe siècle*, 220ff.

37 *Polnoe sobranie zakonov Rossiiskoi imperii s 1649 g.,* 197–198, no. 4406.

... Si tu trouves où attacher tes voeux, ton choix sera le mien, et je ne considérerai ni intérêts d'état, ni avantages d'alliance.

I'm sorry you can think me so bad a Father as to do violence to your Sentiments, and use tyrannically the Power Heav'n has given me over you ... if you pitch upon any one to fix your Inclinations on, your Choice shall be mine, and I'll consider neither Interest of State, nor Advantage of Alliance.[38]

This pastoral ideal is clearly present in the world of *Khorev*. Very early on, Kii shows his approval for the possible marriage of Khorev and Osnelda:

Когда Хорев ей мил, она мила ему,
Досадно ли мне то? ...
Он знает, что его желанью соизволю,
И серце в том ево безспорно удоволю. (2.3.25)

If she loves Khorev, and he loves her, is it harmful to me? He knows I will approve of his wish and bring satisfaction to his heart.

In his turn, the defeated Zavlokh admits he should not have censured their passion:

твой храбрый брат желал
Невольницы своей в жену и испрошал;
Но я ...
Противился ему в желаемой забаве,
И думаю что сим я тако согрешил:
Я может быть союз их бранью разрешил. (5.4.71)

your valorous brother wished to marry his captive and asked my permission, but I ... resisted the pleasure he longed for, and I think I erred and may be destroyed their accord with war.

---

38 Molière, *Œuvres*, 171–172; Molière, *The Works*, 97–99.

In the actual outcome of the play, summed up by Zavlokh, the tragic effect is produced by a precise inversion of the pastoral plot scheme, with the catastrophe brought about by malevolent royal fathers who cannot accept their children's harmless passion. This was a common technique both for the *opera seria* and spoken tragedy. Bonecchi's *Seleuco* bears the name of the king "constant in his cruelty" who "in his awful brutality prefers to die rather than to marry his daughter to … the courageous and magnanimous king," her lover.[39]

More importantly, in Racine's tragedies pastoral couples regularly represent idyllic alternatives to the "tragic" political and dynastic catastrophes finally brought about by their demise. In *Britannicus*, extensively explored by Volker Schröder, the blameless love between Britannicus and Junie represents a promise of prosperity for Rome, obliterated in the end by Nero's dawning tyranny.[40] In *Phédre*, Hippolyte's love for Aricie could have secured dynastic reconciliation, if it was not for Thesée and his terrible act of infanticide. The pastoral focus on the misfortunes of young lovers and their conflict with paternalistic authority—which later allowed Trediakovskii to claim that *Khorev's* "essential basis is Racine's *Phédre*"—already shaped the conception of tragic plots in the anonymous 1739 essay *O pol'ze teatral'nykh deistv i komedii k vozderzhaniiu strastei chelovecheskikh* (*On the Advantages of Plays and Comedies for the Moderation of Human Passions*):

> If an author represents in his play the cruelty of the father who wishes to ruin his children for a passion made excusable by their youth, while for him in his mature age there is no excuse, this action should be shown as horrible as Medea's or other similar crimes; and if the playwright wishes to represent an incident like that on stage and to give his spectators useful lessons, he should … show this action with horrifying traits, and to represent the inevitable punishment or remorse.[41]

---

39 Iosef Bonekki [Giuseppe Bonecchi], *Selevk: Opera predstavlennaia pri Rossiiskom imperatorskom dvore v vysochaishii den' koronovaniya … Elisavety Petrovny … i pri vsenarodnom torzhestvovanii … vechnago mira* (Moscow: Tipografiia Imperatorskoi Akademii nauk, 1744), 35.

40 Volker Schröder, *La tragédie du sang d'Auguste: politique et intertextualité dans Britannicus* (Tübingen: Narr, 1999), 205–254.

41 Trediakovskii, "Pis'mo," 89; *Teatral'naia zhizn' Rossii v epokhu Anny Ioannovny*, 581. On the importance of this plot pattern for Sumarokov's tragedies, see Kasatkina, "Sumarokovskaia

Writing on Corneille's tragedy *Médee*, possibly alluded to in the 1739 essay, Marin suggests that a dramatization of Medea's crimes could be construed "as a demonic perspective on the essence of the political act which unmasks in this fictional form its impossible theory."[42] While in *Khorev* Sumarokov carefully avoids the "demonic" aspects of the genre, represented by Corneille's Médee and Racine's Phédre, the woeful story of Osnelda and Khorev is certainly tailored to provide insights into the *arcana imperii*, the workings of royal rule entrusted in this case to Kii.

---

tragediia 40-kh–nachala 50-kh godov XVIII veka," 225–226; on the links between *Khorev* and *Phédre,* see ibid., 242–244; G. A. Gukovskii, *Rannie raboty po istorii russkoi poezii XVIII veka* (Moscow: Iazyki Russkoi kultury, 2001), 35.

42   Louis Marin, "Théâtralité et pouvoir: Magie, machination, machine: *Médée* de Corneille," in *Politiques de la représentation* (Paris: Editions Kimé, 2005), 264–266.

THE TRAGEDY OF SUSPICION

Sumarokov's attempt to inscribe his tragic plots, evidently fashioned to reflect the conventions of neoclassical drama, into the national past has been a matter of some debate. Whereas Iu. V. Stennik insisted that Sumarokov could not escape the "anti-historicism of artistic thinking characteristic for his time," I. Z. Serman offered a more thoughtful approach, suggesting that Sumarokov's depiction of his characters was dependent on the prevalent conceptualizations of historical developments in general and the primeval origins of royal power in particular.[1] Indeed, Russia's history—centered around Riurik, the medieval founder of the Russian state, and his progeny who ruled Russia for seven hundred years—was the history of an unquestionably absolute monarchy. Manstein, whose *Memoirs of Russia* generally focus on contemporary events, makes a short digression to report that "the government of Russia was always despotic" and that "the respect felt by the Russian people for the descendants of the first Grand Duke Riurik was so high that they were far from any thoughts of even the slightest rebellion until his race lasted, and no one probably ever thought that Russia could be ruled otherwise than by a despotic ruler."[2] Tatishchev, both in the *History of Russia* and in a political pamphlet (apparently written around the same time as Sumarokov's first tragedies) against aristocratic limitations on monarchy proposed by the *verkhovniki* in 1730, used accounts of ancient Russian history to corroborate his unconditional support for absolute royal rule.

---

1   Iu. V. Stennik, *Zhanr tragedii v russkoi literature. Epokha klassitsizma* (Leningrad: Nauka, 1981), 73; Serman, *Russkii klassitsizm*, 122ff.

2   *Perevoroty i voiny*, 268–269.

Tatishchev, who traced the origins of his historiographic project to his time at Peter the Great's court and framed it as a token of dynastic loyalty to the deceased emperor and his successors, viewed it as an antidote against such "harmful" books, already circulating in manuscript translations, as Machiavelli's *The Prince*, Hobbes's *Leviathan*, Locke's *Second Treatise on Government*, and Boccalini's *Ragguagli di Parnasso*, which in 1730 had already led some "perfidious magnates" to unleash the "Leviathan" of aristocratic faction.[3] As Tatishchev's line of reasoning demonstrates, historical knowledge invoked to support the absolutist dogma inadvertently implied and perpetuated the possibility of dissent and revolt it was meant to contain. This was recognized by the authorities, for as Evgenii Anisimov shows, any public reference to Russia's past rulers or historical events could be interpreted as sedition by the secret police. Among the crimes imputed to Artemii Volynskii in 1740 was the fact that he and his companions used to read chronicles and history works and to draw parallels between political situations past and present. (Allegedly, Volynskii further abused his historical knowledge by ordering a genealogical table that proved his rights to the Russian throne.) Although Tatishchev was spared during the Volynskii trial (he was on trial for another charge), his own work on the chronicles relied on the same personal networks of manuscript circulation and shared the same highly politicized approach to ancient history, essentially read as political theory in disguise.[4]

Sumarokov's tragedies, while they certainly lack the *couleur locale* of a Walter Scott historical novel, reveal a stronger historical grounding than critics usually assume. Besieged in Kiev by a contender he had once ousted by force, and questioning the loyalty of his subjects including his own brother, Sumarokov's Kii (like most other rulers of his tragedies) finds himself in a position characteristic of medieval Russian politics and dynastic chronicles. From a theoretical perspective, this position allows for an inquiry into the foundations and stability of royal rule, an issue central both for political practice and readings of history in mid-eighteenth-century Russia. If the

---

3   Tatishchev, "Istoriia rossiiskaia," *Sobranie sochinenii*, 1: 86–89, 359, 362, 368; Tatishchev, "Proizvol'noe i soglasnoe rassuzhdenie i mnenie sobravshegosia shliakhetstva russkogo o pravlenii gosudarstvennom," *Sobranie sochinenii* (Moscow: Ladomir, 1996), 8: 148.

4   Evgenii Anisimov, *Dyba i knut. Politicheskii sysk i russkoe obshchestvo v XVIII veke*, 58–62; Aleksei Tolochko, *"Istoriia Rossiiskaia" Vasiliia Tatishcheva* (Moscow: Novoe literaturnoe obozrenie, 2005).

play's exposition in the first act is dominated by Khorev's and Osnelda's pastoral musings, the second act introduces us to the sinister world of court politics. It opens with a scene of council between Kii and his "first boyar" Stalverkh, who questions the honesty of Zavlokh's promise to withdraw from Kiev once he receives Osnelda and warns Kii against his own subjects: "Bregisia, gosudar', nechaiannykh izmen" (2.1.19; "Beware, my prince, before unlooked-for treachery," 53). Kii at first seems unwilling to share this fears:

Что может, рассуди, изменник учинить?

Народ бесчисленный удобно ль возмутить,

В котором множество мне сердцем покоренно?

Владычество мое любовью утвержденно,

Меня мои раби непринужденно чтят,

Мне верности давно их внутренну явят. (2.1.18)

Consider and reflect; what can the traitor do?

Can he cause to rebel a nation numberless,

Whose hearts unto my rule with faithfulness are humbled?

My sov'reignty in love stands steadfast without challenge.

My followers are true and give me their respect.

Through many years they showed to me their inner selves. (54)

This unclouded vision of rule certainly relies on the Elizabethan gallant idiom of amorous domination and centers on the notion of "sov'reignty in love" and "fidelity," "vernost'," a Russian rendering of the French "foi," "a word entirely precious in its ambiguity, both political and erotic."[5] *The Alliance of Love and Marriage*, Sérigny's 1745 *divertissement*, asserted that "nasha liubeznaia Samoderzhitsa / Umeet shchedrymi svoimi blagodeianiiami / Nad vsekh serdtsami byt' tsaritseiu" ("our beloved empress through her generous deeds reigns over all hearts").[6]

Kii's speech, however, suggests a situation much less serene than it claims and than parallels with court pageantry would seem to imply. In April 1742, soon after Elizabeth's coup, her close confidant Chétardie had to persuade the French court that "the force of her rights and the love of her peoples reassure her

---

5   Barthes, *On Racine*, 72.

6   Starikova, *Teatral'naia zhizn' Rossii v epokhu Elizavety Petrovny*, vol. 2, bk. 1, 102.

so much that she can look forward with so much tranquility as if she had ascended the throne without a revolution."[7] Addressing his superiors in Paris, Chétardie was refuting the widely spread apprehensions of another coup d'état, which would return the throne to Anna Leopoldovna and her son, the infant emperor. Those apprehensions, shared by European diplomats and Petersburg populace alike, including the soldiers of the guards who had brought Elizabeth to power and now felt that the fate of the Russian throne was in their hands, dominated the political sensibilities during the first years of Elizabeth's reign. Chétardie's wording, which draws from the language of Machiavelli's *The Prince*, is itself characteristic of the political language evoked to make sense of the complex and shifting political circumstances in Petersburg.

As Tatishchev's remarks indicate, Machiavelli's work was already well known in Russia. Since Petrine times it appeared in the libraries of educated courtiers, and while an early Russian translation that Volynskii allegedly possessed has not been found, another translation of *The Prince* together with Frederick II's *Anti-Machiavel*, carried out sometime after 1742, survives in the manuscript collection of the Vorontsovs, a clan with close ties to Elizabeth.[8] The French editions of Machiavelli's and Frederick's works were apparently in some demand in the Petersburg foreign book trade in the late 1740s, and Chétardie's sucessor alluded to both of them in a conversation with the empress in 1742.[9] Tatishchev's argument suggests that along with other political treatises Machiavelli's work could be directly associated with the dangers of revolt, but unlike Hobbes or Locke, Machiavelli did not deal with the theory of sovereignty but rather with practical techniques of empowerment. *The Prince* acknowledged and even endorsed the possibility of acquiring supreme authority through conquest and usurpation but provided the contenders for power with clear-sighted advice:

> I say then, that it is a much easier matter to support an hereditary
> State, which has been long accustomed to obey the family of a Prince
> that reigns over it, than such a one as has been newly acquired ... For

---

7   *SIRIO* 100 (St. Petersburg, 1897): 148.

8   On the reception of Machiavelli and European theories of reason of state in general in eighteenth-century Russia, see a very informative source study: Iusim, *Makiavelli v Rossii*, 77–186.

9   N. A. Kopanev, "Rasprostranenie frantsuzskoi knigi v Moskve v seredine XVIII v.," in *Frantsuzskaia kniga v Rossii v XVIII v.: Ocherki istorii* (Leningrad: Nauka, 1986), 133, 148, no. 258–259, 441; *SIRIO* 100 (St. Petersburg, 1897): 425.

a natural Prince neither lies under any necessity, nor can have any motive to oppress or disgust his subjects: from whence it must follow of course, that he will be more beloved by them than another ... Besides, the long succession and duration of his government abolish both the causes and memory of innovations: for one change generally leaves a toothing (as it is called in buildings) and aptitude for another. ... But in the government of a Principality newly-acquired, many difficulties occur. For if it is not absolutely new ... tumults and revolutions will in the first place ensue from the perverseness and instability that are incident to the Subjects of all new States; because, as most men are ready enough to change their masters, in expectation of bettering their condition, such a persuasion induces them to take up arms against their Governors: but they are often deceived in this, and have the mortification to find by experience that they have changed for the worse. ... The most effectual preservative then against conspiracies, is not to be hated and despised by the people: for those that enter into a conspiracy, do it out of a persuasion that the death of the Prince would be acceptable to his Subjects; but when they are convinced, on the contrary, that it would only serve to enrage them, they will be deterred from embarking in any such undertaking ...[10]

In his account of Elizabeth's coup, Chétardie revives—while attempting to obliterate—Machiavelli's distinction between the two types of domination, old and new. A similar attempt frames the position of Kii, who is simultaneously an "old" ruler (he has reigned over Kiev for sixteen years) and a "new" one (he had conquered it by force). Machiavelli's description of the popular craving for upheavals fostered by frequent changes of power seemed to provide an optimal explanation for the Russian tumults of 1740–1741, with Elizabeth overthrowing Anna Leopoldovna only a year after Anna herself had in a similar fashion seized power from the omnipotent regent Biron with the help of Burchard von Münnich. General Löwendahl remarked that Münnich deserved to be punished if only "for having first shown a dangerous example of overthrowing princes and raising them to the throne

---

10   *The Works of Nicholas Machiavel ... Newly Translated ... by Ellis Farneworth* (London: Thomas Davies et al., 1762), 1: 513–514, 516, 638.

with a company of grenadiers."[11] Frederick II, an attentive reader of Machia-velli, commented in his *Histoire de mon temps*:

> Such enterprises, which would appear rash in other governments, may sometimes be accomplished in Russia. The national spirit is inclined to revolt. The Russians, in common with other people, are dissatisfied with the present and hope better from the future.[12]

A Machiavellian vision of popular instincts, confirmed by the seditious talk among the Petersburg soldiers, fundamentally challenged the conception of Russians as a people particularly devoted to its despotic monarchs, suggested by conventional readings of national history.

This tension, negotiated in Tatishchev's juxtaposition of his loyalist historiography to the seditious Machiavelli, is again reenacted in Kii's lines quoted above: entangled in a rhetorical figure, he wishes to assert the fidelity of his subjects but ends up questioning it. Confronted with Stalverkh's allegations against Khorev, he attempts to dismiss them but cannot help admitting that the need to question appearances is inherent in the position of a ruler:

> Сталверх! Ты верен мне, но дело таково
> Восходит выше сил понятья моего.
> Кому на свете сем вдруг верити возможно?
> Хочу равно и ложь и истину внимать
> И слепо никого не буду осуждать.
> Мятусь, и лютого злодея видя в горе.
> Князь—кормщик корабля, власть княжеская—море,
> Где ветры, камни, мель препятствуют судам,
> Желающим пристать к покойным берегам.
> Но часто кажутся и облаки горами,
> Летая вдалеке по небу над водами,
> Которых кормщику не должно обегать;
> Но горы ль то иль нет, искусством разбирать.

---

11   *Perevoroty i voiny*, 477.
12   [Frederick II], "History of my Own Times," 170.

Хоть все б вещали мне, там горы, мели тамо,
Когда не вижу сам, плыву без страха прямо. (2.1.20–21)

You have been true to me, Stalverkh, but such a thing
Beyond my understanding far exceeds the bounds.
Who dwells upon the earth whose word can now be trusted?
If I could but believe both falsehood and the truth
That I might not be forced disheartened to condemn!
I am perplexed to see in grief even a villain.
The prince pilots the ship; his power is the ocean,
Where winds and rocks and shoals obstruct the passing boats,
Whose only goal is this: to reach a tranquil shore.
But sometimes even clouds appear to us as mountains,
Drifting through distant skies above the churning waters,
Which he, the helmsman, must discern to guide his ship,
Distinguishing with skill the mountain from the cloud.
And though the world should shout: "There lie the rock and shallows!"
If I discern them not, I sail on fearing nothing. (55–56)

In Levitt's words, "In *Khorev* … seeing correctly or being blinded by appearances—whether intentionally or not—emerges as one of the fundamental problems of being a good ruler."[13] As was customary for early modern drama, Sumarokov's construction of tragic plot and characters resonated with what Benjamin describes as a Machiavellian political anthropology, produced and disseminated across Europe by innumerable treatises, avidly read and oftentimes translated in early eighteenth-century Russia.[14] Among the works that have survived in these never published and barely studied manuscript translations is Diego de Saavedra Fajardo's emblematic treatise *Idea de un príncipe político cristiano*, widely known in Europe (it is cited by Benjamin in his analysis of the "tragic drama") and rendered into Russian as *Izobrazhenie*

---

13 Levitt, *Visual Dominant in Eighteenth-Century Russia,* 95–96.

14 On "political anthropology" at the core of early modern tragedy, see Benjamin, *Origin of German Tragic Drama,* 100; Alain Viala, "Péril, conseil et secret d'État dans les tragédies romaines de Racine: Racine et Machiavel," *Littératures classiques* 26 (1996): 91–113.

khristiana politicheskago vlastelina by none other than Feofan Prokopovich on the personal orders of Peter the Great. One of Saavedra Fajardo's emblems, instructing the ruler to "think always he may be deceived," shows a boat stern ("korma," the position of Sumarokov's "pilot" or "helmsman" ["korm-schik"]) and explains that a prince should not

> be too positive in his opinions, but believe that he may easily be deceiv'd in his Judgment, either through Affection, or Passion, or false Information, or Flattery, and Insinuation ... because few things are really what they appear, especially in Policy, which is now a-days nothing but the art of cheating, or not being cheated; wherefore they ought to be viewed in different lights, and a Prince ought carefully to consider and weigh them not slightly to pass them over, least he should give credit to appearances and groundless stories ... How often have Waves of Envy and Jealousy been interpos'd between the Eyes of the Prince, and the Minister's actions, making those appear crooked and disloyal which are drawn by the rule of Justice and his Service. Thus Virtue suffers, the Prince loses a good Minister, and Malice triumphs in its Practices; which that he may practically know, and not suffer Innocence to be wrong'd, I will here set down the most usual.[15]

Discourse of this kind was immediately relevant for post-Petrine court politics. The fall of Artemii Volynskii was precipitated by a letter he wrote in 1739 to Empress Anna, masking an attempt to discredit his enemies at court as a generalized analysis of "kakie pritvorstvy i vymysly upotrebliaemy byvaiut pri vashikh monarsheskikh dvorakh, i v chem vsya takaya zakrytaia bezsovestnaia politika sostoit" ("which ruses and stratagems are employed at your royal courts, and what all this secretive and shameless politics is about"):

> 1: Сколко возможно столко на совестных людей вымышлено затевать и вредить, и всяческии добрые дела их помрачать и опровергать, дабы тем кураж и охоту к службе у них отнять.
> 2: Приводить государей в сомнение чтоб никому верить не

---

15 Diego de Saavedra Fajardo, *Royal Politician Represented in One Hundred Emblems* (London: Matt. Gylliflower et al., 1700), 1: 319–320, 322. For Feofan's translation, see OR RNB, f. 550, OSRK, F II 67.

изволили и всеб подозрением огорчены были и казались всяко милости недостойными, а при том и самея опасности представлять иногда и от таких дел, которыя за самую безделицу почитать можно, однако ж оныя как наиболше расширять … а потом самого толко себя к поправлению или успокоению того дела рекомендовать, и что уж бутто бы в том иному никому поверить невозможно или по крайней мере такия мудрости и затруднении в том деле показать, что иной никто того зделать и исправить не может, а в самом деле вымыслы оных господ политиков, или просто назвать обманщиков в том состоят, чтою тем у государя своего в кредит себя наиболше привести, и показать в том особливую свою, якобы истиннейшую верность и усердие, хотя б и ничего того не было.

Такими безсовестными поступками можно государя в такое состояние привезти, что времянем конечно обманется (каков бы он премудр ни был) подумает, что все то правда, что ему доносят и показывают, и для того принужден преклонится и во всех делах держатся того политика советов разсужаючи так, да кому ж мне поверити стало, когда ни в кому другом верности и радения нет …

1. To conceive as much as possible harmful intrigues against the conscientious, to smear and discredit all their good deeds in order to bereave them of enthusiasm and service zeal. 2. To instill doubt into sovereigns so that they would not believe anyone and all would be tainted with suspicion and would seem unworthy of favor; and sometimes suggest danger on occasions which can be appropriately seen as trifles, exaggerating them … and then to recommend oneself to remedy or appease the said occasion, as if no one else could be trusted or at least no one has enough wisdom to overcome the supposed difficulties. In truth, however, the design of those politicians or, to put it simply, cheats is to acquire favor with the sovereign through the said means, and to show their supposedly superior and true loyalty and zeal, even if there is nothing to worry about.

Through this dishonest conduct a sovereign can be brought to such
a state of mind that he eventually would be deceived (however wise
he is) and would think that all of it is true what they tell and report
him, and will be compelled to yield and on all occasions to follow
the advice of the said politician, thinking: "who else would I believe
if no one else has either loyalty or zeal . . .[16]

The tragic plot of *Khorev* is shaped by this sinister vision of courtly ways. Trediakovskii remarked that the play has two main plotlines: the pastoral love story and "Kii's suspicion of a supposed conspiracy between Khorev and Osnelda."[17] This suspicion, based on malicious exaggeration, is provoked by Stalverkh in the course of what might be seen as a courtly intrigue against a powerful general and a member of the royal family; Khorev complains to Kii that someone "prezhnei milosti tvoei menia lishil" ("has deprived me of your former favor" [2.2.25]). Kii is well aware of the dangerous powers of envy outlined by Saavedra and Volynskii (he even voices the possibility that the charges are "a deception" designed by the guards "to ruin the innocent Khorev" [4.3.52]) and is bent on resisting them, but eventually succumbs to a malicious reading of Khorev's intentions. Once admitted, the assumption that no one "can now be trusted" undermines Kii's belief that his true subjects "showed to me their inner selves," and erases the very possibility to recognize true loyalty and distinguish it from pretense.

In Benjamin's terms, Stalverkh incorporates the type of intriguer who possesses "a mastery of the workings of politics" based on anthropological insights and "corresponds to an ideal which was first outlined by Machiavelli and which was energetically elaborated in the creative and theoretical literature of the seventeenth century." In tragic drama, this intriguer is "the organizer of the plot": "In all circumstances it was necessary for the intriguer to assume a dominating position in the economy of the drama. For according to the theory of Scaliger, which in this respect harmonized with the interests of the baroque and was accepted by it, the real purpose of the drama was to communicate knowledge of the life of the soul, in the observation of which the intriguer is without equal."[18]

---

16   RGADA, f. 6, op. 1, no. 195, l. 8–9ob.
17   Trediakovskii, "Pis'mo . . . ot priiatelia k priiateliu," 100.
18   Benjamin, *Origin of German Tragic Drama*, 95, 98–99.

Duplicating the theatricality of dramatic genre in the play itself, Stalverkh exposes Kii and the play's audience to a "political anthropology," which views political practice as self-interested playacting. It is thanks to this anthropology that Stalverkh's hypothetical representation of the supposed conspiracy, which dangerously departs from truth, can achieve the "probability" ("vraisem-blance") prescribed for tragic plots by Aristotelian theory. As the true author of the *plot*—in the double sense of a political conspiracy and a set of fictional events—which makes *Khorev* a tragedy, Stalverkh follows a procedure similar to the one suggested in the *Poetics* for dramatic compositions. Dacier expressly derived the Aristotelian requirements for the "probability or necessity" of represented action from the secretiveness of courtly politics, the *arcana imperii*:

> a prodigious number of things happen every day, of which we know not the causes, especially those which concern Monarchs, which are properly the Subjects of Tragedy. Now a Poet is obliged to explain all the Causes of the Incidents which enter into the Composition of the Subject; and 'tis just to let him be Master of his Matter, so it should not be required of him to speak things as they are, but as they may, provided he follows either Necessity of Probability; for nothing more can be required of him.[19]

Just as a tragedian—like Sumarokov himself—is invited to inscribe the received plots, in fact fragmented accounts of political events, into a hypothetical set of probable motivations, the denunciator Stalverkh uses an overheard conversation between Osnelda and Khorev, indeed replete with dangerous ambiguities ("Befriend Zavlokh"—"I will raise to the throne your royal blood again … having once obtained this land's possession") to construct a narrative of a conspiracy in progress which can be accepted as plausible by courtly audiences both in Kiev of the dramatic legend and eighteenth-century Petersburg.

In the political idiom of Saavedra's treatise and Volynskii's letter, narratives of this kind are dismissed as malicious lies of evil councilors, and at first glance Sumarokov's Stalverkh seems to illustrate this logic. However, a closer look at his actions suggests a less straightforward—and even more

---

19   *Aristotle's Art of Poetry*, 141; see also *La Poétique d'Aristote*, 135.

disturbing—view of royally sponsored repression. Identifying Stalverkh with the type of the intriguer, Trediakovskii ridicules him for the lack of appropriate slyness: "Stalverkh ... is nothing but a very foolish slanderer. What cunning intriguer ... would smear someone who holds all the power in his hands when it is both impossible to harm him in any way and very probable that he can immediately take revenge when he finds out? And has ever slander stayed in secret?"[20] In fact, nowhere in the play do we find unambiguous proof of Stalverkh's malicious intent. His final suicide ("Half-maddened with remorse ... remembering Osnelda") might be construed as a sign of his secret passion for the captive princess, which would explain his wish to prevent a peace agreement with Zavlokh and to smear Khorev; but it could also be seen simply as a symptom of remorse for the death of an innocent victim. The uncertainty regarding Stalverkh's personal motives fits well with his position of a subordinate character, a function rather than a personality. Even more overtly than others, "Stalverkh, the first boyar of Kiev" is an allegory: his high rank forms the substance of his name, *stal-verkh*, almost literally translated as "upstart" and emphasizing his debt to service hierarchies of preferment rather than royal status or extraction enjoyed by all of the play's principal characters. As an allegory, Stalverkh—who has an unblemished service record ("You have been true to me, Stalverkh")—is able to incorporate at once "the two faces of the courtier: the intriguer, as the evil genius of their despots, and the faithful servant."[21] Whether or not his actions are driven by malice is not important: what matters is his mode of operation embedded in the "absolutist" structure of power.

E. A. Kasatkina has identified Stalverkh's denunciation of Khorev as the principal motor of the play's tragic plot and linked it to the political trials of the 1730s and 1740s and the common practice of "unverified denunciation."[22] Indeed, political trials—alongside triumphal theatrical festivities—shaped the "scenario of power" enacted during the first years of Elizabeth's rule. If Khorev's military feats are to be read as allusions to the victories of Field Marshal Münnich, the allegations raised against him by Stalverkh must have reminded viewers of the hasty trial over the field marshal presided by the empress in

---

20 Trediakovskii, "Pis'mo ... ot priiatelia k priiateliu," 98–99.

21 Benjamin, *Origin of German Tragic Drama*, 98.

22 Kasatkina, "Sumarokovskaia tragediia 40-kh–nachala 50-kh godov XVIII veka," 216; Stennik, *Zhanr tragedii v russkoi literature*, 35.

early 1742, in the first months after her ascension. Along with other high-ranking officials, Münnich was found guilty of treason and sentenced to death, replaced with exile. This was followed in 1743 by the trial of Natalia Lopukhina and several others who were charged with political conspiracy. In these notorious trials as well as in the records of more trivial cases involving seditious gossip constantly investigated and persecuted by the Secret Chancery, the horror scenario of a political conspiracy surfaced time and again.

In Stalverkh's version of events, Khorev, in order to overthrow Kii, conspired with a foreign ruler, Zavlokh, and simultaneously attempted to incite local troops to treason and revolt. Similarly, in the early 1740s there was constant gossip that Anna Leopoldovna and her son, the deposed Emperor Ivan, might be restored to power both by disenchanted guards and by the armed forces of their royal relatives, the kings of Prussia and Denmark and the Empress Queen Maria Theresa. This scenario appears to have been mentioned in public by Lopukhina's son, the lieutenant colonel Ivan Lopukhin, and both of them allegedly acted in accord with the Austrian ambassador Botta.[23] The official narratives behind the two trials concluded by public acts of punishment on the scaffold and publicized through special royal manifestoes were as problematic as Stalverkh's. According to Manstein, for example, Osterman and Münnich "could easily have disproved these accusations, had their defence been listened to; but their condemnation was determined on." Reflecting upon Lopukhina's trial, the Anonym concludes that "however we approach this case, we must admit that there was no apparent conspiracy."[24]

While the highly publicized political trials were little more than "legal fictions," invented stories whose effect on their audiences overshadowed the fragility of their truth claim, Sumarokov centered his dramatic fiction on the prosecution of Osnelda, closely linked to Elizabethan judicial practice. The notorious system of political surveillance and persecution known as "slovo i delo gosudarevo" (literally, "sovereign's word and deed") was designed

---

23 M. I. Semevskii, "N. F. Lopukhina," *Russkaia starina* 11 (1874): 9–10; M. I. Semevskii, "Tainaia kantseliariia v 1741–1761 gg.," *Russkaia starina* 12 (1875): 533–537. For a wealth of similar material, and for the following discussion of judicial practices, see two recent monographs: Evgenii Anisimov, *Dyba i knut. Politicheskii sysk i russkoe obshchestvo v XVIII veke veke* (Moscow: Novoe literaturnoe obozrenie, 1999); Elena Nikulina and Igor Kurukin, *Povsednevnaia zhizn' tainoi kantseliarii XVIII veka* (Moscow: Molodaia gvardiia, 2008).

24 Cristoph Hermann v. Manstein, *Contemporary Memoirs of Russia from the Year 1727 to 1744* (London: Longman et al., 1856), 330; *Perevoroty i voiny*, 487.

to bring any cases of possible lese-majesty to the attention of the Secret Chancery and the sovereign. While recognizing the dangers of slander and threatening slanderers with the worst punishments, royal decrees time and again proclaimed political denunciations a sacred duty of any subject and servitor. Among the offences imputed to Volynskii after he sent his letter to Empress Anna was his equivocal manner of speech: censuring his enemies at court without naming them, he was either smearing the innocent or concealing crimes which he was obliged to openly denounce.

Against this background Stalverkh's denunciation seems a natural course of action for a high-standing official. Lopukhina's case was initiated by Elizabeth's confidant and personal surgeon, Lestocq, who brought the supposed conspiracy to the empress's attention and arranged her personal meeting with an informer, inciting her to quick prosecution.[25] Similarly, Stalverkh reported the conversation between Khorev and Osnelda to Kii, who confirmed his testimony with that of a "captive" who had served as a messenger between Osnelda and Zavlokh. Stalverkh thus triggered a formal legal inquiry personally presided over by the prince, as was often the case in eighteenth-century Russia. In cases of lese-majesty and treason, suspicion ("podozrenie") was recognized as sufficient grounds for prosecution, revealing, as Evgenii Anisimov puts it, "the sovereign's unlimited right to punish and pardon" and "the sovereign will of the autocrat as the ultimate source of law."[26] Petzold, a Saxon representative in Petersburg, gave the following account of Lopukhina's trial conducted under Elizabeth's royal supervision:

> After their arrest the accused had voluntarily admitted everything that they knew. But since those utterances did not extend beyond … general displeasure with the empress' way of life and a wish to see the restoration of the previous government … [the prosecutors], based on the assumption of a certainly existing conspiracy, were not satisfied with this, and asked first the young Lopukhin whether he knew of other accomplices and planned assaults. The empress was present personally, and ignored all the wailing and begging at her feet … Lopukhina and Bestuzheva, as they were

---

25   Semevskii, "N. F. Lopukhina," 6.
26   Anisimov, *Dyba i knut*, 52.

raised on the beams with their arms broken insisted most movingly that they could be torn to pieces but will never slander themselves or admit more than they know or have done.[27]

After Kii recognizes the legal implications of Stalverkh's report—"dnes' nad bratom mne byt' sudieiu dolzhno" ("Today I will have to be the judge over my brother" [2.1.20])—he deals with Osnelda in a scene (4.7) that represents nothing less than a royal interrogation, and in significant points resembles Lopukhina's trial. Osnelda, now a prisoner rather than a captive, is brought to the stage in irons. Kii confronts her with the false charge of conspiracy and treason, based on witness testimony, and attempts to extort a confession of guilt, acknowledged in the Petrine judicial code, the *Kratkoe izobrazhenie protsessov ili sudebnykh tiazheb* of 1716, as "the best testimony in the world." Osnelda, frightened that Khorev might "remain under suspicion" ("v podozrenii ostanetsia"), admits to their mutual love and to their correspondence with Zavlokh but persistently denies any thought of treason, resorting to the only proof of innocence she can produce: the oath ("Klianusia vsem chto est', chto ia ne litsemeriu") which, according to Petrine law, could suffice for a requital. Kii counters this defense by demanding to see Zavlokh's letter that she had already burned; in legal terms it would have been qualified as written proof, "pismennoe svidetel'stvo." Moreover, he produces a charge she cannot refute: she spoke inappropriately about his royal person, an evident case of lese-majesty, specifically identified in Peter's 1716 *Artikul voinskii* and other legal acts as a crime punishable by death.[28] Osnelda must to admit to it, and Kii, who is generally aware of the advantages of clemency in a "just trial" ("Shchedrota khvalitsia na pravednom sude") feels compelled in this case to fulfill his "duty," passing a death sentence upon Osnelda: "Umri, obmanshchitsa!" ("You die, deceitful wretch!") (56–63; 74–78).

Kii's conviction of Osnelda, his most important royal act and the play's primary peripeteia, at once a *coup de théâtre* and a *coup d'état*, represents a

---

27   *SIRIO* 6 (St. Petersburg, 1870): 497–498.

28   *Polnoe sobranie zakonov Rossiiskoi imperii s 1649 g.,* 5 (1713–1719): 394, 400ff., 325, no. 3006. On policies encouraging denunciations, see Nikulina and Kurukin, *Povsednevnaia zhizn',* 158–175; on laws regarding lese-majesty and treason, and personal royal involvement in the persecution, see Anisimov, *Dyba i knut,* 50–57, 95–123.

point at which the dramatic idiom of tragic drama is alone capable to provide insight into the workings of absolutist power. Benjamin has established that the fundamental affinity between tragic drama and political theory was rooted in the vision of sovereignty "which takes as its example the special case in which dictatorial powers are unfolded." This vision, famously explored by Carl Schmitt and later Louis Marin, was developed in Machiavelli's wake by seventeenth-century political thinkers such as Gabriel Naudé and Cardinal Richelieu, whose works were read and translated in eighteenth-century Russia. Their work revolved around the notion of *coup d'état*, which had a broader meaning than today's usage would suggest and often referred to violent persecution of the enemies of the crown. Consequently, Benjamin continues, "[t]he drama makes a special point of endowing the ruler with the gesture of executive power [die Geste der Vollstreckung], and having him take part in the action with the words and behavior of a tyrant even where the situation does not require it." On the other hand, drama constantly shows the prince to be "almost incapable of making a decision," thus revealing a fundamental "antithesis between the power of the ruler and his capacity to rule."[29]

Addressing the major threats inherent in monarchy in his intricate, almost self-contradictory defense of autocracy completed simultaneously with Sumarokov's first tragedies, Tatishchev admitted the inevitable deficiency of a single ruler who would be at best "wise, just, mild and diligent" but not "free from faults," or worse, who "would give free reign to his passions," which would inevitably lead to "unjust violence and ruin of the innocent." Similarly problematic is the institution of councilors ("sovetniki") or favorites ("vremenshchiki"), created to correct the flaws of monarchy but itself prone to abuse by someone who "out of envy inflicts ruin on others … especially persons of distinction and merit." Finally, "the evil and impious" can usurp the royally sanctioned powers of the secret police designed "for the safety of the monarch" and invested with the right to inflict torture and death "for a single carelessly uttered word."[30] All of these issues are reenacted in the catastrophe of Sumarokov's play: judicial abuse brought about by deceitful counsel highlights the troubling incapacity of the solitary ruler.

---

29 Benjamin, *Origin of German Tragic Drama*, 69–71; Marin, "Théâtralité et pouvoir: Magie, machination, machine: *Médée* de Corneille."

30 Tatishchev, "Proizvol'noe i soglasnoe rassuzhdenie," 149.

In the play's finale, Kii himself recognizes the self-destructive implications of his injustice and in a fit of a remorse pledges the victorious Khorev to "cast me from the throne" (84), thus calling for the palace revolution predicted by Stalverkh.

A monarch's tragic failure must not take the form of Hamletian inaction, emphasized in most readings of Benjamin, but it may also emerge as its polar opposite—rash action. Any royal act risks missing the elusive middle ground between the only seemingly opposed vices of weakness and excessive force, upsetting the precarious balance prescribed by Machiavelli: the new prince "ought to be slow in giving credit to reports, not overhasty in his proceedings, and to beware of frighting himself with phantoms of his own raising; tempering his mercy with prudence in such a manner, that too much confidence may not put him off his guard, nor causeless jealousies make him insupportable."[31] In a well-intended but futile pursuit of this golden mean, Kii is trapped in constant chaotic oscillation between the extremes, as Trediakovskii reveals in his assessment of the character:

> As for Kii, his indifference is quite awkward: the Author represents him as good-tempered at one moment and as ill-tempered at the next; at one moment he is a kind man, at the other extremely wicked. This Kii resembles a weather vane: wherever the wind blows, he turns in the same direction. In short, the Author's Kii is a perfect hypochondriac, or a kind of madman.[32]

Trediakovskii's analysis resonates both with Benjamin's discussion of murderous insanity as "characteristic of the idea of the tyrant" in early modern drama[33] and with historical experiences of monarchy in eighteenth-century Russia. Volynskii, for example, argued in 1740 that while Empress Anna ought to judge with "mercy and terror" ("nadobno ei sud s grozoiu i s milostiiu imet'"), she in fact "sometimes becomes angry I do not even know for what reason," and generally "there is nothing worse in a state than inconstancy, and in sovereigns, secrecy."[34] In 1730, Empress Anna excused the Duke of Liria's

---

31   *The Works of Nicholas Machiavel*, 1: 625.
32   Trediakovskii, "Pis'mo," 98.
33   Benjamin, *Origin of German Tragic Drama*, 69.
34   "Zapiska o Volynskom," in *COIDR* 1858, otd. 2, 149.

past disfavor in her eyes by explaining to him "that it was such a critical time that she did not know who is her friend or enemy, and was compelled to believe everything some people said about me and others."[35]

Unlimited and unwarranted trust of some and mistrust of others, as well as the inconstancy of both displayed in Anna's very speech act, propelled the monarchy to regular acts of repression instead of debilitating it. In *Khorev*, its symbolic violence is heightened by a collision between the procedure of political and judicial power, on the one hand, and familial bonds, on the other, recognized by Kii in his statement "dnes' nad bratom mne byt' sudieiu dolzhno" ("Today I will have to be the judge over my brother"). Not surprisingly, Sumarokov follows the pattern prescribed by Aristotle: the principal character of a tragedy should be someone of "Eminent Quality, and of Great Reputation, some Illustrious person," and tragic plots should involve situations when "one Brother kills, or is killed, by his Brother, or a Father his Son, or a Mother her Son, or the Son his Mother, or do any such like thing."[36] However, for Sumarokov and his audiences this perspective on the tragic was not only a matter of literary poetics; rather, tragedy was suited to ventilate the anxieties of a dynastic and paternalistic autocracy that recognized familial relationships as a pattern of absolutist power.

This symbolic perspective, which made any persecution of a subject a potentially tragic violation of familial ties, was reinforced by the very real kinship between the monarchs and the victims of political trials. Natalia Lopukhina, for instance, could have been considered a relative of the royal house, since her husband (convicted during the same trial) belonged to the same noble clan as the first wife of Peter the Great, Tsaritsa Evdokiia Lopukhina. More specifically, Sumarokov's tragedy reveals the tension inherent in the precarious position of the heir to the throne, both an incarnation of dynastic stability and a threat to the current ruler. In 1745 Elizabeth revealed a mistrust of her own heir, Grand Duke Peter, so deep that she was compelled to remind him, according to Catherine's account "that her father, Peter I, had also an ungrateful son, and that he punished him by disinheriting him."[37] What Elizabeth—or, possibly, only

---

35 *Zapiski diuka Liriiskago i Bervikskago vo vremia prebyvaniia ego pri imperatorskom rossijskom dvore . . .* (St. Petersburg: V Gutenbergovoi Tipografii, 1845), 111.

36 *Aristotle's Art of Poetry*, 186–187, 241.

37 [Catherine, Empress of Russia], *Memoirs of the Empress Catherine II*, 55.

Catherine—chose to omit was the fact that Peter I had his son and her brother, Tsarevich Aleksei, tried and killed. (Elizabeth herself must have feared a similar fate when her mother's affair aroused Peter's wrath several years later.)

Aleksei's death—characterized by Teplov in 1765 as an appropriate subject for a tragedy, and indeed dramatized in several French plays—apparently resonated with tragic poetics; specifically, it could have reminded spectators of Racine's *Phédre*, a central text of the French dramatic canon and a model for Sumarokov's *Khorev*, where a royal father sentences to death his son and heir falsely accused in the course of a political intrigue.[38] Similarly, in the demise of Khorev, Kii's "brother and son" (54)—which might be read as a fictionalized reenactment of the unspeakable death of Tsarevich Aleksei—the ultimate political catastrophe is engendered by the abuse of familial power, the paternalistic "sovereign'ty of love," tainted and deluded by the Machiavellian politics of mistrust and suspicion. It is in the Machiavellian discourse of political treatises that we find an answer to the rhetorical question that a later critic used to outline the tragic effects of Sumarokov's play and, specifically, the sentencing of Osnelda as one of *Khorev*'s truly tragic scenes:

> what I do not understand is why Kii is so credulous; why is he so cruel that he ordered Osnelda to be poisoned, who did him no harm, before the battle was over? and, what is even more unjust, he showed himself a tyrant through Osnelda's death without any reliable proof of his brother's treason ... Does not this barbaric act appall all spectators? Do Kii's actions not make him vicious in the eyes of the world?[39]

The false charges brought against the main characters drive *Khorev*'s plot, putting into question the legal procedures that seem to corroborate them. Finally revealed as little more than "legal fiction," these charges provide a

---

38 Kirill Ospovat, "Petr i Aleksei: k literaturnoi semantike istoriograficheskogo siuzheta," *Sobranie sochinenii. K 60-letiiu L. I. Soboleva* (Moscow: Vremia novostei, 2006), 442–455; Alexei Evstratov and Pierre Frantz, "Pierre le Grand au théâtre, entre tragédie encomiastique et comédie bourgeoise," in *Rossiia i Frantsiia: XVIII-XX vv. Lotmanovskie chtenia*, ed. D. Alexander et al. (Moscow: RGGU, 2013), 30–49; Kasatkina, "Sumarokovskaia tragediia 40-kh–nachala 50-kh godov XVIII veka," 243.

39 A. Gruzintsov, "Ekzamen 'Khoreva,'" *Novosti literatury* 4 (1802): 157–158.

nucleus for the tragic fiction that is Sumarokov's play. This was a technique not uncommon to neoclassical drama. The action of Metastasio's *La Clemenza di Tito*, which inaugurated Elizabethan court theater in 1742, focuses on a failed plot against the emperor and its subsequent investigation, which includes a royal interrogation of a falsely accused man subsequently sentenced to death, who is dramatically spared in the play's last moments.

Indeed, the affinity between *Khorev* and the judicial practice of Elizabethan Russia is not a matter of incidental topical allusion, but rather a symptom of the fundamental issues inherent in tragedy as a genre. Aristotle's definition of a tragic catastrophe hinges on the problematization of guilt and retribution: since pity is aroused "by the Misfortunes of those who are like ourselves" and fear "from the Miseries of those who deserve better Luck," the best tragic character is someone "who is become miserable, by some involuntary fault" and not as a result of "a Remarkable Crime."[40] Besides the moral imperfection common to stage characters and spectators, the tragic effect highlights the mysteries of (in)justice, the discrepancy between crime and punishment. In Racinian tragedy, according to Barthes, "Good, Blood, the Father, the Law—in short, anteriority becomes incriminating in essence. This form of absolute guilt suggests what in totalitarian politics is called objective guilt. The world is a tribunal: if the accused is innocent, the judge is guilty; hence the accused takes upon himself the judge's transgression."[41]

The problematization of justice was central for early modern tragedy at least since Guarini's *Il pastor fido*, where Amarillis, the virtuous heroine, is falsely accused of amorous transgression, interrogated and tried by an official, the "Chief Minister to the Priest," and formally sentenced to death, only to be saved at the moment of the execution by a fortunate recognition. Once again, Guarini's interrogation scene is permeated with legal language: the minister asks Amarillis "who hath been the cause of thy offence," and she attempts to draw on witness testimony ("witness without faith," replies the judge) and recourses to an oath. To the judicial approximations of truth based on assumptions of malicious dissimulation, both Amarillis and Osnelda oppose assertions of sincerity akin to Kii's idyllic vision of political order, insights into the inner selves provided by oath and

---

40 *Aristotle's Art of Poetry*, 186–187.
41 Barthes, *On Racine*, 46.

confession: "Actions are false comments on our hearts ... The heart may be seen too with th' eys o' th' mind," says Amarillis, and Osnelda vows: "Klianusia vsem chto est', chto ia ne litsemeriu" ("I swear by all the gods that I am not dissembling" [4.7. 60]). As with Sumarokov's Osnelda, Amarillis's staunch insistence on her innocence ("have not I / Transgrest the Law and innocently dye") provokes the wrath of the prosecutor: "Defence offence doth breed!"[42] Their collision, in many ways central for both plays, radically challenges the validity of established law, incapable of distinguishing between guilt and innocence; as Osnelda says to Kii, "Ty sam sebia vinish', nevinnogo vinia" ("You condemn yourself when you condemn one innocent" [59; 76]).

Osnelda's defense resonates with the critique of law as originating in the "insanity" and "prejudice" of men rather than heavenly justice, voiced by Astrada in her apology of love. Indeed, love played an important role in the pastoral revival and revision of the Aristotelian concept of tragic justice. The 1739 essay on drama cited Racine's *Phèdre* as a good example of dramatic didacticism, and referred to Racine's own assessment of the tragedy in his preface:

> Les moindres fautes y sont sévèrement punies ... Les faiblesses de l'amour y passent pour de vraies faiblesses. Les passions n'y sont présentées aux yeux que pour montrer tout le désordre dont elles sont cause: et le vice y est peint partout avec des couleurs qui en font connaître et haïr la difformité.

> The smallest faults are severely punished ... The weaknesses caused by love are considered true weaknesses. Passions are only displayed to fully reveal the disorder they have caused, and vice is depicted everywhere with such colors which expose its deformity and instill hatred for it.[43]

This condemnation of love not only concerns the pernicious passion that drives Phèdre, but it also includes the blameless pastoral lovers, Hyppolite and Aricie. This directly contradicts the apology of love delivered in the tragedy by

---

42   *Giovanni Battista Guarini's "Il pastor fido,"* 108–110.
43   Racine, *Théâtre complet*, vol. 2.

Théramène and—in a direct allusion to Aristotle's formulations—aligns the conservative moral order that Racine's preface appeals to with an impossible justification of Hyppolite's unmerited death precipitated by sinister suspicions and false accusations. The skillfully orchestrated contradiction between the pastoral vision of an innocent erotic freedom suggested by the text and the established prohibitive morality alluded to in the preface develops a tension crucial for the pastoral tradition. Substituting love for horrible crimes of ancient myth as the "error or frailty" that governs the fate of the principle characters, pastoral plots both reenact and question the idea of guilt inherent in Aristotelian definitions. In *Il pastor fido* love is symbolized by Amarillis's meeting with her lover, Mirtillo, which assumes the appearance of transgression in the eyes of the authorities but is presented as an innocent error to the play's audience. In *Khorev*, in significant respects modeled after *Phédre*, it is love that Kii, misled by Stalverkh's accusations, blames for his future ruin: "Chto delaesh' ty, chto, prokliataia liubov'!" ("What dost thou affect, thou cursed love!" [4.1.50]). The severely punished conspiracy of the pastoral lovers is not an outright fabrication, but rather a malicious misreading of their morally and politically harmless—or, potentially, even beneficent—amorous accord, for as Kii admits: "My vedali uzh to, chto s nei liubilis' vy, / No tainstvu semu davali tolk my lozhno" (5.5.72; We knew / Already of this love, but finding out this secret, / Unwisely gave to it a false interpretation," 83–84).

The error of Osnelda's persecutors, who mistake amorous intrigue for sedition, is inscribed in the precarious dynamic of political containment implied in tragic poetics. According to Riccoboni, stage representations of "Intrigues of Ambition" attract a public that has a claim to "a great Share in the Government," while interest for love stories is natural for a polity content "with their happy Government, through a long Succession of Years under the wise Direction of their Princes."[44] The pastoral love plot implies an idyllic vision of monarchic harmony on and off stage, which—at least in the space of a tragedy like *Khorev*—defuses the threats of sedition associated with the political involvement of subjects. Together with the literary language as such this logic spread from established genres of literary fiction into the discourses of Elizabethan politics, which intertwined power and the erotic. Sumarokov's

---

44 Riccoboni, *An Historical and Critical Account*, 329–330. See also Riccoboni, *Histoire du théâtre*, 1: 314–315.

treatment of Osnelda's trial resembles contemporary interpretations of Lopukhina's case, reported, among others, by the Anonym: "at that time many persons who deserve utmost trust considered this conspiracy as fabricated" and "maintained that the whole case consisted of empty speeches of two discontented ladies," namely Lopukhina herself and her friend Countess Bestuzheva, who resented the fate of Lopukhina's lover, Löwenwolde, and Count Mikhail Golovkin, Bestuzheva's brother (and Sumarokov's one-time patron), both of whom were convicted and exiled in 1742 together with Münnich.[45] In this version of events, just like in Sumarokov's play, political resentment was ventilated in conversations driven by "feminine" motifs of familial and erotic love as opposed to the "masculine" dangers of direct political action.

Sumarokov's dramatization of Osnelda's demise for court performances could have resonated with the spectacular finale of Lopukhina's trial, the public punishment of convicts on a scaffold—designated in official sources as "theater" ("teatr," as Semevskii emphasizes), in August 1743.[46] This event made such an impression on the Russian public that the French astronomer Chappe D'Auteroche, who visited Petersburg eighteen years later, in 1761–1762, was able to give a vivid and detailed description of it in his travelogue:

> Everybody who has been at St. Petersburg, knows that Mad. Lapouchin was one of the finest women belonging to the court of the Empress Elizabeth: she was intimately connected with a foreign ambassador, then engaged in a conspiracy. Mad. Lapouchin, who was supposed to be an accomplice in this conspiracy, was condemned, by the Empress Elizabeth, to undergo the punishment of the knout. She appeared at the place of execution in a genteel undress, which contributed still to heighten her beauty. The sweetness of her countenance, and her vivacity, were such as might indicate indiscretion, but not even the shadow of guilt; although I have been assured by every person of whom I have made inquiry, that she was really guilty. Young, lovely, admired and sought for at the court, of which she was the life and spirit; instead of the number of admirers her beauty

---

45   *Perevoty i voiny*, 486–487.

46   Semevskii, "N. F. Lopukhina," 193; for contemporary accounts of the trial, see M. I. Semevskii, "N. F. Lopukhina. 1699–1763. Epizod iz eia zhizni," *Russkii vestnik* 29 (1860): 17, 5–52.

usually drew after her, she then saw herself surrounded only by executioners. She looked on them with astonishment, seeming to doubt whether such preparations were intended for her: one of the executioners then pulled off a kind of cloak which covered her bosom; her modesty taking the alarm made her start back a few steps; she turned pale, and burst into into tears: her clothes were soon after stripped off, and in a few moments she was quite naked to the waist, exposed to the eager looks of a vast concourse of people profoundly silent. One of the executioners then seized her by both hands, and turning half round, threw her on his back, bending forwards, so as to raise her a few inches from the ground: the other executioner then laid hold of her delicate limbs ... This executioner then took a kind of whip called knout ... and leaping backwards, gave a stroke with the end of the whip, so as to carry away a flap of skin from the neck to the bottom of the back: then striking his feet against the ground he took his aim for applying a second blow parallel to the former; so that in a few moments all the skin of her back was cut away in small ships, most of which remained hanging to the shift. Her tongue was cut out immediately after, and she was directly banished into Siberia.[47]

Chappe's account is both accurate and invested with literary appeal achieved, one might argue, with means akin to those employed by Sumarokov. As all other memoirists, Chappe (who could have seen Lopukhina after her return from exile in 1762) does not fail to mention that the forty-three-year-old lady-in-waiting "was one of the finest women belonging to the court of the Empress Elizabeth"; as Jane Rondeau's earlier impressions of her confirm, she was apparently a paragon of the new courtly gallantry and an object of considerable erotic fascination. Building on the sexual charisma of his heroine, Chappe aligns his depiction of the punishment with the pastoral contrast between the brutal violence of the judicial apparatus—symbolized in plays from *Il pastor fido* to Racine's *Iphigénie* by execution scenes where the heroines nearly die—and female weakness set off

---

47   Chappe d'Auteroche, *A Journey into Siberia: Made by Order of the King of France* (London: T. Jefferys, 1770), 338–339. See also a recent critical edition of Chappe's original: Chappe d'Auteroche, *Voyage en Sibérie: fait par ordre du roi en 1761*, ed. Michel Mervaud (Oxford: Voltaire Foundation, 2004), 2: 447–449.

by the absence of "even the shadow of guilt." If in tragedies like *Khorev* the demise of the *jeune première* becomes a source of aesthetic pleasure, Chappe's punishment scene reveals the workings of this standard yet paradoxical reaction. In a manner that—as Michel Mervaud indicates—directly anticipates de Sade, its audience, replacing the multitudes of Lopukhina's earlier "admirers," takes erotic satisfaction in her nudity, submission, and physical suffering.

This pleasure, conveyed from the immediate eyewitnesses to Chappe's readers and enhanced by an engraving printed in his book, does not, however, imply a straightforward approval of the judicial procedure behind the punishment. Appealing to the conflicted sensibility of the audience, it molds a fascination for suffering with a compassion for the victim, reminiscent of Aristotelian tragic "pity." This complex reaction is implied in an episode recounted by Chappe in the chapter *Of the laws, of punishments, and of exile* next to Lopukhina's punishment: a nameless serf girl was also "stripped ... to the waist" and publicly flogged "on account of some neglect," although her "eyes ... pleaded for mercy; which her beauty should seem to have insured her, independent of her tears."[48]

In Racinian tragedy, as Barthes remarks, the "disrobing" of the female self, including "tears whose erotic power is so familiar," "is always ... an attempt to compel pity (sometimes carried out to the point of sadistic prov-ocation)."[49] This mechanism underlies the aesthetic effects of pastoral tragedy and its stagings of justice. In *Il pastor fido* Amarillis's treatment is summa-rized in this way:

> (Oh
> Sad spectacle!) being brought before the Priest,
> Did not alone from the beholders wrest
> Salt tears; but (trust me) made the marble melt,
> And the hard flint the dint of pity felt,
> Shee was accus'd, convict, and sentence past
> All in a trice.[50]

---

48 D'Auteroche, *A Journey Into Siberia*, 337; d'Auteroche, *Voyage en Sibérie* II, 446.
49 Barthes, *On Racine*, 15.
50 *Giovanni Battista Guarini's "Il pastor fido,"* 133.

In Sumarokov, a mixture of compassion and desire permeates Khorev's heavily eroticized, almost necrophilic, complaint after Osnelda's death:

Толь малодушным быть хоть мужу и не должно,
Но мысли горькия преодолеть не можно:
Оснельда во слезах пред очи предстает,
Которыя она о мне при смерти льет.
Воображаются мне все ея заразы …
И представляются мне все утехи те,
Которых ожидал в драгой я красоте. (5.4.75)

Although a man must not be fainthearted,
I cannot overcome bitter thoughts.
Osnelda comes to me, and she weeps,
Tears shed remembering our love even in death.
All her charms come back, as in a gentle daydream …
And all the joys we sought, and all the joys we planned,
Which I expected from the beloved's beauty. (85)

As Zavlokh immediately makes clear, Khorev's grief provides a pattern for a public emotional response to Osnelda's demise:

Ты сделала, о дщерь! хотя упал наш трон,
И победителям и побежденным стон.
И если в аде глас Хоревов дух твой тронет,
Ликуй что по тебе Герой великий стонет,
Уж не почтет тебя невольницею ад,
Заплачет по тебе с Хоревом весь сей град. (75)

Although our throne is lost, O daughter, you have brought
Conquered and conqueror past limits of despair.
And if into the depths a prince's sobs may reach you,
Rejoice! a hero weeps for that he truly loved you.
The dusky lands you tread will judge you freed at last,
For all the city mourns your loss with Prince Khorev. (85)

In the play's conclusion, Zavlokh's lines provide a blueprint for the emotional effects of tragedy as such, and *Khorev* in particular, as they outline the function that "tragic" compassion is meant to assume both in Sumarokov's Kiev and at Elizabeth's court. Among its audiences Osnelda's death sets in motion a pattern of eroticized collective sensibility shared by the whole polity ("grad"), reaffirming the order of power through a renewed emotional bond between ruler and subjects, "conquered and conqueror." Breaking with the "masculine" hard-heartedness styled as virtue, it recasts pastoral compassion for amorous suffering as a full-fledged "aesthetic ideology," an emotional paradigm of a renewed social coherence.

This renewal of the political order depends on a reassessment of the royal role fulfilled in *Khorev*'s last scenes but prepared from the beginning of the play. If the execution of Osnelda is, according to Gruzintsov, a barbarian act that appalls "all spectators" and presents Kii as "vicious in the eyes of all the world," this perspective is not alien to Sumarokov's tragedy and its original context. In his discussion of the origins of government, Tatishchev distinguished between two types of domination: the power of a conqueror ("preodolitel' ili khishchnik") who subdues his enemies with violence, and that of a "true lord" ("suschii gospodin") who establishes his rule "on the right of charity, like a father over his children," or on "a voluntary compact."[51] Accordingly, the young and gallant Khorev lectures the old warrior Kii on virtuous rule and condemns "brutishness under the guise of courage," which culminates in the lack of empathy at the sight of those in misery ("Nepopechitel'ny zria bednykh v gor'kom plache" [2.2.23; 57]). In a speech to Stalverkh, Kii himself professes compassion: "Smushchaiusia, kak zriu ia i zlodeev v gore" ("I am perplexed to see in grief even a villain" [2.1.20; 55]).

The compassionate royal gaze directed at the miserable and the guilty, emphasized in Sumarokov's play, was institutionalized by court theater centered on tragedies, where it became a matter of display and public performance in its own right. Building on political and poetic visions of pity, Kii's final fit of compassion for Osnelda models the theatrical sensibility of the royal spectator—a new facet of Elizabeth's ambivalent "scenario of power" incorporated by the double figure of Kii, the benevolent monarch and

---

51   Tatishchev, "Istoriia rossiiskaia," 1: 360.

murderous tyrant. In his preface to Aristotle, Dacier recounts the well-known anecdote about Alexander of Pherae, a Greek tyrant who had to leave a performance of a tragedy because "he was asham'd to be seen to weep, at the misfortunes of Hecuba and Polyxena, when he daily imbrud his Hands in the Blood of his Citizens; he was afraid that his Heart should be truly mollify'd, that the Spirit of Tyranny would now leave the possession of his Breast."[52] Conversely, in Elizabethan Russia royal encouragement of national tragedy and court theater developed after the cessation of political trials (Lopukhina's was the last). Tragic theater affirmed the empress's new role as a compassionate ruler and reenhanced her bond with her subjects through collective experiences of pity, while simultaneously upholding and reviving in public imagination the threats of royal terror.

---

52 *Aristotle's Art of Poetry*, preface. This anecdote was, evidently, followed by Shakespeare in the Mousetrap scene of *Hamlet*.

PART III

POETIC JUSTICE: COUP D'ÉTAT, POLITICAL THEOLOGY, AND THE POLITICS OF SPECTACLE IN THE RUSSIAN *HAMLET*

TRAGEDY AND POLITICAL THEOLOGY

Gamlet, a loose but evident adaptation of Shakespeare's *Hamlet*, was Sumarokov's second tragedy published in 1748, soon after *Khorev*, and produced alongside it after the formal inauguration of Russian-language court performances in around 1750. Sumarokov, who shared and himself reiterated commonplace neoclassical criticisms of Shakespeare's "irregularity," greatly simplified the plot and provided it with a happy ending. His Gamlet (Hamlet), informed by his confidant Armans of Klavdii's (Claudius's) crime, is urged by a dream vision of his father to avenge his murder. He confronts Gertruda (Gertrude), compelling her to confess and repent, but out of love for Ofeliia (Ophelia), he hesitates to punish Klavdii and Polonii (Polonius). Meanwhile, the two plan the murder of Gertruda, which would allow Klavdii to marry the virtuous Ofeliia. Dispatching assassins to kill Gamlet, they stay behind to execute Ofeliia for refusing to comply with their plan. The palace is stormed by the triumphant Gamlet backed by the populace. He kills Klavdii off stage, and after a long hesitation, pardons Polonii at Ofeliia's request, but Polonii ultimately takes his own life.

Sumarokov's *Gamlet*, its treatment of the tragic and its relationship to the Shakespearean original have been analyzed by Marcus Levitt in a valuable study that in many respects provides a point of departure for my discussion. Specifically, Levitt addresses the play's happy ending, its single most important deviation from the English *Hamlet*, and points to Trediakovskii's criticism of *Khorev*'s dismal outcome, which in Levitt's terms "may serve as a working description of *[G]amlet*." Indeed, in an internal review of

Gamlet commissioned by the Academy's administration prior to the play's publication in 1748, Trediakovskii contrasted the endings of Sumarokov's two first tragedies, and reiterated his argument in the lengthy 1750 review of Sumarokov's oeuvre:

> According to its most important and primary statute, tragedy is produced in order to inculcate the audience with love for virtue and an extreme hatred for evil and a contempt for it in a pleasant rather than didactic fashion. Therefore ... one must always give the upper hand to good deeds, and evildoing, however many successes it may have, must always end up defeated, in this way imitating the very actions of God.[1]

Levitt draws from Trediakovskii's reasoning to highlight the crucial religious dimension of Sumarokov's *Gamlet*, which, incidentally, happened to be the first Russian example of a Christian tragedy, a relatively rare but important subgenre of classicist tragedy. In a reply to Trediakovskii's critique, Sumarokov claimed that his play resembled Shakespeare's only in the "To be or not to be" soliloquy and Klavdii's "falling down on his knees" in a futile attempt to reconcile with God (2.1). Staging in a parallel scene (2.3) his version of Gertrude's repentance, Sumarokov greatly amplified Shakespeare's laconic reference to religious redemption. Levitt establishes the significance of these scenes and concludes that Sumarokov's *Gamlet* centers on the metaphysical problem of "the existence of evil (for example, in Claudius)" and "the working out of divine theodicy on earth." He further opposes this reading both to the "traditional notions of the tragic" and to the "common Russian view," which stresses the "political message of Sumarokov's plays" so

---

1   Levitt, "Sumarokov's Russianized *Hamlet*: Texts and Contexts," in *Early Modern Russian Letters: Texts and Contexts*, 86–87; V. K. Trediakovskii, "Pis'mo, v kotorom soderzhitsia rassuzhdenie o stikhotvorenii, ponyne na svet izdannom ... pisannoe ot priiatelia k priiateliu," in *Kritika XVIII veka*, ed. A. M. Ranchin and V. L. Korovin (Moscow: Olimp, 2002), 92 (I borrow Levitt's English rendering of both passages with slight emendations). For Trediakovskii's review of *Gamlet*, see P. P. Pekarskii, *Istoriia imperatorskoi Akademii nauk v Peterburge* (St. Petersburg: Tipografiia Imperatorskoi Akademii nauk, 1873), 2: 131–132. For a recent reproduction of a damaged copy, see Starikova, ed., *Teatral'naia zhizn' Rossii v epokhu Elizavety Petrovny*, vol. 2, bk. 1, 793.

that "some commentators have seen in [*Gamlet*] an allegorical defense of Empress Elizabeth's ascension to the throne."[2] While Levitt's emphasis on the play's religious aspects is indeed pivotal, his positioning of the religious, in general, and *Gamlet,* in particular, beyond tragic poetics and politics seems to merit reconsideration.

Indeed, beginning with Benjamin's famous study, scholarship has amply demonstrated the intrinsic relationship of early modern European tragedy to political theology, a sphere where, in Carl Schmitt's well-known formulation, "all significant concepts of the modern theory of state" emerged and functioned as "secularized theological concepts … transferred from theology to the theory of state," so that "the omnipotent God became the omnipotent lawgiver," and the "exception in jurisprudence is analogous to the miracle in theology."[3] Sumarokov's Polonii claims as much (2.2):

> Кому прощать Царя? народ в его руках.
> Он Бог, не человек, в подверженных странах.[4]

> Who's to forgive the king? The nation's in his hands.
> He is not man but God through all the realm he rules. (102)

Drawing on Schmitt, Benjamin centers his reading of tragic drama, *Trauerspiel,* on a political metaphysics that styles political catastrophes on stage as a revelation (*Offenbarung*) of "both history and the higher power which checks its vicissitudes."[5] It is now well established that the parallel and amalgamation of divine and political order resulting in a sacralization of monarchy was fundamental for eighteenth-century Russia.[6] It is hardly

---

2   Levitt, "Sumarokov's Russianized *Hamlet*: Texts and Contexts," 95–96.

3   Carl Schmitt, *Political Theology: Four Chapters on the Concept of Sovereignty*, trans. George Schwab (Cambridge, MA: Harvard University Press, 1985), 36.

4   Sumarokov, *Polnoe sobranie vsekh sochinenii*, 3: 78. I will quote the text of *Gamlet* from this edition, with page numbers in parentheses. I also consult Maksim Amelin's republication of the play, which takes into account Sumarokov's list of corrections to the original edition: *Novaia Iunost'* 4 (2003), accessed June 16, 2015, http://magazines.russ.ru/nov_yun/2003/4/amel.html.

5   Benjamin, *Origin of the German Tragic Drama,* 70.

6   B. A. Uspenskii and V. M. Zhivov, "Tsar' i Bog (Semioticheskie aspekty sakralizatsii monarkha v Rossii)," in B. A. Uspenskii, *Izbrannye Trudy*, vol. 1 (Moscow: Iazyki

surprising, then, that Trediakovskii's vision of tragedy as a display of divine justice is loaded with political overtones. He reinforces his criticism of *Khorev* with a reference to Barclay's *Argenis* (which he was translating around the same time) where the triumph of justice in works of fiction was associated with the monarchy's victory over revolt and dissent (see part 1). While Trediakovskii's political metaphysics differs in its radical optimism from the much more somber "baroque" view reconstructed by Benjamin, they share a fundamental alignment of politics with providence and the focus on sovereignty as manifested in a state of emergency. According to Benjamin, the "theological-juridical mode of thought" derived the idea of royal power from the metaphysically charged tension between catastrophe and restoration, so that the monarch could emerge as "the great restorer of the disturbed order of creation." Consequently, in baroque drama "the conflicts of a state of creation without grace" are relegated to the political sphere of the court where kingship reveals itself as a "secularized redemptive power."[7] Accordingly, the happy endings central for Trediakovskii's view of tragic poetics are brought about by decisionist gestures of power constitutive of sovereignty, both royal and divine, and simultaneously situated on the metaphysical and political planes. Specifically, the triumph of virtue in the finale of Sumarokov's *Gamlet*, praised by Trediakovskii in the 1748 review, amounts to a political act, the seizure of power accompanied by the downfall of the previous ruler presented as an impostor and tyrant, along with his main accomplice. It is the (re)establishment of righteous sovereignty that fulfills divine will, while the finally defeated "evildoing" is identified with the political crimes of usurpation and abuse of royal authority.

This constellation was not incidental to Sumarokov's play or to Trediakovskii's criticism; in fact, it was central for the functioning of tragedy as a political genre. Among political treatises translated into Russian in the early eighteenth century was Innocent Gentillet's *Anti-Machiavel: Discours sur les moyens de bien gouverner et maintenir en bonne paix un royaume ou autre*

---

slavianskoi kultury, 1996); Michael Cherniavsky, *Tsar and People: Studies in Russian Myths* (New Haven: Yale University Press, 1961); Paul Kléber Monod, *The Power of Kings: Monarchy and Religion in Europe, 1589–1715* (New Haven: Yale University Press, 1999); Ernest Zitser, *The Transfigured Kingdom: Sacred Parody and Charismatic Authority at the Court of Peter the Great* (Ithaca, NY: Cornell University Press, 2004).

7   Benjamin, *Origin of the German Tragic Drama*, 62–66, 81, 130.

principauté (*A Discourse upon the Meanes of Wel Governing*, 1576), a work popular across Europe in the French original and translations into Latin and various vernaculars. Gentillet warns against tyranny in the following terms:

> it is impossible ... that a tyrant or cruell prince (for all is one) can long endure ... And if sometimes it please God to suffer him to live long, it is to cause him to take the higher leap, that in the end hee may have the sorer fall: As wee see it well painted in poets tragoedies, where many tyrants are seene ... to drinke the poison, to the stab the dagger in their bosomes, or hang themselves on the gibet, in the sight of all the world ... we must not say, that such tragoedies are but poeticall fictions; for hystories are full of such tragicall ends of tyrants, which have delighted to shed their subjects bloud, and to handle them cruellie.[8]

If tragedy was suited to reveal divine presence in royal history, then the parallel between Sumarokov's *Gamlet* and the scenarios of power enacted by Empress Elizabeth does not appear as superficial or incidental as Levitt seems to suggest. Conceived with an eye for possible performances at court, *Gamlet* could have hardly avoided allusions to the palace revolution of November 1741 that brought Elizabeth to Russia's throne and was revived in public memory through yearly celebrations of the empress's "ascension day."[9] Among other things, Elizabeth's triumph encompassed the punishment of "evildoers": the exile of the Braunschweig dynasty and the widely publicized trial of Münnich, Ostermann, and Golovkin in 1742. The idiom of political theology implying a direct divine supervision of the Russian monarchy and the ruling dynasty was omnipresent in Elizabethan ceremonial culture largely dominated (especially

---

8   Innocent Gentillet, A *Discourse upon the Meanes of Wel Governing* (London: n.p., 1602; reprint Amsterdam: Da Capo Press, 1969), 200. For a scholarly edition of the original, see Innocent Gentillet, *Anti-Machiavel: Discours sur les moyens de bien gouverner et maintenir en bonne paix un royaume ou autre principauté* (Geneva: Droz, 1968). For the unpublished Russian translation, see *Feorimato ili Rassuzhdenie o prostom i mirnom tsarstva ili koe-libo oblasti pravlenii ...*, OR RNB, OSRK, fond II. 27.

9   On political allusions in *Gamlet*, see Vsevoldskii-Gerngross, *Teatr v Rossii pri imperatritse Elizavete Petrovne*, 110–112.

in the first years of the reign) by court sermons.[10] This culture extended to fictionalized dramatic reenactments of her coup, which included the Novgoro-dian baroque drama *Stefanotokos* (*The Crown-bearer*, 1742), Bonecchi's opera *Bellerofonte* staged in 1750 by the Italian court opera company, and, most importantly, a performance of Voltaire's tragedy *Mérope* (1743), chosen by Sérigny and his French actors to celebrate an anniversary of Elizabeth's corona-tion in 1746. This performance was followed by a printing of the festivities' libretto both in French and in the Russian translation carried out by Tredia-kovskii (who, by the way, pointed to *Mérope* as a source for Sumarokov).

The play's plot bears apparent similarities to *Gamlet*: Egiste, the legitimate heir to the throne, has to defeat the upstart usurper Polifonte and restore the kingdom to himself and his oppressed mother, the legitimate queen Mérope (in the Russian context an allusion to Elizabeth and her nephew and heir apparent, Petr Fedorovich).[11] Voltaire, as his recent commentators note with some surprise, develops for his tragedy a "political content," absent from his sources, which involves "the overthrow of the tyrant and the triumph of legitimate monarchy" with an unequivocal divine sanction.[12] Voltaire's characters expressly anticipate the belated divine vengeance for the tyrant that indeed unfolds in the fifth act. In his rendering of the play's summary, Trediakovskii enhances the theological reso-nances of Mérope's triumph with the Church Slavonic term *mzdovozdaianie*, "retribution," a concept current in the homiletic idiom and specifically applied to Elizabeth's ascension in a festive sermon of 1744.[13] Similarly, in Sumarokov's *Gamlet*, the downfall of Klavdii and Polonii is foreshadowed by the repentant Gertruda as divine punishment:

---

10 See N. Popov, "Pridvornye propovedi v tsarstvovanie Elizavety Petrovny," *in Letopisi russkoi literatury i drevnosti,* ed. N. S. Tikhonravov (Moscow: V tipografii Gracheva I Komi, 1859), vol. 2, otd. 3, 1–33; Jelena Pogosjan, "Kniaz' Vladimir v russkoi ofitsial'noi kul'ture nachala pravleniia Elizavety Petrovny," in *Trudy po russkoi i slavianskoi filologii. Literaturovedenie 5* (Tartu: Tartu Ülikooli kirjastus, 2005), 11–36.

11 For the text and analysis of the 1746 Russian summary of *Mérope,* see Kirill Ospovat, "Iz istorii russkogo pridvornogo teatra 1740-kh gg."

12 Jack R. Vrooman and Janet Godden, "Introduction [to *Mérope*]," in Voltaire, *The Complete Works*, 17: 122–124.

13 Pankratii Charnysskii, *Slovo v vysochaishee prisutstvie … Elisavety Petrovny i naslednika eia … Petra Feodorovicha … o delakh mzdovozdaiatel'nykh ot Boga …,* in Arsenii Mogilianskii, *Rech' k eia imperatorskomu velichestvu s ego imperatorskim vysochestvom v monarshei svite k Troitskoi Sergievoi lavre priblizhivsheisia … skazovannaia iiunia 6 dnia, 1744 god*a ([St. Petersburg: Tipografiia Akademii nauk], 1744).

Уже и так Творца ты варвар раздражил,

Брегись, чтоб вскоре он тебя не поразил,

Он терпит; но терпеть когда нибудь престанет,

И в час, когда не ждешь, в твою погибель грянет. (2.2.78)

Sufficient is your wrong to tax our patient God.

Beware, lest He decide to strike you down at last.

His patience has its bounds, and when these have been traversed,

That hour He will decree your unexpected downfall. (103)

Sumarokov's *Gamlet*, then, belongs to the long line of tragedies centered on an experience of history associated with often violent court politics and permeated with a political metaphysics common to the dramatic tradition and the institution of monarchy. This perspective gives consistency to the peculiar genealogy of Sumarokov's play that simultaneously drew on Voltaire's neoclassical drama and Shakespeare's "irregular" masterpiece. (Sumarokov, as Levitt had demonstrated, had access to the 1685 Folio and to the French version of the play in Laplace's *Théâtre anglois*).[14] While Sumarokov corrected those features of the original *Hamlet* that contradicted classicist convention, his very choice of Shakespeare's play as a point of departure attests to the relevance of the English tragedy's fundamental thematic structure for its Russian imitator and his audience. Eliminating plotlines and characters, Sumarokov adopts the the basic premise and outline of Shakespeare's plot, its political situation involving a dynastic crisis and a justified revolt.

In a recent compelling study, Margreta de Grazia disputes the customary yet anachronistic view of Shakespeare's play as a "timeless tragedy" rather than an example of an overtly political history. Rather, she reads it as a political drama, a tragedy of failed succession that threatens, and eventually destroys, the body politic ("Something is rotten in the state of Denmark," 1.4).[15] If compared to the wording of Gentillet's treatise (published in English

---

14   On Sumarokov's direct acquaintance with Shakespeare's text, see Levitt, "Sumarokov's Reading at the Academy of Sciences Library," in *Early Modern Russian Letters: Texts and Contexts,* 25–27, 33. The French translation he used was Pierre-Antoine de La Place, *Théâtre anglois,* vol. 2 (London: n.p., 1746).

15   Margreta de Grazia, *"Hamlet" without Hamlet* (Cambridge: Cambridge University Press, 2007); Shakespeare, *Hamlet,* 184.

a year before *Hamlet*), the terms "tragedy" and "tragic history," intermittently used in the earliest editions of Shakespeare's play, equally evoke a dramatic poetics that overlaps with the divinely ordained logic of history manifested in crises of statehood: "There is no separating tragic action from historical events: both tend toward catastrophe."[16]

For the tumultuous politics of early modern Russia, the relevance of this perspective on history, both "tragic" and "religious," is confirmed by one of the earliest references to the English *Hamlet* in the anonymous tract *Sir Thomas Smithes Voiage and Entertainment in Rushia. With the tragicall ends of two Emperors . . .* (1605). Speaking of the sweeping rise to power of the False Dmitrii and the death of Boris Godunov, the anonymous chronicler attributes to Boris's ill-fated son Feodor the tacit admission

> that his father's Empire and Government was but as the Poeticall Furie in a Stage-action, compleat yet with horrid and wofull tragedies: a first, but no second to any Hamlet; and that now Revenge, just Revenge, was comming with his sworde drawne against him, his royall Mother, and dearest Sister, to fill up those Murdering Sceanes; the Embryon whereof was long since Modeld, yea digested (but unlawfully and too-too vicedly) by his dead selfe-murdering Father.[17]

De Grazia quotes this passage to emphasize "a feature of *Hamlet* rarely noted in modern discussions: its preoccupation with the stuff of history—the fall of states, kingdoms, and empires."[18] In fact, both the parallel between Shakespeare's plot and Russian history (reinforced by the North European geopolitical space, from Denmark to Poland, common to them), and the more fundamental analogy between the patterns of history and tragedy revolve around the notion of divine vengeance that turns "carnal, bloody, and unnatural acts" (5.2) into terrifyingly spectacular revelations of metaphysical harmony.

---

16 De Grazia, *"Hamlet" without Hamlet*, 52.

17 Quoted in David Farley-Hills, ed., *Critical Responses to "Hamlet," 1600–1900*, vol. 1, *1600–1790* (New York: AMS Press, 1997), 7. For the Russian translation, see *Sera Tomasa Smita puteshestvie i prebyvanie v Rossii* (St. Petersburg: Izdanie grafa S. D. Sheremeteva, 1893). In Russian scholarship this passage has been noted, of course, by M. P. Alekseev, *Russko-angliiskie literaturnye sviazi (XVIII vek–pervaia polovina XIX veka)* (Moscow: Nauka, 1982), 33.

18 De Grazia, *"Hamlet" without Hamlet*, 48.

Neither Sumarokov nor Trediakovskii could have known the anonymous English account, but they certainly shared similar patterns of thought. In 1771 Sumarokov wrote a tragedy, *Dimitrii Samozvanets* (*Demetrius the Pretender*), similar to his earlier *Gamlet* in that it was also designed to "show Russia Shakespeare" and staged a successful and legitimate revolt against a tyrant.[19] Indeed, the association of political upheaval with divine vengeance remained central for the treatments of False Dmitrii's story both in drama, including Schiller's *Demetrius* (1805) and Pushkin's *Boris Godunov* (1825), and historiography from Tatishchev to Karamzin's *History of the Russian State* (1818–1829). According to official dynastic mythology, the Time of Troubles associated with Boris Godunov and the False Dmitrii was concluded in 1613 by a manifest act of divine will, the ascent to tsardom of Mikhail Romanov, Elizabeth's great-grandfather. An adaptation of Shakespeare to the ceremonial idiom of the Russian court, Sumarokov's *Gamlet* in fact revives and relies upon more fundamental symbolic patterns that place the genre of tragedy (Benjamin's "tragic drama") in the focus of a political metaphysics that views court politics as a privileged space for spectacles of divine retribution (*mzdovozdaianie*).[20]

Neither Sumarokov's choice of Shakespeare as his model nor the political theology behind it was incidental to his immediate Russian context; rather, they corresponded to contemporary developments in French drama. Levitt opposes the optimistic worldliness of Sumarokov's theological tragedy centered "on a divinely rational utopia" to the Hamletian "things undreamt of in Horatio's philosophy," which allegedly constitute the true spirit of tragedy. In doing so, he relies on George Steiner's generalizing claim that the "triumph of rationalism and secular metaphysics" in the age of Newton and Descartes brought about the end of tragedy.[21] From this perspective, it should seem paradoxical that tragedy was very much alive in eighteenth-century France, a primary space of the Enlightenment, and that none other than Voltaire was the genre's most successful practitioner.

---

19 Makogonenko, ed., *Pis'ma russkikh pisatelei XVIII veka,* 133.

20 On the seventeenth-century readings of tragedy as an image of divine punishment, with specific references to political neostoicism also influential in Russia, see Armin Schäfer, "Wer verübt die Rache? Eine Handlungskette in Andreas Gryphius' Trauerspiel *Leo Armenius*," in *Kulturtechniken des Barock: Zehn Versuche,* ed. Tobias Nanz and Armin Schäfer (Berlin: Kulturverlag Kadmos, 2012), 57–60.

21 Levitt, "Sumarokov's Russianized *Hamlet*: Texts and Contexts," 95–97; George Steiner, *The Death of Tragedy* (New York: Oxford University Press, 1961).

In fact, in his tragedy *Sémiramis*, which took shape concurrently with Sumarokov's *Gamlet* (drafted in 1746, staged in 1748, and published in 1749) and could not have influenced it, Voltaire in emulation of Shakespeare's *Hamlet* introduced a ghost of a murdered king. In the *Dissertation sur la tragédie ancienne et moderne (Dissertation on Ancient and Modern Tragedy)*, printed together with the play, he specifically pointed to his source and (in an evident contradiction to the Enlightenment critique of superstition he could so vigorously propagate) eloquently defended a dramatist's right to take recourse to the supernatural. At first invoking the combined authority of the classical dramatic tradition and Christian religion, he then revealed the political overtones of his theatrical experiment in a discussion of royal ghosts in Aeschylus and Shakespeare:

> ... in Shakespear, the ghost of Hamlet appears to demand vengeance, and to reveal secret crimes. It is neither useless, nor brought in by force, but serves to convince mankind, that there is an invisible power, the master of nature. All men have a sense of justice imprinted on their hearts, and naturally wish that heaven wou'd interest itself in the cause of innocence: in every age therefore, and in every nation, they will behold with pleasure, the supreme being engag'd in the punishment of crimes which cou'd not come within the reach of human laws: this is a consolation to the weak, and a restraint on the insolence and obstinacy of the powerful.
>
> —Heaven
> Will oft suspend its own eternal laws
> When justice calls, reversing death's decree
> Thus to chastise the sov'reigns of the earth,
> And terrify mankind—
>
> Thus Semiramis speaks to the high priest of Babylon, and thus the successor of Samuel might have spoke to Saul, when the ghost of Samuel came to tell him of his condemnation.[22]

---

22 Voltaire, *The Dramatic Works*, trans. Rev. Mr. Francklin: London: J. Newbery et al., 1761), 2: 33–34; see also Voltaire, *The Complete Works*, 30A: 161–162.

Like the happy ending, the royal ghost is a stage metaphor of divine retribution expressly inscribed into a traditional metaphysics of monarchy we would consider obsolete for Voltaire's age. In fact, *Sémiramis* was specifically designed for court festivities, the nuptials of the French dauphin (although the modern commentator is once again discomfited by Voltaire's plot, a story of a murderous and all but incestuous queen, which "may not seem an obvious choice for such an occasion").[23] In Voltaire's theoretical argument, his own verses are amalgamated with a reading of *Hamlet* and Aristotle's discussion of tragic representations of fate with a "baroque" theology of divinely sanctioned kingship.

In *Poetics*, Aristotle suggests that tragedies should profit from the impression that represented events are steered by a divine design rather than mere chance, for example, when "the statue of Mitys at Argos ... fell on his Murderer, and killed him on the spot." As Dacier comments, "Plutarch relates this History in his Treatise, why Justice, oftentimes defers the Punishment of the Wicked ... He attributes this Punishment to Providence."[24] Unlike Plutarch, Aristotle himself—as Dacier emphasizes—hesitates to accept the idea of providence as a metaphysical certitude, just as Gentillet and Voltaire both hover between investing dramatic representations of fate with metaphysical validity and recognizing them as an artfully constructed fiction. The need for this fiction lies not only in the exigencies of tragic poetics but also in commonplace political theology that considered divine will the only power entitled "to chastise the sov'reigns of the earth" and to punish their "crimes which cou'd not come within the reach of human laws." Divine intervention was thus firmly inscribed in the legal discourse of "sacralized" monarchies. Not incidentally, Voltaire situates his ghost at the focus of the intertwined political and religious authority of Semiramis and her high priest, compared to the prototypical politico-theological cooperation of biblical kings and prophets. Royal ghosts, then, appear in tragedies in order to stage divine oversight of monarchies, asserted as a legal principle even when it was not taken at face value as religious truth.

Voltaire's treatment of the supernatural in drama is shaped by the same alignment of the political with the metaphysical that has been delineated by

---

23   Robert Niklaus, "Introduction [to *Sémiramis*]," in Voltaire, *The Complete Works*, 30A: 40.
24   *Aristotle's Art of Poetry*, 140, 156.

Schmitt and Benjamin. The parallel between the two implied in what Schmitt defined as the process of secularization was reinterpreted by Benjamin as the "tension between immanence and transcendence" (*Welt und Transzendenz*) inherent in, rather than resolved by, "the exaggerated forms of baroque Byzantinism," the sacralization of royal power (in Russia's case specifically derived from Byzantine models).[25] This tension is negotiated through tropes that forge the relationship of mutual implication between the political and the metaphysical; thus, it becomes an appropriate subject for tragedy as a genre of "poeticall fiction" equipped to fabricate visions of divine presence and its effects in the political space. Indeed, Benjamin specifically addresses dramatic images of fate and its manifestations in "ghostly apparitions, the terrors of the end" and establishes their importance for the *Trauerspiel* as "transcendental phenomena whose dimension is temporal."[26] As figments of poetic language and dramatic imagination, both more immediately linked to the divine than other characters and more evidently fictional, the ghosts (at least for Voltaire) are overtly and potently metaphorical: like tragic drama itself, they spectacularly evoke the metaphysical and simultaneously expose it as a projection of the political imaginary, a set of fictions and tropes of power and its vicissitudes. In Voltaire, the appearance of the ghost constitutes a metaphysical version of a Schmittian state of exception: "Heaven / Will oft suspend its own eternal laws." Conversely, in Shakespeare the Ghost's mystic apparition and the "fates" behind it are easily (and quite rightly) recognized by Horatio as a political matter, the onset of an imminent state crisis: "In the most high and palmy state of Rome, / A little ere the mightiest Julius fell, / The graves stood tenantless and the sheeted dead / Did squeak and gibber in the Roman streets" (1.1).[27]

This perspective seems crucial for Sumarokov's interpretation of Shakespeare's tragedy and its political mysticism incorporated by the Ghost. As in Shakespeare, in Sumarokov's *Gamlet* the apparition of the murdered royal father also provides the starting point for the play's action. In this case, though, the ghost is reduced to a dream, which Gamlet recounts in his opening monologue and then discusses with his confidant Armans:

---

25 Benjamin, *Origin of the German Tragic Drama*, 66.
26 Ibid., 134.
27 Shakespeare, *Hamlet*, 355; see also, de Grazia, *"Hamlet" without Hamlet*, 50–51.

Отрыгни мне теперь тиранов гнусных злоба,

Свирепство к должности, на жертву к месту гроба,

Где Царь мой и отец себе отмщенья ждет!

Он совести моей покою не дает:

Я слышу глас его и в ребрах вижу рану;

О сын мой! вопиет, отмсти, отмсти тирану

И свободи граждан. … Ужасный сон! своих мечтавшихся мне сил,

Ты ударением несчастна поразил!

Готов к отмщению … (1.1–2.61–62)

Renew in me, O wrath and hatred of foul tyrants,

Passion for right, for sacrifice where lies the coffin,

Where waits to be avenged my father and my king!

He gives no peace at all, my conscience knows no rest.

I hear his voice and see the wound the body suffers.

"My son," he cries, "my son, seek vengeance on a tyrant

And set the people free. …"

O frightful dream! You've struck me down, unfortunate,

With all your power in the dreaming dreamt to me.

I'm ready to avenge. (89–90)

Substituting a dream for a ghost, Sumarokov seems to be diluting the tragedy's mysticism in line with the general rationalizing tendencies that we so easily recognize in eighteenth-century culture. Indeed, Gamlet emphasizes that it was from Armans rather than from his father's apparition that he had learned of Klavdii's crime: "Dovol'no bez mechty / Ko gnevu i togo, chto skazyval mne ty" (1.2.62; "With this dream or without, / There's cause enough for rage in what you told me," 90). In a radical move, Sumarokov exposes the dream as a transparent metaphor for political knowledge, insight into court politics and its horrible secrets, *arcana imperii*: Gamlet only sees in a dream what Armans had told him before. If compared to the presentation of Shakespeare's and Voltaire's ghosts, Sumarokov's dream can at first glance appear as an almost redundant figure of speech; but even (or especially) in this divested form, the royal apparition epitomizes the play's poetics. Refashioning

Shakespeare and depriving himself of the Ghost's imposing appearance and manifest divinity, Sumarokov follows an austere neoclassicist aesthetic, which has immediate ramifications for his representation of the political. Gamlet's account of his dream establishes the tension between traditional tragic mysticism (Benjamin lists "prophetic dreams" that "generally foretell the end of the tyrant" among common devices of baroque drama[28]) and its "rationalist" denial. The now evident precariousness of conventional tragic metaphysics and political theology—further enacted in the "To be or not to be" soliloquy and its close adaptation in the Russian play—is employed to set off and highlight the self-constitutive validity of dramatic and political action, *Gamlet's* actual substance. Anticipating the play's outcome in its first lines, Gamlet's account of his dream follows Aristotle's advice as it simultaneously aligns plot development and suspense with a logic of retribution and allows for an interpretation of divine intervention as a mere projection of human fantasy.[29] Sumarokov's reduction of the metaphysical (especially striking in a religiously charged play) seems to owe as much to Steiner's "triumph of rationalism" as to Carl Schmitt's "secularization": ghost or no ghost, a "tragic" spectacle capable of "terrifying mankind" is reliably provided by a political crisis, a state of exception that results in a violent seizure of power, a coup d'état.

---

28 Benjamin, *Origin of the German Tragic Drama*, 134.

29 For a valuable discussion of political metaphysics in eighteenth-century tragedy, see Albrecht Koschorke, "Das Politische und die Zeichen der Götter. Zum 'Lied der Parzen' in *Iphigenie auf Tauris*," in *Die Gabe des Gedichts: Goethes Lyrik im Wechsel der Töne*, ed. Gerhard Neumann and David E. Wellbery (Freiburg: Rombach, 2008), 143–159.

THE DRAMA OF COUP D'ÉTAT

In a discussion of the political underpinnings of theater in a monarchy, d'Aubignac's *La pratique du théâtre* specifically evokes stage representations of revolt:

> Thus the Athenians delighted to see upon their Theatre the Cruelties of Kings, and the Misfortunes befalling them, the Calamities of Illustrious and Noble Families, and the Rebellion of the whole Nation for an ill Action of the Prince, because the State in which they liv'd being Popular, they lov'd to be perswaded that Monarchy was always Tyrannical ... Whereas quite contrary among us, the respect and love which we have for our Princes, cannot endure that we should entertain the Publick with such Spectacles of horror; we are not willing to believe that Kings are wicked, nor that their Subjects, though with same appearance of ill usage, ought to Rebel against their Power: or touch their Persons, no not in Effigie; and I do not believe that upon our Stage a Poet could cause a Tyrant to be murder'd with any applause, except he had very cautiously laid the thing: As for Example, that the Tyrant were an Usurper, and the right Heir should appear, and be own'd by the People, who should take that occasion to revenge the injuries that had suffered from a Tyrant.[1]

---

1   [D'Aubignac], *The Whole Art of the Stage*, 70; see also d'Aubignac, *La pratique du théâtre*, 119–120.

D'Aubignac's argument notably blends dramatic and political theory, the mechanics of collective submission to monarchy with the emotional effects of dramatic performance on its audience. The resulting conceptual framework is immediately put to the test through the introduction of a paradox which alone seems to be able to provide a positive source of theatrical interest among prohibitive politically orthodox regulations: a legitimate revolt. This paradox can indeed be central for a vision of royal power that associates it with dramatic performance. Having established that monarchical order rests on the public's "respect and love … for our Princes," d'Aubignac then develops a Schmittian dialectic of the state of exception that both negates the stability of this order (manifested in the public's refusal to accept the overthrow of tyrants even "in Effigie") and restores it through a spectacular act of violence that serves as the monarchy's new point of origin. It revives the solidarity between monarchy and its subjects on stage, who assist the "right Heir," as well as subjects in the audience who applaud this revolt as a counterintuitive triumph of the monarchic principle.

This pattern necessarily shaped Elizabeth's "scenario of power," centered on a palace revolution, and its dramatic reenactments, including Sumarokov's *Gamlet*. In this version, Gamlet emerges as a winner in his struggle with Klavdii after he is able to mobilize popular support: "Vse zdeshne zhitel'stvo na pomoshch' mne predstalo … Edinodushno vse na tron menia zhelali" (5. 5.116; "All of the citizens did rally to support me … all expressed the wish to crown me king of Denmark," 132). Reenacting in his tragedy the "theatrical" conception of royal power dependent on the approval of the public, Sumarokov—just like d'Aubignac—attempts to assimilate it with absolutist orthodoxy, yet it cannot but evoke a much more disillusioned and disturbing, Machiavellian analysis of monarchy.

In an important study of the aesthetic dimensions of early modern statehood, Susanne Lüdemann draws attention to a passage in *The Prince*:

> It is not at all necessary therefore, that a Prince should be actually possessed of all the good qualities … but highly so, that he should have the appearance of them … mankind in general form their judgment rather from appearances than realities: all men have eyes, but not many have the gift of penetration: every one sees your

exterior, but few can discern what you have in your heart; and those few dare not oppose the voice of the multitude, who have the Majesty of their Prince on their side: besides, the actions of all men, but particularly of Princes (of which no private Judge can properly take cognizance) are generally condemned or approved by the event of them. Let it then be the chief care of a Prince to preserve himself and his State: the means which he uses for that purpose, whatsoever they are, will always be esteemed honourable, and applauded by every one: for the opinion of the Vulgar is always determined by appearances and the issue of things; and as the world is chiefly composed of such as are called the Vulgar ...[2]

Machiavelli outlines some of the major tensions and ambiguities inherent in the "absolutist" visions of power and played out in Sumarokov's *Gamlet*. The mechanics of illusion, which d'Aubignac would appropriate for a culturally and politically legitimate institution of theater, are represented here as the craft of ruthless political manipulation and calculated deceit. At the same time, its "theatrical" effects on public judgment are seen as the ultimate source of power, while even the slightest reference to divine justice is strikingly absent: the incapacity of subjects to judge their rulers is *not* balanced by the notion of a higher law (as was the case in Voltaire's *Sémiramis*, for example). However, while Machiavelli can be said to derive power from political theatrics, these theatrics are not limited to lies and fabrications: efficacious political action judged by its success, "the issue of things," can provide for its own legitimacy. A forceful act—easily identified as the "conquest" of power, *The Prince*'s most important subject—erases for a spectacular moment the boundary between reality and its representation, the secret mechanics of rule and the carefully forged "appearances" of virtue. It is not that displays of false virtue are staged in order to cover up the ruler's secret evildoing; rather, his public actions simultaneously establish his power and provide for its legitimacy through fictional narratives that thrive on the

---

2   *The Works of Nicholas Machiavel*, 1: 632; Albrecht Koschorke, Susanne Lüdemann, Thomas Frank, and Ethel Matala de Mazza, *Der fiktive Staat. Konstruktionen des politischen Körpers in der Geschichte Europas* (Frankfurt am Main: Fischer Taschenbuch Verlag, 2007), 156–157.

public's need to consider any authority "honourable" and the common desire to agree with "the multitude, who have the Majesty of their Prince on their side." Political order hinges, then, on the ability of the collective political imagination to inscribe royal violence into publicly accepted fictions. It is this aesthetic complicity between ruler and subjects that provides a blueprint for theater as an institution of monarchy, for tragic stagings of royal authority, and for Sumarokov's *Gamlet* in particular.

Indeed, engaging its audience with a fictionalized account of a palace revolution, the play simultaneously profits from the discrepancies between actual events and dramatic plot, and from the fundamental analogy between theatrical and political interest. This analogy was not only accepted by dramatic criticism, but was also used in political discourse to describe and fashion public fascination for monarchs and their life stories. A German biography of Empress Elizabeth published (apparently under the sponsorship of her court) in 1759 begins:

> The histories of the rulers of the Great Russian Empire belong no doubt to the most remarkable events of the European courts. Like in a play, they are so closely intertwined that cannot be well understood outside of the whole. In order to know the motives, actions, and goals of a main actor, one has to know other actors, and already be informed about the contents of the play; in a similar fashion we have to approach our heroine's history. Who can enjoy the history of the mighty daughter of Peter the Great without sufficient knowledge of the actions of her predecessors in government under whose rule this heroic princess has given most worthy signs of her greatness in adversity? Such a depiction of the life of the great Elizabeth would have gaps where the original did not, at a time when the general regard of nations already learned to refer to our heroine with admiration. No, the realm of morality has the most noble rights to the zeal of historical scholarship. ... Accordingly we will not depart in our account from the path prescribed by moral philosophy.[3]

---

3   *Merkwürdige Geschichte ... Elisabeth der Ersten: Nebst einer kurzen Einleitung in die Historie der russischen Regenten von Anfang des Christenthums in diesem nordischen Reiche* (n.p., 1759), 2ff.

The commonplace comparison between theater and political history, intrinsic to the idiom of early journalism exemplified here, is not in fact meaningless or neutral. It inscribes Elizabeth's story, specifically the period of "adversity" before her ascension (corresponding to the first acts of Sumarokov's *Gamlet*), into a Machiavellian vision of power that places more emphasis on extraordinary royal actors and "events" capable of provoking public "admiration" than on legality and dynastic continuity. Evidently, it was this vision that fueled Elizabeth's coup, as all its subsequent legalistic justifications could not possibly conceal. Accordingly, in *Gamlet* and other court-sponsored dramatizations of the coup, the principles of dramatic poetics were activated as a mode of representation that not only relied on but also fostered a fascination for forceful if questionable action. Addressing in a single act of representation political concerns of the audience and its aesthetic sensibilities, early modern tragedy—as demonstrated by Louis Marin, Rüdiger Campe, and Gisbert Ter-Nedden, among others—could constitute an analytical model, or a "theory," of political crisis.[4] Sumarokov's *Gamlet*, a courtier's play about court politics, dissects the coup d'état as a foundational act of rule together with all the tensions inherent in it. It thus assumes a function similar to that of "historical scholarship" (a term that, in this case, refers to accounts of contemporary political events) but, thanks to its status as fiction, or "poetry," is paradoxically exempted from many constraints imposed on directly "historical" speech.

While Levitt argues against an approach to Sumarokov's plays as "allegories on good and bad monarchs," it can in fact prove fruitful if based on an understanding of allegory as a complex trope of generalization as outlined in part 2. A paradoxical situation of legitimate revolt, recommended by d'Aubignac and staged by Sumarokov, necessarily calls into question and suspends the seemingly stable conditions of legitimacy, the very coordinates for distinguishing "good and bad monarchs." D'Aubignac's line of argument

---

4   Marin, "Théâtralité et pouvoir"; Rüdiger Campe, "Theater der Institution. Gryphius' Trauerspiele *Leo Armenius, Catharina von Georgien, Carolus Stuardus und Papinianus*," in *Konfigurationen der Macht in der Frühen Neuzeit*, ed. R. Galle and R. Behrens (Heidelberg: Winter, 2000), 257–287; Gisbert Ter-Nedden, "*Philotas* und *Aias* oder Der Kriegsheld im Gefangenendilemma. Lessings Sophokles-Modernisierung und ihre Lektüre durch Gleim, Bodmer und die Germanistik," in *Krieg ist mein Lied: Der Siebenjährige Krieg in den Zeitgenössischen Medien* (Göttingen: Wallstein, 2007), 317–378.

reveals the crux of the uneasy early modern understanding of monarchy: even a tyrant has a legitimate claim to obedience, "for there is no power but of God: the powers that be are ordained of God. Whosoever therefore resisteth the power, resisteth the ordinance of God" (Rom. 13:1–2). In Shakespeare's Denmark, as de Grazia meticulously shows, "Claudius is the legitimate king; as far is known to the court, he has committed no legal offence in ascending to the throne," and Hamlet himself never accuses him of usurpation.[5] In both Shakespeare's and Sumarokov's *Hamlet*s, King Claudius appropriates the language of legitimacy. Confronting the rebellious Laertes, Shakespeare's Claudius proclaims:

> There's such divinity doth hedge a king
> That treason can but peep to what it would,
> Acts little of his will. (4.5)

G. R. Hibbard finds these words "supremely ironical" since Claudius's faith in divine support for kings is confuted by his own crime.[6] Sumarokov retains this ambiguity when he makes his Klavdii respond to the remorseful Gertruda, who impels him to abdicate and hope for a pardon from the nation:

> Кому прощать Царя? народ в его руках.
> Он Бог, не человек, в подверженных странах.
> Когда кому даны порфира и корона,
> Тому вся правда власть, и нет ему закона. (2.2.78)

> Who's to forgive the king? The nation's in his hands.
> He is not man but God through all the realm he rules.
> Whoever gains the crown and the imperial purple
> Knows no law but his own, his voice alone is justice. (102)

---

5   De Grazia, *"Hamlet" without Hamlet*, 87–88.

6   Shakespeare, *Hamlet*, 304; elsewhere in the play (3.3) conventional praise of monarchy is addressed to Claudius by Rosencrantz and Guildenstern, "by a couple of sycophants to a king who is an usurper and a murderer" (ibid., 271).

The royal prerogatives evoked by both kings are quite real; an absolute monarch is not bound by law and cannot be judged or punished by his subjects. However, in Sumarokov's play—much more clearly than in Shakespeare's—defiled and distorted certitudes of absolutist orthodoxy fail to contain resentment against Klavdii both on stage and in the audience. Instead, this failure unleashes the overtly destructive energies of political violence. The defeated Polonii is not legally wrong when he condemns Gamlet's triumph as mutiny:

> Всходи взносись на трон высокой,
> Когда тебе твоя неправда помогла,
> И дерзостны сердца против Царя зажгла. (5.4.110–111)

> Go, ascend the throne of Denmark,
> If your injustice has helped you gain your end,
> And has inflamed the hearts of traitors to the king. (127)

Fantasies of revolt were anything but irrelevant or harmless in Russia of the 1740s. In 1740, still during Empress Anna's reign, Artemii Volynskii was publicly executed on fabricated charges of conspiracy: allegedly he harbored a dynastic claim to the Russian throne and planned to provoke a popular revolt in order to overthrow the empress, marry the princess Elizabeth, and seize Russia's throne.[7] In this imaginary scenario forged by the collective imagination of the Russian court, Volynskii assumed a role very much similar to Sumarokov's Gamlet, who leads a popular revolt in order to claim his dynastic rights. Another fiction of this kind surfaced in 1748, the year when *Gamlet* was published. At that time Sumarokov served as a high-ranking officer in the *leib-companiia*, a privileged unit of royal bodyguards formed from the soldiers involved in the palace revolution of 1741 and directly supervised by Elizabeth's favorite, Count Aleksei Razumovskii. Sometime during this year, Sumarokov's fellow guardsman Stepanov, possibly the poet's acquaintance if not his subordinate, as he was stationed at the doors of the royal chambers witnessed the empress enter with Razumovskii and received an order to leave the porch. In his own words, reported to the Secret Chancery

---

7   Igor Kurukin, *Artemii Volynskii* (Moscow: Molodaia gvardiia, 2011), 356.

and confirmed and expanded by Stepanov himself during ensuing interroga-
tions, he heard the floor boarding creak and "reckoned that the most gracious
lady is committing fornication with Razumovskii," so that he started trembling
and considered bursting into the room and stabbing Razumovskii with his
bayonet. Afterwards he planned to explain to the empress that he had stabbed
her lover because "he commits fornication with your imperial majesty" and was
hopeful that she would not have him punished. In one version of the story, he
did not execute his plan because he was scared, in another because he was relieved
by the next watch. Evgenii Anisimov, who recounts this case in his study of political prosecution in eighteenth-century Russia, is right to conclude that Stepanov
was frightened by the "contradiction, horrifying for a man of his time, between
the sacred, taboo status of the empress' persona, and the blasphemy of her trivial
sexual intercourse with one of her subjects. Stepanov's intentions clearly affirm
that he considered the empress' coition with a subject as an assault, an act of
violence, and wished to defend the empress in accordance with the statutes and
his oath, as he thought he was expected to when stationed at the doors of the
royal bedroom."[8]

Stepanov's fantasy clearly parallels the plot of both *Hamlet*s and draws
on the deeply rooted political mythology that permeates them. Identifying
sexual possession of the royal female body with the desecration of the
monarchy, he follows the same logic as Hamlet himself in censuring
Gertrude's lustful cohabitation with Claudius. Indeed, as de Grazia shows, in
the world of Shakespeare's play, Gertrude's sexuality is intrinsically linked to
the well-being of the body politic. Claudius addresses her as his "imperial
jointress," a term that identifies her "as what joins him to the empire and
the empire to him." The term alludes to "a legal *jointure*, an estate settled on
a wife which reverts back to her in the event of her husband's death … What
man the 'imperial jointress' chooses to conjoin with, then, would be of
paramount concern for the empire … Union to her in marriage would settle
the realm on her husband."[9] This legal pattern is even more obvious in
Sumarokov than it is in Shakespeare; the Russian Klavdii is not of royal
birth, as Gertruda admits to her son: "Na tsarskii odr, na tron raba ia
voznesla, / Chtob luchshe ia tvoe nasledie pasla," (1.3.66; "Onto the kingly

8   Anisimov, *Dyba i knut,* 64–65.
9   De Grazia, *"Hamlet" without Hamlet,* 105.

bed, onto the throne I've raised / A slave so that I might better guard your inheritance," cf. 93). She reiterates this admission in a speech that exhorts Klavdii to repent and abdicate, and condemns their marriage in terms reminiscent of Stepanov, up to the shaking walls of the royal bedroom:

> Любовь произвело во мне твое злодейство!
> Супружество мое с тобой прелюбодейство. ...
> Как честь мою любовь сквернейша поглотила,
> А я тебя на трон Монаршеский пустила!
> О как тогда, о как не сшел на землю гром,
> И с нами не упал наш оскверненный дом!
> Как стены наших сих чертогов не тряслися!
> И как мы в таковом грехе с тобой спаслися! (2.2.76)

> My love was fashioned when you wrought your greatest evil,
> Our marriage is nothing but adultery ...
> When love profane won out and overcame my honor,
> When I bestowed the throne upon you,
> Where was the thunder then that should have rocked the earth?
> How did our sinful house withstand the wrath of God?
> How did the palace walls that housed our evil-doing
> Shake not, as though our sins were nothing? (100–101)

It is in this perspective that the use of armed force to fend off lovers of the "imperial jointress" can be considered a defense of the royal body and the body politic rather than an attack against them. In fact, Stepanov's imaginary defense of Elizabeth was not unique but represented a pattern often rehearsed by Russian political imagination of the 1740s. As if to make the analogies with *Hamlet* even more evident, popular rumors designated Grand Duke Peter, Elizabeth's nephew and proclaimed heir, as the future avenger of her affair with (or even a morganatic marriage to) Razumovskii. It was said, for example, that Elizabeth planned to abdicate, secluding herself in a convent (similar to Sumarokov's Gertruda) and that her heir, Peter, had already bought an axe for Razumovskii and would have already stabbed him with his sword had not the empress intervened.[10]

The affinity between both *Hamlet*s and the widespread fantasies of legitimate revolt apparently shaped by common patterns of political imagination shared across Europe underscore the drastic differences in the status that these fictions could assume. While Sumarokov's play was published and staged at court with royal approval, rumors of violence in the royal family were investigated and prosecuted by the Secret Chancery as cases of sedition. Anisimov does not relate what happened to Stepanov, but—as the very fact of his interrogation makes clear—even an intention of an armed intrusion into royal quarters fell under the definition of high treason. The practice of massive and violent prosecution of gossip was informed by a systemic fear of dissent and mutiny of the kind that Sumarokov's Gamlet reverts to. As contemporaries reiterate time and again, Petersburg soldiery was invigorated by the series of coups where it played the main part, and constantly evoked the possibility of a next revolt. Stepanov's crime was to revive the role of armed subjects as true judges and true sources of royal power, an admission that could not but put into question its symbolic legitimacy. The same crime, however, was committed on stage by Sumarokov's Gamlet: instead of justifying his revolt with his indisputable dynastic rights, which would have had at least an appearance of legality, he repeatedly emphasizes the need to punish King Klavdii and to "liberate" the country from him—a course of action divinely forbidden to any absolutist subject, even one of royal extraction.

In order to consecrate—rather than obliterate—this potentially dangerous contradiction that underlay Elizabeth's rule, Sumarokov conjures forth the ghost of Gamlet's nameless father:

Родитель мой в крови предстал передо мною
И, плача, мне вещал, о сын! любезный сын!
Познав вину моих несчастливых судьбин,
Почто ты борешься с разсудком толь бесчинно,
Или чтоб и твое мне сердце было винно?

---

10   Semevskii, "Tainaia kantseliariia v tsarstvovanie Elizavety Petrovny. 1741–1761": 529–530.

Отмсти отцову смерть, и мщеньем утуши
Всегдашню жалобу стенящия души,
Прими Геройску мысль, отставь дела любовны,
Воззри на тень мою, и зри потоки кровны,
Которы пред тобой из ребр моих текут
И, проливаяся на небо вопиют.
Сей глас меня воздвиг, ужасна тень пропала;
Но мнилось, что еще и въяве угрожала. (1.2.63)

My father, all in blood, appeared, I dreamt before me,
And tearfully called out: "O son, beloved son!
Once finding out the cause of my most bitter fate,
Why do you struggle so outrageously with reason,
As though somehow your heart were guilty too before me.
Avenge your father's death, and with revenge suppress
The everlasting plaint of my lamenting soul.
Take up heroic thoughts and put aside love's pleasures,
Look at your father's ghost and see the bloody torrents
Which from my side still gush before you where I stand
And flooding like the tide to heav'n raise their appeal."
This voice caused me to rise, and then the ghost departed,
But still it seemed to stay, to linger and to threaten. (91)

Both in Shakespeare's and in Sumarokov's plays the ghost provides the Prince with a reinvigorating perspective on his intricate dynastic situation. Shakespeare's Denmark, as de Grazia elucidates, is an elective monarchy, which makes it "perfectly legal for the kingdom to pass to a collateral relation rather than the lineal … Denmark's elective constitution is crucial to the play's dramatic set-up. It allows for a situation impossible in a primogenitary monarchy: the Prince remains at court in the company of the King who was preferred over him. This is not a comfortable situation for either Prince or King, and for that very reason it provides a tensely dramatic one for the audience."[11] The legal implications of Hamlet's situation, which we tend to overlook,

---

11   De Grazia, *"Hamlet" without Hamlet*, 87–89.

were probably much more meaningful for Sumarokov and his audience, as they closely resembled Russian court politics. Russia was not legally an elective monarchy but it came close to functioning like one in the aftermath of Peter the Great's decision to abolish any regulations on the order of succession, leaving it to each subsequent ruler to choose their own heir. Instead of consolidating royal prerogative, this measure made royal succession dependent on the tumultuous struggle of court factions and, in the years 1728–1730, the decisions of the Supreme Privy Council. (According to de Grazia, Shakespeare's Claudius was also elected by a council, which he addresses in his first scene.) Elizabeth, by 1741 the only surviving child of Peter and his wife and heir, Catherine I, was twice denied the succession rights assured to her by her mother's testament in 1728. After the death of Elizabeth's nephew Peter II in 1730, the Supreme Privy Council passed the crown to her cousin Anna Ioannovna who, in 1740, left the throne to the infant emperor Ivan and his mother, Anna Leopoldovna. By Petrine legislation, Elizabeth did not have legal grounds to claim more legitimacy than her rivals, but she still enjoyed exceptional popularity as the daughter of Peter, comparable in his charisma to Old Hamlet. Like the coup d'état that Shakespeare's Hamlet could not accomplish, Elizabeth's seizure of power was informed by the tension between the law of the land and the mechanics of personal charisma derived from a deceased royal father.

Indeed, the concept of charisma, personal and inherited, famously developed by Max Weber and closely related to the already cited discussions of royal power by Machiavelli and Carl Schmitt, can prove fruitful for our analysis. It has been shown that it is relevant for an understanding of both Russian court politics of the Petrine age and for a reading of Shakespeare's *Hamlet*.[12] Weber's famous theory opposes types of rule ("traditional" or "legal") dependent on institutional and symbolic continuity to charismatic authority, which is originally generated by extraordinary qualities and actions of a single leader but then itself undergoes "routinization" when power is passed to a successor. Of the various types of succession listed by Weber, several were simultaneously in play in eighteenth-century Russia. The first was envisaged but never accomplished by Peter the Great: "designation on the part of the original charismatic leader of his own successor." The second, "[d]esignation of a

---

12 Zitser, *Transfigured Kingdom*; Raphael Falco, *Charismatic Authority in Early Modern English Tragedy* (Baltimore, MD: Johns Hopkins University Press, 2000).

successor by the charismatically qualified administrative staff," which "should quite definitely not be interpreted as 'election,'" resulted in the appointment of Anna Ioannovna in 1730. Finally, Weber mentions "hereditary charisma" invested in the "kinsmen of the bearers, particularly ... closest relatives," and complicated by the necessity "to select the proper heir within the kinship group." This was the case of Elizabeth and her nephew Peter.[13]

Uncertainties of charismatic succession framed the situation of both Hamlets and Elizabeth in 1741. However, contrary to the customary scenario outlined by Weber, the idea of linear succession does not in either of our cases stand for a "routinization" of charisma but rather for its revival. Sumarokov's play, for example, stages the critical moment when hereditary charisma violently asserts itself over other types of legitimacy. A similar situation was played out in Voltaire's *Mérope*, chosen to reenact Elizabeth's coup on the Russian court stage in 1746. This tragedy—another of Voltaire's responses to Shakespeare's *Hamlet*—also depicts an "imperial jointress," Mérope, the queen of Messene, a descendant of the local royal dynasty and the widow of the charismatic King Cresfonte. She struggles for influence with the powerful general Polifonte, the de facto "tyrant of Messene," as he is described in the dramatis personae. In order to consolidate his authority, Polifonte, who officially recognizes Mérope's dynastic legitimacy cherished by the populace, is forcing her to marry him. Cresfonte's legitimate heir, Egiste, suddenly reappears from obscurity, overthrows the tyrant, and saves his mother. In the beginning of the play, the people of Messene are about to chose their ruler after fifteen years of civil strife unleashed by the death of Cresfonte, "the best of our kings," as Mérope's confidant Ismenia reminds her:

> Nos chefs, nos citoyens, rassemblés sous vos yeux,
> Les organes des lois, les ministres des dieux,
> Vont, libres dans leur choix, décerner la couronne.
> Sans doute elle est à vous, si la vertu la donne.
> Vous seule avez sur nous d'irrévocables droits;
> Vous, veuve de Cresphonte, et fille de nos rois;
> Vous, que tant de constance, et quinze ans de misère,

---

13   For these and the following quotations from Weber, see Max Weber, *The Theory of Social and Economic Organization,* trans. A. M. Henderson and Talcott Parsons (New York: Oxford University Press, 1947), 358–366.

Font encor plus auguste, et nous rendent plus chère;
Vous, pour qui tous les coeurs en secret réunis …

… the ministers
Of heav'n, the guardians of our sacred laws,
The rulers, and the people, soon shall meet,
Free in their choice, to fix the pow'r supreme:
If virtue gives the diadem, 'tis thine:
Thine by irrevocable right: to thee,
Tile widow of Cresphontes, from our kings
Descended, must devolve Messene's throne:
Thou, whom misfortunes and firm constancy
Have made but more illustrious, and more dear
Thou, to whom ev'ry heart in secret ty'd …[14]

Ismenia's doubts about Mérope's success, which seem quite reasonable given Polifonte's opposing power, emerge from her bombastic protestations, undermining Mérope's claim to authority before it is confirmed by the play's outcome. The procedure of royal election does not seem to favor a single dynastic line. Consequently, the importance of kinship for Mérope's status is not a matter of law or legal process but one of charisma, defined by Weber as entirely dependent on the collective opinion of its subjects.[15] In this case, popular opinion half-illicitly ("in secret") recognizes Mérope's descent and her misfortunes as a source of an "irrevocable right" to rule, making her such a dangerous rival to Polifonte. After Egiste's assasintion of Polifonte, Mérope justifies his actions and asserts her and her son's hereditary charisma in a final speech addressed to the multitude silently assembled on stage. She simultaneously appeals to divine approval and popular acclaim:

Guerriers, prêtres, amis, citoyens de Messène,
Au nom des dieux vengeurs, peuples, écoutez-moi.
Je vous le jure encore, Égisthe est votre roi:
Il a puni le crime, il a vengé son père.

---

14   Voltaire, *Complete Works* (Oxford: The Voltaire Foundation 1991), 17: 246; Voltaire, *The Dramatic Works,* 4: 2.

15   Weber, *Theory of Social and Economic Organization,* 359, 361.

> Priests, warriors, friends, my fellow-citizens,
> Attend, and hear me in the name of heav'n.
> Once more I swear, Ægisthus [Egiste] is your king,
> The scourge of guilt, th'avenger of his father ...[16]

Like Sumarokov's Gamlet, Egiste accomplishes a double act of revenge and dynastic restoration, which escapes Shakespeare's Prince. This act is not, however, unrelated to Shakespeare's play where Claudius considers his "legal authority" menaced by Hamlet's charisma (4.2):

> Yet must not we put the strong law on him:
> He's loved of the distracted multitude,
> Who like not in their judgment but their eyes ...[17]

As Raphael Falco remarks in his Weberian reading of Shakespeare, "Hamlet has charismatic power with the populace and ... their bond to him is irrational—which is the meaning of 'distracted'—and therefore dangerous to Claudius' rulership. Claudius fears revolution at this juncture just as much as he worries about his own exposure as a murderer."[18] Indeed, as Falco notes, Weber's claim that "charismatic authority repudiates the past, and is in this sense a specifically revolutionary force" is further enacted in Shakespeare by the revolt of Laertes (4.5):

> ... young Laertes, in a riotous head,
> O'erbears your officers. The rabble call him lord;
> And, as the world were now but to begin,
> Antiquity forgot, custom not known,
> The ratifiers and props of every word,
> They cry "Choose we: Laertes shall be king."[19]

In Shakespeare's play, just as absolutist orthodoxy would have it, charismatic upheaval falls short of the legitimacy or power necessary to resolve the

---

16   Voltaire, *Complete Works,* 17: 341–342; Voltaire, *The Dramatic Works,* 4: 87.
17   Shakespeare, *Hamlet,* 292.
18   Falco, *Charismatic Authority,* 111.
19   Shakespeare, *Hamlet,* 302–303; Falco, *Charismatic Authority,* 111, 114–115.

crisis brought about by the desecration of dynastic lineage. On the contrary, Sumarokov's Gamlet and Voltaire's Egiste are both able to exploit popular force to renew the monarchic order. Already in the first act Gertruda warns Klavdii:

Ты в ненависти, Князь мой сын любим в народе,
Надежда всех граждан, остаток в царском роде. (2.2.76)

The prince's lineage win him the people's honor.
He is their fondest hope, you are their greatest hatred. (101)

Elizabeth's coup was also made possible by the favor she enjoyed with the populace and the military, and the French envoy Chétardie described her afterwards as "an amiable princess, legitimate heiress to the throne who has captivated the hearts of the whole empire by her charms as much as by the qualities of her spirit."[20] Accordingly, her first manifesto proclaimed that she only assumed her "legal right" to inherit her "paternal throne" because she had been urged by her "loyal subjects" and, specifically, the "guards regiments" to stop "troubles and perturbations" caused by unable rulers, which would have lead to "a great ruin of the whole state."[21] This argument bases Elizabeth's authority on the same patterns of crisis and action that are outlined by Schmitt and Weber. In Schmitt's terms, forceful action in a state of exception is the ultimate origin of power and legitimacy. In Weber's terms, a ruler's charisma depends on "proof of charismatic qualification," possibly "a brilliant display of his authority," a success attributable to a "gift of grace," which provides him with the "recognition on the part of those subject to authority which is decisive for the validity of charisma."[22]

Weber's analysis of exceptional authority, like Machiavelli's, reveals its fundamental similarity to theater. Machiavelli grounds a prince's "esteem" on "extraordinary actions" that keep his subjects "in continual suspense and admiration."[23] According to Weber, a forceful act engenders charismatic authority only inasmuch as it dazzles the spectator subjects and engages

---

20 *SIRIO* 96 (St. Petersburg, 1896): 662.
21 *Polnoe sobranie zakonov,* 11: 537.
22 Weber, *The Theory of Social and Economic Organization,* 359–360, 362.
23 *The Works of Nicholas Machiavel,* 1: 662.

public emotion: "The corporate group which is subject to charismatic authority is based on an emotional form of communal relationship."[24] Charisma, then, is mediated by a poetics of represented action, a set of techniques tailored to produce an emotional complicity between ruler-as-actor and his subjects. Theatricality of charisma is exposed when dramatic plots reenact a coup d'état: political action and its representations in drama build upon the same visions of extraordinary power and share the same fundamental tension between truth and fiction. The intensified violence of Voltaire's *Mérope* and Sumarokov's *Hamlet*—Egiste and Hamlet publicly kill their adversaries whereas Elizabeth quietly arrested hers in the middle of the night—directs dramatic interest toward the "physical battle of the leaders" identified by Weber as a basic form of charismatic self-assertion.[25] Conversely, the charismatic value of a royal act unfolds in fictions, narratives that both perpetuate self-serving royal violence and align it with visions of public salvation. To quote Machiavelli once more, "Let it then be the chief care of a Prince to preserve himself and his State: the means which he uses for that purpose, whatsoever they are, will always be esteemed honourable, and applauded by every one."[26]

Similarly to Elizabeth's manifesto, Sumarokov's *Gamlet* overtly subordinates absolutist legality to an urge for action that amalgamates Gamlet's familial affair—revenge for his father's murder—with public interest, the overturn of Klavdii's tyranny. Revolt of a legitimate heir, recommended by d'Aubignac as a topic of absolutist drama, is in fact—both on and off stage—a revolt that constitutes its own legitimacy, as both political event and its representation. In 1742 Elizabeth's ascension and its effect on the populace was symbolized by yet another kind of spectacle, fireworks designed to revive the "most vivid joy" experienced, according to the official description, by all loyal subjects when they witnessed as the true heiress to the empire "lays the crown due to [her] upon [herself] through [her] own natural force" (instead of receiving it in regular succession, that is).[27] While Elizabeth's or Gamlet's revolt could hardly be justified by written law, this deficit

---

24 Weber, *Theory of Social and Economic Organization*, 360.
25 Ibid., 361.
26 *The Works of Nicholas Machiavel*, 1: 632
27 Starikova, *Teatral'naia zhizn' Rossii v epokhu Elizavety Petrovny*, vol. 2, bk. 2, 416–421.

is compensated by a symbolic pattern validated by the collective political imagination: the inheritance of paternal charisma incorporated by the ghost. In Shakespeare, the Ghost is easily recognized as an omen of political disaster, but it fails to bring about a resolution of the dynastic crisis. In Sumarokov, the striking dramatic effect associated with this figure is reinterpreted as an indisputable source of both poetic justice and political authority.

The effect of this dramatic fiction on the play's audience recreates and intensifies the workings of hereditary charisma in Elizabethan Russia. Elizabeth made a point of publicly cultivating the memory of her father, and in panegyric poetry of the era, the ghost of Peter the Great often appeared to consecrate her coup, reinterpreting a spectacular breach of law as an extraordinary act of providentially sanctioned dynastic continuity. Sumarokov's ghost fulfills a similar function, glorifying a transmission of paternal charisma in an act of violence rather than legal procedure. Just as Voltaire would have it, the ghost uses his dual authority as a royal father and a divine messenger to proclaim a double state of exception that brings about the downfall of a villainous ruler and suspends the divine prohibition of revolt. As a device conjured forth to establish legitimacy for illicit political success, Sumarokov's ghost conflates images and symbolic patterns of charisma with dramatic poetics in a stage metaphor epitomizing theatricality itself along with its political consequences—a metaphor whose lack of metaphysical or juridical validity is outweighed by its spectacular appeal, the vivid cogency of fiction.

ANATOMY OF MELANCHOLY, OR GAMLET THE HERO

While Sumarokov's Gamlet certainly differs from his Shakespearean proto-
type, the actions of both characters are shaped by the same challenges arising
from the exigencies of charismatic succession made manifest by the ghosts.
In both plays, dramatic suspense originates in the Prince's famous hesitation
to fulfill his filial calling, which aligns dramatic and political patterns of
expectation. As Falco concludes, because of the ambiguous dynastic status of
Shakespeare's Hamlet, it is only natural that Claudius and his courtiers
would expect him to revolt: "Hamlet's refusal to act organizes those expectations ... The court and indeed the populace all function as Hamlet's
charismatic group, bound in an intersubjective structure by the anticipation
of Hamlet's action."[1] Although Falco himself insists on disassociating
Hamlet's stage audience (the Danish court) from the theatrical audience
of the play, it seems evident—especially within the institutional framework
of court theater, one of the original contexts of Shakespeare's tragedy—that
the play coordinates the two audiences who are made to share a similar set
of expectations (described in the neoclassical theoretical idiom by the
concept of "verisimilitude" or *vraisemblance*). De Grazia also illuminates
political aspects of Hamlet's behavior, drawing attention to his dialogue with
Rosencrantz (3.4):

Rosencrantz
Good my lord, what is your cause of distemper? ...

---

1 . Falco, *Charismatic Authority*, 110–111, 103.

Hamlet
Sir, I lack advancement.

Rosencrantz
How can that be, when you have the voice of the King himself for
your succession in Denmark?

Hamlet
Ay, sir, but "while the grass grows,"—the proverb is something
musty.[2]

Hamlet himself explains his "distemper," the tragedy's psychological crux, as
a consequence of his dynastic situation. As de Grazia comments, "for the play's
first audiences, at least, what Hamlet keeps within himself might have gone
without saying … As he puts it bitterly to Horatio, his only confidant, Claudius
'[p]opp'd in between the election and my hopes.'"[3] While the endless interpretations warranted by Shakespeare's play and its principal character definitely should
not be reduced to court politics, it is useful (especially for those interested in the
play's early modern contexts and readings) to keep in mind that they arise from
a dramatic premise that is fundamentally political. Sumarokov's adaptation of
Shakespeare, while manifestly lacking its wealth of psychological nuance (for
example, Hamlet's ambiguous madness is completely absent from the Russian
play), retains as its central theme a psychological issue relegated by Benjamin in
his reading of early modern drama to "political anthropology": the tension
between extraordinary powers within the prince's reach and inner doubts which
make him "almost incapable of making a decision."[4]

In Sumarokov's *Gamlet*, this tension is played out—and resolved—in the
second of the two passages that Sumarokov admits to have directly modeled
on Shakespeare, namely his version of the "To be or not to be" soliloquy:

Что делать мне теперь? не знаю, что зачать.
Легколь Офелию навеки потерять!

---

2   Shakespeare, *Hamlet*, 267.
3   De Grazia, *"Hamlet" without Hamlet*, 89–90.
4   Benjamin, *Origin of the German Tragic Drama*, 69–71.

Отец! любовница! о имена драгия!

Вы были счастьем мне во времена другия.

Днесь вы мучительны, днесь вы несносны мне;

Пред кем-нибудь из вас мне должно быть в вине.

Пред кем я преступлю? вы мне равно любезны:

Здержитеся в очах моих потоки слезны!

Не зрюсь способен быть я к долгу своему,

И нет пристанища блудящему уму.

(Хватается за шпагу.)

В тебе едином, меч, надежду ощущаю,

А праведную месть я небу поручаю.

Постой,—великое днесь дело предлежит:

Мое сей тело час с душею разделит.

Отверсть ли гроба дверь, и бедствы окончати?

Или во свете сем еще претерпевати?

Когда умру; засну,—засну и буду спать?

Но что за сны сия ночь будет представлять!

Умреть—и внити в гроб—спокойствие прелестно;

Но что последует сну сладку?—неизвестно.

Мы знаем, что сулит нам щедро Божество:

Надежда есть, дух бодр, но слабо естество.

О смерть! противный час! минута вселютейша!

Последняя напасть, но всех напастей злейша!

Воображение мучительное нам!

Неизреченный страх отважнейшим серцам!

Единым именем твоим вся плоть трепещет,

И от пристанища опять в валы отмещет.

Но естьли бы в бедах здесь жизнь была вечна;

Кто б не хотел иметь сего покойна сна?

И кто бы мог снести зла счастия гоненье,

Болезни, нищету, и сильных нападенье,

Неправосудие безсовестных судей,

Грабеж, обиды, гнев, неверности друзей,

Влиянный яд в серца великих льсти устами?

Когда б мы жили ввек, и скорбь жила б ввек с нами.

Во обстоятельствах таких нам смерть нужна;
Но, ах! во всех бедах еще страшна она.
Каким ты, естество, суровствам подчиненно!
Страшна—но весь сей страх прейдет
—прейдет мгновенно.
Умри!—но что потом в несчастной сей стране
Под тяжким бременем народ речет о мне?
Он скажет, что любовь геройство победила,
И мужество мое тщетою учинила:
Что я мне данну жизнь безславно окончал,
И малодушием ток крови проливал,
Котору за него пролить мне должно было.
Успокоение! почто ты духу льстило?
Не льзя мне умереть; исполнить надлежит,
Что совести моей днесь истинна гласит. (3.7.95–96)

What am I now to do? Where am I to begin?
Is it an easy thing to cast one's love aside?
Father, Ofeliia, of all names to me the dearest,
You were my happiness in other days now vanished.
Now you torment me so, now you are hard to bear;
In front of one of you I am bound to stand in guilt.
Although I love you both, I must offend one of you.
O floodgates of my eyes, restrain the tears from flowing!
I do not seem to be equipped to face my task,
And there's no refuge for my poor distracted mind.
[Reaches for his sword]
In you alone, my sword, I find consolation,
And I entrust to heav'n a just and righteous vengeance.
But wait ..., the matter's grave that lies ahead today,
My body and my soul this very hour will part.
To open up death's door and finish with my suff'ring,
Or in this world of ours to try to bear it longer?
In death I'll fall asleep, asleep I'll slumber on,
But what will be the dreams that restless night will bring?

To die, to find one's peace in death would seem so pleasant,
But what may follow that sweet sleep is unknown to us.
We know the promises of our most gracious God.
There's hope, the spirit's strong, but how the flesh is weak!
O death, O hour of woe, O dreaded final minute,
O agony supreme, of all or woes the greatest!
Even to think of it is torment in itself,
Is fear unspeakable even to bravest hearts!
The very name alone does cause our flesh to tremble,
And from our safe retreat returns us to confusion.
But if our dreary life on earth had not an end,
Who would not long to end it with this peaceful sleep?
For who could long endure the pain of prosecution,
Illnesses, poverty, attacks of all the stronger,
Wrongs and injustices of judges' lawlessness,
Anger, offences, theft, betrayal of best friends,
And poison-hearted knaves who flatter those in power?
If we should just on and on with grief forever,
Then death would be a thing most needful and desired.
But even so, alas, it fills our hearts with fear.
How frail is man before the majesty of nature!
We fear death, yet this fear will pass by in an instant.
If I should die, what would my people say of me,
Under their heavy yoke in this unhappy land?
Their songs would tell how love did vanquish [G]amlet's honor,
How [G]amlet's manliness became love's greatest trophy.
How I gave up my life without a glorious stand,
How from a coward's wounds I caused my blood to flow,
Blood that was meant to flow in honor of my people.
O peace of mind, alas, whom did you think to flatter?
I must not think of death when I hear duty call,
When truth makes itself known and lights my conscience's path.
(115–116)

Like Sumarokov's play itself, this speech is simultaneously a variation of
Shakespeare's original and, in important respects, its opposite. As Gamlet's

hesitation reaches its peak here, together with Shakespearean diction, it assumes the features of melancholy—an emotional state traditionally associated in early modern Europe with tragedy and, as Benjamin reminds us, with court politics. Generally, Sumarokov's adaptation of Shakespeare was made possible by visions of political existence largely common to early seventeenth-century England and mid-eighteenth-century Russia and shaped by Machiavellian (or "Tacitean") apprehensions of ruthless violence. Melancholy provided a speech mode, as well as a metaphor, to voice these apprehensions. Robert Burton's famous compendium *The Anatomy of Melancholy* (1621) stated:

> Kingdoms, Provinces, and Politicke Bodies are likewise sensible and subject to this disease ... For where you shall see the people civill, obedient to God and Princes, judicious, peaceable and quiet, rich, fortunate, and flourish, to live in peace, in unity and concord ... that Country is free from melancholy; as it was in Italy in the time of Augustus, now in China, now in many other flourishing kingdomes of Europe. But whereas you shall see many discontents, common grievances, complaints, poverty, barbarism, beggary, plagues, wars, rebellions, seditions, mutinies, contentions, Idleness, riot, Epicurisme ... ; that Kingdome, that Country, must needs be discontent, melancholy, hath a sick body, and had need to bee reformed.[5]

Denmark under the rule of Klavdii—according to Gamlet as well as Gertruda—seems to be as plagued by this disease as the disinherited prince himself. In Shakespeare's version, Hamlet famously considers committing suicide in order to free himself from "The oppressor's wrong, the proud man's contumely ... the law's delay, The insolence of office, and the spurns That patient merit of the unworthy takes" (3.1).[6] As we have seen in Part I, a "melancholic" view of the existing order of things was not incompatible with

---

5   Robert Burton, *The Anatomy of Melancholy,* ed. Thomas C. Faulkner (Oxford: Clarendon Press, 1997), 1: 66–67. On the politics of melancholy in Burton, see Angus Gowland, *The Worlds of Renaissance Melancholy: Robert Burton in Context* (Cambridge: Cambridge University Press, 2006), 205–245.

6   Shakespeare, *Hamlet*, 240.

a position of power (especially in a state like Petrine Russia where the monarchy openly regarded the majority of its subjects and their way of life as barbaric). Quite characteristically, Hamlet's and Gamlet's discontent arises from the frustrated promises of power associated with their birth and status.

In his insightful analysis of the political use of melancholy in eighteenth-century Russia, David Griffiths specifically refers to the "lack [of] advancement" resented by Shakespeare's Prince. Fifty years after the appearance of Sumarokov's play, Catherine II (who had been among its first spectators) drew from the idiom of melancholy to explain the actions of Aleksandr Radishchev, a conscientious government official who had published his now famous *Puteshestive iz Peterburga v Moskvu* (*Journey from Petersburg to Moscow*, 1790), a vehement critique of Russian autocracy and social order. Catherine, who was herself intimately familiar with melancholy and its discourses, concluded that Radishchev acted out of hypochondria "nurtured by his frustrated ambition." As Griffiths himself indicates, "such an explanation was not alien to Russia where the psychosomatic origins of melancholy tended to be accepted. Countess Rumiantseva reported that S. R. Vorontsov was weak with hypochondria because he had been passed over for promotion."[7] Decades earlier, Prince Boris Kurakin (1676–1727), an elite servitor under Peter the Great and at some point the tsar's brother-in-law, in his astrologically informed autobiography used the medical concept of melancholy to express his disaffection with his position at court. According to Ernest Zitser, Kurakin was "unfriendly to the government," more precisely "the tsar's inner circle," although he "was never involved in any sort of overt political opposition."[8] Melancholic resentment was situated, then, in the perilous zone where a nobleman's legitimate ambition bordered on "political opposition," or simply sedition. This ambiguity was spectacularly

---

7   Devid Griffits [David Griffiths], "Ekaterina II i melankholiia, ili Anatomiia politicheskoi oppozitsii," in Devid Griffits [David Griffiths], *Ekaterina II i ee mir: Stat'i raznykh let* (Moscow: Novoe literaturnoe obozrenie, 2013), 109–110.

8   Ernest Zitser, "The Vita of Prince Boris Ivanovich 'Korybut'-Kurakin: Personal Life-Writing and Aristocratic Self-Fashioning at the Court of Peter the Great," *Jahrbücher für Geschichte Osteuropas 59*, no. 2 (2011): 177–178; Robert Collis, "'Stars Rule over People, but God Rules over the Stars': The Astrological Worldview of Boris Ivanovich Kurakin (1676–1727)," *Jahrbücher für Geschichte Osteuropas 59*, no. 2 (2011): 195–216.

enacted by Volynskii's fateful letter to Empress Anna written in 1739, another first-person representation of a courtier's melancholy:

> откровенно доношу (как мне пред богом стать) что я так опечален и в такое крайнее состояние рассуждения моего пришел, что мне временем бывает ничто на свете не мило поистинне ни живот мой, и сколько по слабости ума моего могу рассудить, кажется иногда, что лучшеб хотел умереть нежели беспокойную и вредительную мне жизнь мою с такою горестию продолжать знаючи себя каков я совестен и доброжелателен к вам государыне и отечеству моему и какую я крепкую рабскую верность мою имею к вашему величеству, а вижу что безсовестные льстецы нерадетели добра и безполезные отечеству своему тунеядцы некоторые лучше живут и больше довольства имеют нежели я.

> I openly report (as if standing before God) that I am so distressed and have come to such an extreme condition of my mind that at times nothing in the world pleases me, even my very life, and judging with my weak mind, it seems sometimes that it would be better to die than to continue this restless and self-harming life in such sorrow, knowing how conscientious and good willed I am towards you my sovereign and my country and how slavishly loyal I am to your majesty, while I see how shameless flatterers who ignore [public] good, parasites of no use to their fatherland, live sometimes better and are more satisfied than me.[9]

This letter, accompanied by the denunciation of courtly ways quoted in Part I, was interpreted by Volynskii's adversaries and the empress herself as seditious and provided the first impetus for charges of conspiracy and high treason that lead Volynskii to the scaffold. Evidently, however, this was not the effect Volynskii anticipated: he devised this confession in order to secure royal favor in the constant competition for ranks and money, and apparently

---

9   RGADA, fond 6, op. 1, ed. khr. 195, 6ob–7.

considered "melancholic" death wish an acceptable trope for legitimate grievances of a high-ranking royal servitor. Indeed, respect for melancholic resentment was implied in the early references to melancholy in Petrine legislation on suicide discussed by Susan K. Morrissey. She shows that while all suicide was qualified as a crime against the combined sovereignty of tsar and God, melancholy (*melankholiia*) was considered a mitigating circumstance alongside madness (*bespamiatstvo*) as well as *styd, mucheniie i dosada*, apparent equivalents of "shame and disgrace" as well as "discontents, cares, miseries" listed by Burton as melancholy's common causes. Someone who attempted suicide for one of these reasons would not be punishable by death if he survived the attempt, and if not, his body would not be buried in a dishonorable place.[10]

The tension between dissent and conformity negotiated (but not erased) by the language of melancholy spectacularly erupted in Volynskii's trial as well as in Sumarokov's *Gamlet*. For Volynskii as for Gamlet, a longing for death (Sumarokov consistently uses "death" [*smert'*], for suicide) represents the peak of a rhetorical thrust that starts from an individual's claim for "advancement" and proceeds through a general resentment of "patient merit" against "the insolence of office" (to use Shakespeare's terms). On its way, it erases the distinctions between resentment and dissent, suicide and sedition, already blurred in official discourse and political imagination. Fabricated charges against Volynskii and Sumarokov's dramatic fiction both link the language of melancholic resignation ("words, words, words") to its opposite: a scenario of violent insurrection.

One of the dramatic celebrations of Elizabeth's coup, the allegorical drama *Obraz torzhestva rossiiskogo* (*The Image of the Russian Triumph*, 1742), featured the future empress as the Knight who "speculates how to attain the crown" and bitterly complains about the endless impediments to his task, while Glory and Love promise him a crown and remind him of the adversities overcome by the heroes of ancient fable: Jason, Hercules,

---

10 Burton, *Anatomy of Melancholy*, 1: 261–263, 270–279; Susan K. Morrissey, *Suicide and the Body Politic in Imperial Russia* (Cambridge: Cambridge University Press, 2006), 42–44; *Polnoe sobranie zakonov*, 5: 370, no. 3006, art. 164.

and the conquerors of Troy.[11] In Sumarokov's version of Hamlet's grand soliloquy, melancholic resentment is also amalgamated with the political deliberation that is a necessary step towards final action: after his speech Gamlet leaves the stage only to reappear as a victor over Klavdii. This reinterpretation of Hamlet's melancholy drives Sumarokov's deviations from Shakespeare's original. Albeit for different reasons, neither of the Hamlets actually commits suicide at the end of this speech. Shakespeare's prince famously concludes that

> conscience does make cowards of us all;
> And thus the native hue of resolution
> Is sicklied o'er with the pale cast of thought,
> And enterprises of great pitch and moment
> With this regard their currents turn awry,
> And lose the name of action. (3.1)[12]

Sumarokov's Gamlet operates with similar concepts but interprets them differently. In his comparative discussion of the two soliloquies and Voltaire's French adaptation that mediated between them, Levitt notes that Shakespeare's "undiscovered country," a metaphor for afterlife, is substituted in the Russian play with "this unhappy land," which signifies "Russia herself, and the sufferer 'pod tiazhkim bremenem' [is] not [G]amlet but Russian people."[13] The erroneous allocation of *Gamlet*'s action to Russia instead of Denmark is characteristic of the immediately political implications of Sumarokov's text, which are evident from Levitt's reading of it even though he downplays them elsewhere. Interestingly, in the First Quarto text of *Hamlet* the Ambassador describes Denmark's state at the end of the play in terms similar to Sumarokov's (5.2): "Oh, most unlooked-for time! Unhappy country!," and Horatio then recasts this assessment into a theatrical metaphor: "I'll show to all the ground, / The first beginning of this tragedy."[14] Although Sumarokov

---

11 O. A. Derzhavina, A. S. Demin, and A. N. Robinson, eds., *P'esy shkol'nych teatrov Moskvy* (Moscow: Nauka, 1974), 440–443.

12 Shakespeare, *Hamlet*, 241.

13 Levitt, "Sumarokov's Russianized *Hamlet*: Texts and Contexts," 83.

14 William Shakespeare, *Hamlet. The Texts of 1603 and 1623*, The Arden Shakespeare, ed. Ann Thompson (London: Bloomsbury, 2006), 171.

could not have known this text, its association of the time and space of tragedy with those of a political crisis was fundamental for his dramatic poetics.

Instead of an "abstract metaphysical ratiocination about the other world," Levitt continues, Sumarokov's Gamlet "struggles with the problem of his country's fate [and] the opposition between heroism and cowardice (*geroistvo* versus *malodushie*) ... Sumarokov's protagonist worries about his honor and posthumous national reputation rather than the limits of his reason."[15] A central role in this "secularization" belongs to the concept of conscience, *sovest'*. While in Shakespeare it stands for consciousness, the faculty of thought that impedes action, both Voltaire's and La Place's French versions discussed by Levitt render it as a reference to religiously charged self-discipline. Sumarokov retains this overtone but shifts the signification of the concept and inverts its dramatic function. His *sovest'* is an imperative for political action, the driving force behind Gamlet's final triumph.

The transition from metaphysical doubt in the English original and reflective heterodoxy in the Russian adaptation[16] to political action enacts a trajectory outlined in the "baroque" political discourse adopted in Petrine and post-Petrine Russia. Saavedra Fajardo, for example, while he instructs the prince to "think always he may be deceived," specifically warns him against debilitating philosophical doubt: "Nor that I would have a Prince a Sceptick, for he who doubts all determines nothing; nor is there any thing more pernicious to Government, than Hesitation in resolving and executing."[17] Sumarokov's use of *sovest'*, which balances between the religious and the political, corresponds to the logic of Petrine secularization, and specifically reflects the reliance of Petrine political ethics on a secularized idiom of religious duty.[18] This was, of course, a common feature of absolutist political theology across Europe. Among the books owned by Elizabeth during the first years of her reign (or, possibly, even earlier) was the political testament

15   Ibid., 83–84.
16   Sumarokov's text seems to imply a possibility of eternal bliss for a suicide, an assumption incompatible with the official Orthodox doctrine.
17   Diego de Saavedra Fajardo, *Royal Politician Represented in One Hundred Emblems* (London: Matt. Gylliflower et al., 1700), 1: 320.
18   B. P. Maslov, "Ot dolgov khristianina k grazhdanskomu dolgu (ocherk istorii kontseptual'noi metafory)," in *Ocherki istoricheskoi semantiki russkogo iazyka rannego Novogo vremeni,* ed. V. M. Zhivov (Moscow: Iazyki slavianskikh kultur, 2009), 238–258.

of Cardinal Richelieu, who epitomized this development in his double status as a church dignitary and powerful first minister. The apocryphal text associated with his name aligned personal conscience and political duty in a passage that directly prefigures the concepts and conclusions of the last, most non-Shakespearean part of Sumarokov's soliloquy:

> Men must behave themselves in all things with Vigor, principally seeing that tho Success should not answer our expectation, at least we will have this advantage that having omitted nothing to make it succeed, we will avoid the shame ... on the contrary what ever Success a Man could have, in deviating from that which he is obliged to out of Honour and Conscience, he ought to be esteemed unhappy ...[19]

The decision to act taken by Sumarokov's Gamlet is also driven by a political ethos that associates conscience with honor ("posthumous national reputation," in Levitt's terms) and is intensified by a possibility of failure, as implied in Gamlet's willingness to shed blood for his people. This hypothetical scenario of self-sacrifice is further evoked in Act 5 where Gamlet's triumphant entry is preceded by rumors of his death that incite both popular upheaval and Ofeliia's mourning.

Sumarokov's radical reinterpretation of Shakespeare's character was anticipated in La Place's French version where, according to Helen Bailey, "Hamlet's metaphysical musings are condensed or omitted, yielding first importance to the progress of the plot. As a result, the hero's character is severely simplified. Physically 'robuste et alerte' (La Place's translation of 'He's fat, and scant of breath'), Shakespeare's 'sweet' prince becomes the 'noble' prince of French tradition: a normally fearless man of resolution and of action ... He has no need to look into his soul for the cause of his procrastination; he knows at all times exactly what he is about and why he behaves as he does."[20] Stripping the central character of psychological nuance, both continental versions realign

---

19   *The Political Will and Testament of that Great Minister of State, Cardinal Duke de Richelieu* (London: n.p., 1695), 2: 7–8; see also Françoise Hildesheimer, ed., *Testament politique de Richelieu* (Paris: Champion, 1995), 247.

20   Helen Bailey, *Hamlet in France from Voltaire to Laforgue* (Geneva: Droz, 1964), 10–11.

him with the political situation that forms the substance of the play's plot. Consequently, the Russian Gamlet's suspension of action, which both impedes "the progress of the plot" and conditions it as a source of dramatic suspense, is itself construed in terms of "political anthropology," a Machiavellian poetics of political action evoked in court politics no less than on the court stage.

Similar issues were at stake during the months before Elizabeth's coup, as the reports of French envoy Chétardie demonstrate. In a situation report sent in June 1741, Chétardie, closely involved in the preparation of the coup, emphasized the general dissatisfaction with the current rule ("la fermentation et le mécontetement qu'il y a dans l'interieur") and Elizabeth's popularity. At the same time he bitterly derided her "weakness" and "irresolution," which undermined her own protestations that she and her supporters were prepared to act "with all possible courage." Chétardie even concluded that Elizabeth was in fact unworthy to rule, and should have been excluded from succession in favor of her nephew.[21] Around the same time the English diplomat Edward Finch expressly drew from a Shakespearean representation of conspiracy to describe Elizabeth's conduct:

> For, as she is addicted to her pleasures, she will squander all the money she can get upon them; which may not only lessen her character, and of course diminish her popularity, but also, while she is not pinched in her extravagances, we may say of her, as Shakspeare's Julius Caesar says, "Her highness will be too fat to be in a plot."[22]

Finch apparently refers to the exchange between Caesar and Antony in 1.2:

> Caesar
> Let me have men about me that are fat,
> Sleek-headed men and such as sleep a-nights:
> Yon Cassius has a lean and hungry look;
> He thinks too much. Such men are dangerous.

---

21 *SIRIO* 96 (St. Petersburg, 1896): 169–170; P. Pekarskii, *Markiz de la Shetardi v Rossii 1740–1742 godov* (Riazan', Aleksandriia, 2010), 260–261.

22 *SIRIO* 91 (St. Petersburg, 1894): 106–107.

Antony
Fear him not, Caesar, he's not dangerous;
He is a noble Roman, and well given.

Caesar
Would he were fatter![23]

This motif resurfaces at an important juncture in *Hamlet*, as Gertrude questions her son's ability to assert his manly virtues in the duel with a famous formula we have already encountered: "He's fat, and scant of breath" (5.2).[24] Hamlet's fatness functions here as yet another medical trope for political impotence. Characteristically, though, all of the mentioned speakers except Caesar (Chétardie, Finch, Antony, and Gertrude) are proven wrong, while Cassius, Hamlet, and Elizabeth each turn out to be quite capable of bringing down their adversaries. Indeed, *Hamlet* is replete with references to *Julius Caesar*, which include Horatio's reading of the Ghost's appearance and Polonius' admission to Hamlet that he once "did enact Julius Caesar" and "was killed i' th' Capitol" (3.2)—a passage that clearly anticipates both Polonius's own demise and the death of Claudius.[25] In Shakespeare, Hamlet's madness oscillates between reality and deceit, resembling the feigned idiocy of Lucius Junius Brutus, the ancestor of Caesar's assassin and the founder of the Roman republic, who had assumed it as a disguise while planning the overthrow of Rome's last king. Similarly, the Russian princess Elizabeth shared with Shakespeare's Hamlet a "fatness," which in her case stood for political weakness originating in an "addiction to pleasures" but could also be construed as a mask for a political strategy.[26]

---

23 William Shakespeare, *Julius Caesar*, ed. Arthur Humphreys The Oxford Shakespeare, (Oxford: Clarendon Press, 1984), 112–113.
24 *Hamlet*, The Oxford Shakespeare, 248.
25 Ibid., 253; de Grazia, *"Hamlet" without Hamlet*, 67.
26 This is an approach recently suggested by K. A. Pisarenko, who insists that Elizabeth's well known hedonism and fear of direct action were only a disguise for cold-blooded strategy adopted from political and historical writings she had in her library. See, K. A. *Pisarenko, Povsednevnaia zhizn' russkogo dvora v tsarstvovanie Elizavety Petrovny* (Moskva: Molodaia gvardiia, 2003), 608–632. Of course, hopes for succession and intrigues to that end were not incompatible either with a sincere fear of failure and ruin or a true

Building on this parallel, Sumarokov takes pains to refashion and justify in political terms the reluctance to act imputed to both his prototypes, Shakespeare's Prince Hamlet and Empress Elizabeth. In this version, the soliloquy that questions the very possibility of action represents a momentary delusion occasioned by Gamlet's encounter with Ofeliia. While his ensuing speech showcases the fundamental tension between personal sensibilities—and specifically love, analogous to Elizabeth's "private" pleasures—and political duty, its doubts do not dominate Gamlet's character. Instead, from the very first scene Gamlet is mostly driven by a rage that must be tempered with considerations of prudence and efficacy. This function is assumed by the prince's confidant, Armans, as he himself explains to Gertrude's servant and his accomplice Ratuda:

Ратуда
Но что ему взойти на свой престол претит?

Арманс
Доколь с ним истина народ не съединит,
Все предприятии ево Ратуда тщетны;
В пути ему стоят препятствии безсметны.
Уже я множеству народа то открыл,
И силою присяг в них тайну заключил.
Одно лишь то меня тревожа устрашает,
Что Князь разгневанный терпение теряет.
Уж алчный меч его был в гневе обнажен,
И на врагов его жестоко устремлен.
Но иль нещастье их еще от них бежало,
Иль щастие ево ему то даровало,
Что меч без добычи в влагалище вмещен
И в ярости из них никто не поражен. (3.4.92–93)

---

propensity for pleasures, the only licit occupation accessible to a disinherited princess of royal blood. However, it also true that a high degree of pretense and duplicity was always in play in court politics. Moreover, Pisarenko's proposal to view Elizabeth's library as a source for practical political wisdom and strategy is certainly warranted by courtly approaches to psychology and the uses of literature as described by Norbert Elias in *The Court Society*, 104sqq.

Ratuda

But what prevents him now from ascending his throne?

Armans

Until the truth unites him with the people's goal,

His efforts are in vain to occupy the throne.

He faces obstacles that may prove serious hardships.

Many I've told the truth, the true state of affairs,

And under solemn oath I've made the secret known.

But one thing I fear most, and that's the prince's anger.

I fear lest he become enraged and lose his patience.

Already he has bared his sword that seeks revenge,

He's raised it up in wrath against his enemies,

But either their bad luck still skirted them or shunned them,

Or Gamlet's luck was kind enough to spare his victims,

And put his sword unstained with blood back in the sheath,

And all his foes remained unscathed by Gamlet's wrath.

(113–114)

Quite surprisingly for a model character of a court play, Armans lectures his audience on the arts of political conspiracy. Gamlet's delay is accounted for by the necessity to consolidate supporters and preserve secrecy; it is in this perspective that abstention from violence can be attributed to his "luck"—a notion reminiscent of Machiavellian "fortune," another mystified term for paradoxes and vicissitudes of political success (which, by the way, reappears as Fortuna in *Obraz torzhestva rossiiskogo*). As if addressing the likes of Finch and Chétardie, who criticized Elizabeth's indecision in the months before the coup, Armans evokes the wisdom of court politics in order to argue for strategic advantages of circumspection. Saavedra Fajardo, for example, engages in an intricate discussion of royal anger which, as he claims at first, should "submit to reason":

'Tis not thus sickle pettish Passion obtains Victories, triumphs over enemies, nor is that really Courage that is without Reason provoked. ... Anger is a short Madness, directly opposite to mature Deliberation; there is no better Antidote against it than prudent Reflection; that the Prince be not too hasty in Execution, before he has Council to examine a matter thoroughly. … Ministers [should] endeavour not only to moderate Princes Anger, but cover and conceal it handsomely.[27]

This pattern is both implied in Armans's speech to Ratuda and enacted in an earlier episode he refers to. In 1.3 Gamlet, apparently in a fit of rage, draws his sword and prepares to mount an immediate attack on Klavdii only to be held back by Armans:

Остановися здесь. Князь! что ты предприемлешь?
Ты в исступлении едину ярость внемлешь. (66)

Stop it, my Prince! I beg you study what you are doing,
For in your frenzied rage you listen only to passion. (94)

However, neither Armans nor Saavedra believe that royal anger should be in fact extinguished or debilitated. Rather, in Saavedra's words,

Anger is to be commended when kindled by Reason, and moderated by Discretion; without such as that, there can be no Justice. … To continue in Anger when 'tis to punish Offences, or make Examples of such as Affront Regal Authority is no Vice, but a Virtue, and by no means derogates from Mildness and Clemency. … That Anger too is praise-worthy in Princes, and profitable to a State, which kindled by incentives of Glory, elevates the Mind to difficult and noble Enterprizes, for without it nothing extraordinary, nothing great, can be undertaken … That, that is it which nourishes the Heart of generous Spirits, and raises it above its self to despise Difficulties. … Injuries done … to his Dignity or Publick Station, he ought not to vindicate as a private Person, so as in a transport of Passion to think his Honour and Reputation lost, except he have immediate satisfaction, especially when it were fitter to be deferred; for Anger should not be a Motion

---

27   Saavedra Fajardo, *Royal Politician Represented*, 1: 55, 57, 61.

of the Mind, but of the Publick Good and Advantage. . . . Nor is it less prudent to dissemble Anger, when one has reason to presume, that a time will come when it will be for our disadvantage to have shown it … A generous mind hides its Resentment of Injuries, and strives not by the impetuousness of Anger, but rather by noble Actions to smother them; the best, certainly, and a truly heroical kind of Revenge.[28]

This vision of royal conduct defines both the politics and the poetics of Sumarokov's *Gamlet* and its outcome. The transition from the prince's hesitation in the first four acts to his spectacular (though off-stage) coup in the fifth aligns the techniques of dramatic suspense with visions of power which feed on the tension between patient deferral and "extraordinary" actions. This pattern underlay the glorifying narratives of Elizabeth's conduct leading to her ascension. The German history quoted above characteristically speaks of the period when "this heroic princess has given most worthy signs of her greatness in adversity." Similar to *Gamlet*, dramatic celebrations of Elizabeth's coup, such as *Obraz torzhestva rossiiskogo* or Bonecci's opera *Bellerofonte* (1750), also highlighted her protracted "ordeals" as a setting for her momentous victory. Indeed, it is only this deferral that by contrast makes postponed violence "extraordinary" and, thus, a lasting source of power. This is why a reluctance to act immediately constitutes for Saavedra a specific feature that distinguishes the prince from a "private person." Accordingly, Gamlet's "noble Action" in the play's finale is anticipated by Armans as a Schmittian state of exception, a (re)constitution of royal authority in a single "hour" that disrupts the orderly course of political "times":

Снимай желанный час с народа бремена
И скончивай страны сей злые времена!
Дай небо, чтоб жил Князь с Офельей неразлучно
И правил скипетром своим благополучно! (3.5.93)

O long-awaited hour, remove the people's yoke,
And put an end to all the evil times we've known!

---

28 Ibid., 57–61.

May God grant to the prince and to the fair Ofeliia
A reign of plenty and a happy life together! (114)

At this juncture political discourse and dramatic poetics drew on the same fundamental distinction between two opposite modes of temporality, developed in antiquity and adopted by early modern political thought: "Whereas *chronos* denotes a linear and progressive sense of time, *kairos* stands in opposition as a rare singularity."[29] From Plutarch to Machiavelli and "thinkers ... associated with the spread of Machiavellianism and reason of state" (including Saavdera Fajardo), this distinction was employed to grasp the challenges of political practice.[30] In his chapter on "new Principalities acquired by one's own conduct and arms" Machiavelli speaks of skillful use of opportunity:

Such occasions made these great men successful, and their wisdom taught them how to improve those opportunities to the reputation and deliverance of their respective Countries. It is a difficult matter indeed for other people to raise themselves to dominion in the same heroic manner that they did; but when they succeed, it is very easy to maintain it.[31]

This language shaped the perceptions of Elizabeth's position before the coup. If in June 1741 Chétardie feared that she was missing a unique occasion ("il est difficile de retrouver de pareilles circonstances quand on les laisse échapper"), in October he was somewhat more optimistic and sounded like Sumarokov's Armans:

The minute to act openly, after the difficulties I have overcome, has arrived ... one should not lose a single moment to come to terms with one's supporters; this would be the occasion to assert and convince them that there is no such effort that they should avoid in order to cast off the yoke of the foreigners ... One should come

---

29 Joanne Paul, "The Use of Kairos in Renaissance Political Philosophy," *Renaissance Quarterly* 67, no. 1 (Spring 2014): 45–46.

30 Ibid., 46; Horst Bredekamp, "Von Walter Benjamin zu Carl Schmitt, via Thomas Hobbes," *Deutsche Zeitschrift für Philosophie* 46, no. 6 (1998): 901–916.

31 *The Works of Nicholas Machiavel*, 1: 541.

and support through one's presence the power of this noble resolution, which would simultaneously command respect and inspire. This advice ... does not exclude any measures of prudence and precaution ... first of all one has to ensure the firmness of those who value the fortune of the fatherland and their own.[32]

The encomiastic *Portrait naturel,* composed to publicize Elizabeth's rule soon after the coup, recast these concepts of practical politics into a celebration of royal will:

Toute la terre a admiré sa conduite sage et circonspecte, lorsqu'après la mort de l'empereur Pierre Second, elle se vit exclue du trône de ses augustes parens. Tems d'adversité et de soufrance, qui dura pres d'onze ans, pendant lequel elle eut besoin de toute la prudence humaine pour conserver sa liberté et son droit. Sa prudence est soutenue per une fermeté mâle et une courage heroïque; qualités, qu'elle fit briller a travers de l'obscurité de la nuit, memorable a jamais, dans laquelle la courageuse resolution de revendiquer le trône fut executée avec une hardiesse et un bonheur, dont on ne trouve pas d'exemple dans les histoires.

All the world admired her wise and circumspect conduct when after the death of the Emperor Peter II she was denied the throne of her august parents. The times of adversity and suffering lasted for more than eleven years when she needed all human prudence to retain her freedom and her rights. Her prudence was supported by valorous constancy and heroic courage—qualities which allowed her to shine in the darkness of the night, forever memorable, when her courageous resolve to reclaim the throne was executed with daring and good fortune unparalleled in history.[33]

The precarious balance between patience and impulse, courage and prudence recommended by Machiavellian political idiom could not in fact

---

32 *SIRIO* 96, 169. Pekarskii, *Markiz de la Shetardi v Rossii 1740–1742 godov,* 328–329.
33 *Portrait naturel,* 4–5.

be achieved in theory but only in action, in the moment of a "noble Enter-prize." However, for all its disillusionment, this idiom did not reduce political success to mere chance but—by way of "political anthropology"—supposed an equivalence between "Regal Authority" and the character of its holder. This person has to be endowed with a "generous spirit" and an "elevated mind": "Spirit—such was the thesis of the age—shows itself in power; spirit is the capacity to exercise dictatorship."[34]

It is this alignment of—and tension between—ostensible action and modes of interiority that is explored in early modern tragedy, and specifically frames Sumarokov's reading and adaptation of *Hamlet*. Sumarokov shares with Chétardie (not to mention the English translators of Saavedra and Machiavelli) a concept that played a central role at this juncture of political and literary anthropology, that of a *hero*. As Levitt notes, in his central mono-logue, the Russian Gamlet opposes "cowardice" (*malodushie*) to "heroism" (*geroistvo*). This concept retains the reference to violent self-sacrifice most familiar to us. Polonii says: "No s smertiiu i muk bezstrashno zhdet geroi" (2.1.74), "A hero awaits death and torments without fear" (99), and in La Place's French version of Shakespeare, Fortinbras, arriving after the duel scene, calls the deceased Hamlet a "hero."[35] There are, however, other mean-ings at stake. They are manifested in the exhortation that Sumarokov's Gamlet receives from his father's ghost and that anticipates the play's outcome:

Прими Геройску мысль, отставь дела любовны,
Воззри на тень мою, и зри потоки кровны … (63)

Take up heroic thoughts and put aside love's pleasures,
Look at your father's ghost and see the bloody torrents … (91)

The term *heroic* is associated here with a genealogical myth, requiring a half-divine, half-fictional apparition in place of a father, a specific type of political action, and a specific emotional mode ("put aside love's pleasures"). This was quite standard for the time. The 1762 edition of the *Dictionnaire de l'Académie française*, for example, outlined the genealogy of the term *héros* and

---

34 Benjamin, *Origin of the German Tragic Drama*, 98.
35 De La Place, *Théâtre anglois*, 2: 416.

its doubly figurative meaning. While in antiquity it stood for the fiction of divine extraction, contemporary usage revived this fiction as a metaphor for military feats or public displays of "grande noblesse d'âme" ("great nobility of the soul"). Accordingly, in Chétardie's correspondence with his court in 1741 the term *l'héros* was used to refer to Elizabeth as a future leader of a coup. Rather transparent as a cipher, Chétardie's usage both evoked the violent "scenario of power" that the French diplomacy had in mind for Elizabeth and revealed its fundamental dependence on a trope. Weber's analysis, which lists "heroic power" as a form of charismatic authority, suggests that it originates—both as a notion and function—in a metaphorical procedure that infers "exceptional" personal qualities of the leader (and her divine, or dynastic, legitimation) from successful displays of force.[36] This political trope underlay panegyric celebrations of Elizabeth's coup, both lyric and dramatic, which often styled her a "heroine," attributed to her divine birth, and compared her to heroes of ancient myth, paragons of violence rather than dynastic stability (Hercules, Jason, or Bellerophon). The same trope shaped the dramatic poetics of Sumarokov's *Gamlet*, a play which refashions its political and literary prototypes in terms of a general "political anthropology," and Gamlet, a *hero* whose interiority is defined by the challenges of political action.

---

36 Weber, *Theory of Social and Economic Organization*, 358–362.

INVESTIGATIONS OF MALICE

Trediakovskii's definition of tragedy as a reenactment of divine justice, an abbreviated theory of the genre's of its aesthetic and moral effect, resonates with a remark made in 1730 by the Duke of Liria, the Spanish ambassador to Petersburg:

> June 6 sealed the final ruin of the house of Dolgorukii. Prince Aleksei, the father of the betrothed bride of Peter II, was exiled with all his family to the Berezov island which before that had harbored the unfortunate Menshikov ... This was the tragic end of this branch of the house of Dolgorukii, favored by Peter II, and it seems that its fall was effected by divine justice, to punish them for their mischief and boundless haughtiness and vanity.[1]

Liria's association of the fall of Dolgorukiis with tragedy was not incidental, and Jane Rondeau concurred that it would "make a pretty story for a tragedy."[2] Apparently, the language of Horatian poetics evoked by Trediakovskii was intrinsically related to the common experience of European court politics. (The Duke of Liria, a Spanish diplomat and a member of the house of Stuart, who wrote in French and spoke English, was the epitome of the cosmopolitan European aristocracy.) A space where secularization of theology into political theory was played out, tragedy staged the link between divine justice and court politics, particularly the fall of the great. Shakespeare's *Hamlet*, as de

---

1   *Zapiski diuka Liriiskago*, 103.
2   Vigor, *Letters from a lady*, 64.

Grazia demonstrates, built on visions of history suggesting that "the lives of the highborn had a cadential structure."[3] Tragedy and dramatic introspection as its central technique were aligned with forensic narratives of political crime, and depended on a generally accepted "political anthropology" that shaped public perception of actions and events on and off stage. This is how Liria's account of the Dolgorukiis' disgrace is structured. He first reports the events and then provides a political-theological interpretation for them (introduced, characteristically, with the phrase "it seems"). What follows is an act of introspection that justifies the act of punishment by fashioning the Dolgorukiis as "tragic" villains driven by "limitless ambition."

A similar procedure underlies Sumarokov's *Gamlet*. As in *Khorev*, Sumarokov draws on the fundamental affinity between tragedy and political prosecution, but he reinterprets it in light of Trediakovskii's critique, distancing himself from any suspicion of dissent. In *Khorev*, political prosecution constituted a ruler's tragic error, underscoring the need for clemency. In *Gamlet*, the ruin of Klavdii and Polonii, evidently an allusion to the overthrow of the Braunschweig dynasty and spectacular prosecution of Münnich and Ostermann after the coup of 1741, is represented as the triumph of political and divine justice. Accordingly, if in *Khorev* Stalverkh's Machiavellian suspicions against Khorev and Osnelda are exposed as a malicious distortion of their pastoral intentions, in *Gamlet* a sinister "political anthropology" of malice and intrigue indeed drives the play's central conflict originating in Klavdii's and Polonii's struggle for power. The unambiguously negative representation of their conduct aligns the perspective suggested to the audience with that of Gamlet, their triumphant accuser, and reproduces constructions of criminal interiority established and propagated in various court-sponsored discourses.

Münnich and Ostermann were tried and convicted for a conspiracy to obliterate the testament of Elizabeth's mother, Catherine I. According to the order of succession established by Catherine, Elizabeth would have ascended to the throne eleven years earlier, in 1730, after the death of Peter II. As Münnich and Ostermann reminded their prosecutors, Catherine's regulation was invalidated by Petrine law, which allowed every subsequent monarch a free choice of a successor. However, Elizabeth was persistent in orchestrating the trial, which

---

3   De Grazia, *"Hamlet" without Hamlet*, 52.

reinterpreted the complex dynastic politics of the 1730s as the outcome of a protracted and targeted conspiracy against her succession rights. This reading of events was first presented to the public immediately after Elizabeth's ascension, and the prosecution of the alleged conspirators—publicized through further royal manifestoes—was a logical second act of her "scenario of power." The inculpatory narrative that underlay the trial centered on the repeated usurpation of Elizabeth's sovereignty by powerful subjects who ignored their duty of obedience to the deceased monarch and the dynastic principle. It was imputed to Ostermann, for example, that he "did not defend as was his duty" the testament that he among others "had signed and confirmed with a solemn oath" as Anna Ioannovna was elected to the throne in 1730, and again when Ivan Antonovich was chosen as her heir in 1740.[4] Once again, the manifesto relies on a semi-mystical notion of dynastic succession rather than legal procedure as the true source of kingship—just as in Shakespeare's *Hamlet* an apparently lawful election fails to invest Claudius with an ultimate, sacred legitimacy.

Similar issues were negotiated in Voltaire's *Mérope* (and Trediakovskii's Russian summary of it). Attempting to restrain the powerful general Polifonte, the politically weak, yet legitimate queen, Mérope reminds him of his sacred obligations to the ruling dynasty (3.1):

> Un parti! Vous barbare, au mépris de nos lois!
> Est-il d'autre parti que celui de vos rois?
> Est-ce là cette foi, si pure et si sacrée,
> Qu'à mon époux, à moi, votre bouche a jurée?
> La foi que vous devez à ses mânes trahis …

> Is there a party which thou dar'st support
> Against the king's, against the royal race?
> Is this thy faith, thy solemn vows, thy oath,
> Sworn to Cresphontes, and to me; the love,
> The honour due to his illustrious shade …[5]

Generally, Polifonte and his role in the play's political cosmos closely resemble the wide-spread assessments of Münnich's conduct that fueled the

---

4   *Polnoe sobranie zakonov* (1740–1743), 11: 568, no. 8506.
5   Voltaire, *Complete Works*, 17: 255; Voltaire, *The Dramatic Works*, 4: 13.

narrative of his crimes in Elizabethan manifestos. Polifonte is a general who has established peace in Messene and suppressed civil strife unleashed by the murder of King Cresphontes. As a savior of the city he claims the right to partake of royal sovereignty:

> La fière ambition, dont il est dévoré
> Est inquiète, ardente, et n'a rien de sacré.
> S'il chassa les brigands de Pylos et d'Amphrise;
> S'il a sauvé Messène, il croit l'avoir conquise.
> Il agit pour lui seul, il veut tout asservir:
> II touche à la couronne; et pour mieux la ravir,
> II n'est point de rampart que sa main ne renverse,
> De lois qu'il ne corrompe, et de sang qu'il ne verse ...

> Restless ambition, that holds nothing dear
> Or sacred but itself, has sill'd his foul
> With bitterness and pride: because he drove
> The ruffian slaves from Pylos and Amphrysa,
> And sav'd Messene from a band of robbers,
> He claims it as his conquest: for himself
> Alone he acts, and wou'd enslave us all:
> He looks towards the crown, and to attain it
> Wou'd throw down ev'ry fence, break every law ...[6]

Similarly, Münnich established his military fame during the Crimean campaigns of 1735–1739, and after overthrowing Biron's regency in 1740 rose to the rank of Russia's "first minister" under Anna Leopoldovna's weak rule. Münnich, who prided himself on being known as the "pillar of the Russian empire," was famous for his "great ambition."[7] Manstein wrote of him:

> There is not another man in the world of so high a soul, and yet he has been guilty of paltry acts. His dominating vice is pride. Devoured

---

6 Voltaire, *Complete Works*, 17: 252; Voltaire, *The Dramatic Works*, 4: 10–11.
7 Maréchal de Münnich, *Ebauche de gouvernement de l'Empire de Russie*, commentary and notes by Francis Ley (Geneva: Droz, 1989), 93; Pekarskii, *Markiz de la Shetardi v Rossii*, 228.

by an ambition beyond all bounds, he sacrifices everything in the
world to gratify it. What be best loves is his own interest ...[8]

This assessment is supported with a characteristic episode illustrating
Münnich's aspirations to a royal title:

> The ambitious schemes of marshal Munich had gone still farther in the
> life of the Empress Anne. When he entered Moldavia with his army,
> even before he had effected the conquest of that duchy, he proposed to
> the empress to make him hospodar [ruler] of it ... He asked for the
> title of duke of Ukrain, and explained his views to the duke of Cour-
> land, when he enclosed him the request to be presented to the empress.
> The duke, accordingly, gave it into the hands of the empress, who said,
> on seeing it, "Marshal Munich is still excessively modest; I thought he
> would have asked me for the title of grand-duke of Muscovy."[9]

Manstein's report is marked by a rising degree of fictionality: it recounts
an uncorroborated rumor that figures the empress exaggerating Münnich's
ambition in an ironic fantasy of her own. It is all the more significant that this
account shares a fundamental symbolic pattern with other narratives of political crime and retribution, including the official charges against Münnich in
1741–1742 and the staging of *Mérope* in 1746. Voltaire's Polifonte offers to
marry Mérope so that his dictatorial power would support her weakened
dynastic authority instead of undermining it; Mérope declines "with contempt,"
as Trediakovskii puts it. Münnich was also represented as someone who
attempted to usurp royal sovereignty while pretending to uphold the rights of
a "weak" yet dynastically legitimate candidate. According to Elizabeth's manifesto, he failed to protect her rights in the succession struggles of 1740–1741,
although he had "all the power in his hands" and recognized the legitimacy of
her claims to the throne. Allegedly, he had even attracted the loyalty of the
guards by affecting the wish to reinstate Elizabeth in her rights, while in fact
only pursuing his own goals.[10] Like the fictional Polifonte, Münnich came to

---

8   Manstein, *Contemporary Memoirs of Russia*, 331.
9   Ibid., 274.
10   *Polnoe sobranie zakonov*, 11: 571–572. For a recent well informed account of Münnich's
     trial, see Brigitta Berg, *Burchard Christoph Reichsgraf von Münnich (1683–1767). Ein*

be associated with the general apprehensions of excessive political ambition inappropriate for subjects, which—as Liria's phrasing affirms as well—seemed to threaten monarchic order and to warrant violent prosecution.

In his well-known essay "Invisible Bullets," Stephen Greenblatt discusses the cultural (and specifically theatrical) patterns behind early modern political prosecution: "when a hated favorite … was accused of treason what was looked for was not evidence but a performance, a theatrical revelation of motive." These expectations, Greenblatt argues, were often driven by a common "cultural conceit, the recurrent fantasy of the archcriminal as atheist," because "no one who loved and feared God would allow himself to rebel against an anointed ruler."[11] A similar alignment of political offence with religious transgression was pivotal for political discourses adopted and employed in early modern Russia. Gentillet argued that "the cause … that commonly princes and great lords have no the feare of God" is "the want of Faith: for if a prince beleeved verely the paines of hell, to bee such as indeed they are, he would doe no wrong to noe man."[12] Furió Ceriol's sixteenth-century treatise on royal "counsel" extant in an early eighteenth-century Russian translation titled *Nastavlenie tsaria o tvorenii sovetov i o izbranii sovetnikov*, asserted:

> князь и советники истинные суть служитилие Божии. Противным же образом, злым советом неточию княжое достоинство растлевается, но и весма изнуряется … Народ убо разоряется, и в последнюю пагубу приходит: Сия же двоица сие есть князь и советницы, отпадением от воле Божой пленниками диаволскими стаетъся.

> the prince and the councilors are the true servants of god. Conversely, evil council not only corrupts the prince's stature but weakens it as well … For the people is impoverished and comes to utter ruin, while this pair, the prince and his councilors, as they depart from divine will become devil's prisoners.[13]

Oldenburger in Zarendiensten (Oldenburg: Isensee, 2011), 353–361.

11 Greenblatt, *Shakespearean Negotiations*, 25.

12 Gentillet, *A Discourse upon the Meanes of Wel Governing*, 245; Gentillet, *Anti-Machiavel*, 430.

13 OR RNB, OSRK, q. II. 25, ll. 2ob-3. On Furió Ceriol and his work, see Ronald W. Truman, *Spanish Treatises on Government, Society, and Religion in the Time of Philipp II:*

The allegations against Münnich and Ostermann followed the same pattern. A royal manifesto accused them of "machinations both impious and detrimental to our state" ("Bogu protivnyia i gosudarstvu nashemu vreditel'n yia intrigi").[14] Court preachers called upon to justify Elizabeth's ascension and the punishment of her enemies pictured Ostermann and Münnich—Protestant ministers in an Orthodox state—as demonic adversaries of Christian faith, "devil's emissaries" sent to destroy the divinely sanctioned order of dynastic succession and the Orthodox Church.[15]

Before Greenblatt, the religious perspective on courtly intrigue and its significance for early modern drama was explored by Benjamin. He observed that "the court official, the privy councilor who has access to the prince's cabinet where the projects of high politics are conceived, is presented ... his power, knowledge, and will intensified to demonic proportions ... The drama of the German protestants emphasizes the infernal characteristics of the councilor." This motif culminates in the parallel between Cain and the courtier, who often shares the "curse which God laid upon the murderer."[16] Indeed, Shakespeare's Hamlet muses in the graveyard scene (5.1):

> That skull had a tongue in it, and could sing once. How the knave
> jowls it to th' ground, as if it were Cain's jaw-bone, that did the first
> murder. It might be the pate of a politician, which this ass now
> o'er-offices, one that would circumvent God, might it not?[17]

In Benjamin's analysis, the demonic councilor accompanies an even more troubling figure of the tyrant, one of the necessary "incarnations of the princely essence." Just as Cain is the archetypal courtier, the monarch dangerously resembles "the figure of Herod as he was presented throughout the European theater of the time, which is characteristic of the idea of the tyrant.

The "De Regimine Principum" and Associated Traditions (Leiden: Brill, 1999), 89–116.

14   Polnoe sobranie zakonov, 11: 568.

15   Popov, "Pridvornye propovedi v tsarstvovanie Elizavety Petrovny," 5ff.

16   Benjamin, Origin of the German Tragic Drama, 97–98.

17   Shakespeare, Hamlet, 324.

It was this story which lent the depiction of the *hubris* of kings its most powerful features. Before being seen as a mad autocrat and a symbol of disordered creation, he had appeared in an even crueler guise to early Christianity, as the Antichrist." [18] The dramatic tradition outlined by Benjamin was not extinct by the eighteenth century. Sumarokov lists among Voltaire's best plays the tragedy *Hérode et Mariamne* (1724–1725).[19] It is from baroque dramatic forms discussed by Benjamin that eighteenth-century tragedy, and Sumarokov in particular, inherited its visions of the monarchy's darker aspects.

Although Sumarokov did not retain Shakespeare's graveyard scene (and his Klavdii, unlike Cain, does not kill his own brother), the representation of illicit ambition in his *Gamlet* builds upon the same idea of a "politician … that would circumvent God." His villains, Klavdii and Polonii, much more than his Gamlet, are shaped by their relationship to the divine, as they seem to illustrate Furió Ceriol's concept of an evil monarch and his councilor as a pair of "devil's prisoners." Once again, we must review Polonii's profession of his political theology:

Кому прощать Царя? народ в его руках.
Он Бог, не человек, в подверженных странах.
Когда кому даны порфира и корона,
Тому вся правда власть, и нет ему закона. (2.2.78)

Who's to forgive the king? The nation's in his hands.
He is not man but God through all the realm he rules.
Whoever gains the crown and the imperial purple
Knows no law but his own, his voice alone is juctice. (102)

Just as the demonic only exists as a perversion of the divine, tyranny corrupts—rather than extinguishes—the truths of sacred kingship. In a sense, Polonii merely reiterates accepted definitions of royal power, emphasizing its "absolute" status above any law, supported by the parallel

---

18   Benjamin, *Origin of the German Tragic Drama*, 69.
19   Sumarokov, *Izbrannye proizvedeniia*, 126.

between royal and divine sovereignty. The problematic aspects of this doctrine are manifested in the Machiavellian dictum "his will alone is justice," or even "power is his only law," where the tensions implicit in Schmittian "secularization" are negotiated through poetic polysemy and nuance. Besides juridical meaning most familiar to us, the eighteenth-century Russian concept of law, or *zakon*, held strong religious connotations: in fact, it could stand for religion itself.[20] Consequently, in Polonii's Russian phrasing the commonplace legal argument in favor of absolute monarchy comes to suggest a negation, or usurpation, of divine authority. This usurpation is directly played out in the identification of the monarch with God. While it was, generally, a legitimate political trope widely spread in early modern Russia,[21] Sumarokov subtly shifts conventional phraseology and turns Polonii's words into outright blasphemy. In denying his own humanity ("he is not man, but God"), his divine monarch pretends to more than Christ himself does. (Several years earlier, a court preacher claimed that Osterman and Münnich had been worshipped as pagan gods who had assumed human form, and were in fact Russia's "golden idols," ["kumiry zlatyia"].[22]) Polonii, who is no atheist and does not shy away from references to divine justice on other occasions, is here carried away by Machiavellian (de)mystification of politics, which—paradoxically—undermines rather than reinforces his calculation. While he is right to assert that the people are not entitled to judge the king, he forgets about a higher power—even as he evokes its name—which in the end of the play manifests itself in the "wonder" of a successful and legitimate insurrection.

For Klavdii, whose appearance as tyrant is largely shaped by Polonii's speeches, forceful assertion of royal status also requires a violation of worldly and divine law. In his scheme to kill off Gertruda and marry Ofeliia, he not only discards moral obligations to restrain his passions and abstain from

---

20 *Slovar' russkogo iazyka XVIII veka* (St. Petersburg: Nauka, 1992), 7: 244–246. On religious connotations of law in medieval and early modern Russia, see V. M. Zhivov, "Istoriia russkogo prava kak lingvosemioticheskaia problema," in *Razyskaniia v oblasti istorii i predystorii russkoi kul'tury* (Moscow: Iazyki slavianskoi kultury, 2002), 187–305.

21 Uspenskii and Zhivov, "Tsar' i Bog."

22 Popov, "Pridvornye propovedi v tsarstvovanie Elizavety Petrovny," 10.

murder, but also endangers the only legal grounds for his rule as Gertruda's husband. This plot line, one of Sumarokov's most significant additions to Shakespeare's plot, does not have any consequences (Ofeliia is rescued by the revolting populace) yet occupies a significant space within the play. Apparently, its dramatic function is to reveal the inner workings of tyrannical violence. Although Sumarokov's Klavdii is not represented as mad, his actions definitely correspond to the "Herodian" visions of monarchy reconstructed by Benjamin:

> At the moment when the ruler indulges in the most violent display of power, both history and the higher power, which checks its vicissitudes, are recognized as manifest in him. And so there is one thing to be said in favour of the Caesar as he loses himself in the ecstasy of power: he falls victim to the disproportion between the unlimited hierarchical dignity, with which he is divinely invested and the humble estate of his humanity.[23]

The "tension between immanence and transcendence" inherent in the doctrinal parallel between God and sovereign (as reiterated by Polonii) is specifically addressed in Sumarokov's *Gamlet*. Polonii's Machiavellian assertion of the king's divinity is rebutted by the repentant Gertruda:

> Царь мудрый есть пример всей области своей …
> То помня завсегда, что краток смертных век,
> Что он в величестве такой же человек. (78)

> The wise king sets his land examples how to live …
> He knows that the life of man is but a flash of time,
> That kings are also men in their majesty. (102)

It would be wrong, however, to suppose that Gertruda (or Sumarokov) aims to divest kingship of its religious mystique. While Polonii's monstrous

---

23 Benjamin, *Origin of the German Tragic Drama*, 70.

falsehood discredits both God and king, Gertrude revives the political theology of the king's double nature, modeled on the double nature of Christ.[24] If the ideal of kingship is shaped by the harmonious coexistence of the worldly and the divine, it is the distortion of their relationship which makes Klavdii a tyrant. This is the substance of his first meaningful exchange with Polonii:

Полоний
Имей великий дух приявши скипетр в руки,
Будь мужествен по гроб, и не страшися муки.
Не тот отважен, кто идет безстрашно в бой;
Но с смертию и мук безстрашно ждет герой.
Забудь и светския и Божески уставы,
Ты Царь противу их; последуй правам славы.

Клавдий
Наполнен злобою жизнь вечную губя,
Будь бодр, мой томный дух, и не щади себя!
Довольствуйся одним ты, Клавдий щастьем света
И уж не отрицай днесь пагубна совета!
Не представляй злых следств, и жизни сей конца,
Вся часть твоя есть честь державы и венца.
Наполним щастием здесь житие толь кратко,
Чтоб при конце сказать: я жил на свете сладко.
Но кая фурия стесненну грудь грызет?
И кая скорбь во мне всю внутренную рвет?
О небо! не тревожь меня, оставь в покое!
Уже не превратишь мое ты сердце злое.
Не обличай меня; спасенья не хочу,
И что я зделал, то во аде заплачу. (2.1.74–75)

Polonii
You've picked the scepter up. Now let your spirit triumph.

---

24 Ernst Kantorowicz, *The King's Two Bodies: A Study in Mediaeval Political Theology* (Princeton: Princeton University Press, 1957).

Be brave even to death, and brook no fear of torment.
The one who's not afraid of war is not so brave;
A hero awaits death and torments without fear.
Forget the law of God, forget the rules of humans,
For you alone are king, and you must live for glory.

Klavdii
With evil in my heart, I lose eternal life
And steel my weary soul for all that is to come.
My happiness must be fulfilled within my lifetime,
And I will heed the words of wise Polonii's counsel.
O tell me not the way this life of mine must end,
This life which has no worth beyond the throne and crown.
With this rare happiness I'll feel my life so fleeting,
And when the end draws near, I'll say I've lived completely.
But I, what pain is this, what fury gnaws my heart,
What sorrow tears my soul, what thoughts oppress my mind?
O heaven, spare my soul this ever-growing anguish,
For yours is not the craft to change my murky spirit.
Call me not by my name, I care not to be saved,
And all that I have done, in hell will be repaid. (99)

Contrary to Polonii's later claims of Klavdii's divinity, these lines highlight human frailty as the core of his inner self, the moral source for his
crimes and the ensuing political crisis. His ambition compels him, literally,
to "circumvent God" and adopt a specific ethic which values the pleasures
of earthly power over salvation. Elsewhere, when Ofeliia rejects the plans
of her marriage to Claudius on moral and religious grounds, Polonii
derides her attachment to traditional religion as it complicates her way to
the throne:

Подобьем таковым младенцы рассуждают,
Которы все дела грехами поставляют,
И что безумие жен старых им втвердит,
Все мыслят, что то им в них совесть говорит. (3.2.86)

> This is the away affairs are understood by infants,
> Who think that everything is villainous and sinful,
> And whatever old women teach them,
> They believe it is the voice of their conscience. (109)

Homiletic denunciations of Münnich and Ostermann similarly linked their political practice to a blasphemous "Epicureanism":

> Christian dogmas which lead us to eternal salvation, they considered fables and trifles … Eat, drink, feast, there is no consolation after death: and those who would rave in this way would enjoy favor with our enemies [Münnich and Ostermann], those would acquire ranks … Who would fast, would be considered a hypocrite; who would speak to God in prayer, superstitious …[25]

Political crime only exists in confrontation with the sacred order. The tyrant's anticipation of torment in the afterlife makes him, in Benjamin's terms, into a martyr to his own worldliness ("A hero awaits death and torments without fear"), as it reestablishes the retributive power of divine law disputed by Polonii. Curiously enough, the religious perspective on tyranny was not extinct in Enlightenment tragedy. For all his audacity, Voltaire's Polifonte also fears that "heav'n, / By slow and solemn steps, may bring down vengeance" (4.1).[26] Frederick of Prussia agreed in his critique of *Mérope* that it is natural for a tyrant to be superstitious, that is, to fear divine punishment.[27] Similarly, in Sumarokov's play, the dual law of divine and worldly justice, circumvented by Klavdii's actions, reemerges under the name of conscience in the focus of his troubled interiority. The conversation quoted above immediately follows Klavdii's prayer, which Sumarokov adopted from Shakespeare:

> Се Боже! пред Тобой сей мерзский человек,
> Который срамотой одной наполнил век,
> Рушитель истинны, бесстыдных дел рачитель,

---

25 Popov, "Pridvornye propovedi v tsarstvovanie Elizavety Petrovny," 13.

26 Voltaire, *The Dramatic Works*, 4: 17; Voltaire, *Complete Works*, 17: 259.

27 Voltaire, *Complete Works*, 17: 309.

Враг твой, враг ближняго, убийца и мучитель!
Нет силы больше дел злодейских мне носить;
Принудь меня, принудь прощения просить!
Всели желание искать мне благодати;
Я не могу в себе сей ревности сыскати!
Противных божеству исполнен всех страстей,
Ни искры добраго нет в совести моей.
При покаянии ж мне что зачати должно?
Мне царствия никак оставить невозможно.
На что ж мне каяться и извергати яд;
Коль мысли от тебя далеко отстоят? (74)

O God, behold this man who kneels before You now,
This villain who has filled his life with shameful vice,
Destroyer of the truth, of wickedness a zealot,
Tormentor, murderer, a foe to God and neighbor.
I cannot bear the weight of any further sin.
Help me to find forgiveness, O Almighty God,
Fill me with desire to seek Your grace and mercy,
For I cannot pretend to feel religious fervor.
My instincts are the ones which God does most detest,
And in my conscience shines no spark of good at all.
In laying bare my sins what can I do about them?
I can't give up the throne, nor can I yield the kingdom.
What good is to repent, to cast the venom out,
If all my inner thoughts are so remote from You? (98–99)

What can seem a rather naïve representation of a villain's self-denunciation in front of his accomplice and the audience is in fact central for Sumarokov's tragic poetics inherited to a large degree from "baroque" allegorical drama.[28] Klavdii's outburst, surprising for a politician of Machiavellian cunning, is a psychological projection of the state of exception whereby the seemingly

---

28 Klein, *Puti kul'turnogo importa*, 375–376, draws attention to the demonic aspects of the tragic tyrant as exposed by another of Sumarokov's Shakespearean usurpers, Dimitrii Samozvanets, and concludes that Sumarokov largely depended on the poetics of "baroque" drama.

suppressed divine authority manifests itself in the tyrant's conduct. This is the fundamental paradox behind Klavdii's speech. Though he professes to have lost access to divine will, and is accordingly punished at the play's end, it is his prayer that ultimately establishes divine judgment (evoked earlier by Gertruda) as the frame of reference for his actions. In fact, Klavdii's tyrannical self emerges from an inversion of the Davidic royal prayer that secured divine support for the ruler and his land in the course of the coronation rite (most recently, at Elizabeth's coronation in 1742, publicized by a lavish album printed in 1745). Thus, Klavdii's prayer does not lead away from the political, as we would expect, as he concludes that he "can't give up the throne." Instead, it stages the link between individual interiority and the "divine" foundations of political order, which cannot but assimilate "the law of God" with the "rules of humans." As Levitt concludes in his analysis of this scene, "when Sumarokov's characters evoke the afterlife, it is as the place where evil is unequivocally punished or good rewarded, and hence an eloquent argument for proper behavior in the here and now."[29] A similar symbolic pattern was played out during another high profile trial of the preceding decades, the prosecution of Prince Dmitrii Golitsyn, one of the leaders of the aristocratic opposition of 1730. Arrested in 1737 on not altogether unfounded charges of corruption, Golitsyn made a comment under enhanced interrogation that was then reproduced in the inculpatory manifesto:

> князь Дмитрий, не ужасаясь страшнаго суда Божия, так Богу противно сказал, что будто совесть надлежит до одного суда Божия, а не до человеческаго, ведая, что суд гражданский суд Божий есть. … и злея того яд свой изблевал, объявляя перед судом, что когда б из ада сатана к нему пришел, то бы хотя он пред Богом и погрешил, однако ж и с ним бы для пользы своей советовал, и советов от него требовал и принимал.

> Prince Dmitry, not fearing God's terrible judgment claimed blasphemously that conscience is only a matter of divine judgment and not human, [despite] knowing that civil court is the court of God … and he vomited even more evil venom when he declared before

---

29 Levitt, "Sumarokov's Russianized *Hamlet*: Texts and Contexts," 85.

the court that if Satan would come to him from hell he would, even if he sinned against God, consult him for his own benefit, and would have asked and accepted his council.[30]

Golitsyn's outburst, like Klavdii's, both unmasks his criminal interiority and aligns it with the most exaggerated demonic visions of corrupt council, for the abuse of authority, as the manifesto suggests, is never far from a pact with Satan. Golitsyn himself resorted to this ultimate trope of dissent in an attempt to question the identification of faith and conscience with political discipline. This was a central point of the political theology of "secularized" absolute statehood, styled here as self-evident religious orthodoxy. Accordingly, Golitsyn's doubts are only reiterated to reemphasize the outlines of the triumphant authority he had momentarily challenged, the symbolic validity of royally sponsored repression amalgamated with divine retribution: "civil court is the court of God." Acting in the name of this dual law (the "law of God, rules of humans" evoked by Polonii), the procedures of royal prosecution both rely on the notion of conscience and replace the act of self-analysis it simultaneously represents and requires. It is only during interrogation that the offender's guilt is confirmed, and his inner self is revealed to his judges. In "historical reality," Foucault writes, "the modern 'soul' … unlike the soul represented by Christian theology, is not born in sin and subject to punishment, but is born rather out of methods of punishment, supervision and constraint."[31] Judicial introspection and the punitive gaze, divine and prosecutorial, which shapes it, were shared in the manifestos with the general public—the same people who, according to Foucault, "were summoned as spectators" to "the liturgy of torture and execution" because they "must be the witnesses, the guarantors, of the punishment, and because they must to a certain extent take part in it."[32] Similar patterns of introspection and engagement, both political and aesthetic, were at stake in tragedy, and in Sumarokov's *Gamlet* in particular.

---

30 *Polnoe sobranie zakonov*, 10: 11–12.
31 Michel Foucault, *Discipline and Punish: The Birth of the Prison*, trans. Alan Sheridan (New York: Vintage Books, 1979), 29.
32 Ibid., 49, 58.

THE CATHARSIS OF PARDON

The play's culmination, Gamlet's triumph over his enemies in the fifth act, takes a double form. Behind the scenes he kills Klavdii and overtakes the Danish throne, and reappears on stage only to deal with Ofeliia's insistent pleas to pardon her captive father. Only after he does so out of love for her does she show an interest in his exploits and allow the audience to hear the details of the revolt. It can be said that dramatic representation inverts the spatial pattern of events. Gamlet's coup, which is hidden from the audience, originates in the public spaces of the city and is made possible by the immediate involvement of the populace, whereas the prince's conversation with his mistress and his decision made in secluded royal chambers are opened to the public eye. This inversion follows the classicist convention that did not permit violence on stage. At the same time it reveals a fundamental logic of monarchic representation: the universally known but questionable origin of royal power in popular violence is overshadowed by a display of singular royal sovereignty over Polonii's life and death. The play's last spark of suspense is provided for by Gamlet's verbose wavering between punishment and pardon, which takes up a whole scene. Here, Sumarokov's tragedy reenacts a tension that underlay manifestations of sovereignty in rituals of punishment, as described by Foucault:

> sovereign power ... never appeared with more spectacular effect than when it interrupted the executioner's gesture with a letter of pardon. The short time that usually elapsed between sentence and execution (often a few hours) meant that the pardon usually arrived

at the very last moment. But the ceremony, by the very slowness of its progress, was no doubt arranged to leave room for this eventuality. … The sovereign was present at the execution not only as the power exacting the vengeance of the law, but as the power that could suspend both law and vengeance.[1]

Indeed, the proximity of dramatic poetics to procedures of spectacular punishment was made evident to the Russian public in the months after Elizabeth's ascension. Her newly acquired sovereignty was manifested in two parallel stagings of royal justice: the pardon and exile of Münnich and Ostermann on January 18, 1742, and, starting in May of the same year, repeated productions of the festive opera *La Clemenza di Tito* (*The Clemency of Titus*), which, according to Stählin, "represented a live image of the glorious Empress's benevolent spirit." Stählin (who happened to author the prologue articulating the analogy between Elizabeth and Titus) reports that a theater specially built in Moscow and intended for 5,000 spectators was overcrowded on the first three performances, and the opera enjoyed general approval among the empire's nobility.[2] In Metastasio's libretto, published in Russian translation soon afterwards, the emperor Titus investigates a failed conspiracy against him and at the last moment pardons the main suspect. With this plot, *La Clemenza di Tito*, originally written for the Habsburg court and loosely modeled on the French dramatic classic, Corneille's *Cinna* (1642), became one of the most popular scripts for festive celebrations of monarchy across Europe. It was also recognized as a dramatic masterpiece: thus, Voltaire in his *Dissertation sur la tragédie ancienne et moderne* praised Metastasio as a worthy rival of Greek tragedians and singled out Titus's profession of clemency as "an eternal lesson for kings, and the admiration of all mankind": "To take the life of a fellow-creature is in the power of the vilest being upon earth: to give it belongs only to the gods

---

1   Foucault, *Discipline and Punish*, 53.
2   *Beylagen zum Neuveränderten Rußland* (Riga and Leipzig: Johann Friedrich Hartknoch, 1770), 2: 94–95; Vsevolodskii-Gerngross, *Teatr v Rossii pri imperatritse Elizavete Petrovne*, 19–25. For the Russian version, see [Pietro Metastasio], *Miloserdie Titovo: Opera s prologom: Predstavlennaia vo vremia vysokotorzhestvennago dnia koronatsii e. i. v. Elisavety Petrovny* … (Moscow: Tipografiia Akademii nauk, [1742]).

and to kings."[3] Merging dramatic poetics with the workings of royal charisma, clemency functioned as the ultimate "scenario of power"—the institutional act of sovereignty in its double status as earthly authority and an incarnation of divine will.

The demand for such a performance no doubt propelled the prosecution of Münnich and Ostermann on false charges, resulting in what an informed eyewitness, the Saxon diplomat Petzold, called a "spectacle" ("Schauspiel"), a "terrifying play" ("schauderhafte[s] Spiel"), and a "tragic action" ("tragischer Aktus"). It was announced before the crowd gathered for the promised execution that lethal torture for all offenders would be substituted with "perpetual banishment" (to quote Finch's report) and a confiscation of property. The intricate phrasing of the manifesto is reduced by Petzold to a laconic formula: "God and the Empress grant you your life." Even before he received a printed copy of the manifesto with the official interpretation of events, Petzold was easily able to outline it: the empress has shown her magnanimity and clemency (*Clemenz*) and, in commemoration of her peaceful ascension, taken mercy on those who have been found guilty.[4] In what is simultaneously an emotionally charged firsthand account and a circumspect political commentary, Petzold singles out the same qualities of the empress as Stählin in his record of *La Clemenza di Tito*.

However, there were important differences between the two performances of royal justice, providing for a tension that complicated the very notion of clemency. In Corneille, Augustus pardons the guilty Cinna and restores him to his high ranks. Similarly, in Metastasio, Titus repeals the painful, and public, death sentence he has ordered for the main suspect because he is at the last moment proven innocent. On the Petersburg scaffold, however, the concept of clemency comes to designate a penalty known in Russian judicial practice as "political death." In fact, the trial of Münnich and Ostermann was a starting point for Elizabeth's famous suspension of capital punishment and reinstitution of political death in its stead as the

---

3   Voltaire, *The Dramatic Works*, 2: 11; Voltaire, *The Complete Works*, 30A: 146; Pietro Metastasio, *The Clemency of Titus from the Italian by a Lady* (Liverpool: George Smith, 1828), 51.

4   Ernst Herrmann, *Geschichte des russischen Staates* (Hamburg: Perthes, 1853), 5: 5; *SIRIO* 6 (St. Petersburg, 1870): 408.

harshest penalty imposed by the state. As Finch's overtly critical dispatches demonstrate, the outlines of Russian judicial order were at stake from the very beginning of the trial. In December 1741, he reported that the empress herself—just like Metastasio's Titus—was directing the "examinations," and concluded that "there is nothing in this country, at least on such occasions, which deserves the name of the court of justice" but only of "inquisition."[5] After the scene on the scaffold Finch pointed to obvious cruelty of Elizabeth's "clemency": "If leading a wretched life in perpetual banishment and the remotest parts of Siberia may appear to any of these unhappy persons a more eligible fate, than a speedier end of their misery, it is entirely owing to her Majesty."[6]

Elizabeth's handling of Münnich and Ostermann's case relied on the same deeply ambiguous view of clemency that was explored in drama and theorized in political literature starting from Seneca's *De Clementia* (*On Clemency*, 55–56 CE), a treatise characteristically addressed to Nero and revived by early modern political thought. Praising clemency as an ultimate gesture of domination, Seneca's treatise amalgamates it with its opposite, suppression:

> to owe your life to someone is the same as to have lost your life. Anyone thrown down from the heights to his enemy's feet and made to wait for a verdict about his life and his kingdom from someone else increases the glory of the preserver by living on.[7]

Similarly, as Hélène Merlin-Cajman demonstrates, in Corneille's *Cinna* (which, just like Metastasio's Titus libretto afterwards, closely followed Seneca), Augustus's clemency is styled as an "extraordinary form of punishment" and, as such, "a revelation of sovereignty."[8] The same perspective is

---

5 *SIRIO* 91, 386.
6 Ibid., 422.
7 Seneca, *De clementia*, ed. Susanna Braund (Oxford: Oxford University Press, 2009), 133.
8 Hélène Merlin, *Public et littérature en France au XVIIe siècle* (Paris: Les Belles Lettres, 1994), 297. On the politics of royal clemency in early modern drama, see further Armin Schäfer, "Der Souverän, die *clementia* und die Aporien der Politik. Überlegungen zu Daniel Casper von Lohensteins Trauerspielen," in *Theatralität und die Krisen der Repräsentation*, ed. Erika Fischer-Lichte (Stuttgart: Weimar, 2001), 101–124; Armin Schäfer "Die Wohltat in der Politik. Über Souveränität und Moral im barocken Trauerspiel," in *Imaginem. Bildlichkeit und Souveränität*, ed. Anne von der Heiden (Zürich: Diaphanes, 2005), 79–99.

manifested in the final scenes of *Gamlet*: Polonii receives pardon from the triumphant Gamlet but commits suicide rather than acknowledge Gamlet and Ofeliia as his "sovereigns" ("vladeteli"). At this point his daughter, who earlier felt obliged to plead for her criminal father's life, sums up the play's action with a formula which could be borrowed from Trediakovskii's (or Liria's) discussion of tragedy as a staging of divine retribution. She exclaims:

Ты само небо днесь Полонья покарало!
Ты, Боже мой! ему был долготерпелив!
Я чту судьбы твои! твой гнев есть справедлив! (5.6.119)

Heaven, you have yourself wrought justice on my father!
Your patience has been tried, your judgment slow to come.
I know your wrath is just, I know God's will is done! (134)

Thus, the play has a double ending: Gamlet's hesitant act of pardon is balanced in the very last lines by Polonii's terrifying and ambiguous death, which simultaneously represents a last doomed attempt at emancipation and an ultimate divine punishment. If Seneca and Metastasio associated the divinity of kingship with pardon, in *Gamlet*'s ending divine will is expressly assigned responsibility for the criminal's death. Indeed, according to Finch similar arguments were employed by the Petersburg public to justify the evident injustice of Münnich's fate:

Upon this occasion, those whose humanity and generosity lead them rather to insult than pity people in distress, affect to talk much of the providence of God and His divine judgments, which I believe it would better become them to adore, than to pretend to penetrate …[9]

Polonii's death represents the affinity between "political death" imposed after a pardon and the death penalty it ostensibly suspends, as well as the common visions of divine wrath as the ultimate reason behind royally

---

9 *SIRIO* 91, 423.

sanctioned political prosecution. In his argument with Ofeliia, Gamlet evokes divine vengeance epitomized by his father's ghost as the main ground for punishing Polonii, so that retribution rather than clemency is exalted as the sacred principle of royal justice. Later, Sumarokov would express similar views in his *Slovo na den koronovaniia … Ekateriny II* (*Oration on the Coronation Day of Catherine II*, 1762), censored at the time of its original composition. Rearranging the commonplaces of the official political theology, he develops a parallel argument against an overreliance on divine forgiveness, and an understanding of royal clemency ("milost'"), as leniency: "i milost' nakazaniia opredeliaet" ("clemency, too, imposes punishments"). To illustrate his point, Sumarokov refers to none other than Titus, the paragon of clemency: "Plakal Tit, kogda bezzakonnikam podpisyval kazni; plakal, no podpisyval" ("Titus wept when he had to sign death warrants for the criminals; wept but signed them").[10] Referring to an episode that figures in Metastasio's libretto, Sumarokov makes a point of circumventing the play's famous ending: while Titus could have once pardoned the innocent, he still had to execute the guilty.

In his *Gamlet*, however, Sumarokov associates the pattern of spectacular punishment unrestrained by clemency with the tyrannical ways of Klavdii and Polonii. As Polonii prepares to execute Ofeliia for her refusal to marry Klavdii he speaks to the guards present at the scene:

Вы воины смотрите
Позорище сие, и в нем пример возьмите,
О правосудии народу возвестить,
Которо над собой я вам хочу явить.
Единородна дочь моя в преступок впала:
Она владетелю досаду показала,
Непослушанием устав пренебрегла … (5.2.108)

Soldiers, behold this spectacle, and learn from this a lesson.
To all the people tell of justice that was done
By one who had to make the judgment on himself.

---

10 Sumarokov, *Polnoe sobranie vsekh sochinenii,* 2: 230–232.

My only daughter has into transgression fallen
By showing the king a heart filled up with anger,
By disobedience to the imperial will ... (125)

While King Gamlet and Empress Elizabeth certainly share Polonii's belief in harsh and public punishment, they both feel compelled to resort to conspicuous if seemingly pointless gestures of clemency. Their logic, explored in Sumarokov's play, had less to do with the fate of particular offenders than with specific "scenarios of power," quasi-theatrical patterns of emotional engagement evoked by the monarchy to fashion its relationship with the public of spectator subjects.

Sumarokov's punishing Titus has to weep in order to manifest the divine duality of the sovereign who combines heavenly justice with human empathy (as Gertruda reminds Klavdii in 2.2: "Vragov svoikh proshchat' est' dolzhnost' nashei very," 77; "Forgiving enemies is part of our religion, 102). In Ofeliia's argument with Gamlet, the sentimental idiom of love tragedy is used to expose this empathy as an intrinsic attribute of royal politics that merges personal emotion and the strategies of power in the public performance of royal selfhood. In order to obtain Polonii's pardon, Ofeliia invokes Gamlet's love for her and reminds him that Polonii's execution would make their marriage impossible. As Gamlet holds to his notions of duty and vengeance, Ofeliia brings forth her last argument:

Сего ли для ты жизнь нещастныя продлил,
Чтоб ты свирепея мя с нею разлучил,
Чтоб я лютейшее терзание вкусила,
И очи, ах! в тоске несносной затворила?
Какое бедство я стране сей приключю!
Все радости в тебе народны помрачю.
Никто уже меня без злобы не вспомянет,
Коль из любви моей толь вредный гром здесь грянет.
Когда над сердцем я твоим имею власть;
Яви любезный Князь, яви мне ону страсть!
Иль на Полония железом изощренным,
Дай прежде смерть вкусить тобою чувствам пленным!

Отмщай! но прежде ты любовь мою забудь,
И проколи сперва Офелиину грудь! (5.5.115).

Today you saved my life, a life of the distressed.
Was this to kill me later with more savageness?
To make me know the taste of unimagined torment,
To make my eyes to close at last in bitter anguish?
How great will be the woe I cause to this poor land!
All of our country's joys will fade and die with you.
No one will think of me without a flush of hatred.
Out of my love for you will roar a fearful thunder.
If I still have the power left to sway your heart,
Show me, my dearest prince, the love that I once knew.
And if you will avenge, if your sword has been sharpened,
Then take your sweet revenge! But first do me this favor,
Forget my captive heart, forget the love it holds,
And pierce it with your sword before my father's death. (131)

Commonplace tropes of tragic sensibility are interwoven here with an interrogation of the newly established civic peace. While Ofeliia does not question Polonii's guilt ("Ia, Kniaz', zlodeia v nem, kak ty unichtozhaiu," 5.3.111; "like you I do disdain in him the villain," 128), she insists on the broader political resonances of his execution that would affect the innocent. In the pathetic evocation of her own near death, a metaphor of amorous longing amounts to a formula of royal terror capable of indiscriminate brutality, that is to say, Gamlet's torture and murder of his own faithful bride:

Уже не чувствуешь любезной огорченья,
И становишься сам виной ея мученья.
Жалей меня, жалей, не дай мне умереть! (5.5.113)

No longer do you feel the grief of your beloved,
And you yourself become the cause of her affliction.
Take pity on me, Hamlet, do not let me die! (129)

Like Gamlet himself in his grand soliloquy, Ofeliia uses intimations of suicide as a trope for general political resentment, and—in an otherwise obscure threat—styles her future death as a hopeless yet imposing act of defiance. Invoking the fundamental patterns of clemency, punishment, and domination, she reveals the dependence of Gamlet's sovereignty on public emotion—"joy" or "hatred"—which can, and must, be steered by extraordinary and spectacular actions. If imputed to Gamlet, as Ofeliia suggests, her death beside her father would make her an innocent victim of royal terror, undermining the people's attachment for their king and, thus, producing a political calamity, "fearful thunder." Indeed, Ofeliia draws on an argument commonly made in political philosophy. Frederick the Great in his famous *Anti-Machiavel* (1740) advised against royal cruelty:

> I conclude then, that a cruel Prince is much more exposed to treason and other dangers, than one that is tender and merciful: for cruelty is insupportable, and people soon grow tired of fear: but goodness is always amiable, and subjects are never weary of being affectionate. It is much to be wished, therefore, for the happiness of mankind, that all Princes were good, without being too indulgent: that so their lenity might always be regarded as a virtue, rather than despised as a weakness.[11]

It is not surprising, then, that Gamlet, after distancing himself from a suspicion of leniency, or weakness, succumbs at this point to Ofeliia's arguments and gives free reign to pity and love ("Vladychestvui, liubov' ... !" 115; "O love, yours is the power," 131"), which are through his very choice of words inscribed in, rather than opposed to, the logic of rule and kingship. This display of royal emotion does not save Polonii (Heaven itself takes care of that), but it does reestablish Gamlet's affective relationship with the rest of the polity. Instead of terror, Gamlet now inspires public joy, as Ofeliia exclaims: "Preobrashchaisia, plach, ty v radosti i smekhi!" (115; "Weeping, give way to sounds of thankfulness and laughter," 131). In *Gamlet* just as in *Cinna* and *La Clemenza di Tito*, the

---

11   *The Works of Nicholas Machiavel*, 1: 630.

gesture of clemency functions as a theatrical device that grounds sovereignty upon a strong emotional affect evoked among the publics on and off stage.[12]

A quasi-theatrical view of royal justice, including both punishment and pardon, was not, however, peculiar to the dramatic tradition, but was also shared by legal and political discourses which shaped the official documentation of Elizabethan political trials. Among the works read in post-Petrine Russia was Justus Lipsius's *Monita et exempla politica* (1605), translated into Russian in 1721 as *Uveshchaniia i priklady politicheskiia*.[13] Lipsius, an editor and commentator of Seneca, engages in a lengthy discussion of royal justice and its effects on the populace. He first pleads for direct royal involvement in the administration of justice because it allows the king to claim the respect due to all judges, so that "his words, gestures, or even his gaze gives rise to fear in the heart of men." He then elaborates on the workings and effects of royal terror:

> неправда то яко грозная казнь раждает царю ненависть от народа, паче же противное видим в человецех правду любящих, иже радуются и благодарят, егда видят грозное и жестокое злым наказание. Самый точию взор жестокия казни умиляет нас и смущает. ... Аще же царь иногда покажет ослабу согрешившему, не будет то во образ прочим согрешати понеже там велии страх и срам ослабу или прощение предварят. Простит кому царь, обаче страха прежде и безчестие исполнивши, простит кому царь, но царь ... человеколюбия точию и милости ради, сие убо самое коликую любовь у всех исходатайствует, аще точию благовременне случится.

> it is not true that a terrifying punishment instills the people with hatred for the king; on the contrary we may see that people who value justice rejoice and express gratitude when they see the punishment of the wicked. The very spectacle of a severe punishment moves

---

12 Merlin, *Public et littérature en France au XVIIe siècle*, 297.

13 On early Russian translations of Lipsius, see O. E. Novikova, "Lipsii v Rossii pervoi poloviny XVIII veka," in *Filosofskii vek*, vol. 10 (St. Petersburg: Sankt-Peterburgskii Tsentr istorii idei, 1999).

and agitates us. … Even if the king does show leniency towards a criminal, that will not be an example for others to sin because in that case pardon will be preceded by great fear and shame. The king can pardon, yet he will first inflict fear and infamy; the king can pardon but it will be the king … [acting] out of sheer humanity and mercy, which will evoke general love, if the timing is right.[14]

Like Empress Elizabeth or Sumarokov, Lipsius does not see repression and clemency as mutually exclusive but rather as complementary elements of royal justice. His vision of authority builds upon the strategic manipulation of opposite emotions stirred by the "spectacle of a severe punishment" (or pardon), which "moves and agitates us" enough to mold "fear and infamy" into their opposite, a manifold public affection (love, joy, gratitude) for the ruler endowed with such "humanity and mercy."

Lipsius's interrogation of judicial authority develops along the same lines as Aristotelian definitions of the tragic effect canonized by classicist literary theory. This parallel, already discussed in part 1, both illuminates the logic of the trials and explains the functions claimed by the newly imported tragedy in the Elizabethan "theater of power." According to Aristotle, tragedy had to evoke both pity and fear in order to "purge" the emotions of the spectators. Dacier's authoritative interpretation of Aristotle's ideas inscribed this literary doctrine into the Platonic debate on the status of poetry in the political order and concluded that "the Passions when regulated [a]re useful, nay necessary," while tragedy's aim is to "Curb the Excess, by which they err'd, and to reduce them to a Just Moderation … In whatsoever Condition a Man may be, yet when he shall see, an Oedipus, a Philoctetes, an Orestes, he can think his own afflictions light in Comparison with theirs."[15] In René Rapin's wording, tragedy represents "the unforeseen Disgraces to which the most important Persons are subject" and, among other things, teaches "Men not to fear too weakly the common Misfortunes, and manage their Fear; it makes account also to teach them to spare their Compassion, for Objects that deserve it not."[16] Similar effects were achieved by the punishment of Münnich and Ostermann. Petzold reported,

---

14   OR RGB, fond 354, no. 233, ll. 277–279.

15   *Aristotle's Art of Poetry*, 78–79.

16   Rapin, "Reflections upon Poetry," 205; René Rapin, *Les réflexions sur la poétique de ce temps, et sur les ouvrages des poètes anciens et modernes* (Geneva: Droz, 1970), 98.

In all his life he did not experience anything more dismal than this
spectacle; aside for the raging mob, even among Russian nobles
there were few who left the square indifferent or without
compassion.[17]

Apparently, differences in emotional reaction corresponded to, and reaffirmed, different positions of the spectator groups in relationship to royal
violence. While the populace assembled to witness a public execution was
prepared to endorse royal punishment of the powerful, the nobility could
not escape compassion for the convicts as it could not but feel immediately
threatened. Indeed, since ministers on trial had long occupied the highest
positions in military and civil administration, many of the capital's serving
nobles had to be their former clients or subordinates. Sumarokov himself
started his career as a protégé of the vice-chancellor Golovkin, who in 1742
stood on the scaffold beside Münnich and Ostermann.

Finch's sarcastic advice to those who justified the trial "to reflect seri-
ously on which of them the lot may fall next"[18] points to a reaction both
natural for subjects of an autocracy and appropriate for spectators of a
tragedy. Dacier defines tragic pity as "a Sense of Pain, which the sufferings
of a Man who does not deserve it, produces in us; since that Evil is of such
a Nature, that it may happen to us, and which we may reasonably fear."[19]
In fact, Aristotle discusses and compares various possible emotional reactions to public misfortunes of others, and advises against the display of the
"misfortunes of a very wicked Man" since it "may give some Pleasure, but
it will produce neither Fear nor Pity." The ruin of the guilty, Dacier
explains,

will never stir us up to Compassion, because he has only what he
deserved ... and consequently all good Men ought to be pleased at
it. If his Misery does not excite Pity, it will much less excite Fear,
and so cannot refine the Passions, for the Spectators knowing
themselves not to be wicked as that Man, will never fear those evils,

17   Herrmann, *Geschichte des russischen Staates*, 5: 5.
18   *SIRIO* 91, 423.
19   *Aristotle's Art of Poetry*, 189–190.

which he has drawn on him by his Crimes, nor endeavour to make themselves better.[20]

If so, not only pure "pleasure" at the ruin of the "wicked," but also compassion and fear of fellow subjects who felt threatened by disproportionate or plainly unjustified royal violence was a proper reaction to public punishments staged with Lipsius, if not Aristotle, in mind. Just like Aristotelian theory, the idiom of judicial terror amalgamated fear and pleasure. As Lopukhina and her accomplices were prosecuted in 1743 for expressions of resentment after the Münnich trial, the royal manifesto read:

> мы … уповали, что показанное Наше к ним милосердие не токмо им самим и их фамилиям, но и друзьям их за наичуствительнейшим удовольствие быть имело, что и без сомнение целой свет засвидетельствовать может …

> We … had hoped that the clemency we have shown would be accepted with an utmost pleasure not only by the convicted but also by their families and friends, which, no doubt, the whole world can confirm …[21]

In his *Gamlet* Sumarokov both ignores Aristotle's advice in order to comply with Trediakovskii's criticism and to elicit moral *pleasure* originating from the ruin of the wicked, and stages the political effects of *pleasure* originating in the act of false pardon. His Ofeliia seems to be modeled on Lopukhina and her accomplice, Countess Bestuzheva, who gave a female voice to the resentment of the "families and friends" of the convicts in the first trial, numerous and influential noble clans. In this case, Ofeliia's death threat alludes to Lopukhina's publicly known and all but blatantly suicidal defiance of Elizabeth, and simultaneously points to the dangers for civic peace inherent in the false logic of escalating repression. Ofeliia's reconciliation with Gamlet precisely reproduces the pattern of appeasement outlined

---

20 Ibid., 192.
21 *Polnoe sobranie zakonov*, 11: 881, no. 8775.

in the 1743 manifesto: a suspension of the death penalty is represented as a symbolic gesture strong enough by itself to produce a general "pleasure" among the political class affected by the trials, just as it is designed to please the audience of the play's fifth act.

Sumarokov's tragic poetics relied on the same patterns of public sensibility that were affirmed and explored by judicial terror. Characteristically, in his 1756 madrigal celebrating a court production of his opera, the notion of pleasure ("udovol'stvie") makes one of its first appearances in Russian as an aesthetic concept, describing the fine effects of musical and dramatic performance on the court public and on the author himself.[22] Neither in the idiom of terror nor in Aristotelian poetics, however, is *pleasure* considered to be the primary or the best possible effect of the spectacle upon the audience. Aristotle suggested that the sight of another's undeserved ruin is beneficial as it evokes *catharsis*, a "purgation of the passions," which, in Dacier's words, inspires the spectators to "to make themselves better." Dacier inscribes Aristotle's poetics into a Christianized discussion of moral discipline: since it is impossible, he writes, "to oblige Men to follow the Precepts of the Gospel," tragedy has been introduced in order to provide them with "Diversions, where there is Order, and Shows, where Truth is to be found." In this way, it is a remedy against general moral corruption. Consequently,

> Tragedy does not only represent the Punishments, which voluntary Crimes always draw on their Authors ... But it sets forth the misfortunes which even involuntary crimes, and those committed by Imprudence, draw on such as we are, and this is perfect Tragedy. It instructs us to stand on our guard, to refine and moderate our Passions, which alone occasion'd the loss of those unfortunate ones. Thus the aspiring may learn to give bounds to his Ambition; the Prophane to fear God; the Malicious to forget his Wrongs; the Passionate to restrain his Anger; the Tyrant to forsake his Violence and Injustice.[23]

---

22 Sumarokov, *Izbrannye proizvedeniia*, 181.
23 *Aristotle's Art of Poetry*, preface.

Levitt draws attention to Sumarokov's direct paraphrase of this doctrine in a 1755 epistle that "specifically described the action of the tragic poet in terms of compulsion":

В героях кроючи стихов своих творца,
Пусть тот трагедией вселяется в сердца:
Принудит чувствовать чужие нам напасти
И к добродетели направит наши страсти.

Speaking in verse through his heroes, the creator of a tragedy should enter [his audience's] hearts, compel us to feel alien misfortunes and direct our passions toward virtue.[24]

According to Levitt's reading of these lines, "The tragedian, like the divine Creator, actively 'sows' emotions into the hearts of his audience and compels them towards virtue 'by means of tragedy,' thus 'imitating the very actions of God' [as Trediakovskii advised]."[25] While Sumarokov's regular use of the word "tvorets" ("creator") for author hardly supports a theological reading, a parallel between the effects of faith and tragedy is in this case certainly warranted and particularly relevant for *Gamlet*. In his Gertruda, Sumarokov vividly stages the alignment of dramatic representation and effect with disciplinary introspection, both divine and judicial.

In a variation of Shakespeare's closet scene with its famous formula of self-knowledge ("Thou turn'st mine eyes into my very soul"), she is already in the first act confronted by Gamlet and Armans and must admit her crimes:

Покров безстыдных дел Гертрудиных низпал,
Проклятая душа открылась пред тобою ... (1.3.68)

The curtain that concealed my shameful deeds has dropped,
And you have seen the scars that left my soul accursed ... (94)

---

24 Sumarokov, *Izbrannye proizvedeniia*, 130. I borrow Levitt's translation with slight emendations.

25 Levitt, "Sumarokov's Russianized *Hamlet*: Texts and Contexts," 87.

As for Gamlet, in this first encounter with the crime he is destined to purge, he anticipates his actions in the fifth act and pardons Gertruda. In an oddly sacerdotal gesture, he and Armans speak in the name of divine justice and lecture her on the political theology of repentance that closely associates divine will with earthly compliance:

> Признание вины к прощению успех,
> Кто плачет о грехе, тот чувствует свой грех . . . .
> Безсмертный милосерд, и гнев его смягчится,
> Коль грешник перед ним всем сердцем сокрушится.
> Покайся, и коль смерть супругу ты дала,
> Превысь блаженными злодейские дела. (68–70)

> Confession of one's guilt leads others to forgive,
> Who truly rues his sin has won the right to grace. . . .
> God's mercy knows no bounds, and his wrath shall be softened,
> When sinners truly feel with all their hearts contrition.
> Repent, and if you've killed your husband, still repent,
> Exceed your evil deeds with deeds of blessedness. (94–96)

In response to these admonitions, Gertruda, in Levitt's words, "truly engages the issue of whether or not she is in a condition to pray" and "is able finally to reconcile divine commandment and the voice of heaven with her inner voice of repentant conscience to overcome her passionate self."[26] While she may indeed embody the "traditional Russian Orthodox values of kenotic humility," as Levitt claims, it is crucial that she only repents when her crime is exposed and she considers herself to be in immediate danger of violent punishment. As Gamlet confronts her, he is armed and raging against his enemies, so that the desperate Gertruda even suggests that he should kill her himself: "Zabud', chto mat' tvoia, kazni svoei rukoi" (68; "Forget that you're my son and kill me now, at once," 95). While he does not physically harm his mother (a barbaric gesture reminiscent of the ancient Orestes and prohibited by Shakespeare's Ghost), he makes sure to exercise his nascent authority

---

26 Ibid., 91.

over her. Promising her a remission of sins in the afterlife, Gamlet through Armans sentences Gertruda to what sounds like perpetual exile ("Ostavi svet drugim, i plach' v pustyniakh vvek," 71; "leave the world behind forever for some wilderness," 97)—a measure which reminds the spectator of Elizabeth's treatment of her overthrown predecessor, Anna Leopoldovna, who was spared a public punishment but sent away from Petersburg and imprisoned.

Confronted with pardon and punishment, a dual gesture of Gamlet's sovereignty, Gertruda experiences a conversion which simultaneously inscribes into several disciplinary paradigms—religious, political, and aesthetic—and showcases their mutual alignment in the symbolic structure of autocracy. Confessing her sins to a legitimate successor to the throne, she reenacts the crossover of religious discipline and political order found in practices of justice and penitence characteristic for early modern Europe, and specifically for eighteenth-century Russia where obligatory confessions were introduced as a measure of state control over the nation.[27] At the same time, Gertruda's self-exposure before the retributive gaze of royal and divine authority leads her to experience what Aristotelian criticism understood to be *catharsis*, a purgation of passions. Excessive fear of a criminal in hiding ("Razversty propasti, i ad menia pozhret," 69; "Hell's portals open wide and draw me to my home," 95) evoked by Gamlet's account of her crime resolves itself in a moral transformation associated with a righteous fear of God:

Но все, что ни страшит в смятении меня,
Чего себе ни ждет душа моя стеня,
Ни что в толикий страх злочастну не приводит,
Как то, когда сие на мысль мою приходит,
Что, ах! не буду зреть Творца я своего. (71)

But there's one thing I fear beyond all other fears,
Whatever else my soul may suffer in distress,
And nothing grieves me more in all my tribulations

---

27 Viktor Zhivov, "Handling Sin in Eighteenth-Century Russia," in *Representing Private Lives of the Enlightenment, Studies on Voltaire and the Eighteenth Century*, ed. Andrew Kahn, no. 11 (Oxford: Voltaire Foundation, 2010).

Than when I sometimes chance to think of what I'd suffer,
If I should never see my Maker and my God ... (97)

Conversely, this intimately felt fear of God is inscribed into a vision of
moral discipline that embraces political existence along with religious experience. Gertruda's spectacular conversion represents a mode of subjectivity posed
equally by judicial terror and Aristotelian theory. The vices that she urges her
accomplices, Klavdii and Polonii, to repudiate with her are precisely those that
Dacier listed in his didactic interpretation of catharsis: "Thus the aspiring may
learn to give bounds to his Ambition; the Prophane to fear God; the Malicious
to forget his Wrongs; the Passionate to restrain his Anger; the Tyrant to forsake
his Violence and Injustice." The act of repentance, or purgation, fulfilled by
Gertruda on stage, was implied in tragedy as its primary effect on its audience.
In this respect, too, tragedy was aligned with political trials that, as can be seen
from the Münnich manifesto, aimed for a similar effect:

И чтоб все верныя Наши подданные, смотря на то призна-
вали, что Бог клятвопреступникам не терпит, и что мудрым
Его промыслом скрытыя в сердцах их умышления к времян-
ному и вечному их осуждению всегда откровенны бывают, и
дабы опасаясь того от всяких таких Богу противных поступок
конечно остерегались, и во всем бы так поступали, как то
верным подданным и прямым сыновьям отечества по
присяжной их должности принадлежит, за что от Бога во
всех своих предприятиях благословенны, также и Нашею
Императорскою милостию всегда награждены будут.

Let all our true subjects see this and acknowledge that God does
not tolerate perjurers and that evil intentions hidden in their hearts
are always revealed through his wise Providence to their temporal
and eternal blame, and that they [subjects] should abstain from
actions of this kind which are repugnant to God, and should always
act as true subjects and sons of their fatherland ought according to
their sworn duty, and they will be blessed by God and will be
always rewarded with our royal favor.[28]

---

28 *Polnoe sobranie zakonov*, 11: 575, no. 8506.

Appealing to the subjects' inner selves in an attempt to impose upon them an orthodoxy of autocratic obedience amalgamated with divine justice, the spectacle of disproportionate repression drew on emotional scripts common to drama and the "theater of power." The spectacular nature of political trials proved to be an intrinsic element of autocratic domination which could not be dispensed with even when the pattern of constant repression was suspended. With all their exaggerated or outright false accusations and unjustified punishments, the political trials of 1742–1743 functioned as scenarios, or "fictions," carefully crafted to call forth and regulate public anxiety for the benefit of the monarchic order. Emerging after the cessation of high-profile trials in the wake of the Lopukhina case, Russian tragedy with its plea for mercy both supplanted them as a performative genre and took over their function of fashioning public sensibilities. The scaffold provided a blueprint for the genre of tragedy and a point of departure for the institution of court theater. If protocols of pleasure established there were free from physical violence and displaced suffering into the realm of fiction, theater as a space simultaneously enhanced the ruler's physical and emotional control over the public, which itself literally became—along with actors on stage— subject to the interrogating royal gaze.[29]

---

29 On the link between the disciplinary effects of public punishment and early modern drama, as well as on the amalgamation of dramatic, religious and judicial introspection, see Steven Mullaney, "Apprehending Subjects, or the Reformation in the Suburbs," in Steven Mullaney, *The Place of the Stage: License, Play, and Power in Renaissance England* (Ann Arbor: University of Michigan Press, 1995), 88–115; Debora Kuller Shuger, *Political Theologies in Shakespeare's England: The Sacred and the State in "Measure for Measure"* (New York: Palgrave, 2001).

THE THEATER OF WAR AND PEACE: THE "MIRACLE OF THE HOUSE OF BRANDENBURG" AND THE POETICS OF EUROPEAN ABSOLUTISM

TRAGEDY AND POLITICAL THEOLOGY ON THE BATTLEFIELD

In the preceding chapters, I have discussed the import of tragedy into Russia against the background of court politics, pageantry, and theatrical and judicial practices of the 1740s. I would like to conclude my study with an episode that provides an inverted perspective on the intrinsic affinity of tragedy with royal politics. Throughout this book, I have argued that tragedy never amounted to a straightforward glorification of power—it actually entailed a complex interrogation of its hidden workings and tensions. Conversely, actual royal conduct could possess immediate dramatic and theatrical implications. In Part I, I discussed the theatrical underpinnings of the 1741 coup that inaugurated the two decades of Elizabeth's reign. In this concluding part, I investigate a historical episode taking place immediately after her death and ostensibly having little to do with the practice of court theater, but which was aligned with dramatic images of sovereignty canonized during her reign.

Upon succeeding to the Russian throne in early 1762, Elizabeth's heir, Peter III, an outspoken admirer of Prussia and its king Frederick II, withdrew from the anti-Prussian coalition formed by France and Austria and thus effectually ended the Seven Years' War. Restoring all occupied Prussian territory, including East Prussia with its capital Königsberg, Peter prevented the imminent ruin of the Prussian state, instead allowing Frederick to conclude an honorable peace. Peter's gesture, usually judged as catastrophic by historians of Russia but known as "the miracle of the house of

Brandenburg" in Germany, is routinely explained by the new emperor's anecdotally exaggerated Prussophilia. As I will argue, this approach is not sufficient to account for the emergence and manifold implications of Peter's spectacular (if indeed very misfortunate) gesture. In fact, it drew upon patterns of political action developed in dramatic tradition equally familiar to Peter, his Prussian adversary, and their pan-European audience. As it was, tragedy provided both a common political idiom and a pattern of communication for contending sovereigns. This was far from incidental: it has recently been argued that the "origins" of tragedy in the seventeenth century were fundamentally linked to the emergence of international relations as a conceptual framework and discursive sphere.[1]

Once again, an elusive yet suggestive argument to that effect is found in Walter Benjamin. He detects a contradiction between the "theocratic" exaltation of singular sovereignty and the "political wisdom" of the age, which admitted the necessity for relations of equality or even dependence between specific rulers. Benjamin quotes Saavedra Fajardo, an author whose relevance for early Russian tragedy I have attempted to demonstrate: "An Interview of two Princes, is almost like a Duel, in which they fight with Ceremonies, each endeavoring to conquer t'other."[2] This statement reveals the tension inherent in diplomatic protocols of friendship between rulers that fail to obliterate the fierce competition for singular sovereignty associated with armed violence and tragic plots. Alongside tragedy, international relations, and warfare in particular, represented a rare field within the absolutist political experience where established authority was routinely and legitimately confronted with fundamental challenges. In this setting, royal conduct at war, which we most often assess in practical terms of achievement and error, easily amounted to a reassertion of sovereignty, a symbolic performance of the royal role addressed to a mixed audience of affected and distanced publics both at home and abroad.

When Peter the Great assumed his imperial title in 1721, after signing the Nystad treaty that sealed his victory over Sweden, he was credited with

---

1   Timothy Hampton, "*La foi des traités*: Baroque History, International Law, and the Politics of Reading in Corneille's *Rodogune*," in *Walter Benjamin's Imaginary French Trauerspiel*, ed. Katherine Ibbett and Hall Bjornstad (New Haven: Yale University Press, 2013), 135–151.

2   Benjamin, *Origin of the German Tragic Drama*, 68.

introducing Russia to the "theater of glory." During the Seven Years' War, Frederick II used a similar trope in a letter to Voltaire written after the bloody battle of Zorndorf. The king compared his situation to a tragedy by Racine (where, as the letter's editors put it, "the mortality . . . equals that of *Hamlet*") and himself to an actor:

> This Don Quixote leads the life of a country comedian, playing in one theater as often as another, sometimes booed, sometimes applauded. The last play in which he performed was *Thebaïde*; hardly the extinguisher of candles was left.[3]

The persistence of "the old form of tragedy—and the way of defining it" in the eighteenth century, as Matthew Wikander has suggested, arose from continued public fascination for "the mystique of royalty" and "the royal role."[4] Conversely, during the war and its resolution, both Frederick and his Russian counterpart, Emperor Peter III, largely relied on established patterns of action and domination elaborated in tragedy and *opera seria*. This type of dramatic patterning, Wortman's "scenarios of power," was calculated to reaffirm royal charisma by means of artfully manipulated public emotion.[5]

---

3   Voltaire, *Complete Works*, vol. 103 (*Correspondence*, vol. 19) (Oxford: The Voltaire Foundation, 1971), 192–193 (D7884). The importance of French tragedy for Frederick's political self-fashioning has been often noted by scholars, from Wilhelm Dilthey and Norbert Elias to Christiane Mervaud. See Wilhelm Dilthey, "Friedrich der Grosse und die deutsche Aufklärung," in *Gesammelte Schriften: Studien zur Geschichte des deutschen Geistes* (Göttingen: Vandenhoeck & Ruprecht, 1992), 3: 103–104; Norbert Elias, "The Fate of German Baroque Poetry: Between the Traditions of Court and Middle Class," in *The Collected Works* (Dublin: University College Dublin Press, 2010), 12: 8–9; Christiane Mervaud, *Voltaire et Frédéric II: une dramaturgie des lumières, 1736–1778*, Studies on Voltaire and the Eighteenth Century, vol. 234 (Oxford: Oxford University Press, 1985), 274.

4   Matthew H. Wikander, *Princes to Act: Royal Audience and Royal Performance, 1578–1792* (Baltimore, MD: Johns Hopkins University Press, 1993), 12.

5   On *opera seria* and the artistic (de)mystification of sovereignty, see Ethel Matala de Mazza, "Die Regeln der Ausnahme. Zur Überschreitung der Souveränität in Fénelons *Télémaque* und Mozarts *Idomeneo*," in *Transgressionen. Literatur als Ethnographie*, ed. Gerhard Neumann and Rainer Warning (Freiburg: Rombach, 2003), 257–286; Martha Feldman, *Opera and Sovereignty: Transforming Myths in Eighteenth-Century Italy* (Chicago: University of Chicago Press, 2007).

Summarizing the political developments following Peter III's succession to the Russian throne, Frederick wrote to his field marshal, Prince Ferdinand of Braunschweig-Lüneburg, in May 1762: "Ce changement qui m'arrive, est ce que les Grecs appellent dans leur tragédies péripetie. Le Ciel nous seconde encore et mène tout à une bonne fin!" ("This change which occurred with me, is what the Greeks call in their tragedies 'peripeteia.' Heaven still supports us and leads everything to a good end!").[6] By the time Elizabeth died, Frederick, who was increasingly overstrained by the prolonged war against overwhelming enemy forces, had already several times conjured a "miracle of the house of Brandenburg." Judging by Johannes Kunisch's well-known monograph, this concept has not lost its viability for discussing the events of 1762, even in the era of rationalist historiography. The notion of "miracle," a figment of self-referential discoursivity inimical to any elucidation, conveys the powerful presence of symbolic patterns, which inform the experience of history beyond explanations and—contrary to Hayden White's assertion that "stories are not lived"—embed tropes of representation into the very core of fact, the "factum."[7] As Reinhold Koser has established, Frederick's own miracle belonged to an archaic political theology that was modeled after a long-standing tradition of the "miracles of the House of Austria," which proved the divine election of the Habsburgs.

However, unlike some of his pious subjects, who literally accepted and propagated this theology, Frederick—himself a man of letters, philosopher, poet, and historian—was schooled in skepticism and keenly appreciated the powers of manipulation and distortion accessible to authority and authorship.[8] These powers were revealed and tested on the occasion of the war: as

---

6   [Frederick II], *Politische Correspondenz Friedrich's des Großen* (Berlin: Duncker & Humblot, 1894), 21: 462; Johannes Kunisch, *Das Mirakel des Hauses Brandenburg: Studien zum Verhältnis von Kabinettspolitik und Kriegführung im Zeitalter des Siebenjährigen Krieges* (Munich: Oldenbourg, 1978), 12.

7   Hayden White, "Literary Theory and Historical Writing," in *Figural Realism: Studies in the Mimesis Effect* (Baltimore, MD: Johns Hopkins University Press, 1999), 9.

8   Reinhold Koser, *Geschichte Friedrichs des Großen*, Bd. 3 (Stuttgart: Cotta'sche Buchhandlung Nachfolger, 1913), 38; Kunisch, *Mirakel*, 12. The distortions inherent in Frederick's double role as his own chronicler were recognized by Klopstock in an ode addressed to the king: "Mehr trübt der Nebel, wenn, was du tatest, du / Selbst redest." Friedrich Gottlieb Klopstock, "Die Verkennung (1779)," in Frederick II, *Friedrich II, König von Preußen, und die deutsche Literatur des 18. Jahrhunderts. Texte und Dokumente*, ed. Horst Steinmetz (Stuttgart: Reclam, 1985), 57.

its instigator—its *auteur*—Frederick devised both its military operations and its glorifying narrative, culminating in his own (*Histoire de la guerre de Sept Ans* (1763). In his letter to Braunschweig, the suggestion of divine intervention is both diluted by a vague reference to *le ciel*, a mere figure of speech as much as a confession of faith, and—in a self-conscious reminder of the authorial powers of representation—counterbalanced by the notion of "péripetie," a technical term from pagan poetics. It is a reference to tragedy and its Aristotelian theory that allows Frederick to grasp the fateful events that saved his kingdom from the brink of ruin. Indeed, tragedy as it was practiced and theorized in early modern Europe provided a paradigm for a historical sensibility dominated (as White argues) by the tension between a methodology of historical representation dependent on "classical rhetoric and poetics," on the one hand, and a mistrust of the irrational and "the fabulous" in history, on the other.[9] Walter Benjamin has demonstrated that tragedy was conceived of as a medium of reflection on history identified with "the insight into diplomacy and the manipulation of all the political schemes." Moreover, this vision of history centered upon the figure of the sovereign, its "principal exponent" and "representative," and thus "the main character of the *Trauerspiel*."[10] The royal history of the *Trauerspiel* is permeated with a constant "tension between immanence and transcendence," which shapes the troubled status of the sovereign, who cannot cast off his own "immanence," or "the disproportion between the unlimited hierarchical dignity, with which he is divinely invested and the humble estate of his humanity."[11]

This tension was reenacted in Frederick's intellectual trajectory during the Seven Years' War. As the records of Henri de Catt, the king's reader, confirm, his self-consciousness as a political actor and a "warrior king" was largely shaped by a constantly reconsidered relationship with the divine. Frederick's view oscillated between his usual metaphysical skepticism (which informs many of his poems composed during the war) and occasional

---

9   Hayden White, "The Irrational and the Problem of Historical Knowledge in the Enlightenment," in *Tropics of Discourse: Essays in Cultural Criticism* (Baltimore, MD: Johns Hopkins University Press, 1985), 142–143.
10 Benjamin, *Origin of the German Tragic Drama*, 62–65.
11 Ibid., 67–70.

outbreaks of religious zeal reinforced by the political theology of divine election. On July 28, 1760, Frederick said, for example: "Pour me tirer d'affaire, il faut un miracle, et il ne s'un fait plus" ("In order to get out of this business, I need a miracle, and there are no more").[12] Frederick's response to tragedies, mostly Racine's, which were known to have been his favorite reading in the war years, reflected this set of issues.[13] Among the tragedies he recited to de Catt, he especially favored Racine's *Athalie* (1691), which adopted a biblical plot and staged the restoration of the divine kingship of the house of David, which became emblematic of direct divine intervention into royal politics. In 1758 Frederick "fervently" quoted the prayer of the high priest Joad directed against the usurper Queen Athalie and her councilor Mathan, adapting the verses to include a reference to Empress Queen Maria Theresa, the leader of the anti-Prussian coalition, and her minister Kaunitz:

Daigne, daigne, mon Dieu, sur Kaunitz et sur elle
Répandre cet esprit d'imprudence et d'erreur,
De la chute des rois funeste avant-coureur!

Deign, Deign, My God, to shine your light on Kaunitz and on her
And on this spirit of imprudence and error,
A fateful precursor of the fall of kings![14]

It is the idiom of tragedy that allows Frederick to interpret political events in a theological perspective. Joad's prayer provided a pattern for the king's assessment of his position a year later when he wrote that things were

---

12   Reinhold Koser, ed., *Unterhaltungen mit Friedrich dem Grossen: Memoiren und Tagebücher von Heinrich de Catt* (Leipzig: Hirzel, 1884), 432. On the religious and metaphysical issues in the cultural experience of the Seven Years' War, see Karl Schwarze, *Der Siebenjährige Krieg in der zeitgenössischen deutschen Literatur. Kriegserleben und Kriegserlebnis in Schrifttum und Dichtung des 18. Jahrhunderts* (Berlin: Junker und Dunhaupt, 1936), 94–116.

13   On Frederick's reading, see Jorg Ulbert, "Friedrichs Lektüren während des Siebenjährigen Krieges," in *Friedrich der Große als Leser*, ed. Brunhilde Wehinger and Günther Lottes (Berlin: Akademie Verlag, 2012), 71–98.

14   Koser, *Unterhaltungen*, 130; *Frederick the Great: The Memoirs of His Reader, Henri de Catt (1758–1760)*, trans. F. S. Flint (Boston: Houghton Mifflin, 1917), 1: 238. See also Jean Racine, *Athalie*, 1: 2, in Racine, *Théâtre complet*, ed. Jean-Pierre Collinet (Paris: Gallimard, 1983), 2: 420.

going so badly that a favorable outcome could only originate from "quelque miracle ou de la divin ânerie des mes ennemis" ("some miracle or the heaven sent imbecility of my enemies").[15] Anticipating the "miracle" of 1762, the king's use of tragic discourse nourished a fascination with political mysticism quite remote from his usual skeptical intellectual stance. He enthusiastically recited to de Catt verses from *Athalie* on the divine supervision of earthly rulers and immediately declared them to be false.[16] In 1763, in an intriguing train of thought, he told D'Alembert that he would rather have written *Athalie* than have won the war, since the war was mostly a work of chance. Thus, he simultaneously negated the divine intervention that he had so often conjured forth, while affirming the value of its tragic representation.[17] The parallel between drama and the war (meant to problematize the comparative strengths and weaknesses of authorial and royal agency) relied on the intrinsic affinity between the literary mode of tragedy and the experience of history: "The *Trauerspiel*, it was believed, could be directly grasped in the events of history itself; it was only a question of finding the right words."[18] In the letter to Braunschweig, Frederick juxtaposes "miracle" with "péripetie," thereby linking it to a mode of representation that simultaneously functioned as a performative theory of political action. In 1778, writing amidst a political crisis where Frederick II figured prominently, another German statesman and man of letters, Johann Wolfgang Goethe, noted: "It seems that I am approaching closer and closer the aim of dramatic essence, as I am more and more affected by the ways in which the great play with men, and the gods play with the great."[19] Goethe summarizes his experience of absolutist politics with a reference to dramatic "essence," which again discerns a divine will behind political shifts and then reduces it to a poetic trope.

In characterizing the "miracle of the house of Brandenburg" with a term of tragic poetics signifying a reversal of a dramatic situation, Frederick

---

15 [Frederick II], *Politische Correspondenz Friedrich's des Großen*, 18: 516, no. 11403.

16 Koser, *Unterhaltungen*, 132; Koser, *Frederick the Great*, 243.

17 Marie de Vichy Chamrond Du Deffand, *Correspondance complète de la Marquise du Deffand avec ses amis* (Paris: Henri Plon, 1865), 1: 276.

18 Benjamin, *Origin of the German Tragic Drama*, 63.

19 Goethe to Charlotte von Stein, letter of May 14, 1778, cited in Katharina Mommsen, *Goethe und der Alte Fritz* (Leipzig: Lehmstedt, 2012), 71. On the political context of Goethe's phrase, see ibid., 69–81.

exposed the very notion of miracle as a trope of political triumph. The triumph of sovereignty in a state of emergency, its ultimate action, was often conceived in early modern thinking as a "miraculous" restoration after a cosmic catastrophe.[20] Aligning this analogy with "peripeteia," a technique of dramatic representation, Frederick fashioned the genre of tragedy as an aestheticized paradigm for the interpretation of political crises. Several decades later another warrior monarch and an interested spectator of tragedies, Napoleon, in his conversations with Goethe and others condemned appeals to fate in contemporary drama since "in our age … politics is fate" and "the principle of political necessity is … a fertile germ of the most dramatic situations, a modern fate no less imperious, no less ineluctable than that of the ancients."[21]

20   Benjamin, *Origin of the German Tragic Drama*, 65–66.
21   Quoted in J. Christopher Herold, *The Age of Napoleon* (Boston: Houghton Mifflin Harcourt, 2002), 121; Frank George Healey, *The Literary Culture of Napoléon* (Geneva: Droz, 1959), 103–104.

FREDERICK, OR THE PERFORMANCE OF DEFEAT

In October 1757, when Frederick's military situation after his defeat at Kolin in June of the same year was nearly catastrophic, he wrote and sent to Voltaire what is probably his best and best-known poem:

Croyez que si j'étais Voltaire,
Particulier aujourd'hui,
Me contentant du nécessaire,
Je verrais envoler la fortune légère,
Et m'en moquerais comme lui.
Je connais l'abus des richesses,
Je connais l'ennui des grandeurs
Le fardeau des devoirs, le jargon des flatteurs . . .
La vive et naïve allégresse,
Ont toujours fui des grands la pompe et les faisceaux.
Nés pour la liberté, leur troupe enchanteresse
Préfère l'aimable paresse
Aux austères devoirs, guides de nos travaux. . . .
Mais notre état nous fait la loi;
Il nous oblige, il nous engage
A mesurer notre courage
Sur ce qu'exige notre emploi.

Voltaire, dans son ermitage,
Dans un pays dont l'héritage
Est son antique bonne foi,
Peut s'adonner en paix à la vertu du sage,
Dont Platon nous marqua la loi.
Pour moi, menacé du naufrage,
Je dois, en affrontant l'orage,
Penser, vivre et mourir en roi.[1]

A soon-to-follow English translation read:

Voltaire, believe me, were I now
In private life's calm station plac'd,
Let Heav'n for Nature's wants allow,
With cold indifference would I view
Departing Fortune's winged haste,
And at the Goddess laugh like you.
Th' insipid farce of tedious state,
Imperial duty's real weight,
The faithless courtier's supple bow,
The fickle multitude's caress,
And flatt'rer's wordy emptiness,
By long experience well I know ...
Sweet ease, and unaffected joy,
Domestic peace and sportive pleasure.
The regal throne and palace fly,
And, born for liberty, prefer
Soft silent scenes of lovely leisure
To, what we Monarchs buy so dear,
The thorny pomp of scepter'd care. ...
But from our stations we derive

---

1   For the most recent scholarly edition of the poem, see Voltaire, *Complete Works*, 102
    (*Correspondence*, vol. 18) (Oxford: The Voltaire Foundation, 1971), 198 (D7414). For its
    insightful and informed discussion, see Mervaud, *Voltaire et Frédéric II*, 276–278.

Unerring precepts how to live,
And certain deeds each rank calls forth,
By which is measur'd human worth.
Voltaire, within his private cell,
In realms where ancient honesty
Is patrimonial property,
And sacred Freedom loves to dwell,
May give up all his peaceful mind,
Guided by Plato's deathless page,
In silent solitude resign'd
To the mild virtues of a sage;
But I, 'gainst whom wild whirlwinds wage
Fierce war with wreck-denouncing wing,
Must be, to face the tempest's rage,
In thought, in life, and death a King.[2]

Written in the lighter diction of *poésie légère* and conceived as little more than a trifle reiterating the political stoicism of Frederick's grand epistles (*Épître à ma sœur de Baireuth*, 1757; *Épître sur le hasard. À ma sœur Amélie*, 1760), this poem claims a central place in the complex dynamic of literary authorship and political (self-)representation that permeated the king's oeuvre. As Brunhilde Wehinger suggests, the verses to Voltaire ostensibly amount to the king's renunciation of authorship, driven by social protocols that made it impossible to combine public literary ambition with royal status. However, on another level the royal persona fashions itself through a speech act, both drawing from and relying on techniques of poetic expression. This reading, which confirms the general approach to Frederick's writings suggested by Andreas Pečar, is enhanced by what seems to be the text's special status. While Frederick generally avoided wide dissemination of his poems and only published an authorized collection after a pirated edition had appeared in 1760, the verses in question were printed in January 1758 as "Réponse de

---

2 [Frederick II], "Epistle from the King of Prussia to Monsieur Voltaire. Translated by J. G. Cooper, Esq.," *The Annual Register, or A View of the History, Politicks and Literature of the Year 1758* (London: J. Dodsley, 1759), 413–414.

S. M. le roi de Prusse au M. de Voltaire" in Berlin's semi-official news-paper *Vossische Zeitung*.[3]

In a dialogue that has been qualified as a *dramaturgie des lumières*, Frederick taps into older but still meaningful "tragic" and "baroque" visions of sovereignty to style his public performance in a way that associates it with martyrdom. Benjamin discerns a paradoxical relationship among these concepts in that sovereignty as a worldly institution becomes aligned with martyrdom, but martyrdom itself, as understood in "baroque" discourse, was aligned to the "sphere of immanence" and conceived in stoic rather than truly religious terms. Frederick's reference to "l'ennui des grandeurs" ("the tedium of grandeur") and "le fardeau des devoirs" ("the burden of duty") inscribes into a baroque tradition that viewed the prince as the "paradigm of the melancholy man." Benjamin illustrates this point with a passage from Pascal's *Pensées* (1669), arguing that if a king should be left alone, "l'on verra, un Roi qui se voit, est un homme plein de misères" ("one will see that a king who sees himself, is a man full of misery"), and further draws four lines from a seventeenth-century emblem book that serve as a commentary for a picture of a crown:

> Ce fardeau paroist autre à celuy qui le porte,
> Qu'à ceux qu'il esblouyt de son lustre trompeur,
> Ceuxcy n'en ont jamais conneu la pesanteur,
> Mais l'autre sçait expert quel tourment il apporte.

> This burden appears differently to him who bears it,
> Than to those who are dazzled by its deceptive brilliance,

---

3   Brunhilde Wehinger, "Denkwürdigkeiten des Hauses Brandenburg—Friedrich der Große als Autor der Geschichte seiner Dynastie," in *Vom Kurfürstentum zum Königreich der Landstriche. Brandenburg-Preußen im Zeitalter von Absolutismus und Aufklärung*, ed. Günther Lottes (Berlin: Berliner Wiss.-Verlag, 2004), 147–148; Andreas Pečar, "Friedrich der Große als Autor. Plädoyer für eine adressatenorientierte Lektüre seiner Schriften," in *Friedrich300—Eine perspektivische Bestandsaufnahme. Beiträge des ersten Colloquiums in der Reihe "Friedrich300" vom 28./29. September 2007*, ed. Michael Kaiser und Jürgen Luh, accessed August 28, 2013, http://www.perspectivia.net/content/publikationen/friedrich300-colloquien/friedrich-bestandsaufnahme.

These men have never known that weight,
But the other knows expertly what torment he carries.[4]

This tradition was still quite alive in the eighteenth century. Frederick is known to have read Pascal during the war, and his instructor in poetic art, Voltaire (also an avid reader of the *Pensées*), wrote in his 1740 poem "Sur l'usage de la vie" some lines that could have provided a model for Frederick's own verses:

On voit souvent plus d'un roi
Que la tristesse environne;
Les brillants de la couronne
Ne sauvent point de l'ennui:
Ses valets de pied, ses pages,
Jeunes, indiscrets, volages,
Sont plus fortunés que lui.

One often sees a king
Surrounded by sorrow;
The diamonds of a crown
Cannot save from tedium:
His footmen, his pages,
Young, indiscreet, flighty,
Are more fortunate than he.[5]

However, it was ultimately the tragedy rather than *poésie légère* that provided the literary pattern for the double act of royal introspection and self-exposure suggested by Pascal. In conversations with de Catt, Frederick bitterly derided the common opinion of those "stupid people" who wish to "be happy as a king," complained about "this burden that weighs on me so," the moral corruption of the courts, the anxiety engendered even in peaceful years by premonitions of "the storm," and "since then, what troubles, what unprecedented fatigues, and what reverses!" He would conclude: "As a private individual—which I have often

---

4   Benjamin, *Origin of the German Tragic Drama*, 72–73, 142–145.
5   Voltaire, *Complete Works*, 16: 313.

desired to be—I should live in quiet and as I pleased." The royal poet, who readily admitted to imitating Racine's tragic diction even in shorter lyric pieces, often adorned the laments for private happiness unattainable by kings, which he summarized in his "Réponse ... au M. de Voltaire," with Agamemnon's lines from Racine's *Iphigénie* (1674; 1.1, 1.5):

> Heureux! qui, satisfait de son humble fortune,
> Libre du joug superbe où je suis attaché,
> Vit dans l'état obscur où les dieux l'ont caché ...
> Triste destin des rois!

> Oh Happy Man! He who is satisfied with his humble fortune,
> Free of the supreme yoke to which I am bound,
> He lives in the obscure state in which the gods have hidden him ...
> Sad destiny of kings![6]

References to the tragic figure of Agamemnon, a king and commander of the Greek army who is compelled by a divine decree to sacrifice his daughter to secure military success, permitted Frederick to inscribe his personal suffering into a "scenario of power," a recognizable royal role. The inherent theatricality of this emotional pattern was revealed when Frederick quoted *Iphigénie* to convey his grief over the death of his deeply loved sister and then immediately came to speak of theater and the opera. This time the reference was taken from a scene where Ulysses urges Agamemnon to overcome his hesitation and accomplish the horrific sacrifice in exchange for royal glory and military triumph.[7] The "Réponse ... au M. de Voltaire" reenacts a similar emotional dynamic in which the ruler's public "austères devoirs" ("austere obligations") subordinate his own "private" emotions. In this way, the violence of war molds Frederick's intimate emotional experience into a culturally charged public spectacle of sovereignty, as announced by the last verse: "vivre et mourir en roi" ("to live and die as king").

---

6   *Frederick the Great: The Memoirs of His Reader*, 1:86; Koser, *Unterhaltungen*, 48, 350, 366, 374, 409; see also Racine, *Théâtre complet*, 2: 207, 219. On Frederick's imitation of Racine, see Koser, *Unterhaltungen*, 300, 423.

7   Koser, *Unterhaltungen*, 379.

The tragic resonance of the poem's finale was evident to its contemporaries. Voltaire wrote later: "Rien n'est plus beau que ces derniers vers; rien n'est plus grand. Corneille dans son bon temps ne les eût pas mieux faits. Et quand, après de tels vers, on gagne une bataille, le sublime ne peut aller plus loin" ("Nothing is as beautiful as these last lines; nothing is more grand. Corneille in his time could not have crafted them better. And when, after such verses, one wins a battle, the sublime could go no further").[8] Elias, whose fundamental studies of court culture reflect a specific interest in Frederick II and his relationship to belles lettres, discussed the same lines in one of his less-known essays: "Here, the tragic pathos of Corneille, which sometimes seems over-theatrical to later generations, served as a pattern to a real king in expressing his agitated feelings with great reserve in an extremely real and entirely untheatrical situation."[9]

In his poetic staging of kingship, Frederick relied on performative techniques of tragedy where sovereignty itself is constituted by acts of speech.[10] While older scholarship, which made "Réponse … au M. de Voltaire" a matter of some debate, failed to identify the poem's tragic models, Christiane Mervaud points to a scene in Corneille's *Sophonisbe* (1663), where a king and his queen share a common vow before a decisive battle: "je sais vivre et mourir en reine" ("I know how to live and die as a queen"), and "je saurai, pour vous, vaincre ou mourir en roi" ("I know, for you, how to conquer or die as a king," 1.4). An abbreviated version of this vow reappears in Racine's second tragedy, *Alexandre le Grand* (1665), which shows the Indian king Porus engaged in heroic but hopeless resistance to Alexander's overwhelming forces. Like Corneille's Sophonisbe, Porus's lover, Queen Axiane, assures him that the conquering enemy "me verra, toujours digne de toi, / Mourir en reine, ainsi que tu mourus en roi" ("will see me, always worthy of you, / Dying as a queen, just as you die as a king," 4.1). In Racine's play, which was closer to Frederick's reading habits, although certainly not

---

8 Voltaire, *Écrits autobiographiques*, ed. Jean Goldzink (Paris: Flammarion, 2006), 157–158.

9 Elias, "The Fate of German Baroque Poetry," 8.

10 Rüdiger Campe, "Der Befehl und die Rede des Souveräns im Schauspiel des 17. Jahrhunderts. Nero bei Busenello, Racine und Lohenstein," in *Übertragung und Gesetz. Gründungsmythen, Kriegstheater und Unterwerfungstechniken von Institutionen*, ed. A. Adam and M. Stingelin (Berlin: Akademie Verlag, 1995), 55–71.

his favorite, this line resonated with a later scene where victorious Alexander questions the captive Porus:

Alexandre
... Parlez donc, dites—moi:
Comment prétendez—vous que je vous traite?

Porus
En roi.

Alexander
So, speak, tell me:
How do you claim that I should treat you?

Porus
As a king. (5.3)[11]

Racine borrows Porus's famous answer from Plutarch, whose *Parallel Lives*, including the "Life of Alexander," were well known to the European courtly audiences. Frederick found inspiration in them during the war.[12] The last line of the "Réponse ... au M. de Voltaire," both a poetic and a political gesture, reenacts the powerful rhetorical effect of Porus's laconic formula, an assertion of royal grandeur paradoxically reaffirmed by the momentarily suspended reality of defeat.

Frederick's insistence on his ability to "die as a king" referred to the plans of suicide that he contemplated during the war and often discussed in his conversations and correspondence, making them an important element of his self-dramatization.[13] Once again, visions of historical and political action were aligned with tragic patterns. Referring to the historical suicides of Cato the Younger and the Emperor Otho (recorded by Plutarch), Frederick

---

11 Racine, *Théâtre complet*, 1: 166.
12 [Frederick II], *Œuvres de Frédéric le Grand* (Berlin: Imprimerie royale, 1852), 19: 311; Ulbert, "Friedrichs Lektüren während des Siebenjährigen Krieges," 96.
13 Florian Kühnel, *Kranke Ehre? Adlige Selbsttötung im Übergang zur Moderne* (Munich: Oldenbourg Verlag, 2013), 135–170.

applauded them and even used his own poetic voice to embody them in two *heroides*, in essence, isolated tragic monologues, written in their names.[14] The possibility of his own suicide he often justified with a couplet from Voltaire's tragedy *Mérope* (1743): "Quand on a tout perdu, quand on n'a plus d'espoir, / La vie est un opprobre et la mort un devoir" ("When one has lost everything, when one has no more hope, / Life is a disgrace and death an obligation").

Frederick repeatedly claimed his suicide would "end the tragedy."[15] In a letter to Voltaire composed shortly before the "Réponse," the king suggested that his ruin would make "a good subject for a tragedy" characteristic of the times when "the common man would have been broken on the wheel for having committed a hundredth of the evil that these masters of the earth commit with impunity."[16] Frederick blamed the anti-Prussian coalition for the beginning of hostilities, and resorted in his accusations to the commonplace critique of war and conquest popular in early modern literature.

This critique was utilized in Racine's *Alexandre le Grand*, in which Porus exposes the destructive ambition of Alexander, the paragon of military valor and triumph: "nous l'aurons vu, par tant d'horribles guerres, / Troubler le calme heureux dont jouissaient nos terres" ("We have seen him, through so many horrible wars, / disrupt the happy peace of our lands," 1.2.) Just as Porus is prepared to perish for "la liberté de l'Inde" ("the freedom of India") and despises the "esclavage" ("slavery") imposed by Alexander (1.1–2), Frederick in a bombastic poem incites the Germans to resist the ambition of the Habsburgs and their allies, whom he calls "éternels ennemis / De votre liberté, de vos droits, de vos princes" ("the eternal enemies / of your freedom, of your rights, of your princes").[17] The drama of Porus, a performative

---

14 [Frederick II], "Discours de l'empereur Othon à ses amis, après la perte de la bataille de Bédriac" and "Discours de Caton d'Utique à son fils et à ses amis, avant de se tuer," in *Œuvres de Frédéric le Grand*, 12: 237–245; Werner Langer, *Friedrich der Große und die geistige Welt Frankreichs* (Hamburg: Seminar für romanische Sprachen und Kultur, 1932), 142.

15 Koser, *Unterhaltungen mit Friedrich dem Grossen*, 374. The references to *Mérope* are notable, as Voltaire's play also portrays an oppressed heroic prince who proudly proclaims: "je sais mourir en roi" (Voltaire, *The Complete Works*, 17: 319).

16 Voltaire, *The Complete Works*, 102 (*Correspondence*, vol. 18): 152 (D 7373).

17 Racine, *Théâtre complet*, 1: 122–124; [Frederick II], "Ode aux Germains," in *Œuvres*, 12:20. On the contexts of Porus's denunciation of conquest, see Pia Claudia Doering, *Jean Racine zwischen Kunst und Politik: Lesarten der Alexandertragödie* (Heidelberg: Winter, 2010),

reenactment, or "emplotment," of this conceptual framework, includes the verbal gesture of royal self-sacrifice as a *coup de théâtre*, a ploy which, instead of annihilating royal charisma, only reinforces it through an intrinsically theatrical appeal to the emotions of an audience transformed into a political community. This mechanism was explored by the pan-European court theater, an institution equally important for the dramatist Racine and King Frederick, who inaugurated his reign by establishing an opera theater under his own close supervision and famously encouraged the "reformed" *opera seria* modeled on French neoclassical tragedy.

Among the operas performed in Berlin before the beginning of the Seven Years' War were two different musical settings of Pietro Metastasio's libretto *Alessandro nell'Indie* (1729), which also treated the Porus plot and loosely followed Racine's tragedy. The opera opens with a scene on a "Field of Battle on the Banks of Hydaspes, with the Remains of Porus's Army, defeated by Alexander," to quote a contemporary English translation. Porus attempts to stop his fleeing soldiers, crying out to them,

> Stay, ye pale Cowards! I command ye, stay!
> Life is Dishonour when bestow'd by Flight ...
> His Term of Life is full that dies in Freedom!
> (Offers to kill himself.)

He is interrupted by his general, Gandarte, who rushes to save his king and partake of the royal sacrifice, assuming "the Regal Diadem, that now, / Points all the Danger at your sacred Head." Gandarte's actions are immediately explicated in terms of monarchist political morality:

> A Subject pays for Publick Good,
> A frugal Purchase with his Blood,
> If, by a private Death alone,
> His Prince preserves the Indian Throne.[18]

155–172. On the concept of liberty in Frederick's political rhetoric during the Seven Years' War, see Ullrich Sachse, *Cäsar in Sanssouci: die Politik Friedrichs des Großen und die Antike* (Munich: Allitera Verlag, 2008), 213–216.

18 [Pietro Metastasio], *Poro, Re Dell'Indie. Drama ... Done Into English by Mr. Humphreys* (London: Wood, 1731), 9–10. On Frederick's opera and its repertoire, see Michele Calella,

The spectacular effects of stage drama provided the blueprint for the emotional economy of monarchy. In a scene that is itself a tragedy in miniature, the display of a king in danger evokes pity and fear, the two fundamental emotions that shaped the aesthetic effects of tragedy in Aristotelian theory. The Porus plays converted them into a political senti- ment, pro-royalist enthusiasm enacted on stage by Gandarte and suggested to the play's audience. This fundamentally theatrical vision of the mobilizing effects of the threatened royal charisma on a nation of subjects was developed in Thomas Abbt's vigorous manifesto of Prussian martial patriotism published during the Seven Years' War, *Vom Tode fürs Vaterland* (*On Dying for the Fatherland,* 1761). Abbt specifically refers to the Porus plot, writing:

> Porus und seine Untertanen teilen mit Alexanders Armee die Lorbeern, mit welcher sich die letztere umkränzt hat. Denn nach einem tapfern Widerstand überwunden werden, heißt nicht, seine Größe verlieren … Ich erinnere mich noch mit dem melan- cholischen Vergnügen, das unsre Seele bei der Vorstellung einer Tragischen Begebenheit überströmt, eine ganze Stadt über die falsche Nachricht von dem Unglück ihres Friederichs in Bestür- zung, Greise in Tränen zerfließend, und Jünglinge in männlichen Ernst gesehen zu haben. … Hier sehe ich nicht nur mein Vaterland vor mir, ich sehe auch meinen König. Sein Anblick ist beredter, als Demosthene, und erregt die Leidenschaften heftiger. Mit der Blut- fahne in der Hand geht er vor seinem Heer dem Feind entgegen. Die Gefahren umzingeln ihn; jedes tödtliche Blei, das neben ihm niederfällt, schlägt den Gedanken meiner eigenen Gefahr aus mir heraus. Ich sehe auf sein Leben, und vergesse darüber, daß das meinige vielleicht den nächsten Augenblick mir entrissen wird. … Aus dieser Denkungsart, aus dieser Leidenschaft, die allezeit unter einem guten, einem tapfern, Monarchen entstehen muß, rührt es

---

"Metastasios Dramenkonzeption und die Ästhetik der friderizianischen Oper," in *Metas- tasio im Deutschland der Aufklärung: Bericht über das Symposium Potsdam 1999,* ed. Laurenz Lütteken and Gerhad Splitt (Tübingen: Niemeyer, 2002), 103–123. The settings in question are Graun's *Allesandro e Poro* and Agricola's *Cleofide*.

her, daß die Soldaten Alexanders, wenn sie sein Leben in Gefahr sehen, mit einer Wut fechten, welche kaum bey Republikanern angetroffen wird . . .

Porus and his subjects share with Alexander's army the laurels that it has crowned itself with. For to be defeated after a brave resistance does not mean to lose your greatness . . . I still remember with a melancholic delight that overwhelms our soul when a tragic event is presented to us, seeing a whole city thrown into confusion by a false news of their Frederick's misfortune, the elderly shedding tears, the young in manly earnestness. . . . Here I do not only see my fatherland before me, I also see my king. His look is more eloquent than Demosthenes, and he awakens stronger passions. With a banner in his hand, he rides towards the enemy ahead of his troops. Dangers surround him; each deadly bullet which falls near him drives the thoughts of my own danger away from me. I look after his life, and I forget that my own could be taken from me in the next moment. . . . This sentiment, this passion, which always inevitably arises under a good and valorous monarch, is the reason why Alexander's soldiers, when they saw his life at risk, fought with a rage that could scarcely be seen among republicans . . .[19]

Abbt's influential treatise occupies an important place in the early history of German national sentiment. In it, he outlines what has been called an "aesthetic patriotism," grounding the monarchist solidarity of Prussia's subjects in the mechanics of collective sensibility. These mechanics are paradigmatically developed in tragedy, the genre where "tragic events" indeed appear as fictional representations tailored to arouse a public reaction of "melancholic delight." As the influential Gottsched argued, the Porus plot was well suited for public theater in absolutist polities, and audiences' admiration for Porus's resistance to Alexander provided an aesthetic

---

19 Thomas Abbt, "Vom Tode für das Vaterland," in *Aufklärung und Kriegserfahrung. Klassische Zeitzeugen zum Siebenjährigen Krieg*, ed. Johannes Kunisch (Frankfurt am Main: Deutscher Klassischer Verlag, 1996), 612, 615, 633.

paradigm for the exalted public devotion to Frederick II as it was fashioned in different genres and media.[20]

During the battle of Kolin in June 1757, Frederick experienced his first major defeat, one that eventually compelled him to resort to the rhetoric of desperation that he would come to use in his "Réponse ... à M. de Voltaire." The king supposedly attempted to stop his fleeing soldiers with a risk of his own life, shouting to them: "Rascals, would you live forever?"[21] This phrase entered into Friderician lore after it appeared in print, only days after the battle. It appears to translate into colloquial German the operatic exclamations of Metastasio's Porus, balancing between Porus's praise of a death on the battlefield over a life of disgrace and the implication of immortal fame suggested in Frederick's own "Ode à mon frère Henri" written later that year. The king writes that calamities and defeats, identified once again with "images tragiques" ("tragic images"), inevitably occur in the history of any great nation and must be overcome with "noble désespoir" ("noble despair") and heroic patriotism, which acknowledge that "La mort est un tribut qu'on doit à la nature ... Aucun

---

20 Johann Christoph Gottsched, "Die Schauspiele und besonders die Tragödien sind aus einer wohlbestellten Republik nicht zu verbannen," [1729], in *Schriften zur Literatur* (Stuttgart: Ph. Reclam, 1972), 7. On Abbt's construction of patriotism, see Eva Piirimäe, "Dying for the Fatherland: Thomas Abbt's Theory of Aesthetic Patriotism," *History of European Ideas* 35 (2009): 194–208; Klaus Bohnen, *Von den Anfängen des Nationalsinns*, "Von den Anfängen des Nationalsinns. Zur literarischen Patriotismus-Debatte im Umfeld des Siebenjährigen Kriegs," in *Dichter und ihre Nation*, ed. Helmut Scheuer (Frankfurt am Main: Suhrkamp, 1993), 121–137; Kunisch, [Kommentar], *Aufklärung und Kriegserfahrung*, 971–1008. On Abbt and the cult of Frederick, which emphasized royal grief and martyrdom, see Eckhart Hellmuth, "Die 'Wiedergeburt' Friedrichs des Großen und der 'Tod fürs Vaterland.' Zum patriotischen Selbstverständnis in Preußen in der zweiten Hälfte des 18. Jahrhunderts," in *Nationalismus vor dem Nationalismus?*, Aufklärung. Interdisziplinäre Halbjahresschrift zur Erforschung des 18. Jahrhunderts, vol. 10, no. 2 (1998), ed. E. Hellmuth and R. Stauber, 21–52. On the Seven Years' War as a crucial juncture for the emergence of printed mass media and the corresponding modes of public reaction, see Wolfgang Adam and Holger Dainat, eds., *"Krieg ist mein Lied": der Siebenjährige Krieg in den zeitgenössischen Medien* (Göttingen: Wallstein-Verlag, 2007); Manfred Schort, *Politik und Propaganda: der Siebenjährige Krieg in den zeitgenössischen Flugschriften* (Frankfurt am Main: Lang Verlag, 2006). For more on the public image and perception of Frederick, see Bernd Sösemann and Gregor Vogt-Spira, eds., *Friedrich der Große in Europa: Geschichte einer wechselvollen Beziehung* (Stuttgart: Steiner, 2012), vols. 1–2.

21 On the origins and history of this anecdote reported, among others, by Goethe, see Gerhard Knoll, "'Hunde, wollt Ihr ewig leben?' oder Goethe und die 'Hunde' des Großen Königs," *Aus dem Aniquariat. Zeitschrift für Aniquare und Büchersammler* 2 (2005): 22–27.

n'en fut exempt" ("Death is a tribute one owes to nature ... No one is exempt from it"), while a death suffered for the fatherland secures immortality.[22]

Reducing dramatic polyphony to a unity of poetic voice and political perspective appropriate for the occasion, the lyrical idiom of the war nevertheless built upon the emotional economy of tragic representation in order to mobilize and manipulate public sensibilities. Whereas Frederick exploited this aestheticized fascination for military adversity for a limited readership, Johann Wilhelm Ludwig Gleim explored it in his *Preußische Kriegslieder* (*Prussian War Songs*, 1758), lyric utterances of Prussian martial sentiment published in the course of the war for the use of broader German audiences. Styling Frederick's battles as a "great tragedy" ("große[s] Trauerspie[l]"), Gleim once again represented the threat to the body of the king as a spectacle with mobilizing effects:

> Da, *Friedrich*, gieng dein Grenadier
> Auf Leichen hoch einher.
> Dacht, in dem mörderischen Kampf,
> Gott, Vaterland, und Dich;
> Sah, tief in schwarzem Rauch und Dampf,
> Dich seinen Friederich.
> Und zitterte, ward feuerroth,
> Im kriegrischen Gesicht,
> (Er zitterte vor Deinem Tod,
> Vor seinem aber nicht.)
> Verachtete die Kugelsaat,
> Der Stücke Donnerton,
> Stritt wütender, that Heldenthat,
> Bis deine Feinde flohn.

> Then, Frederick, your grenadier
> Climbed over the corpses.
> He thought in the midst of a murderous battle
> Of God, of the Fatherland, and of you;

---

22 [Frederick II], *Œuvres*, 12:1–8.

> Deep in black smoke and fumes he saw
> You, his Frederick.
> He trembled, his warlike face
> Turned red as fire
> (He trembled for your life,
> Not for his own.)
> He despised the crop of bullets
> And the cannons' thunder,
> He fought with even more rage, and performed heroic deeds
> Until your enemies fled.[23]

It is the "tragic" fear for the chief actor that overwhelms the grenadier when he momentarily finds himself a spectator of the battle, which intensifies his patriotic fervor and incites him to action. He emulates the show of royalist self-sacrifice put on by Metastasio's Gandarte, achieving victory where operatic heroes failed. While this emotional economy was unsuccessful on the battlefield (at Kolin the soldiers allegedly told Frederick they had done enough for their miserable salaries), it was crucial for the public resonance of Gleim's immensely popular songs.[24]

Aesthetic mobilization of pro-Prussian political sentiment during the Seven Years' War largely contributed to the emergence of public opinion in Germany. According to Goethe's famous formulation, it also shaped the development of German "national poetry" in which the "war-songs struck by Gleim maintain so high a rank" because Frederick's military exploits for the first time provided them with "true and really vital material of a higher

---

23 Wilhelm Ludwig Gleim, *Preußische Kriegslieder von einem Grenadier* (Heilbronn: Henninger, 1882; rpt. Nendeln/Liechtenstein: Kraus Reprint, 1968), 9, 15.

24 On Gleim and the Prussian martial patriotism of the Seven Years' War, see Hans-Martin Blitz, *Aus Liebe zum Vaterland: die deutsche Nation im 18. Jahrhundert* (Hamburg: Hamburger Ed, 2000), 145–280; Jörg Schönert, "Schlachtgesänge vom Kanapee. Zu den 'Preußischen Kriegsliedern' des Kanonikus Gleim," in *Gedichte und Interpretationen. Aufklärung und Sturm und Drang*, ed. Karl Richter (Stuttgart: Reclam, 1983), 126–139; Hans Peter Herrmann, "Individuum und Staatsmacht. Preußisch-deutscher Nationalismus in Texten zum Siebenjährigen Krieg," in *Machtphantasie Deutschland. Nationalismus, Männlichkeit und Fremdenhaß im Vaterlandsdiskurs deutscher Schriftsteller des 18. Jahrhunderts*, ed. Hans Peter Herrmann, Hans Martin Blitz, and Susanna Moßmann (Frankfurt am Main: Suhrkamp, 1996), 66–79.

order." Goethe explains further that poetry becomes "hollow" unless it is based upon subjects such as "the events of nations and their shepherds, when both stand for one man. Kings are to be represented in war and danger, where on that account they appear as the first, because they determine and share the fate of the very least, and therefore become much more interesting than the gods themselves."[25] In this way, literature (*Dichtung*) is entrusted with upholding the royalist mystique of political incorporation and forging a community of subjects. Royal charisma is produced as an equivalent of literary "interest" through the techniques of aesthetic engagement. Along these lines, Frederick's charismatic popularity during the war was propelled by the public fascination for adversity, crystallized in tragedy, and exploited in poetic dramatizations of his royal role.[26]

---

25 Johann Wolfgang von Goethe, *Poetry and Truth from My Own Life*, trans R. O. Moon (Washington, DC: Public Affairs Press, 1949), 241.

26 Gisbert Ter-Nedden in an important essay discusses the processing of the conceptual challenges posed by the war in drama (namely, in Lessing's *Philotas* and responses to it), and points to the public interest in calamity as a driving force behind the war's media impact: Gisbert Ter-Nedden, "*Philotas* und *Aias* oder Der Kriegsheld im Gefangenendilemma." On the affinities between royal charisma and dramatic interest, see Greenblatt, *Shakespearean Negotiations: The Circulation of Social Energy in Renaissance England*, 62–65.

PETER, OR THE TRAGEDY OF TRIUMPH

Peter III's withdrawal from the Seven Years' War was the earliest among the startling measures that shaped his short reign. This unpopular decision contributed to Peter's fall six months later, when he was overthrown by his wife, the future Catherine II, and assassinated. However, contrary to a popular anecdotal view of events, the politically tactless peace was more than the emperor's personal whim. In fact, Chancellor Mikhail Vorontsov had elaborated plans for a separate peace with Frederick and the restitution of East Prussia even before Elizabeth's death.[1] Vorontsov, the cautious and experienced master of foreign affairs who kept his post under Peter III, had ties to Prussia dating back to the 1740s. Generally, pro-Prussian sympathies were not uncommon at the Russian court, despite the personal animosity towards Frederick affected by Empress Elizabeth.

These sympathies, strengthened after 1756 by the empress's serious illness and the constant expectation of Peter's succession, stimulated interest in Frederick's literary works. In 1756–1757, in the course of an ambitious and dangerous pro-Prussian intrigue, Catherine (at that point still Peter's political ally), entertained a secret correspondence with the English ambassador,

---

1   P. I. Bartenev, ed., *Arkhiv kniazia Vorontsova* (Moscow: Tip. A. I. Mamontova, 1872), 4: 173–178. Arguments for a favorable view of the peace (as well as all other measures undertaken by Peter) have been assembled by Carol Leonard, *Reform and Regicide: The Reign of Peter III of Russia* (Bloomington: Indiana University Press, 1993), 117–137. On the shifting logic behind Russian involvement in the war, see Michael Müller, "Rußland und der Siebenjährige Krieg. Beitrag zu einer Kontroverse," *Jahrbücher für Geschichte Osteuropas* 28 (1980): 198–219.

Hanbury Williams. Among other things, their letters refer to Frederick's "writings" ("écrits") secretly procured by the ambassador for the heir apparent and his spouse. Catherine professed to share the ambassador's admiration for Frederick, who "écrit aussi bien qu'il se bat" ("writes as well as he fights"), and to read his works "avec le meme empressement que ceux de Voltaire" ("with the same eagerness as those of Voltaire").[2] Even as a code, this confession certainly attested to the relevance of Frederick's double performance as a political actor and writer for Russia's courtly public.

According to Stanisław Poniatowski (Catherine's lover, who was also involved in Williams's intrigue), Peter's fascination with Prussia was so focused on the military that he refused to believe that Frederick enjoyed reading and wrote poetry. This suggests that Frederick's intellectual standing and poetic compositions were at least a matter of some debate in Petersburg.[3] This half-illicit interest must have provided the backdrop for the Russian reception of the "Réponse … au M. de Voltaire." By March 1758 Gottsched forwarded it from Leipzig to Sumarokov. As a Prussian subject (he was born in East Prussia) and a resident of a city occupied by Prussian troops, Gottsched was compelled by signs of favor shown to him by Frederick to employ his influential journal, *Das Neueste aus der anmuthigen Gelehrsamkeit* (*The News of Delightful Learning*), and his wide network of correspondents for the king's publicity. Gottsched contributed to the propagandistic success of Frederick's poem, which "soon splashed across the pages of European journals, in the original French and in translations" (including the English rendering quoted above). Gottsched reprinted the "Réponse … au M. de Voltaire" with a translation into German verse and sent it to Russia at a time when, as Lessing reported, his relationship with Frederick grew "immer bekannter, immer vertrauter" ("closer and more intimate by the minute").[4]

2   [Catherine, Empress of Russia], *Correspondance de Catherine Alexéievna, Grande-Duchesse de Russie, et de Sir Charles H. Williams, Ambassadeur d'Angleterre, 1756 et 1757* (Moscow: Lissner & Sobko, 1909), 241, 281.

3   Stanislas Auguste [Poniatowski], *Mémoires*, ed. Anna Grześkowiak-Krwawicz (Paris: Institut d'Études Slaves, 2012), 129.

4   Ulf Lehmann, *Der Gottschedkreis und Russland* (Berlin: Akad. Verlag, 1966), 102; Aleksandr Sumarokov, " "Prilozhenie: Redaktsii i varianty, Dopolneniia. Kommentarii," in Aleksandr Sumarokov, *Ody torzhestvennyia. Reprintnoe vosproizvedenie sbornikov 1774 goda* (Moscow: OGI, 2009), 42, 46; Amanda Ewington, *A Voltaire for Russia: A. P. Sumarokov's Journey from Poet-Critic to Russian Philosophe* (Evanston, IL: Northwestern University Press, 2010), 154;

Sumarokov, recently elected a member of Gottsched's *Deutsche Gesellschaft* sought the patronage of Peter's and Catherine's "young court," and in 1759 dedicated to Catherine his own journal, *Trudoliubivaia pchela* (*The Industrious Bee*). Reflecting the tensions of the political thinking at the Russian court, Sumarokov paradoxically combined exalted martial patriotism with an undercurrent of admiration for Frederick in his odes commemorating Russia's involvement in the "Prussian war." At one point, he apostrophized the enemy king: "Velik ty, ia skazhu to smelo" ("Great you are, I will say it boldly"), and elsewhere praised his courage in facing three hostile powers, thus reproducing a central motif of Frederick's own narrative of the war. At some point, Sumarokov drafted a translation of the "Réponse ... au M. de Voltaire," which was not finished and was published posthumously, possibly because it would have broadcasted all too potently the heroic self-dramatization of a longtime adversary to the Russian general public.[5]

The response of the ruling elite, however, did not depend on Russian translations. Frederick's literary display of valor and endurance, enhanced by the appearance of the first publicly available editions of his poetry during the war in 1760, was not lost on the Russian court. If Frederick resorted to the rhetoric of hopeless resistance associated with Porus, the peace offered to him by Peter III, which included the restoration of territory officially known as the "Kingdom of Prussia," resembled the benevolent actions of Alexander, who accepted the defeated Porus as his friend and returned him his kingdom "through the Admiration he conceived of his extraordinary Courage in his Adversity":

He that could preserve,
Amidst such Injuries of adverse Fate,
A royal Soul, is worthy of a Crown.
I give thee Freedom with thy Queen and Kingdom ...[6]

Lessing to Ewald von Kleist, 14 März 1758, in Gotthold Ephraim Lessing, *Werke* (Wiesbaden: Der Tempel-Verlag, n.d.), 1: 1079; *Das Neueste aus der anmuthigen Gelehrsamkeit* 3 (1758), 214–218. On Gottsched and Frederick, see Werner Rieck, "Gottsched und Friedrich II," *Wissenschaftliche Zeitschrift der Pädagogischen Hochschule Potsdam, Gesell.-Sprachw. Reihe* 2 (1966): 221–230.

5   Sumarokov, *Polnoe sobranie vsekh sochinenii*, 1: 309–310.

6   [Metastasio], *Poro, Re Dell'Indie*, 6, 66.

Alexander's treatment of Porus, as reported by Plutarch and Quintus Curtius, who were both well known to eighteenth-century Russian audiences (Curtius was twice translated into Russian by 1750), presented the most famous case in a "scenario of power" often enacted by Alexander. According to Curtius, Alexander tended to show "clemency towards the vanquished ... returning so many kingdoms to those from whom he had taken them in war."[7] The Alexander-Porus plot often served for absolutist representation. Specifically, Racine's tragedy emerged from a vibrant cult of Louis XIV as Alexander, also reflected in a series of monumental paintings by Charles Le Brun, which included *Alexandre et Porus* (1673). In 1738 this plot was revived by Charles André van Loo, a painter with close ties the French court.[8]

The same patterns of domination and representation were explored all over absolutist Europe, including mid-eighteenth century Russia. In 1743, shortly after the new empress Elizabeth summoned the future Peter III and proclaimed him her heir apparent, the festivities commemorating her ascension were amplified by the military triumph over Sweden, followed by the Peace of Abo in which Elizabeth affected a magnanimous concession of the conquered territory to the defeated enemy in exchange for the designation of a pro-Russian successor to the Swedish crown.[9] This symbolic scenario was celebrated in the opera *Seleuco* (1744), specifically written for the occasion by

---

7   Quintus Curtius, [*History of Alexander*], trans. John C. Rolfe (Cambridge, MA: Harvard University Press, 1985), 2: 523 (10: 5, 28).

8   On the absolutist uses of the Alexander legend, see Chantal Grell, Christian Michel, and Pierre Vidal-Naquet, eds., *L'école des princes, ou Alexandre disgracié: essai sur la mythologie monarchique de la France absolutiste* (Paris: Les Belles Lettres, 1988); Doering, *Jean Racine zwischen Kunst und Politik*. Both works emphasize the fundamental ambiguity of Alexander's image, which simultaneously stood for successful rule and the destructive violence of conquest. Thanks to this ambiguity, comparisons to Alexander proved an important and meaningful political trope in the literature of the Seven Years' War. They were often applied to Frederick himself, a conscientious ruler and a foolhardy invader of Silesia and Saxony. Prince de Ligne, fascinated with the Prussian king, wrote that in the future "au lieu de la bataille de Porus, on saura celle de Lissa," a battle won by Frederick in 1757 (Charles-Joseph de Ligne, *Mes écarts ou ma tête en liberté: et autres pensées et réflexions*, ed. Jeroom Vercruysse and Daniel Acke [Paris: H. Champion, 2007], 146). In Russia, Sumarokov recognized Frederick as the "new Alexander" and simultaneously denied him any superiority over the Russian empress and her troops (Sumarokov, *Ody torzhestvennyia. Prilozhenie*, 46, 263).

9   S. M. Solov'ev, *Istoriia Rossii s drevneishikh vremen*, Kniga XI (Moscow: Prosveshchenie, 1993), 212. The relevance of the Swedish peace for Peter was enhanced by the fact that it immediately concerned his dynastic status as a possible heir to the Swedish throne.

Bonecchi, in which a victorious king cedes occupied lands to the legitimate heir. In this case, foreign policy was reconciled with operatic poetics in a finale imitating Metastasio's *Alessandro nell'Indie*. In its turn, *Alessandro* was twice performed and printed in Petersburg in 1755 and 1759, the second time during the Seven Years' War on direct orders from the heir apparent and on his very own stage at the summer residence of Oranienbaum, as the title page of the respective printing announced.[10]

Operatic reenactments restored the theatricality inherent in Alexander's conduct: according to Curtius, Alexander himself professed to be acting "in the theater of the whole world."[11] Racine's tragedy, conceived as a dramatic reenactment of the emerging cult of the Sun King, fashioned his charisma in theatrical terms, grounding royal "majesté" on a display of "présence auguste": "Ses yeux comme son bras font partout des sujets" ("august presence": "His eyes, as his arms make him subjects everywhere," 3.3).[12] The final reconciliation with Porus, amalgamating military domination with a personalized sway over the emotions of subjects, represented both the peak of dramatic action and a foundational act of Alexander's power, the essential "gesture of executive power," "die Geste der Vollstreckung," which, in Carl Schmitt's political theory and Benjamin's reading of early modern tragedy, is constitutive of sovereignty.[13] The French version of the 1759 Petersburg edition of Metastasio's libretto praised Alexander's act as a model for rulers:

> Que d'un Héros si magnanime
> Les grands exploits soient célébrés ...

---

10   Pierre Metastasio, *Alexandre aux Indes, opera ... representé ... par ordre de Son Altesse Imperiale monseigneur le grand duc de toutes les Russies ...* (St. Petersburg: l'Academie Imperiale des Sciences, 1759); V. N. Vsevolodskii-Gerngross, *Teatr v Rossii pri imperatritse Elizavete Petrovne* (St. Petersburg: Giperion, 2003), 52–54, 107; L. M. Starikova, ed., *Teatral'naia zhizn' Rossii v epokhu Elizavety Petrovny. Dokumental'naia khronika. 1751–1761*, vol. 3, bk. 1 (Moscow: Nauka, 2011), 291–295, 318–321. A German company, which occasionally played in Petersburg, is known to have performed Racine's Alexander tragedy in Riga on Elizabeth's coronation day; see Vsevolodskii-Gerngross, *Teatr v Rossii*, 173. This tragedy was certainly known to the Russian public, along with other plays by Racine. Sumarokov translated an excerpt from it into Russian: Sumarokov, *Polnoe sobranie vsekh sochinenii*, 1: 316.
11   Quintus Curtius, [*History of Alexander*], 2: 421 (9: 6, 21).
12   Racine, *Théâtre complet*, 1: 145.
13   Benjamin, *Origin of the German Tragic Drama*, 69–71.

D'un si beau nom que la douce harmonie
Inspire tous les Courtisans:
Aux plus grands vertus si la gloire est unie,
Que tous les souverains en soient les partisans.

Of a hero so magnanimous
Let the exploits be renown.
Of one such beautiful name the sweet harmony
Inspires all those at Court,
If glory is united with such great virtues
Let all sovereigns partake of it.[14]

In the opera, according to these verses, the aesthetic effects of musical drama ("douce harmonie") are merged with the effects of Alexander's charisma, which should be emulated by sovereigns whose power rests on the emotional engagement of their subjects. The Porus plays dramatized this mechanism of emotional submission. In Racine's rendering, overwhelmed by Alexander's display of "vertu" and "amitié" ("virtue" and "friendship"), Porus recognizes his dominion and joins his military effort in order to give the world "un maître aussi grand qu'Alexandre" ("a master as great as Alexander"). In his response to Peter's advances, Frederick, who once noted that Charles XII of Sweden was so fond of Alexander that he made Stanisław Leszczyński king of Poland "d'après Porus" ("after Porus"), resorted to a similar rhetoric, praising Peter who "donne un exemple de vertu à tous les souverains" ("gives an example of virtue to all sovereigns") and declaring himself the emperor's "ami inseparable et qui coopérera … à tous ce Votre Majesté désirera," "j'irais moi-même contre Ses ennemis" ("inseparable friend who cooperates with all Your Majesty would desire, I would go [to war] myself against Your enemies").[15]

---

14 Metastasio, *Alexandre aux Indes*, 123. On the staging of sovereignty in Metastasio's *Allesandro*, see Reinhard Wiesend, "Metastasios Alexander: Herrscherfigur und Rollentypus. Aspekte der Rezeptionsgeschichte," in *Opernheld und Opernheldin im 18. Jahrhundert. Aspekte der Librettoforschung*, ed. K. Hortschansky (Hamburg: Eisenach, 1991), 139–152; Martha Feldman, *Opera and Sovereignty* (Chicago: University of Chicago Press, 2007), 255–258.

15 [Frederick II], *Politische Correspondenz*, 21:314, 391, 413 (no. 13552, 13637, 13656); [Frederick II], "Réfutation du prince de Machiavel," in *Œuvres*, 8:222. Frederick's remark

The instant reconciliation with Frederick, usually considered as a sign of Peter's inadequacy, could be construed as a spectacular manifestation of his recently acquired sovereignty. The Alexander of the Porus plot, as Racine makes clear in the dedication of his play to Louis XIV, combined the two faces of royal power, the glorious yet violent conqueror and the wise peacemaker. Peter's actions displayed a similar combination: a German oration commemorating the Russo-Prussian peace contrasted the "Verwüstungen und Verheerungen ganzer Länder" ("devastation and ruin of entire nations") by conquerors to the policy of the Russian monarch, who had demonstrated "daß Tapferkeit mit Menschenliebe verknüpffet, einen Helden in seiner Größe darstelle" ("that valor combined with charity shows a hero in his greatness").[16]

Peter's peace initiative—which seemed to make Russia "la bienfaitrice de l'Europe" ("the benefactress of Europe") and "l'arbitre du nord" ("the arbiter of the north"), as Voltaire put it—was only one of several measures devised for a spectacular inauguration of his reign and aligned with a common "scenario of power," which was largely inherited from Elizabeth and revolved around the notion of clemency. According to a contemporary account, the empress extracted from her successor "la promesse de pardonner à ses Ennemis, et de ne point affermir son trône par le sang de ses Sujets" ("the promise of pardoning his enemies, and of not affirming his throne with the blood of his subjects").[17]

---

on Charles and Porus was corrected by Voltaire, who in his own earlier *Histoire de Charles XII, Roi de Suede,* instead of Porus mentions Abdalonymus, a poor nobleman enthroned by Alexander. His story, too, was dramatized by Metastasio in *Il re pastore,* most famous in Mozart's setting. Frederick referred to Abdalonymus's story and its operatic treatments during the war: *Unterhaltungen mit Friedrich dem Grossen,* 345.

16   Racine, *Théâtre complet,* 1: 113–114; Samuel Tiefensee, [Carl Wilhelm Schulz], *Rede und Ode auf den zwischen den hohen Höfen Berlin und Petersburg Anno 1762. glücklich geschlossenen Frieden abgelesen in dem Gröningischen illustren Collegio zu Stargard an der Jhna* (Stargard: n.p., 1762), 19. The same author compares the Seven Years' War to a "traurige Schauspiel" (15).

17   Voltaire, *Complete Works,* vol. 108 (*Correspondence,* vol. 24) (The Voltaire Foundation, 1972), 330 (D10369), 326 (D10366); [Christophe Friedrich Schwan], *Anecdotes russes, ou lettres d'un officier allemand à un gentilhomme livonien, écrites de Petersbourg en 1762; tems du règne & du détrônement de Pierre III. Empereur de Russie* (London: Aux dépens de la compagnie, 1764), 10. Peter's double role as conqueror and peacemaker, as well as his claims to a hegemonic position in European politics, was broadcast in contemporary Russian panegyrics, first of all the odes by Sumarokov, Lomonosov, and Ivan Barkov. Barkov also authored the Russian translation of the festive opera written for the peace celebrations: *Mir geroev. Drama na muzyke predstavlennaia vo vremia torzhestva blagopoluchno zakliuchennago mira mezhdu ... Petrom*

Under Elizabeth this scenario was both reflected in policy, most famously in the suspension of death sentences, and reenacted on court stages. Indeed, *Alessandro nell'Indie* belonged to a rich tradition of dramatic representations of royal clemency that derived from Corneille's tragedy *Cinna* (1639) and its operatic imitation, Metastasio's *La clemenza di Tito* (1734), performed at Elizabeth's coronation.

Peter's reconciliation with Frederick stood for a scenario of clemency developed with an eye for internal use, just as Alexander's treatment of Porus could be construed as an allegory for the monarchy's relations to its subjects. (Racine's play, for example, glorified Louis XIV's handling of the Fronde of the Princes.) According to commonly held political conceptions, clement actions reinforced subjects' obedience to the monarchy with emotionally charged allegiance, or "love," for the ruler. This pattern could be recognized as the driving force behind Peter's policies. In the words of another contemporary, "Wer sollte nun nicht glauben, daß die guldenen Zeiten in Rußland angehen und die Anstalten, Großmuth und Milde des Kaisers ihm Liebe und Treue in allen Herzen erwerben würden?" ("Who would not believe that the golden age is coming to Russia, and that the emperor's measures, his magnanimity and mildness would earn him love and loyalty in all hearts?").[18]

Traditional measures such as gifts, promotions, and the restitution of political exiles were reinforced by two legislative acts published one after another in February 1762. The first decree, the Manifesto on the Freedom of the Russian Nobility, allowed the nobles to retire from state service and to travel abroad, whereas the second abolished the secret police, together with the notorious system of political surveillance and persecution known as "slovo i delo." Both decrees were recognized as displays of royal clemency ("shchedrost'" or "shchedrota," in contemporary encomiastic idiom), strong gestures inscribed into the complex dynamic of collective emotion crucial for the functioning of Russian monarchy. The second decree claimed a semi-theatrical effect, attempting to reform any dissenters by a public "example" ("primerom")

---

tret'im ... i ... Friderikom Tret'im korolem prusskim ... Prelozhenie rossiiskimi stikhami ... Ivana Barkova (St. Petersburg: Pri Imperatorskoi Akademii nauk, 1762).

18 [Georg A. Will], *Merkwürdige Lebensgeschichte Peter des Dritten, Kaiser ... aller Reußen* (Frankfurt: n.p., 1762), 19. On political contexts of Racine's play, see the much-mocked but still valuable René Jasinski, *Vers le vrai Racine* (Paris: A. Colin, 1958), 1: 101–120.

of royal "mildness" (a scenario dramatized in *Cinna* and *La clemenza di Tito*).[19] In one of the many odes celebrating Peter's ascension, Aleksei Rzhevskii, a young nobleman and aspiring servitor, praised the royal decision to "forgive the guilty" and "accept the enemies as sons" ("Ty vinnykh poshchadil s okhotoi, / I prinial v synov'ia vragov"), reviving the pattern of power symbolized by Alexander's pardon for Porus. In another ode, Rzhevskii exalted the Manifesto on the Freedom of the Russian Nobility as a centerpiece of Peter's rule, rooted in the nation's "love" for him rather than armed force:

> Иной себя прославил,
> Кровь неповинных лив;
> Но славу Ты возставил
> Меча не обагрив;
> Щедротою одною,
> Над подданной страною,
> Героев превзошел,
> С мечем не кровавленным,
> В храм славы ты вошел,
> И мил своим плененным.
> Ты вольность даровавши,
> Всех вольность погубил,
> И всем свободу давши,
> Всех ныне нас пленил:
> Пленил ты нас любовью.
> Своей готовы кровью
> Мы то Тебе воздать,
> Трудом все безконечным,
> Мы будем исполнять
> С желанием сердечным.
> Ко смертоносну ль бою

---

19 *Polnoe sobranie zakonov Rossiiskoi imperii*, 15: 917–918. On the undercurrent of public perception of Peter's two decrees as foundational acts of a benevolent monarchy a generation later, see Iu. M. Lotman, "Cherty real'noi politiki v pozitsii Karamzina 1790-kh gg. (K genezisu istoricheskoi kontseptsii Karamzina)," in *Karamzin* (St. Petersburg: Isskustvo-SPB, 1997), 479, 481; "A. S. Kaisarov i literaturno-obshchestvennaia bor'ba ego vremeni," in ibid., 658–660.

Охотно все идем,
Охотно пред тобою
Кровь нашу всю прольем.

Others have attained fame
By shedding innocent blood
But you have established your glory
Without bloodying your sword.
By sheer clemency
To your dominion
You have surpassed heroes and
With a sword pure from blood
You entered into the temple of fame
Dear to your captives.
Having granted us freedom
You have taken it from us, and
Having taken us all captive,
You made us love's captives.
Ready with our own blood,
We will repay you
With endless toil
Accomplished with heartfelt zeal.
If we go into deadly battle,
We will gladly, before your very eyes
Pour out all of our own blood.[20]

Rzhevskii's lyric idiom was artfully tuned to authentic political sensibilities of the Russian public. A Russian diplomat in Vienna admitted in a private letter that upon receiving news of the manifesto he was "overwhelmed" ("enthousiasmé") with Peter's "grandeur" and "une clemence aussi inatendue que surprenant" ("a clemency as unexpected as [it was] surprising"), and that the "chaines" ("chains") abolished by the decree have to be replaced in the hearts of the nobility "avec de beaucoup plus fortes qui sont ceux de

---

20 Aleksei Rzhevskii, "Oda … imperatoru Petru Feodorovichu … na vseradostnoe vosshestvie na vserossiiskii prestol," *Poleznoe uveselenie* (March 1762): 99; ibid., 109–110.

devoir de sujets fidel, zelé et reconaissant [*sic*]" ("by those much stronger, namely those of the duty of loyal subjects, zealous and grateful").[21] In order to convey this new understanding of obedience, Rzhevskii adapts an erotic conceit (underscored by a meter unusual for political panegyric but common for "tender" songs and arias). In rejecting customary coercion, Peter's gift of freedom redefines his sway over his "captives," or subjects, in terms of love, conventionally described by the paradox of voluntary captivity. While Rzhevskii's verses do not necessarily refer to Racine's *Alexandre le Grand*, this play notably explored the affinities between the idioms of gallant love and political submission in the subplot of Queen Cléofile, who, after her kingdom was conquered by Alexander, fell in love with him and gladly accepted "ses fers" ("her bonds"), "sa liberté perdant le souvenir" ("losing the memory of her liberty," 2.1).[22] Showcasing the collective experience of subjection refashioned by the manifesto, the lyric idiom once again unmasked the quasi-theatrical dynamic of royal gesture and public emotional engagement. This dynamic, which blurred the boundary between action and representation, was equally important for dramatic reenactments of monarchy and its actual functioning.

The political anthropology of monarchy, as outlined in classical histories and explored by political theory from Machiavelli to Frederick's *Anti-Machiavel*, implied a constant oscillation between peace and conquest, clemency and violence, as foundations of sovereignty. It is deeply characteristic that Peter both mitigated political persecution and privately deplored his own "abuse of clemency," declaring that he should again "take to the gallows."[23] Just as in the Alexander plays, his reconciliation with the enemy was to be followed by its direct opposite: a war with Denmark for Holsteinian interests in which Peter could rely on his newly won ally. Peter's handling of the Prussian peace brought to light what Greenblatt calls "paradoxes, ambiguities, and tensions of authority"[24] and proved concomitantly to be both the central act of his reign and the ultimate manifestation of his failed sover-

---

21   I. G. Chernyshev to I. I. Shuvalov, February 1762, *Russkii arkhiv* (1869): 1822–1823.

22   Racine, *Théâtre complet*, 1: 131–132.

23   Ja. Shtelin [Jacob Stählin], "Zapiski o Petre III," *Ekaterina. Put' k vlasti* (Moscow: Fond Sergeia Dubova, 2003), 37.

24   Greenblatt, *Shakespearean Negotiations*, 65.

eignty. His rapid fall in June 1762 was made possible by the public disapproval for the emperor's exaggerated Prussophilia.[25]

In order to defend Peter's decisions, his contemporary biographer had to remind readers that a "Souverain absolû" ("absolute sovereign") is not obliged to ask "ses Sujets la permission ... de donner la paix à son païs" ("his subjects for permission ... to give peace to his [own] country") and that they do not possess "le pouvoir de le punir, parce qu'il ne veut pas s'accommoder à leur caprice" ("the power to punish [the monarch], when he does not wish to give in to their caprice").[26] In displays of clemency, the idea of absolute royal sovereignty was reconciled with the monarchy's practical dependence on public approval. A semi-official account of Peter's Manifesto heralded "un Monarque qui a l'âme assez grande, pour renoncer à un droit aussi étendu dans la seule vue de rendre se sujets plus heureux" ("a monarch who has a soul grand enough to renounce his privilege so vast in the only goal of making his subjects happier").[27] Unlike his Prussian counterpart, Peter, however, proved unable to fully acknowledge and master the patterns of performative engagement of the public. The peace with Prussia, juxtaposed with his favor for his German entourage, was largely perceived as a violation of the body politic rather than a show of clemency.

In his poetic defense of Catherine's coup, the classically trained Mikhail Lomonosov complained that under Peter "torzhestvuiushchii narod / Predalsia v ruki pobezhdennykh ... / O styd, o strannoi oborot!"("a people of victors had submitted to the defeated, what a shame, a strange twist"), echoing the Macedonian troops' reproaches to Alexander as they rebelled against his acceptance of the customs of conquered lands, which "by a novel fashion made the victors pass under the yoke."[28] In a gesture equally eccentrically theatrical and drastically differing from public sensibility, Peter's failure to accommodate the

---

25 I build on the reading of Peter's fall suggested by Ronald Vroon, who demonstrates the importance of literary evidence for its comprehension: Ronald Vroon, "'Ekaterina plachet yavno …': k predystorii perevorota 1762 g.," *I vremia i mesto: Istoriko-filologicheskii sbornik k shestidesiatiletiiu A. L. Ospovata* (Moscow: Novoe Izdatel'stvo, 2008), 40–54.

26 [Schwan], *Anecdotes russes, ou lettres d'un officier allemand*, 205–206.

27 François Pierre Pictet to Voltaire, 2 March 1762, in Voltaire, *The Complete Works* 108 (*Correspondence*, vol. 24): 312 (D10355).

28 Mikhail Lomonosov, *Izbrannye proizvedeniia*, ed. A. A. Morozov (Leningrad: Sovetskii pisatel', 1986), 170; Quintus Curtius, [*History of Alexander*], 2: 295 (8: 7, 11).

attitudes of his audience fundamentally undermined his performance of sovereignty. While Frederick II successfully exploited dramatic patterns to refashion his defeat as a source of charisma, a misguided display of triumph precipitated Peter's ruin. If, as Benjamin suggests, tragic visions of kingship revolved around the "antithesis between the power of the ruler and his capacity to rule," Voltaire was right to remark: "Si Pierre III n'avait pas été un ivrogne, son aventure serait un beau sujet de tragédie" ("If Peter III had not been a drunkard, his story would have made a great subject for a tragedy").[29]

---

29 Benjamin, *Origin of the German Tragic Drama,* 70; Voltaire, *The Complete Works,* 109 (*Correspondence,* vol. 25): 198 (D10685).

CONCLUSION: TRAGEDY, HISTORY, AND THEORY

Even as a courtly entertainment, early Russian tragedy poses conceptual challenges not only to students of literary or theater history. However artistically imperfect or derivative Sumarokov's plays might seem in comparison to his models, Shakespeare, Corneille, and Racine, they still fulfilled the pivotal function of early modern tragic drama, voicing fundamental tensions that informed and underlay established visions of authority and political order. Throughout my study, I have consistently drawn upon Walter Benjamin's discussion of *Trauerspiel*, which places this dramatic form, a slightly earlier version of the genre adopted by Sumarokov, on the crossroads of aesthetic and political thinking. Forcefully denying any continuity between early modern drama and classical tragedy it claimed to revive, Benjamin refused to seek its "origin" (*Ursprung*) in literary genealogies but rather situated it in "baroque" political imagination. His archaeology of tragedy was shaped by the same political concerns that drove the much more general inquiry into political theory in his essay "Zur Kritik der Gewalt" ("Critique of Violence," 1920–1921). Translated, for a lack of a better equivalent, as "violence," its central concept, *Gewalt*, conflates in fact what are for Benjamin two inseparable facets of power: the stable order of authority, associated with law (*Recht*), and foundational violence that is—unavoidably—its source, or "origin" (*Ursprung*).[1] While "Critique of Violence" is primarily concerned with the political

---

1   Walter Benjamin, "Critique of Violence," in *Reflections: Essays, Aphorisms, Autobiographical Writings*, trans. Edmund Jephcott (New York: Schocken Books, 1986), 277–300. For a similar

struggles in Weimar Germany, if read alongside the contemporaneous *The Origin of German Tragic Drama* it manifestly resonates with and enhances Benjamin's insights into early modern, or "baroque," economy of power.

The emerging Russian tragic drama, as I have argued, reflected a symbolic economy of rule that relied on a machinery of disproportionate violence and brutal repression just as it developed festive "scenarios of rejoicing" and benevolence to captivate the subjects' hearts. While both faces of Russian autocracy have been separately, and extensively, explored in historical scholarship, it is their coexistence that complicates the conventional notion of (post-)Petrine rational statehood. Only recently, Kevin Platt's study of historical perceptions of Ivan the Terrible and Peter the Great has highlighted "the intimate connection between greatness and terror in Russian historical mythology and in Russian political practice."[2] In the preceding chapters I have assembled cases of royal prosecution that throughout the first decades of the eighteenth century involved executions and maiming of high-standing members of the court (including an heir to the throne) on invented or exaggerated charges of conspiracy and treason. From Aleksei Petrovich in 1718 to Artemii Volynskii in 1740 to Natalia Lopukhina in 1743, these and other, less prominent cases of perceived royal injustice haunted the imagination of Russia's elite, who time and again evoked the notion of tragedy to process them. Both as a concept and textual mode, tragedy points to a conundrum that pervades various periods of Russian history: the spectacular, "irrational" redundancy of state-sponsored violence manifestly unwarranted either by judicial custom or any actual resistance. Precisely this incommensurability of violence as a means with the presumed ends that are expected to justify it is a pivotal issue of Benjamin's analysis of power:

> It is at the same time the question of the truth of the basic dogma common to both theories: just ends can be attained by justified means, justified means used for just ends. How would it be, therefore, if all the violence imposed by fate, using justified means, were

---

argument on the semiotics of seventeenth-century French absolutism, see Louis Marin, *Portrait of the King*, trans. Martha Houle (Minneapolis: University of Minnesota Press, 1988).

2   Kevin Platt, *Terror and Greatness: Ivan and Peter as Russian Myths* (Ithaca, NY: Cornell University Press, 2011), 3.

of itself in irreconcilable conflict with just ends, and if at the same time a different kind of violence came into view that certainly could be either the justified or the unjustified means to those ends, but was not related to them as means at all but in some different way? ... The nonmediate function of violence at issue here is illustrated by everyday experience. As regards man, he is impelled by anger, for example, to the most visible outbursts of a violence that is not related as a means to a preconceived end. It is not a means but a manifestation.[3]

With the concept of *manifestation* Benjamin introduces a logic of power distinct from commonly assumed political rationality of means and ends. A mode of action that constitutes its own value, contingent violence, usually relegated beyond the sphere of signification, moves to occupy the symbolic center of the political order. Its paragon, the angry man, is easily recognized as a version of the baroque monarch whose "dictatorial powers" culminate in the figure of Herod "falling into insanity, holding two babes in his hands in order to batter out their brains." Even "where the situation does not require it," the monarch speaks and acts as a tyrant because his royal essence depends on "the gesture of executive power," *die Geste der Vollstreckung*, which is also the gesture of execution.[4] To quote a historically relevant example, Jean Bodin, an influential sixteenth-century theorist of absolute sovereignty whose works were well known in early eighteenth-century Russia, recounts the election ritual of "a Great King of Tartary" (a toponym inviting comparisons with Russia's "Oriental" despotism, which Bodin expressly refers to on numerous other occasions). The new king proclaims his authority to the assembled people as follows: "you must be ready to do as I command, and whom I order killed must be killed forthwith and without delay, and the whole kingdom must be entrusted to me and put into my hands."[5]

---

3   Benjamin, "Critique of Violence," 293–294.

4   Benjamin, *Origin of German Tragic Drama*, 69–70; Haverkamp, *Shakespearean Genealogies of Power*, 79.

5   Jean Bodin, *On Sovereignty: Four Chapters from the Six Books of the Commonwealth*, ed. and trans. Julian H. Franklin (Cambridge: Cambridge University Press, 1992), 8. On the affinity of Bodin's account to the poetics of tragedy, see Campe, "Der Befehl und die Rede des Souveräns," 59–60. On the knowledge of Bodin in Russia, see Iusim, *Makiavelli*

Accordingly, Benjamin argues in "Critique of Violence" that it is in the death penalty "where the highest violence, that over life and death, occurs in the legal system, the origins of law jut manifestly and fearsomely into existence." Due to this logic of manifestation, "in primitive legal systems" capital punishment "is imposed even for such crimes ... to which it seems quite out of 'proportion.' ... For in the exercise of violence over life and death more than in any other legal act, law reaffirms itself."[6] Quite notably, Benjamin anticipates Foucault's famous discussion of early modern public executions as a ceremonial that "restores ... sovereignty by manifesting it at its most spectacular" and through disproportionate violence "bring[s] into play ... the dissymmetry between the subject who has dared to violate the law and the all-powerful sovereign who displays his strength." Similar to Benjamin, Foucault concludes:

> The fact that the crime and the punishment were related and bound up in the form of atrocity ... was the effect, in the rites of punishment, of a certain mechanism of power: of a power ... which, in the absence of continual supervision, sought a renewal of its effect in the spectacle of its individual manifestations; of a power that was recharged in the ritual display of its reality as "super-power."[7]

If so, our vision of the "regular state" of the eighteenth century must be modified to accommodate the defining role of arbitrary judicial violence, or terror, in the symbolic economy of rule and domination. Though high-profile political prosecution was not everyday practice, and had become exceedingly rare between Lopukhina's trial in 1743 and the 1790s, it was all the more suited to represent the institutional power of monarchy as rooted in the violence of the state of exception. The last trial of its kind for decades, the fall and execution of Volynskii and his alleged accomplices in 1740 made such a

---

v Rossii, 93, 100, 103. On Bodin's extended (and pioneering) endorsement of Russian despotism, see Marshall Poe, *A People Born to Slavery: Russia in Early Modern European Ethnography, 1476–1748* (New York: Cornell University Press, 2000), 169–174.

6 Benjamin, "Critique of Violence," 286.

7 Foucault, *Discipline and Punish*, 48–49, 57.

lasting impression on the Russian imagination that it was still discussed at court in the 1760s, and seemed an appropriate subject for a tragedy to Ozerov in the 1800s. Another three decades later, it provided subject matter for one of Russia's first historical novels in the manner of Walter Scott, Ivan Lazhechnikov's *Ledianoi dom* (*The Ice House*, 1835), not to mention a marginal appearance in another novel published the next year, Aleksandr Pushkin's *Kapitanskaiia dochka* (*The Captain's Daughter*).[8]

The symbolic logic that grounded the political status quo in self-constitutive manifestations of "original" violence unfolded both in ritual (Foucault aligns executions with a "whole series of great rituals" such as "coronation [and] entry of the king into a conquered city"[9]) and in aesthetic, specifically dramatic fictions: tragedies (as well as novels). Sumarokov (and Ozerov after him) built upon a well-established tradition that associated the emotional effects of tragedy and judicial violence. The influential Aristotelian theorist Daniel Heinsius mentioned in his 1611 treatise that ancient "tyrants" used to include real and painful executions in the performances of tragedies "for the oblectation and the pleasure of theaters."[10] The very notion of catharsis was interpreted accordingly; to quote Gerhard Vossius's authoritative definition from 1647, "The listener is shocked by the dreadfulness [*atrocitas*] of the deed itself, while the dignity of the characters increases the outrageousness of the situation."[11] Commenting on one of the primeval scenes of absolutist violence, the execution of Egmont and Horn in 1568, Montaigne described it as a "tragedy" staged by the Spanish governor of the Netherlands, the Duke of Alba.[12] Two centuries later, in the chapter "Of the Effects of Tragedy" in his *Philosophical Enquiry into the Origin of Our Ideas of the Sublime and Beautiful* (1757), Edmund Burke argued that even "the most sublime and affecting tragedy" would not be able to exercise an emotional

---

8 A. L. Ospovat, "Iz materialov dlia kommentariia k 'Kapitanskoi dochke' (1–5)," in *Tekst i kommentarii: Kruglyi stol k 75-letiiu Viach. Vs. Ivanova*, ed. V. N. Toporov (Moscow: Nauka, 2006): 247–266.

9 Foucault, *Discipline and Punish*, 48.

10 Daniel Heinsius, *De constitutione tragoediae. La constitution de la tragédie: dite La poétique d'Heinsius*, ed. and trans. Anne Duprat (Geneva: Droz, 2001), 35, 240–241.

11 Gerardus Joannes Vossius, *Poeticarum institutionum libri tres. Institutes of poetics in three books*, ed. and trans. Jan Bloemendal with Edwin Rabbie (Leiden: Brill, 2010), 1, 510–511.

12 Montaigne, *Essais*, I, 7.

attraction comparable to that of a public execution of a "state criminal of high rank." Not incidentally, Burke's definition of the sublime included a vision of royal power expressly associated with "terror": "Sovereigns are frequently addressed with the title of *dread majesty*."[13]

By staging judicial violence, works of fiction both explored its symbolic implications and provided it with the potent legitimacy of an aesthetic event. In "Critique of Violence" Benjamin suggests that it is in myth that the establishment of power, rather than justice, is revealed as the inherent aim of violence, while the very discrepancy between power and justice is negotiated through the concept of fate:

> Mythical violence in its archetypal form is a mere manifestation of the gods. ... their violence establishes a law far more than it punishes for the infringement of one already existing. ... Laws ... remain, at least in primeval times, unwritten laws. A man can unwittingly infringe upon them and thus incur retribution.... But however unluckily it may befall its unsuspecting victim, its occurrence is, in the understanding of the law, not chance, but fate showing itself once again in its deliberate ambiguity.[14]

This argument clearly resonates with discussions of tragic justice in Aristotle's *Poetics* and its early modern (mis)interpretations, which underlay the practice of tragedy. Using the notion of *mythos* to designate both the "received legends" a dramatist inherits and the poetic plot he ends up constructing, Aristotle suggests it should focus on a character "who is become miserable, by some involuntary fault" rather than as a result of "a Remarkable Crime." Elsewhere, he recommends that tragic representation should suggest the workings of fate behind events aligned by mere chance, such as when "the statue of Mitys at Argos ... fell on his Murderer, and killed him on the spot."[15] In this notion of fate, techniques of dramatic fiction coincided with and gave voice to fundamental, if terrifying, notions of power. Benjamin discusses the

---

13 Edmund Burke, *A Philosophical Enquiry Into the Origin of Our Ideas of the Sublime and Beautiful*, ed. J. T. Boulton (London: Routledge & Paul, 1958), 47, 67.
14 Benjamin, "Critique of Violence," 296.
15 *Aristotle's Art of Poetry*, 186–187, 140.

"mythical violence" of the gods as "closely related, indeed identical to lawmaking violence," while *fate* designates, among other things, unpredictable prosecutorial procedure: "there is always hope of eluding its arm. This makes it all the more threatening, like fate, on which depends whether the criminal is apprehended."[16] This symbolic pattern, as we have seen, largely shaped early Russian tragedies and the discourses of judicial terror it relied upon: arbitrary prosecution was regularly interpreted, both by prosecutors and bystanders, as immediate divine intervention. In tragedy, this pattern unfolded into a myth in both the Aristotelian and Benjaminian sense: in its overtly fictional, or mythistorical past terror could be both acknowledged as the ultimate manifestation of royal authority and mystified as its mythical point of origin, *Ursprung*. In Russia's first tragedy, Sumarokov's *Khorev*, the legendary founder of its monarchy, Kii—similar to Bodin's Great King of Tartary—exercises his royal power primarily through judicial murder of the innocent Osnelda, a murder not found in Sumarokov's sources and devised specifically for the purposes of his tragedy.

In his critique of *Gewalt*, the institutionalized order of power and violence, Benjamin exposes *fate* as its central symbolic concept, an evil twin of true, "divine" justice, by definition unattainable with legal means: "there is only one fate and that what exists, and in particular what threatens, belongs inviolably to its order."[17] If it is fate rather than justice that "in all cases underlies legal violence" and "decides on the justification of means," it is because "violence crowned by fate, is the origin of law." The king of Tartary asserts his right to kill after he receives his authority by chance of election. Kii's unwarranted prosecution of Osnelda is made possible by a military victory that years earlier made him the ruler of Kiev in place of Osnelda's father Zavlokh. *Fate*—in eighteenth-century Russian discourse conventionally assimilated with divine will—stands for a potent pattern of political legitimacy that recognized repression and usurpation (as opposed to due judicial process and legally regulated succession) as valid sources of royal charisma. Without this pattern, usually underestimated in historical scholarship, one can hardly explain the instant and virtually unreserved public acceptance of palace revolutions that secured the throne for Elizabeth in 1741

---

16   Benjamin, "Critique of Violence," 285.
17   Ibid., 285–286.

and the dynastically illegitimate Catherine II in 1762. Quite notably, in both cases the original overthrow and imprisonment (and, in Catherine's case, murder) of legitimate rulers was followed by further acts of self-constitutive violence: the trial of Münnich and Osterman in 1742 and Lopukhina in 1743; the murder of the second living lawful emperor, Ivan VI, in 1764; followed by the public execution of his failed liberator, Vasilii Merovich.

The figure of the tyrant was central, as Benjamin argues in *The Origin of German Tragic Drama*, for both theoretical assessments and dramatic representations of sovereignty in baroque Europe. In "Critique of Violence," Benjamin explores the political and aesthetic implications of a cognate figure of "the 'great' criminal," who, "however repellent his ends may have been, has aroused the secret admiration of the public." This aesthetic appeal results from his usurpation of violence that threatens the "law," or political order, "by its mere existence outside the law." This symbolic patterns unfolds in

> heroic legends in which the hero—for example, Prometheus—challenges fate with dignified courage, fights it with varying fortunes, and is not left by the legend without hope of one day bringing a new law to men. It is really this hero and the legal violence of the myth native to him that the public tries to picture even now in admiring the miscreant.[18]

In this reading, Prometheus resembles early modern usurpers, equally heroic and villainous, as theorized by Machiavelli and represented in dramas, including those staged at the Russian court to celebrate the successful coups d'état. Among them was Sumarokov's *Gamlet*, whose successful protagonist, a stage double of Empress Elizabeth, conflates the features of Hamlet with those of Laertes:

> The rabble call him lord;
> And, as the world were now but to begin,
> Antiquity forgot, custom not known,

---

18   Benjamin, "Critique of Violence," 281, 294–295.

The ratifiers and props of every word,
They cry 'Choose we: Laertes shall be king.'[19]

Order, a new order, is expected at this moment to emerge from an outburst of unlawful violence, legitimated in advance by the audience's sympathy for what is presented as a right cause. Decades later after his *Gamlet* but still addressing a court where the inherently problematic origin of any given status quo was as memorable as ever, Sumarokov tackled the issue in another tragedy with Shakespearean overtones, *Dimitrii Samozvanets*. Its protagonist is the historical seventeenth-century usurper who conquered Moscow with the support of Polish troops. Represented as a blood-thirsty tyrant, a "miscreant" modeled after Shakespeare's Richard III, he still deserves an odd apology from his virtuous, if speedily alienated confidant, Parmen:

Когда владети нет достоинства его,
Во случае таком порода ничего.
Пускай Отрепьев он, но и среди обмана,
Коль он достойный царь, достоин царска сана.

If in those qualities a tsar should have to rule
He is found lacking, then his birthright counts for naught.
Suppose he's Otrepev, but even amidst deceit
If he rules well, he is worthy to be a monarch.[20]

For a *raisonneur* of a court play, this argument is drastically at odds with the monarchy's official discourses. While distancing himself from Dimitrii's atrocities, Parmen does not disavow the act of armed conquest (accompanied by foreign invasion) that lay the foundations for his tyrannical rule. Instead, Parmen continues to defend it, arguing with conviction against the principle of dynastic continuity that was still proclaimed in Catherinian Russia to be the principal source of political legitimacy. At the same time, however, by contrasting political ability to lineage as a true

---

19   Shakespeare, *Hamlet*, 302–303.
20   Sumarokov, *Dramaticheskie sochineniia*, 266; Sumarokov, *Selected Tragedies*, 207; quoted with emendations.

source of power, Parmen (and Sumarokov) validates Catherine's own position as a ruler, shaped by her coup and the latent rivalry with her dynastically legitimate son Paul (whose own descent she would ultimately call into question in her memoirs). Much more than an occasional compliment, Parmen's words attest to the unique capability of tragedy to reveal the fundamental ambiguity of political order through non-authorial voices. In fact, Sumarokov adapted his lines from Corneille's *Cinna*, a classic of the genre that explored the origins of the prototypical monarchy, Augustus's principate in Rome:

> Vos armes l'ont conquise, et tous les conquérants
> Pour être usurpateurs ne sont pas des tyrans;
> Quand ils ont sous leurs lois asservi des provinces,
> Gouvernant justement, ils s'en font justes princes ...

> Your arms have conquered her, and conquerors,
> Although usurpers, are not thereby tyrants;
> When they have brought domains beneath their sway,
> By ruling justly they become just princes ...[21]

The striking analogy between the Shakespearean villain Dimitrii and Augustus, the paragon of benevolent monarchy, is firmly grounded in both texts and revolves around the Benjaminian concept of tyranny. Not only are both rulers—each of them in the focus of the respective play—conquerors of their own people and usurpers, but they both rely on terror, indiscriminate persecution of helpless subjects, to secure their authority. While Augustus renounces the legacy of his famous proscriptions to assume the guise of "justice," and Dimitrii is ruined by his reluctance to do just that, both figures stage what Giorgio Agamben defines as "the hidden paradigm guiding every ... definition of sovereignty: the sovereign is the point of indistinction between violence and law, the threshold on which violence

---

21   [Pierre] Corneille, *Cinna*, ed. Alain Couprie (Paris: Le Livre de poche, 1987), 34; Pierre Corneille, *Seven Plays*, trans. Samuel Solomon (New York: Random House, [1969]), 219.

passes over into law and law passes over into violence."[22] In eighteenth-century Russia, this fundamental indistinction was both indefensible in terms of "rational" political discourse, which obsessively pretended to separate the good monarch from the tyrant, and literally unspeakable. (A direct characterization of a monarch in Parmen's terms would constitute a capital offense punishable by maiming and penal labor.) Only in immediate terror and in literary circumlocution could the double face of sovereignty manifest itself and unfold what has to be understood as its aesthetic appeal.

This complex *dispositif* is reflected and reenacted in Parmen's utterance. It occupies a double position: pronounced by a stage figure in front of a broad public of theatergoers and readers, it simultaneously belongs to a secretive conversation held in secluded chambers of the royal palace by two experienced and cunning political practitioners—Parmen and Vasilii Shuiskii, who in the play's finale leads a successful revolt against Dimitrii to become the next tsar. It is in this space of *arcana imperii*, "mysteries of state," that deceit (*obman*) can be outspokenly acknowledged as a valid foundation of domination and legitimacy. A historical reference to Dimitrii's false identity as Ivan the Terrible's son, "deceit" is conceptually linked to Machiavellian discussions of technologies of empowerment through skillfully managed appearances. Paradoxically, however, even after it is revealed to the public gaze of Sumarokov's audience, the principle of deceit does not discredit the sovereignty that benefits from it. In fact, strategies of manipulation recommended in *The Prince* (itself open to general readership) cannot be reduced to mere falsehoods, but amount rather to a poetics of action and effect grounding the ruler's position in the carefully forged collective sentiment of the subjects. Akin to theatrical illusion itself, "deceit," which allows Dimitrii (as well as Catherine) to be recognized as a monarch by the populace, involves much more than lies. Rather, it stands for the semi-aesthetic effects of royal performance, which Parmen expressly recognizes as the ultimate touchstone of sovereignty instead of dynastic legitimacy and legal procedure. Whatever his hidden vices, the Machiavellian ruler must effectively provide for his subjects' satisfaction, through both policy and propaganda, in order to secure their obedience. Under the name of "justice" this compact emerges as the true foundation of

---

22 Giorgio Agamben, *Homo Sacer: Sovereign Power and Bare Life*, trans. Daniel Heller-Roazen (Stanford: Stanford University Press, 1998), 31–32.

authority and implies a specific Machiavellian form of popular consensus indifferent to the distinction between truth and lie but sensitive to the monarchy's "theater of power."

Far from reiterating an insipid orthodoxy, Parmen (as well as his French source) in a bold move reveals and justifies the true principles of the political order, quite remote from the vision of a sacred dynastic monarchy propagated in ceremonial discourse. Machiavellian pragmatism was not, however, opposed to aesthetic manipulation. The ambiguities of the new benevolent order were incorporated in dramatic fictions (just as in Machiavelli's treatise) by the inherently ambivalent royal figures whose claims to power and aesthetic appeal derived from the inseparability and mutual implication of "justice" and terror. This pattern permeated both the productions of Russian court stages and historical performances of sovereignty during the reigns of Elizabeth and Catherine II. Both empresses centered their "scenarios of power" on "justice" and "clemency," a suspension of terror that they nevertheless wielded spectacularly on singular—and thus symbolically charged—occasions. In Russian "myths" regarding early modern history, Platt is right to discern "a unique affective power" deriving from a "concatenation of triumphal celebration and historical suffering," "subterranean flows which linked terror and greatness together" and thus covertly benefitted "a regime founded on continuing violence."[23] As I have attempted to show, this double emotional effect had as much to do with Russia's unique history and collective identity as with common modern notions of sovereignty and their reenactments in European tragedy—a genre that unfolded, to quote yet another of Shakespeare's murderous kings, "in equal scale weighing delight and dole."

---

23 Platt, *Terror and Greatness*, 52–53.

BIBLIOGRAPHY

Abbreviations

COIDR—*Chteniia v Obshchestve istorii i drevnostei rossiiskikh*
OR RGB—Otdel rukopisei Rossiiskoi gosudarstvennoi biblioteki
OR RNB—Otdel rukopisei Rossiiskoi natsional'noi biblioteki
RGADA—Rossiiskii gosudarstvenyoi arkhiv drevnikh aktov
SIRIO—Sbornik imperatorskago russkago istoricheskago obshchestva.

Abbt, Thomas. "Vom Tode für das Vaterland." In *Aufklärung und Kriegserfahrung. Klassische Zeitzeugen zum Siebenjährigen Krieg*, edited by Johannes Kunisch, 598–650. Frankfurt am Main: Deutscher Klassischer Verlag, 1996.

Adam, Wolfgang and Holger Dainat, eds. *"Krieg ist mein Lied": der Siebenjährige Krieg in den zeitgenössischen Medien*. Göttingen: Wallstein-Verlag, 2007.

Aercke, Kristiaan. *Gods of Play: Baroque Festive Performances as Rhetorical Discourse*. Albany: SUNY Press, 1994.

Agamben, Giorgio. *Homo Sacer: Sovereign Power and Bare Life*. Translated by Daniel Heller-Roazen. Stanford: Stanford University Press, 1998.

Alekseev, M. P. *Russko-angliiskie literaturnye sviazi (XVIII vek–pervaia polovina XIX veka)*. Moscow: Nauka, 1982.

Alt, Peter-André. *Tragödie der Aufklärung: eine Einführung*. Tübingen: Francke, 1994.

———. *Der Tod der Königin: Frauenopfer und politische Souveränität im Trauerspiel des 17. Jahrhunderts*. Berlin: Walter de Gruyter, 2004.

Anisimov, Evgenii. *Dyba i knut. Politicheskii sysk i russkoe obshchestvo v XVIII veke.* Moscow: Novoe literaturnoe obozreniie, 1999.

Apostolidès, Jean-Marie. *Le prince sacrifié: théâtre et politique au temps de Louis XIV.* Paris: Éd. de Minuit, 1985.

Aristotle. *Aristotle's Art of Poetry: Translated from the Original Greek... Together with Mr. D'Acier's notes from the French.* London: D. Browne and W. Turner, 1705.

———. *La Poétique d'Aristote traduite en françois avec des remarques critiques... par André Dacier.* Paris: Claude Barbin, 1692; reprinted Hildesheim: Olms, 1976.

Bailey, Helen. *Hamlet in France from Voltaire to Laforgue.* Geneva: Droz, 1964.

Barclay, John. *Argenis.* Edited and translated by Mark Riley and Dorothy Pritchard Huber. Assen: Royal van Gorcum, 2004.

Barklai, Ioann [John Barclay]. *Argenida: Povest' geroicheskaia...perevedennaia...ot Vasil'ia Trediakovskago.* St. Petersburg: Pri Imp. Akademii nauk, 1751.

Bartenev, P. I., ed. *Arkhiv kniazia Vorontsova.* Moscow: Tip. A. I. Mamontova, 1872.

Barthes, Roland. *On Racine.* Translated by Richard Howard. Berkeley: California University Press, 1992.

Bayle, Pierre. *The Dictionary Historical and Critical of Mr. Peter Bayle.* London: J. J. and P. Knapton et al., 1736.

Béhar, Pierre and Helen Watanabe-O'Kelly, eds. *Spectaculum Europaeum: Theatre and Spectacle in Europe (1580–1750).* Wiesbaden: Harrassowitz, 1999.

Beise, Arnd. *Geschichte, Politik und das Volk im Drama des 16. bis 18. Jahrhunderts.* Berlin: Walter de Gruyter, 2010.

Benjamin, Walter. "Critique of Violence." In *Reflections: Essays, Aphorisms, Autobiographical Writings*, 277–300. Translated by Edmund Jephcott. New York: Schocken Books, 1986.

———. *The Origin of the German Tragic Drama.* Translated by John Osborne. London: Verso, 1985.

Berg, Brigitta. *Burchard Christoph Reichsgraf von Münnich (1683–1767). Ein Oldenburger in Zarendiensten.* Oldenburg: Isensee, 2011.

Berns, Jörg Jochen and Thomas Rahn, eds. *Zeremoniell als höfische Ästhetik im Spätmittelalter und Früher Neuzeit.* Tübingen: Niemeyer, 1995.

Beylagen zum Neuveränderten Rußland. Riga and Leipzig: Hartknoch, 1770.

Blitz, Hans-Martin. *Aus Liebe zum Vaterland: die deutsche Nation im 18. Jahrhundert.* Hamburg: Hamburger Ed, 2000.

Blocker, Déborah. "Dire l'«art» à Florence sous Cosme I de Médicis: une *Poétique* d'Aristote au service du Prince." *AISTHE* 2 (2008).

———. *Instituer un "art." Politiques du théâtre dans la France du premier XVIIe siècle.* Paris: Champion, 2009.

Bodin, Jean. *On Sovereignty: Four Chapters from the Six Books of the Commonwealth.* Edited and translated by Julian H. Franklin. Cambridge: Cambridge University Press, 1992.

Bohnen, Klaus. "Von den Anfängen des Nationalsinns. Zur literarischen Patriotismus-Debatte im Umfeld des Siebenjährigen Kriegs." In *Dichter und ihre Nation*, edited by Helmut Scheuer, 121–137. Frankfurt am Main: Suhrkamp, 1993.

Bonekki, Iosef [Giuseppe Bonecchi]. *Selevk: Opera predstavlennaia pri Rossiiskom imperatorskom dvore v vysochaishii den' koronovaniya … Elisavety Petrovny … i pri vsenarodnom torzhestvovanii … vechnago mira.* Moscow: Tipografiia Imperatorskoi Akademii nauk, 1744.

Bredekamp, Horst. "Von Walter Benjamin zu Carl Schmitt, via Thomas Hobbes." *Deutsche Zeitschrift für Philosophie* 46, no. 6 (1998): 901–916.

Brown, Jane K. *The Persistence of Allegory: Drama and Neoclassicism from Shakespeare to Wagner.* Philadelphia: University of Pennsylvania Press, 2007.

[Brumoy, Pierre]. *The Greek Theatre of Father Brumoy.* London: Millar et al., 1759.

———. *Théâtre des Grecs.* Paris: n.p., 1785.

Burke, Edmund. *A Philosophical Enquiry Into the Origin of Our Ideas of the Sublime and Beautiful.* Edited by J. T. Boulton. London: Routledge & Paul, 1958.

Burton, Robert. *The Anatomy of Melancholy.* Edited by Thomas C. Faulkner. Oxford: Clarendon Press, 1997.

Campe, Rüdiger. "Der Befehl und die Rede des Souveräns im Schauspiel des 17. Jahrhunderts. Nero bei Busenello, Racine und Lohenstein." In *Übertragung und Gesetz. Gründungsmythen, Kriegstheater und Unterwerfungstechniken von Institutionen*, edited by A. Adam and M. Stingelin, 55–71. Berlin: Akademie Verlag, 1995.

———. "Theater der Institution. Gryphius' Trauerspiele Leo Armenius, Catharina von Georgien, Carolus Stuardus und Papinianus." In *Konfigurationen der Macht in der Frühen Neuzeit*, edited by R. Galle and R. Behrens, 257–287. Heidelberg: Winter, 2000.

[Catherine, Empress of Russia]. *Memoirs of the Empress Catherine II*. London: Trübner & Company, 1859.

———. *Correspondance de Catherine Alexéievna, Grande-Duchesse de Russie, et de Sir Charles H. Williams, Ambassadeur d'Angleterre, 1756 et 1757*. Moscow: Lissner & Sobko, 1909.

Chantalat, Claude. *A la recherche du goût classique*. Paris: Klincksieck, 1992.

Cherniavsky, Michael. *Tsar and People: Studies in Russian Myths*. New Haven, CT: Yale University Press, 1961.

Collis, Robert. "'Stars Rule over People, but God Rules over the Stars': The Astrological Worldview of Boris Ivanovich Kurakin (1676–1727)." *Jahrbücher für Geschichte Osteuropas* 59, no. 2 (2011): 195–216.

Corneille, Pierre. *Oeuvres completes*. Paris: Éditions du Seuil, 1963.

———. *Nicomede: a tragi-comedy*. Translated by John Dancer. London: Francis Kirkman, 1671.

———. *Cinna*. Edited by Alain Couprie. Paris: Le Livre de poche, 1987.

———. *Seven Plays*. Translated by Samuel Solomon. New York: Random House, 1969.

Danzel, Theodor Wilhelm. *Gottsched und seine Zeit: Auszüge aus seinem Briefwechsel*. Leipzig: Dyk, 1848.

[D'Aubignac, François-Hédelin]. *The Whole Art of the Stage*. London: n.p., 1684. Reprint, New York: Blom, 1968.

———. *La pratique du théâtre*. Edited by Hélène Baby. Paris: Champion, 2001.

D'Auteroche, Chappe. *A Journey Into Siberia: Made by Order of the King of France*. London: T. Jefferys, 1770.

———. *Voyage en Sibérie: fait par ordre du roi en 1761*. Edited by Michel Mervaud. Oxford: Voltaire Foundation, 2004.

De Catt, Henri. *Unterhaltungen mit Friedrich dem Grossen: Memoiren und Tagebücher von Heinrich de Catt*. Edited by Reinhold Koser. Leipzig: Hirzel, 1884.

———. *Frederick the Great: The Memoirs of his Reader, Henri de Catt (1758–1760)*. Translated by F. S. Flint. Boston: Houghton Mifflin, 1917.

De Grazia, Margreta. *"Hamlet" without Hamlet*. Cambridge: Cambridge University Press, 2007.

De La Place, Pierre-Antoine. *Théâtre anglois*. Vol. 2. London: n.p., 1746.

De Ligne, Charles-Joseph. *Mes écarts ou ma tête en liberté: et autres pensées et réflexions*. Edited by Jeroom Vercruysse and Daniel Acke. Paris: H. Champion, 2007.

De Saavedra Fajardo, Diego. *Royal Politician Represented in One Hundred Emblems*. London: Matt. Gylliflower et al., 1700.

Dens, Jean Pierre. *L'honnête homme et la critique du goût: Esthétique et société au 17e siècle*. Lexington: French Forum, 1981.

———. Derzhavina, O. A., A. S. Demin, and A. N. Robinson, eds. *Pervye p'esy russ-kogo teatra*. Moscow: Nauka, 1972.

———. Derzhavina, O. A., A. S. Demin, and A. N. Robinson, eds. *P'esy stolichnykh i provintsial'nykh teatrov*. Moscow: Nauka, 1975.

O. A. Derzhavina, A. S. Demin, A. N. Robinson, eds. *P'esy liubitelskikh teatrov*. Moscow: Nauka, 1976.

Dictionnaire de L'Académie française. Paris: Coignard, 1694.

Dilthey, Wilhelm. "Friedrich der Grosse und die deutsche Aufklärung." In *Gesammelte Schriften 3: Studien zur Geschichte des deutschen Geistes*, 81–205. Göttingen: Vandenhoeck & Ruprecht, 1992.

Doering, Pia Claudia. *Jean Racine zwischen Kunst und Politik: Lesarten der Alexandertragödie*. Heidelberg: Winter, 2010.

Dmitriev, A. Iu. ed., *F. G. Volkov i russkii teatr ego vremeni. Sbornik dokumentov*. Moscow: Akademii Nauk, 1953.

Du Deffand, Marie de Vichy Chamrond. *Correspondance complète de la Marquise du Deffand avec ses amis*. 2 vols. Edited by Mathurin Francois Adolphe de Lescure. Paris: Plon, 1865.

Eagleton, Terry. *The Ideology of the Aesthetic*. Oxford: Oxford University Press, 1990.

Edgerton, William. "Ambivalence as the Key to Kniazhnin's Tragedy 'Vadim Novgorodskii.'" In *Russia and the World of the Eighteenth Century*, edited by Roger Bartlett, Anthony G. Cross, and Karen Rasmussen, 306–315. Columbus, OH: Slavica, 1988.

Elias, Norbert. *The Court Society*. Translated by Edmund Jephcott. New York: Pantheon Books, 1983.

———. *The Civilizing Process: Sociogenetic and Psychogenetic Investigations*. Revised Edition. Translated by Edmund Jephcott. Edited by Eric Dunning, Johan Goudsblom, and Stephen Menell. Malden, MA: Blackwell, 2003.

———. "The Fate of German Baroque Poetry: Between the Traditions of Court and Middle Class." In *The Collected Works*, vol. 12, 1–28. Dublin: University College Dublin Press, 2010.

Elmarsafy, Ziad. *Freedom, Slavery, and Absolutism: Corneille, Pascal, Racine*. Lewisburg, PA: Bucknell University Press, 2003.

Evstratov, Alexei. "Ekaterina II i russkaia pridvornaia dramaturgiia v 1760-kh–nachale 1770-kh godov." PhD diss. Russian State University for the Humanities (RGGU), 2009.

———. *Le théâtre francophone à Saint-Petersbourg sous le règne de Catherine II (1762– 1796). Organisation, circulation et symboliques des spectacles dramatique.* PhD diss. Université Paris Sorbonne (Paris IV), 2012.

Evstratov, Alekei and Pierre Frantz. "Pierre le Grand au théâtre, entre tragédie encomiastique et comédie bourgeoise." In *Rossiia i Frantsiia: XVIII-XX vv. Lotmanovskie chtenia*, edited by D. Alexander et al., 30–49. Moscow: RGGU, 2013.

Ewington, Amanda. *A Voltaire for Russia: A. P. Sumarokov's Journey from Poet-Critic to Russian Philosophe.* Evanston, IL: Northwestern University Press, 2010.

Falco, Raphael. *Charismatic Authority in Early Modern English Tragedy.* Baltimore, MD: Johns Hopkins University Press, 2000.

Fallot, Léopold-Frédéric. *L' Innocence opprimée, ou La mort d'Iwan Empereur de Russie: Tragédie.* N.p: 1765.

Farley-Hills, David, ed. *Critical Responses to "Hamlet" 1600–1900.* vol. 1, *1600–1790.* New York: AMS Press, 1997.

Feldman, Martha. *Opera and Sovereignty: Transforming Myths in Eighteenth-Century Italy.* Chicago: University of Chicago Press, 2007.

Fletcher, Denis. "Voltaire et l'opéra." In *L'opéra au XVIIIe siècle*, 547–558. Aix-en-Provence: Université de Provence, 1982.

[Frederick II]. "Epistle from the King of Prussia to Monsieur Voltaire." In *The Annual Register, or A View of the History, Politicks and Literature of the Year 1758*, 413–414. Translated by J. G. Cooper. London: J. Dodsley, 1759.

———. *Friedrich II, König von Preußen, und die deutsche Literatur des 18. Jahrhunderts. Texte und Dokumente.* Edited by Horst Steinmetz. Stuttgart: Reclam, 1985.

———. "History of my Own Times." In *Posthumous Works of Frederic II King of Prussia*, vol. 1. Translated by Thomas Holcroft. London: Robinson, 1789.

———. *Œuvres de Frédéric le Grand.* 30 vols. Berlin: Imprimerie royale, 1846–1856.

———. *Politische Correspondenz Friedrich's des Großen.* Berlin: Duncker & Humblot, 1879.

———. "Reponse de S. M. le Roi de Prusse." *Das Neueste aus der anmuthigen Gelehrsamkeit* 3 (1758): 214–218.

Foucault, Michel. *Discipline and Punish: The Birth of the Prison.* Translated by Alan Sheridan. New York: Vintage Books, 1979.

Gentillet, Innocent. *Anti-Machiavel: Discours sur les moyens de bien gouverner et maintenir en bonne paix un royaume ou autre principauté.* Geneva: Droz, 1968.

———. *A Discourse upon the Meanes of Wel Governing.* London: n.p., 1602. Reprint, Amsterdam: Da Capo Press, 1969.

Gleim, Wilhelm Ludwig. *Preußische Kriegslieder von einem Grenadier.* Heilbronn: Gebr. Henninger, 1882. Reprint, Nendeln: Kraus, 1968.

Goethe, Johann Wolfgang. *Poetry and Truth from my Own Life.* Translated by R. O. Moon. Washington, DC: Public Affairs Press, 1949.

———. *Wilhelm Meister's Apprenticeship.* Translated and edited by Eric A. Blackall. New York: Suhrkamp Publishers, 1989.

Gottsched, Johann Christoph. *Schriften zur Literatur.* Stuttgart: Ph. Reclam, 1972.

Gowland, Angus. *The Worlds of Renaissance Melancholy: Robert Burton in Context.* Cambridge: Cambridge University Press, 2006.

Gozenpud, A. A. *Muzykal'nyi teatr v Rossii ot istokov do Glinki: Ocherk.* Leningrad: Muzgiz, 1959.

Graf, Ruedi. *Das Theater im Literaturstaat: literarisches Theater auf dem Weg zur Bildungsmacht.* Tübingen: Walter de Gruyter, 1992.

Grasshoff, Helmut. *Russische Literatur in Deutschland im Zeitalter der Aufklärung.* Berlin: Akademie-Verlag, 1953.

Greenblatt, Stephen. *Shakespearean Negotiations: The Circulation of Social Energy in Renaissance England.* Berkeley: University of California Press, 1988.

Grell, Chantal, Christian Michel, and Pierre Vidal-Naquet. *L'école des princes, ou Alexandre disgracié: essai sur la mythologie monarchique de la France absolutiste.* Paris: Les Belles Lettres, 1988.

Griffits, Devid [David Griffiths]. "Ekaterina II i melankholiia, ili Anatomiia politicheskoi oppozitsii." In *Ekaterina II i ee mir: Stat'i raznykh let,* 102–118. Moscow: Novoe literaturnoe obozrenie, 2013.

Gruzintsov, A. "Ekzamen 'Khoreva.'" *Novosti literatury* 4 (1802): 157–158.

Gukovskii, G. A. *Russkaia literatura XVIII veka.* Moscow: Aspekt Press, 1998.

———. *Ocherki po istorii russkoi literatury XVIII veka: dvorianskaia fronda v literature 1750-kh–1760-kh godov.* Moscow: Izd-vo Akademii nauk, 1936.

———. *Rannie raboty po istorii russkoi poezii XVIII veka.* Moscow: Iazyki Russkoi kultury, 2001.

Guarini Battista Giovanni. *A Critical Edition of Sir Richard Fanshawe's 1647 Translation of Giovanni Battista Guarini's Il pastor fido.* Edited by Walter F. Staton and William E. Simeone. Oxford: Oxford University Press, 1964.

———. "Russkaia literatura v nemetskom zhurnale XVIII veka." In *XVIII vek*, vol. 3, 380–415. Moscow: Izd-vo AN SSSR, 1958.

Hampton, Timothy. "*La foi des traités*: Baroque History, International Law, and the Politics of Reading in Corneille's *Rodogune*." In *Walter Benjamin's Imaginary French Trauerspiel*, edited by Katherine Ibbett and Hall Bjornstad, 135–151. New Haven: Yale University Press, 2013.

Hartter, Christiane. "Deutschsprachiges Theaterleben in Russland in der Mitte des 18. Jahrhunderts. Der Prinzipal und Geschäftsmann Johann Peter Hilferding und seine Theaterunternehmen." In *Deutsches Theater im Ausland vom 17. zum 20. Jahrhundert*, edited by Horst Fassel et al., 47–64. Berlin: International Specialized Book Service Incorporated, 2007.

Haverkamp, Anselm. *Shakespearean Genealogies of Power: A Whispering of Nothing in "Hamlet, Richard II, Julius Caesar, Macbeth, The Merchant of Venice, and The Winter's Tale."* London: Routledge, 2011.

Healey, Frank George. *The Literary Culture of Napoléon.* Geneva: Droz, 1959.

Heinsius, Daniel. *De constitutione tragoediae. La constitution de la tragédie: dite La poétique d'Heinsius.* Edited and translated by Anne Duprat. Geneva: Droz, 2001.

Heldt, Kerstin. *Der vollkommene Regent. Studien zur panegyrischen Casuallyrik am Beispiel des Dresdner Hofes Augusts des Starken (1670–1733).* Tübingen: Niemeyer, 1997.

Hellmuth, Eckhart. "Die 'Wiedergeburt' Friedrichs des Großen und der 'Tod fürs Vaterland.' Zum patriotischen Selbstverständnis in Preußen in der zweiten Hälfte des 18. Jahrhunderts." In *Nationalismus vor dem Nationalismus?*, edited by E. Hellmuth and R. Stauber, 21–52. Hamburg: Meiner, 1998. Aufklärung: interdisziplinäres Jahrbuch zur Erforschung des 18. Jahrhunderts und seiner Wirkungsgeschichte 10, no. 2.

Herder, Johann Gottfried. *Briefe zur Beförderung der Humanität.* Frankfurt am Main: Deutscher Klassiker Verlag, 1991.

Herrmann, Ernst. *Geschichte des russischen Staates.* Vol. 5. Hamburg: Perthes, 1853.

Herrmann, Hans Peter. "Individuum und Staatsmacht. Preußisch-deutscher Nationalismus in Texten zum Siebenjährigen Krieg." In *Machtphantasie Deutschland.*

Nationalismus, Männlichkeit und Fremdenhaß im Vaterlandsdiskurs deutscher Schriftsteller des 18. Jahrhunderts, edited by Hans Martin Blitz and Susanna Moßmann, 66–79. Frankfurt am Main: Suhrkamp, 1996.

Herold, J. Christopher. *The Age of Napoleon.* Boston: Houghton Mifflin Harcourt, 2002.

Hoffman, Kathryn A. *Society of Pleasures: Interdisciplinary Readings in Pleasure and Power during the Reign of Louis XIV.* New York: St. Martin's Press, 1997.

Horace. *Satires, Epistles and Ars poetica.* Translated by H. Ruston Fairclough. London: Heinemann, 1961.

Itigina, L. A. "K voprosu o repertuare oppozitsionnogo teatra Elizavety Petrovny v 1730-e gody." In *XVIII vek*, vol. 9, 321–331. Leningrad: Nauka, 1974.

Iusim, M. A. *Makiavelli v Rossii: moral' i politika na protiazhenii piati stoletii.* Moscow: Rossiiskaia akademiia nauk, 1998.

Jasinski, René. *Vers le vrai Racine.* Paris: A. Colin, 1958.

Jobez, Romain. *Le théâtre baroque allemand et français. Le droit dans la littérature.* Paris: Classiques Garnier, 2010.

Kahn, Victoria. "The Passions and the Interests in Early Modern Europe: The Case of Guarini's *Il Pastor fido.*" In *Reading the Early Modern Passions: Essays in the Cultural History of Emotion*, edited by Gail Kern Paster, Katherine Rowe, and Mary Floyd-Wilson, 217–239. Philadelphia: University of Pennsylvania Press, 2004.

[Kantemir, A. D. and Ch. F. Gross]. "Tak nazyvaemye 'Moskovitskie pis'ma.'" In *Rossiia i Zapad: gorizonty vzaimopoznaniia. Literaturnye istochniki XVIII v. (1726–1762).* Moscow: Nasledie, 2003.

Kantorowicz, Ernst. *The King's Two Bodies: A Study in Mediaeval Political Theology.* Princeton, NJ: Princeton University Press, 1957.

Kapp, Volker. "Die Idealisierung der höfischen Welt im klassischen Drama." In *Französische Literatur in Einzeldarstellungen*, vol. 1, edited by Peter Brockmeier and Hermann H. Wetzel, 115–176. Stuttgart: Metzler, 1981.

Karamzin, N. M. *Sochineniia.* Vol. 2. Leningrad: Khudozhestvennaia literatura, 1984.

Karin, A. "Pis'mo." Poleznoe uveselenie 12 (1761).

Kasatkina, E. A. "Sumarokovskaia tragediia 40-kh–nachala 50-kh godov XVIII veka." In *Uchenye zapiski Tomskogo pedagogicheskogo instituta*, vol. XIII, 213–261. Tomsk: TGPI, 1955.

Klein, Ioakhim [Klein, Joachim]. *Puti kul'turnogo importa. Trudy po russkoi literature XVIII veka.* Moscow: Iazyki slavianskoi kul'tury, 2005.

Knoll, Gerhard. "'Hunde, wollt Ihr ewig leben?' oder Goethe und die 'Hunde' des Großen Königs." *Aus dem Aniquariat. Zeitschrift für Aniquare und Büchersammler* 2 (2005): 22–27.

Kolesch, Doris. *Theater der Emotionen: Ästhetik und Politik zur Zeit Ludwigs XIV.* Frankfurt and New York: Campus Verlag, 2006.

Kopanev, N. A. "Rasprostranenie frantsuzskoi knigi v Moskve v seredine XVIII v." In *Frantsuzskaia kniga v Rossii v XVIII v.: Ocherki istorii*, edited by Sergei Luppov, 59–172. Leningrad: Nauka, 1986.

Korndorf, A. S. *Dvortsy Khimery. Illuzornaia arhitektura i politicheskie alluzii pridvornoi stseny.* Moscow: n.p., 2011.

Korsakov, D. A. *Iz zhizni russkikh deiatelei XVIII veka.* Kazan': Tipografiia Imperatorskogo Universiteta, 1891.

Koschorke, Albrecht. "Das Politische und die Zeichen der Götter. Zum 'Lied der Parzen' in *Iphigenie auf Tauris*." In *Die Gabe des Gedichts: Goethes Lyrik im Wechsel der Töne*, edited by Gerhard Neumann and David E. Wellbery, 143–159. Rombach, 2008.

Koschorke, Albrecht, Susanne Lüdemann, Thomas Frank, and Ethel Matala de Mazza. *Der fiktive Staat. Konstruktionen des politischen Körpers in der Geschichte Europas.* Frankfurt am Main: Fischer Taschenbuch Verlag, 2007.

Koser, Reinhold. *Geschichte Friedrichs des Großen.* Vol. 3. Stuttgart: Cotta'sche Buchhandlung Nachfolger, 1913.

Kostin, Andrei. "Moskovskii maskarad 'Torzhestvuiushchaia Minerva' (1763) glazami inostrantsa." *Russkaia literatura* 2 (2013): 80–112.

Krebs, Roland. *L'Idée de "Théâtre National" dans l'Allemagne des Lumières.* Wiesbaden: Harrassowitz, 1985.

Kühnel, Florian. *Kranke Ehre? Adlige Selbsttötung im Übergang zur Moderne.* Munich: Oldenbourg Verlag, 2013.

Kunisch, Johannes. *Das Mirakel des Hauses Brandenburg: Studien zum Verhältnis von Kabinettspolitik und Kriegführung im Zeitalter des Siebenjährigen Krieges.* Munich: Oldenbourg, 1978.

Kurukin, Igor. *Artemii Volynskii.* Moscow: Molodaia gvardiia, 2011.

———. *Epokha "dvorskikh bur'": Ocherki politicheskoi istorii poslepetrovskoi Rossii, 1725–1762 gg.* Riazan': NRIID, 2003.

Lang, D. M. "Sumarokov's *Hamlet*: A Misjudged Russian Tragedy of the Eighteenth Century." *Modern Language Review* 43, no. 1 (1948): 67–72.

Langer, Werner. *Friedrich der Große und die geistige Welt Frankreichs*. Hamburg: Seminar für romanische Sprachen und Kultur, 1932.

Lazaroni, Lodovico. *Mir geroev. Drama na muzyke predstavlennaia vo vremia torzhestva blagopoluchno zaklyuchennago mira mezhdu … Petrom tret'im … i … Friderikom Tret'im korolem prusskim … Prelozhenie rossiiskimi stikhami … Ivana Barkova*. St. Petersburg: Pri Imperatorskoi Akademii nauk, 1762.

Leben, Thaten, und Betrübter Fall des Weltberufenen Russischen Grafen Burchards Christophs von Münnich. Bremen: Nathaniel Saurmann, 1742.

Lehmann, Ulf. *Der Gottschedkreis und Russland*. Berlin: Akademie Verlag, 1966.

Leonard, Carol. *Reform and Regicide: The Reign of Peter III of Russia*. Bloomington: Indiana University Press, 1993.

Lessing, Gotthold Ephraim. *Werke*. Tempel Klassiker Sonderausgabe. Wiesbaden: Der Tempel-Verlag, n.d.

———. *Hamburgische Dramaturgie*. Stuttgart: Reclam, 1981.

Levitt, Marcus. *Early Modern Russian Letters: Texts and Contexts*. Boston: Academic Studies Press, 2009.

———. *The Visual Dominant in Eighteenth-Century Russia*. DeKalb: Northern Illinois University Press, 2011.

Liebler, Naomi Conn. *Shakespeare's Festive Tragedy: The Ritual Foundations of Genre*. London, Routledge, 1995.

Litzmann, Berthold. "Die Neuberin in Petersburg." *Archiv für Litteraturgeschichte* 12 (1884): 316–318.

Lomonosov, Mikhail. *Izbrannye proizvedeniia*. Edited by A. A. Morozov. Leningrad: Sovetskii Pisatel', 1986.

Lomonosov, M. V. *Sochineniia … s ob'iasnitel'nymi primechaniiami M. I. Sukhomlinova*. Vol. 2. St. Petersburg: Imperatorskaia Akademiia Nauk, 1891.

Lotman, Iu. M. *Izbrannye stat'i*. Vol. 1. Tallinn: Aleksandra, 1992.

———. *Karamzin*. St. Petersburg: Isskustvo-SPB, 1997.

Lütteken, Laurenz, ed. *Metastasio im Deutschland der Aufklärung*. Tübingen: Walter de Gruyter, 2002.

Lyons, John D. *The Tragedy of Origins: Pierre Corneille and Historical Perspective*. Stanford: Stanford University Press, 1996.

Machiavelli, Niccolò. *The Works of Nicholas Machiavel … Newly Translated … by Ellis Farneworth*. Vol. 1. London: Thomas Davies et al., 1762.

Manstein, Cristoph Hermann v. *Contemporary Memoirs of Russia from the Year 1727 to 1744.* London: Longman et al., 1856.

Marin, Louis. *Portrait of the King.* Translated by Martha Houle. Minneapolis: University of Minnesota Press, 1988.

———. "Théâtralité et pouvoir: Magie, machination, machine: *Médée* de Corneille." In *Politiques de la representation*, 263–285. Paris: Editions Kimé, 2005.

Maslov, B. P. "Ot dolgov khristianina k grazhdanskomu dolgu (ocherk istorii kontseptual'noi metafory)." In *Ocherki istoricheskoi semantiki russkogo iazyka rannego Novogo vremeni*, edited by V. M. Zhivov, 201–270. Moscow: Iazyki slavianskikh kultur, 2009.

Matala de Mazza, Ethel. "Die Regeln der Ausnahme. Zur Überschreitung der Souveränität in Fénelons Télémaque und Mozarts *Idomeneo*." In *Transgressionen. Literatur als Ethnographie*, edited by Gerhard Neumann and Rainer Warning, 257–286. Freiburg: Rombach, 2003.

Maurer, Karl. "Die verkannte Tragödie. Die Wiedergeburt der Tragödie aus dem Geist der Pastorale." In *Goethe und die romanische Welt*. Padeborn: F. Schöningh, 1997.

Mauvillon, Eléazar de. *Histoire de la vie, du règne et du détrônement d'Iwan III, empereur de Russie, assassiné à Schlüsselbourg dans la nuit du 15 au 16 juillet (NS.) 1764.* London: n.p., 1766.

Mémoires de Louis XIV pour l'instruction du Dauphin. Vol. 2. Edited by Charles Dreyss. Paris: Didier, 1860.

Menke, Bettine. *Das Trauerspiel-Buch: der Souverän—das Trauerspiel—Konstellationen—Ruinen.* Bielefeld: transcript, 2010.

Merckwürdiges Leben und trauriger Fall des russischen StaatsMinisters Andreae Grafen v. Ostermann. Bremen: Nathaniel Saurmann, 1742.

Merkwürdige Geschichte I. M. Elisabeth der Ersten: Nebst einer kurzen Einleitung in die Historie der russischen Regenten von Anfang des Christenthums in diesem nordischen Reiche. N.p., 1759.

Merlin, Hélène. *Public et littérature en France au XVIIe siècle.* Paris: Les Belles Lettres, 1994.

Merlin-Kajman, Hélène. *L'absolutisme dans les lettres et la théorie des deux corps. Passions et politique.* Paris: Champion, 2000.

Mervaud, Christiane. *Voltaire et Frédéric II: une dramaturgie des lumières, 1776–1778.* Oxford: The Voltaire Foundation; Paris: J. Touzot, 1985.

[Metastasio, Pietro]. *Poro, Re Dell'Indie. Drama . . . Done Into English by Mr. Humphreys*. London: Wood, 1731.

———. *Miloserdie Titovo: Opera s prologom: Predstavlennaia vo vremia vysokotorzhestvennago dnia koronatsii e. i. v. Elisavety Petrovny . . .* Moscow: Tipografiia Akademii nauk, [1742].

———. *Alexandre aux Indes, opera . . . representé . . . par ordre de Son Altesse Imperiale monseigneur le grand duc de toutes les Russies*. St. Petersburg: De l'imprimerie de l'Academie impériale des Sciences, 1759.

———. *The Clemency of Titus, from the Italian by a Lady*. Liverpool: Smith, 1828.

Molière. *The Works*. London: John Watts, 1748.

———. *Œuvres*. Paris: Hachette, 1878.

Mommsen, Katharina. *Goethe und der Alte Fritz*. Leipzig: Lehmstedt, 2012.

Monod, Paul Kléber. *The Power of Kings: Monarchy and Religion in Europe, 1589–1715*. New Haven, CT: Yale University Press, 1999.

Morel, Jacques. *Agréables mensonges. Essais sur le théâtre français du XVIIe siècle*. Paris: Klincksieck, 1991.

Morrissey, Susan K. *Suicide and the Body Politic in Imperial Russia*. Cambridge: Cambridge University Press, 2006.

Mullaney, Steven. "Apprehending Subjects, or the Reformation in the Suburbs." In *The Place of the Stage: License, Play, and Power in Renaissance England*, 88–115. Ann Arbor: University of Michigan Press, 1995.

Müller, Michael. "Rußland und der Siebenjährige Krieg. Beitrag zu einer Kontroverse." *Jahrbücher für Geschichte Osteuropas* 28 (1980): 198–219.

Mulryne, J. R., Helen Watanabe-O'Kelly, and Margaret Shewring, eds. *Europa Triumphans: Court and Civic Festivals in Early Modern Europe*. Vols. 1–2. London: MHRA, 2004.

Münnich, Maréchal de. *Ebauche de gouvernement de l'Empire de Russe*. Geneva: Droz, 1989.

Nebrig, Alexander. *Rhetorizität des hohen Stils: der deutsche Racine in französischer Tradition und romantischer Modernisierung*. Göttingen: Wallstein Verlag, 2007.

Neill, Michael. *Issues of Death: Mortality and Identity in English Renaissance Tragedy*. Oxford: Clarendon Press, 1997.

Neufanger, Dirk. *Geschichtsdrama der frühen Neuzeit, 1495–1773*. Tübingen: De Gruyter, 2005.

Nikulina, Elena and Igor Kurukin. *Povsednevnaia zhizn' tainoi kantseliarii XVIII veka*. Moscow: Molodaia Gvardiia, 2008.

Novikova, O. E. "Lipsii v Rossii pervoi poloviny XVIII veka." In *Filosofskii vek* 10, 146–160. St. Petersburg: Sankt-Peterburgskii Tsentr istorii idei, 1999.

Ogarkova, N. A. *Tseremonii, prazdnestva, muzyka russkogo dvora, XVIII–nachalo XIX veka.* St. Petersburg: Bulanin, 2004.

Orgel, Stephen. *Illusion of Power.* Berkeley: University of California Press, 1975.

Ospovat, A. L. "Iz materialov dlia kommentariia k 'Kapitanskoi dochke' (1–5)." In *Tekst i kommentarii: Kruglyi stol k 75-letiiu Viach. Vs. Ivanova*, edited by V. N. Toporov, 247–266. Moscow: Nauka, 2006.

Ospovat, Kirill. "Iz istorii russkogo pridvornogo teatra 1740-kh gg." In *Memento vivere: sbornik pamiati L. N. Ivanovoi*, 9–36. St. Petersburg: Nauka, 2000.

———. "Petr i Aleksei: k literaturnoi semantike istoriograficheskogo siuzheta." *Sobranie sochinenii. K 60-letiiu L. I. Soboleva.* 442–455. Moscow: Vremia novostei, 2006.

———. "Gosudarstvennaia slovesnost': Lomonosov, Sumarokov i literaturnaia politika I. I. Shuvalova v kontse 1750-kh gg." In *Evropa v Rossii*, edited by Pekka Pesonen, Gennadii Obatnin, and Tomi Khuttunen, 6–65. Moscow: Novoe literaturnoe obozrenie, 2010.

Pankratii (Charnysskii). *Slovo v vysochaishee prisutstvie…Elisavety Petrovny i naslednika eia…Petra Feodorovicha…o delakh mzdovozdaiatel'nykh ot Boga…* In Arsenii (Mogilianskii), *Rech' k eia imperatorskomu velichestvu s ego imperatorskim vysochestvom v monarshei svite k Troitskoi Sergievoi lavre priblizhivsheisia…skazovannaia iiunia 6 dnia, 1744 goda,* [St. Petersburg]: Tipografiia Akademii nauk, 1744.

Paul, Joanne. "The Use of Kairos in Renaissance Political Philosophy." *Renaissance Quarterly* 67, no. 1 (Spring 2014): 43–78.

Pečar, Andreas. "Friedrich der Große als Autor. Plädoyer für eine adressatenorientierte Lektüre seiner Schriften." In *Friedrich300—Eine perspektivische Bestandsaufnahme. Beiträge des ersten Colloquiums in der Reihe "Friedrich 300,"* edited by Michael Kaiser and Jürgen Luh. Accessed August 28, 2013. http://www.perspectivia.net/content/publikationen/friedrich300-colloquien/friedrich-bestandsaufnahme.

Pekarskii, P. P. *Nauka i literatura v Rossii pri Petre Velikom.* Vol. 1. St. Petersburg: Tipografiia Tovarishchestva "Obshchestvennaia pol'za," 1862.

———. *Istoriia imp. Akademii nauk v Peterburge.* Vol. 2. St. Petersburg: Tipografiia Tovarishchestva "Obshchestvennaia pol'za," 1873.

————. *Markiz de la Shetardi v Rossii 1740–1742 godov*. Riazan': Aleksandriia, 2010.

Perella, Nicolas J. *The Critical Fortune of Battista Guarini's "Il pastor fido."* Florence: L. S. Olschiki, 1973.

Piirimäe, Eva. "Dying for the Fatherland: Thomas Abbt's Theory of Aesthetic Patriotism." *History of European Ideas* 35 (2009): 194–208.

Pisarenko, K. A. *Povsednevnaia zhizn' russkogo dvora v tsarstvovanie Elizavety Petrovny*. Moscow: Molodaia gvardiia, 2003.

————. "Pis'ma ober-gofmeistera Kh. V. Minikha Ioganne-Elizavete printsesse Angal't-Tserbstskoi, 1745–1746 gg." In *Rossiiskii Arkhiv: Istoriia Otechestva v svidetel'stvakh i dokumentakh XVIII–XX vv.,* vol. XVIII. Moscow: Studiia Trite, 2009.

Pis'ma russkikh pisatelei XVIII veka. Edited by G. P. Makogonenko. Leningrad: Nauka, 1980.

Platt, Kevin. *Terror and Greatness: Ivan and Peter as Russian Myths*. Ithaca, NY: Cornell University Press, 2011.

Pleschka, Alexander. *Theatralität und Öffentlichkeit: Schillers Spätdramatik und die Tragödie der französischen Klassik*. Berlin: De Gruyter, 2013.

Pogosjan, Jelena. *Vostorg russkoi ody i reshenie temy poeta v russkom panegirike 1730–1762 gg*. Tartu: Tartu Ulikooli Kirjastus, 1997.

————. "Kniaz' Vladimir v russkoi ofitsial'noi kul'ture nachala pravleniia Elizavety Petrovny." In *Trudy po russkoi i slavianskoi filologii. Literaturovedenie* 5. Tartu: Tartu Ülikooli kirjastus, 2005.

————. "Masks and Masquerade at the Court of Elizabeth Petrovna (1741–1742)." In *Russian and Soviet History: From the Time of Troubles to the Collapse of the Soviet Union*. Edited by Steven Usitalo and W. B. Whisenhunt. Lanham, MD: Rownman and Littlefield, 2008.

Poe, Marshall. *A People Born to Slavery: Russia in Early Modern European Ethnography, 1476–1748*. New York: Cornell University Press, 2000.

Poisson, Philippe. *L'Impromptu de campagne*. In *Répertoire du Théâtre François . . .* Paris: Didot l'ainé, 1804.

Polnoe sobranie zakonov Rossiiskoi imperii s 1649 g., [Sobranie I], [Sankt-Petersburg,] 1830.

[Poniatowski], Stanislas Auguste. *Mémoires*. Edited by Anna Grześkowiak-Krwawicz. Paris: Institut d'Études Slaves, 2012.

Popov, N. "Pridvornye propovedi v tsarstvovanie Elizavety Petrovny." In *Letopisi russkoi literatury i drevnosti*, edited by N. S. Tikhonravov, vol. 2, part 3, 1–33. Moscow: V Tipografii Gracheva i Komi, 1859.

Poroshin, S. A. "Zapiski, sluzhashchie k istorii velikogo kniazia Pavla Petrovicha." In *Russkii Gamlet*. Moscow: Fond Sergeia Dubova, 2004.

Portrait naturel de l'Imperatrice de Russie Glorieusement Régnante... Hambourg: n.p., n.d.

Prokopovich, Feofan. *Sochineniia*. Moscow: Izd. AN SSSR, 1961.

Proskurina, V. Iu. *Mify imperii: literatura i vlast' v epochu Ekateriny II*. Moscow: Novoe literaturnoe obozrenie, 2006.

Pumpianskii, L. V. "Trediakovskii i nemetskaia shkola razuma." In *Zapadnyi sbornik*, 157–186. Moscow: Izd-vo AN SSSR, 1937.

———. "Lomonosov i nemetskaia shkola razuma." In *XVIII vek*. Vol. 14, 3–44. Leningrad: Nauka, 1983.

Quintus Curtius. [*History of Alexander*]. Translated by John C. Rolfe. Cambridge, MA: Harvard University Press, 1985.

Racine, Jean. *Racine, Théâtre complet*. Edited by Jean-Pierre Collinet. Paris: Gallimard, 1983.

———. *The Dramatic Works...A Metrical English Version by Robert Bruce Boswell*. London: G. Bell and Sons, 1897.

Rahn, Thomas. *Festbeschreibung. Funktion und Topik einer Textsorte am Beispiel der Beschreibung höfischer Hochzeiten (1568–1794)*. Tübingen: Niemeyer, 2006.

Rapin, René. "Reflections upon Poetry." In *The Whole Critical Works*, vol. 2. Translated by Basil Kennet. London: J. Walthoe et al., 1731.

———. *Les réflexions sur la poétique de ce temps, et sur les ouvrages des poètes anciens et modernes*. Geneva: Droz, 1970.

Richelieu. *The Political Will and Testament of that Great Minister of State, Cardinal Duke de Richelieu*. London: n.p., 1695.

———. *Testament politique de Richelieu*. Edited by Françoise Hildesheimer. Paris: Champion, 1995.

Riccoboni, Louis. *Histoire du théâtre italien...et une dissertation sur la tragedie moderne*. Vol. 1. Paris: André Cailleau, 1730.

———. *An Historical and Critical Account of the Theatres in Europe, together with... A Comparison of the Ancient and Modern Drama*. London: T. Waller, 1741.

———. *De la réformation du théatre*. [Paris]: n.p., 1743.

Rieck, Werner. "Gottsched und Friedrich II." *Wissenschaftliche Zeitschrift der Pädagogischen Hochschule Potsdam, Gesell.-Sprachw. Reihe* 2 (1966): 221–230.

Rzhevskii, Aleksei. "Oda … imperatoru Petru Feodorovichu … na vseradostnoe vosshestvie na vserossiiskii presto." In Poleznoe uveselenie, 99. Moscow: Pechatana pri Imperatorskom Moskovskom Universitete, 1762.

Sachse, Ullrich. *Cäsar in Sanssouci: die Politik Friedrichs des Großen und die Antike.* Munich: Allitera Verlag, 2008.

Sanchez, Melissa E. *Erotic Subjects: The Sexuality of Politics in Early Modern English Literature.* Oxford: Oxford University Press, 2011.

Sbornik imperatorskago russkago istoricheskago obshchestva. Vol. 6. St. Petersburg: n.p., 1870.

———. Vol. 91. St. Petersburg: n.p., 1894.

———. Vol. 96. St. Petersburg: n.p., 1896.

———. Vol. 100. St. Petersburg: n.p., 1897.

———. Vol. 105. Iur'ev: n.p., 1899.

Schäfer, Armin. "Der Souverän, die clementia und die Aporien der Politik. Überlegungen zu Daniel Casper von Lohensteins Trauerspielen." In *Theatralität und die Krisen der Repräsentation*, edited by Erika Fischer-Lichte, 101–124. Stuttgart: Weimar, 2001.

———. "Die Wohltat in der Politik. Über Souveränität und Moral im barocken Trauerspiel." In *Imaginem. Bildlichkeit und Souveränität*, edited by Anne von der Heiden, 79–99. Zürich: Diaphanes, 2005.

———. "Wer verübt die Rache? Eine Handlungskette in Andreas Gryphius' Trauerspiel *Leo Armenius*." In *Kulturtechniken des Barock: Zehn Versuche*, edited by Tobias Nanz and Armin Schäfer, 57–70. Berlin: Kulturverlag Kadmos, 2012.

Schings, Hans-Jürgen. "Consolatio Tragoediae. Zur Theorie des barocken Trauerspiels." In *Deutsche Dramentheorien. Beiträge zu einer historischen Poetik des Dramas in Deutschland*, edited by Reinhold Grimm. Frankfurt am Main: Atheneum, 1971.

Schlegel, Johann Elias. *Werke.* Vol. 1. Kopenhagen and Leipzig: Christian Gottlob Prost, 1761.

———. *Aesthetische und dramaturgische Schriften.* Edited by J. von Antoniewicz. Heilbronn: Gebr. Henninger, 1887.

Schmitt, Carl. *Political Theology: Four Chapters on the Concept of Sovereignty*. Translated by George Schwab. Cambridge, MA: Harvard University Press, 1985.

Schöne, Albrecht. *Emblematik und Drama im Zeitalter des Barock*. München: Beck, 1993.

Schönert, Jörg. "Schlachtgesänge vom Kanapee. Zu den 'Preußischen Kriegsliedern' des Kanonikus Gleim." In *Gedichte und Interpretationen. Aufklärung und Sturm und Drang*, edited by Karl Richter, 126–139. Stuttgart: Reclam, 1983.

Schort, Manfred. *Politik und Propaganda: der Siebenjährige Krieg in den zeitgenössischen Flugschriften*. Frankfurt am Main: Lang Verlag, 2006.

Schröder, Volker. *La tragédie du sang d'Auguste: politique et intertextualité dans Britannicus*. Tübingen: Narr, 1999.

[Schwan, Christophe Friedrich]. *Anecdotes russes, ou lettres d'un officier allemand à un gentilhomme livonien, écrites de Petersbourg en 1762; tems du règne & du détrônement de Pierre III. Empereur de Russie*. Londres: Aux dépens de la Compagnie, 1764.

Schwarze, Karl. *Der Siebenjährige Krieg in der zeitgenössischen deutschen Literatur. Kriegserleben und Kriegserlebnis in Schrifttum und Dichtung des 18. Jahrhunderts*. Berlin: Junker und Dunhaupt, 1936.

Seebald, Christian. *Libretti vom "Mittelalter": Entdeckungen von Historie in der (nord) deutschen und europäischen Oper um 1700*. Tübingen: Walter de Gruyter, 2009.

Semevskii, M. I. "N. F. Lopukhina. 1699–1763. Epizod iz eia zhizni." *Russkii vestnik* 29 (1860), book 17: 5–52.

———. "N. F. Lopukhina." *Russkaia starina* 11 (1874): 1–42, 191–235.

———. "Tainaia kantseliariia v tsarstvovanie Elizavety Petrovny. 1741–1761." *Russkaia starina* 12 (1875): 523–539.

Seneca. *De clementia*. Edited with translation and commentary by Susanna Braund. Oxford: Oxford University Press, 2009.

Sera Tomasa Smita puteshestvie i prebyvanie v Rossii. St. Petersburg: Izdanie grafa S. D. Sheremeteva, 1893.

Sergei Polskoi, "*Rassuzhdenie o pravlenii gosudarstvennom*" V. N. Tatishcheva i dvorianskoe politicheskoe dvizhenie 1730 goda. *Izvestiia Samarskogo nauchnogo tsentra RAN*, 8 (2006), 3: 690–697.

Serman, I. Z. "Lomonosov i pridvornye italianskie stikhotvortsy 1740-kh godov." In *Mezhdunarodnye sviazi russkoi literatury*, 112–134. Leningrad: Izd. AN SSSR, 1963.

———. *Russkii klassitsizm. Poeziia. Drama. Satira*. Leningrad: Nauka, 1972.

Shakespeare, William. *Julius Caesar*. Edited by Arthur Humphreys. The Oxford Shakespeare. Oxford: Clarendon Press, 1984.

———. *Hamlet*. Edited by G. R. Hibbard. The Oxford Shakespeare. Oxford: Oxford University Press, 1987.

———. *Hamlet. The Texts of 1603 and 1623*. Edited by Ann Thompson. The Arden Shakespeare. London: Bloomsbury, 2006.

Shakhovskoi, Ia. P. "Vospominaniia." *Imperiia posle Petra*. Moscow: Fond Sergeia Dubova, 1998.

Shcherbatov, M. M. *On the Corruption of Morals in Russia*. Translated and edited by Antony Lentin. Cambridge: Cambridge University Press, 1969.

Shliapkin, I. A. *Tsarevna Natal'ia Alekseevna i teatr ee vremeni*. [St. Petersburg]: Balashev i Ko., 1898.

Shtelin, Ja. [Jacob Stählin]. *Muzyka i balet v Rossii XVIII v.* St. Petersburg: Soiuz khudozhnikov, 2002.

———. "Zapiski o Petre III." In *Ekaterina. Put k vlasti*, 9–50. Moscow: Fond Sergeia Dubova, 2003.

Shuger, Debora Kuller. *Political Theologies in Shakespeare's England: The Sacred and the State in "Measure for Measure."* New York: Palgrave, 2001.

Sinopsis. Kiev: n.p., 1681. Reprint, Cologne and Vienna: Böhlau, 1983.

Slovar' russkogo iazyka XVIII veka. Vol. 7. St. Petersburg: Nauka, 1992.

Solov'ev, S. M. *Istoriia Rossii s drevneishikh vremen*. Moscow: Prosveshchenie, 1993.

Sommer-Mathis, Andrea, ed. *Pietro Metastasio—uomo universale (1698–1782)*. Vienna: Verlag der Osterrichisches Akademie der Wissenschaften, 2000.

Sösemann, Bernd and Gregor Vogt-Spira, eds. *Friedrich der Große in Europa: Geschichte einer wechselvollen Beziehung*. Stuttgart: Steiner, 2012.

Starikova, L. M., ed. *Teatral'naia zhizn' Rossii v epokhu Anny Ioannovny*. Moscow: Nauka, 1995.

———. *Teatral'naia zhizn' Rossii v epokhu Elizavety Petrovny. Dokumental'naia khronika. 1751EN1761*. Vol. 2, book 1. Moscow: Nauka, 2003.

———. Vol. 2, book 2. Moscow: Nauka, 2005

———. Vol. 3, book 1. Moscow: Nauka, 2011.

———. "Die Neuberin und das 'vorliterarische' Theater in St. Petersburg." In *Vernunft und Sinnlichkeit. Beiträge zur Theaterepoche der Neuberin*, edited by Bärbel Rudin and Marion Schulz, 200–217. Vogtland: Reichenbach i. V. Neuberg Museum, 1999.

Steiner, George. *The Death of Tragedy*. New York: Oxford University Press, 1961.

Stennik, Iu. V. *Zhanr tragedii v russkoi literature. Epokha klassitsizma.* Leningrad: Nauka, 1981.

Stepanov, V. P. "Kritika man'erizma v 'Primechaniiakh k Vedomostiam.'" In *XVIII vek*, vol. 10, 39–48. Leningrad: Nauka, 1975.

Strong, Roy. *Art and Power: Renaissance Festivals 1450–1650.* Woodbridge: Boydell, 1984.

Sumarokov, Aleksandr. *Khorev. Tragediia.* St. Petersburg: n.p., 1747.

———. *Polnoe sobranie vsekh sochinenii.* 10 vols. Moscow: Univ. tip. N. Novikova, 1787.

———. *Izbrannye proizvedeniia.* Edited by P. N. Berkov. Leningrad: Sovetskii pisatel', 1957.

———. *Selected Tragedies.* Translated by Richard and Raymond Fortune. Evanston, IL: Northwestern University Press, 1970.

———. *Dramaticheskie sochineniia.* Edited by Iu. V. Stennik. Leningrad: Iskusstvo, 1990.

———. *Gamlet.* Edited by Maksim Amelin. *Novaia Iunost'* 4 (2003). Accessed on June 16, 2015. http://magazines.russ.ru/nov_yun/2003/4/amel.html.

———. *Ody torzhestvennyia. Elegii lubovnyia. Reprintnoe vosproizvedenie sbornikov 1774 goda.* Moscow: OGI, 2009.

Svodnyi katalog knig na inostrannykh iazykakh, izdannykh v Rossii v XVIII veke. Vol. 2. Leningrad: Nauka, 1985.

Tatishchev, Vasilii. *Sobranie sochinenii.* Moscow: Ladomir, 1994–1996.

Ter-Nedden, Gisbert. "*Philotas* und *Aias* oder Der Kriegsheld im Gefangenendilemma. Lessings Sophokles-Modernisierung und ihre Lektüre durch Gleim, Bodmer und die Germanistik." In *Krieg ist mein Lied: Der Siebenjahrige Krieg in den Zeitgenössischen Medien*, 317–378. Göttingen: Wallstein, 2007.

Tiefensee, Samuel, [Carl Wilhelm Schulz]. *Rede und Ode auf den zwischen den hohen Höfen Berlin und Petersburg Anno 1762. glücklich geschlossenen Frieden abgelesen in dem Gröningischen illustren Collegio zu Stargard an der Jhna.* Stargard: Johann Ludwig Kunst, 1762.

Tikhonravov, N. S., ed. *Russkie dramaticheskie proizvedeniia 1672–1725 godov.* St. Petersburg: Izdanie D. E. Kozhanchikova, 1874.

Tolochko, Aleksei. *"Istoriia Rossiiskaia" Vasiliia Tatishcheva.* Moscow: Novoe literaturnoe obozrenie, 2005.

Trediakovskii, V. K. *Izbrannye proizvedeniia.* Edited by L. I. Timofeev. Moscow: Sovetskii pisatel', 1963.

———. "Pis'mo, v kotorom soderzhitsia rassuzhdenie o stikhotvorenii, ponyne na svet izdannom ... pisannoe ot priiatelia k priiateliu." In *Kritika XVIII veka*, edited by A. M. Ranchin and V. L. Korovin, 29–109. Moscow: Olimp, 2002.

Truman, Ronald W. *Spanish Treatises on Government, Society, and Religion in the Time of Philipp II: The "De Regimine Principum" and Associated Traditions*. Leiden: Brill, 1999.

Ulbert, Jorg. "Friedrichs Lektüren während des Siebenjährigen Krieges." In *Friedrich der Große als Leser*, edited by Brunhilde Wehinger and Günther Lottes, 71–98. Berlin: Akademie Verlag, 2012.

Uspenskii, B. A. and V. M. Zhivov. "Tsar' i Bog (Semioticheskie aspekty sakralizatsii monarkha v Rossii)." In B. A. Uspenskii, *Izbrannye Trudy*. Vol. 1. Moscow: Iazyki slavianskoi kultury, 1996.

Uveselenie, sochinennoe i predstavlennoe ot…frantsusskikh komediantov po vsenarodnom torzhestvovanii…vechnago mira. Moscow: Tipografiia Imperatorskoi Akademii nauk, 1744.

Vetter, Eveline. *Studien zu Sumarokov*. Berlin: Freie Universität, 1961.

Viala, Alain. "Péril, conseil et secret d'État dans les tragédies romaines de Racine: Racine et Machiavel." *Littératures classiques* 26 (1996): 91–113.

———. *La France galante. Essai historique sur une catégorie culturelle, des ses origines jusqu'à la Révolution*. Paris: Presses Universitaires de France, 2008.

Vigor, Jane. *Letters from a lady, who resided some years in Russia, to her friend in England*. London: J. Dodsley, 1777.

———. *Eleven additional letters from Russia, in the reign of Peter II*. London: J. Dodsley, ca. 1785.

Voltaire. *Dramatic Works*. Translated by Rev. Mr. Francklin. London: J. Newbery et al., 1763.

———. *Complete Works*. Vol. 8. Oxford: The Voltaire Foundation, 1988.

———. Vol. 9. Oxford: The Voltaire Foundation, 1999.

———. Vol. 16. Oxford: The Voltaire Foundation, 2003.

———. Vol. 17. Oxford: The Voltaire Foundation, 1991.

———. Vol. 25. Oxford: The Voltaire Foundation, 2012.

———. Vol. 30A. Oxford: The Voltaire Foundation, 2003.

———. Vol. 45A. Oxford: The Voltaire Foundation, 2009.

———. Vol. 46. Oxford: The Voltaire Foundation, 1999.

———. Vol. 93 (*Correspondence*, vol. 9). Genève: Institut et Musée Voltaire, 1970.

———. Vol. 102 (*Correspondence*, vol. 18). Oxford: The Voltaire Foundation, 1971.

———. Vol. 103 (*Correspondence*, vol. 19). Oxford: The Voltaire Foundation, 1971.

———. Vol. 108 (*Correspondence*, vol. 24). Oxford: The Voltaire Foundation, 1972.

———. Vol. 109 (*Correspondence*, vol. 25). Banbury: The Voltaire Foundation, 1973.

———. *Écrits autobiographiques*. Edited by Jean Goldzink. Paris: Flammarion, 2006.

———. *Smert' Cezarja. Eine anonyme frühe russische Übersetzung von Voltaires Tragödie*. München: Fink, 1967.

———. *The Works*. Vol. 30. London: J. Newbery et al., 1763.

Vossius, Gerardus Joannes. *Poeticarum institutionum libri tres. Institutes of poetics in three books*. Edited and translated by Jan Bloemendal with Edwin Rabbie. Leiden: Brill, 2010.

Vroon, Ronald. "'Ekaterina plachet iavno . . .': k predystorii perevorota 1762 g." In *I vremia i mesto: Istoriko-filologicheskii sbornik k shestidesiatiletiiu A. L. Ospovata*, 40–54. Moscow: Novoe Izdatel'stvo, 2008.

Vsevolodskii-Gerngross, V. N. "Politicheskie idei russkoi klassitsisticheskoi tragedii." In *O teatre. Sbornik statei*, 106–133. Leningrad: Iskusstvo, 1940.

———. *Teatr v Rossii pri imperatritse Elizavete Petrovne*. St. Petersburg: Giperion, 2003.

Weber, Friedrich Christian. *The Present State of Russia*. Vol. 1. London: W. Taylor, 1722.

Weber, Max. *The Theory of Social and Economic Organization*. Translated by A. M. Henderson and Talcott Parsons. New York: Oxford University Press, 1947.

Wehinger, Brunhilde. "Denkwürdigkeiten des Hauses Brandenburg—Friedrich der Große als Autor der Geschichte seiner Dynastie." In *Vom Kurfürstentum zum Königreich der Landstriche. Brandenburg-Preußen im Zeitalter von Absolutismus und Aufklärung*, edited by Günther Lottes, 137–174. Berlin: Berliner Wiss.-Verlag, 2004.

White, Hayden. "Literary Theory and Historical Writing." In *Figural Realism: Studies in the Mimesis Effect*, 1–26. Baltimore, MD: Johns Hopkins University Press, 1999.

———. "The Irrational and the Problem of Historical Knowledge in the Enlightenment." In *Tropics of Discourse: Essays in Cultural Criticism*, 142–143. Baltimore, MD: Johns Hopkins University Press, 1985.

Whittaker, Cynthia H. *Russian Monarchy: Eighteenth-Century Rulers and Writers in Political Dialogue*. DeKalb: Northern Illinois University Press, 2003.

Wiesend, Rienhard. "Metastasios Alexander: Herrscherfigur und Rollentypus. Aspekte der Rezeptionsgeschichte." In *Opernheld und Opernheldin im 18. Jahrhundert. Aspekte der Librettoforschung*, edited by K. Hortschansky, 139–152. Hamburg: Eisenach, 1991.

Wikander, Matthew H. *Princes to Act: Royal Audience and Royal Performance, 1578–1792*. Baltimore, MD: Johns Hopkins University Press, 1993.

[Will, Georg A]. *Merkwürdige Lebensgeschichte Peter des Dritten, Kaiser . . . aller Reußen*. Frankfurt: n.p., 1762.

Wirtschafter, Elise Kimerling. *The Play of Ideas in Russian Enlightenment Theater*. DeKalb: Northern Illinois University Press, 2003.

Wolff, Eugen. *Johann Elias Schlegel*. Kiel and Leipzig: Lipsius and Tischer, 1892.

Wortman, Richard. *Scenarios of Power: Myth and Ceremony in Russian Monarchy*. Princeton, NJ: Princeton University Press, 1995.

Zapiski diuka Liriiskago i Bervikskago vo vremia prebyvaniia ego pri imperatorskom rossijskom dvore . . . St. Petersburg: V Gutenbergovoi Tipografii, 1845.

Zelle, Carsten. "Strafen und Schrecken. Einführende Bemerkungen zur Parallele zwischen dem Schauspiel der Tragödie und der Tragödie der Hinrichtung." *Jahrbuch der deutschen Schillergesellschaft* 28 (1984): 76–103.

Zhitie i dela Marka Avreliia Antonina tsesaria rimskago: A pri tom sobstvennyia, i premudryia evo razsuzhdenii o sebe samom. S nemetskago na rossiiskoi iazyk perevel . . . Sergei Volchkov. St. Petersburg: Pri Imperatorskoi Akademii nauk, 1740.

Zhivov, Viktor. "Handling Sin in Eighteenth-Century Russia." In *Representing Private Lives of the Enlightenment*, edited by Andrew Kahn, 123–148. Oxford: Voltaire Foundation, 2010.

———. "Istoriia russkogo prava kak lingvosemioticheskaia problema." In *Razyskaniia v oblasti istorii i predystorii russkoi kul'tury*, 187–305. Moscow: Iazyki slavianskoi kultury, 2002.

Zitser, Ernest. *The Transfigured Kingdom: Sacred Parody and Charismatic Authority at the Court of Peter the Great*. Ithaca, NY: Cornell University Press, 2004.

———. "The Vita of Prince Boris Ivanovich 'Korybut'-Kurakin: Personal Life-Writing and Aristocratic Self-Fashioning at the Court of Peter the Great." *Jahrbücher für Geschichte Osteuropas* 59, no. 2 (2011): 163–194.

Zorin, Andrei. "Catherine II versus Beaumarchais: The Scandal at the St. Petersburg Court at the Time of the French Revolution." In *Russia and The West. Missed Opportunities. Unfulfilled Dialogues*. Brussels: Konninklijke Vlaamse Akademie van Belgie, 2006.

———. *Kormia dvuglavogo orla . . . : literatura i gosudarstvennaia ideologiia v Rossii v poslednei treti XVIII–pervoi treti XIX veka*. Moscow: Novoe literaturnoe obozrenie, 2001.

INDEX

CPSIA information can be obtained
at www.ICGtesting.com
Printed in the USA
BVOW06*2243271016
466258BV00001B/7/P